RALPH de S. CHILDS
COOPER UNION

AMERICAN THOUGHT

Civil War to

World War I

AMERICAN THOUGHT

Civil War to World War I

EDITED WITH AN INTRODUCTION BY

PERRY MILLER

NEW YORK   *Rinehart & Co., Inc.*   TORONTO

Third Printing, July 1957

Introduction copyright, 1954, by Perry Miller
Typography and Cover Design by Stefan Salter
Printed in the United States of America
Library of Congress Catalog Card Number: 54-7243

For the Memory of
Harold J. Laski

FOREWORD

This anthology is designed to represent the basic configuration of thought in America between the end of the Civil War and America's entrance into the First World War. Every editor of a collection must fight against the insuperable limitation of space and the irresistible desire to get in as much as possible. Every student will agree that the value of a work like this diminishes in proportion to the minuteness of the selections from particular authors. Better, they all say in chorus, a substantial piece of each of the major thinkers than an array of meaningless snippets from a multitude. Yet no two will draw up the same list of the indispensable names. Even though it be universally conceded that this volume may safely leave out technical works on logic or metaphysics and proclaim itself addressed to the general reader or to the student of main currents, every specialist will have his favorites. My "Introduction" must bewail the several exclusions I have found regrettable. I have consulted various colleagues, and have been influenced by the recent scholarship; yet, in the final analysis, responsibility for the selection not only of writers but of passages rests with me.

The principal difficulty, as I have sadly discovered, that a student of ideas encounters in endeavoring to analyze the thought of this country is that a vast variety of historians have lately taken unto themselves the prerogative of chronicling the life of the mind without distinguishing between the mind and the market place. Assuredly, if one is concerned with events and elections and measures, the so-called ideas of Theodore Roosevelt and Woodrow Wilson, even those of Andrew Carnegie and Mark Hanna, are more "important" than those of Chauncey Wright and Lester Ward. But there is, I am convinced, a perspective in which the speculations of a serious and competent (all the more if he be a great) thinker have an intrinsic worth that has nothing to do with their direct impact upon politics or programs. Were this small volume to be expanded tenfold, a place could be found for ten times as many publicists and spokesmen. Whether in that case the result could really be called a record of the intellect would remain a question. What I have aimed at is that each of the controlling conceptions—those by which, in the end, politicians, statesmen, theologians, and all lesser intelligences were governed—shall have at least one explicit statement.

There is a further problem—which I do not pretend to have solved: even if my irreducible cast of thirteen characters be confessed the minimum, most of them were fairly voluminous, and no one excerpt—or at the best two—can pretend to speak for their entire output. In some cases, as with Royce and Brandeis, we have the consolation that they always said their essential idea in any sustained essay. In other cases, I am obliged to pick something which the consensus of scholarship holds to be the principal utterance, or else to choose something which I myself find so characteristic as to believe that from it the over-all position, or at least the prevailing temper, can be deduced. As for Holmes, Dewey, and Brandeis, the problem is complicated by the fact that they spoke their best known (not necessarily their best) words after the First World War, but I have summarily dismissed that worry by taking only pieces that come out of the ethos of the earlier time.

It may be a lame defense—if defense be needed—but I am persuaded that, granting such omissions as of Fiske, Lloyd, Croly, Rauschenbusch, the thirteen statements here reprinted do expound the crucial points of view by which Americans between 1865 and 1917 were ruled. It is not necessary for me to add, although even so I shall venture, that these points of view, however modified by later domestic developments and altered by new importations, remain fundamental to any comprehension of the life of the mind in a subsequent America.

P. M.

INTRODUCTION

I

It is a curious fact that one of the most radical revolutions in the history of the American mind took place in the two or three decades after the Civil War without exciting appreciable comment: the philosophy and the philosophers of Scottish Realism vanished from the American colleges, leaving not even a rack behind, and were swiftly replaced by expounders of some form of Idealism.

The Scottish method was brought to America by President John Witherspoon of Princeton, and came into absolute domination of academic curricula by about 1820. Sometimes lecturers used the original works of Thomas Reid, Dugald Stewart, or Sir William Hamilton, but more often employed one or another redactions prepared by an American professor or president, advertised as especially "collected, arranged, and abridged, for the use of colleges and private students." For five or possibly six decades these tomes constituted what must be called the official metaphysic of America —the chief distinction between them and the Scottish originals being a subordination of such metaphysical portions as the latter contained to their cosmological and ethical sections. Witherspoon's successor at Princeton, Samuel Stanhope Smith, and Levi Hedge at Harvard (the first to be called "Professor of Philosophy") sealed the triumph of the school and set the precedent for their successors, Francis Bowen and James Walker at Harvard, Francis Wayland at Brown, James McCosh at Princeton, and Noah Porter at Yale. The Presbyterian Church made the Scottish doctrine virtually synonymous with Protestantism, with the result that the other denominations, even the most Evangelical, incorporated it into their teaching when their institutions also offered courses in "philosophy." During all these years, it was resolutely unaffected by the Idealistic movements which ran riot in Europe, and it especially set a stern face of disapproval against the flutter of literary Idealism among the Transcendental fraternity of New England.

This Realism could be so widely and uncritically accepted because, for one reason, it was based upon John Locke; during the Revolution, America had embraced him as its own political theorist and moralist. For another and more important reason, Scottish Realism was a philosophy of "common sense"—forthright, down-to-earth, rational, and yet pious. It supported orthodoxy in theology, raised no dangerous questions, invited no intellectual adventures. It was enlightened, and yet conservative. It was a restatement of Locke against David Hume, and contradicted Hume's scepticism by a blanket assertion that idea and object correspond so faithfully that Americans, intent upon their business, need never give a second thought to so unprofitable a worry. Berkeley and Hume, said Samuel Stanhope Smith, construct "visionary systems" out of the erroneous notion that the immediate objects of the senses are not external things but only images of those things. "Let the common apprehensions of mankind be received as truth," he declared, and then we shall see, in our common certitude, that external things are indeed the objects of our perceptions, that "the whole foundation of the ideal theories is removed." In this sense the Scottish system was a "Realism," meaning that man does perceive reality and need never bother about what Whitman called "the terrible doubt of appearances."

The Scots and their American interpreters acknowledged that men make mistakes, but they attributed these not to failures in the mechanism of human understanding but to errors of association and inference; they were the marks of original sin, and were to be overcome by the combined help of divine grace and of study and education. The Realists were not anti-intellectuals, but they had no use for the extravagances of Emerson and Bronson Alcott. Philosophy was adequately comprised in the course usually offered in the senior year of the college (generally given by the president), entitled "Mental and Moral Philosophy." This correlated Christian morality with the faculty psychology and "the law of nature." In ethics it taught the automatic operation of the pain-pleasure principle, and in economics translated this principle into a codification of Adam Smith, thus inculcating laissez faire as the supreme law of morals and religion as well as of business. A Whitman or a Melville, as well as a few Transcendentalists in New England, might protest, but their dissent was utterly ignored.

Nevertheless, this American ideology crumbled rapidly after 1870, and by 1890 had disappeared—except as it might survive in the dogmatic assurances of politicians and preachers. One may say that it expired mainly because the behemoths of the system failed to train up successors, so that with the death of McCosh in 1894 there was no one to carry on. But a more cogent reason is the fact that younger intellects—even those who might otherwise have been temperamentally sympathetic with Bowen, Porter, and McCosh—realized that in the rapidly altering circumstances a naïve Realism was no longer a match for the two challenges which so pressed upon the culture that America could no longer live in philosophical isolation. These were, first, the thrust of organized Idealism, particularly in its Hegelian and post-Hegelian formulations, and second, the devastating upset of the Scottish methods of reasoning contained in Charles Darwin's *The Origin of Species,* published in 1859. If America had, intellectually speaking, any traditions of its own on which it had dreamed of making a stand, these suddenly appeared provincial, plebeian, shallow, compared with the vigor and the comprehensiveness either of the European Hegelians or of Darwin's English exponents, Herbert Spencer and Thomas Huxley.

II

Both America and England absorbed during the nineteenth century two separate "Germanic invasions." The first came in the form of literature—poetry, drama, and especially the "romance"—with some metaphysical trimmings; it worked mainly upon poets and popularizers, Coleridge and Carlyle in England, Emerson and Theodore Parker in America, but to the mass of citizens, as also to those whom the masses regarded as their sort of philosophers, this Germanism seemed too fantastic to be taken seriously, except as it corrupted aesthetes. The second invasion came armed with a dialectic, a severe discipline, a rationale of history, and a technique of disputation powerful enough to shatter all opposition. One should further emphasize that this version of the German genius gloried in being no anarchy of the emotions but a solid conservatism. The support which a righteous America had formerly received from Scottish Realism was now promised in a much more invincible form by this massive Idealism—even though, in order to appropriate it, the American mind had to master a more precise and infinitely subtler kind of reasoning than any for which it had hitherto (except possibly among Puritan theologians) shown the slightest aptitude.

Realists like Bowen and Porter lectured on Kant, and so helped to dig their own graves. In 1849 Laurens Perseus Hickock, professor at Union College, published *Rational Psychology,* which was distinctly Hegelian; and in 1869 Charles Carroll Everett brought out *The Science of Thought.* But the first real assault in the name of Kant and Hegel was launched just after the Civil War by a group in St. Louis, most of them self-educated, centering about the boisterous figure of an eccentric immigrant, Henry Brokmeyer, who could read the texts in the original. Barred from the ordinary periodicals, the group published its own organ, *The Journal of Speculative Philosophy,* from 1867 to 1893. The most articulate was William Torrey Harris (1835–1909); he invaded the Concord School of Philosophy and wrested the leadership of American Idealism from the fumbling hands of Bronson Alcott, last pathetic survivor of Transcendentalism. As United States Commissioner of Education, Harris ultimately exerted a still wider influence upon the country. Most of his writing is too technical for so general a work as this; yet he and the *Journal* prepared the way for the triumph of Idealism, which by the end of the century was symbolized in the capture of the major academic posts by philosophers trained—many of them in Germany—in the dialectic. George Trumbull Ladd at Yale, Borden Parker Bowne at Boston University, George Sylvester Morris at Michigan, James Edwin Creighton at Cornell, George Holmes Howison at California were only the best known of a regiment. That these men had much effect outside the colleges may be doubted, but among their students were many leaders of society and business. Undoubtedly the one who stood out, in the eyes both of the profession and of the public, as the foremost Idealist was Josiah Royce, born in California in 1855, who taught at Harvard from 1882 to his death in 1916, and who made many forays into the Chautauqua and the lecture platform.

Idealists disagreed passionately among themselves, staged heroic disputations, and contradicted each other's publications. Still, on the large outlines they were at one in holding that the structure of the human mind so corresponds with the objective fact of the universe that the true constitution of reality is mental. As Morris put it, "Knowledge and being are correlative terms." Standing firm, though in various fashions, upon this solution of the epistemological doubt, they celebrated the enduring verities of religion and morality. Sometimes (except for Bowne) their systems do not seem conspicuously Christian; they found themselves more comfortable pressing the sufficiency of the "Absolute" rather than the glory of God. Nevertheless, they were filled with a sense of mission, and so devoted philosophy to asserting that if eternal right were constantly done, the heavens would never fall.

Royce first expounded his system in *The Religious Aspect of Philosophy* (1885), and most elaborately in *The World and the Individual* (1900–1901). His was a mind of depth and fertility, yet it is not unfair to say that he reproduced his whole thought in every chapter and in every article. The essence of his position is expressed most readably in "The Problem of Job," originally given, interestingly enough, as an address to a convention of ministers, and published in 1898. It is a particularly good example of a tactic which, at the time, looked like the great strength of Idealism: the Idealist was confident that in the climax of his argument he could resolve every contradiction, every objection, into an all-inclusive and affirmative synthesis, and therefore was generously prepared, in the opening portions of his discourse, to acknowledge to the limit the seeming evils of existence.

Today we are annoyed with philosophies which tell us, at the end, that God is in His heaven and all's well with the world—although we desperately seek such assurance. In most quarters,

Royce's stock is probably now at a low point. Yet one cannot read this essay without acquiring a respect for the sincerity of the man, his human sympathy, his ethical fervor, and his resolution to blink no fact, to accept no cheap way out. "The Problem of Job" makes clear why to hundreds Royce appeared *the* philosopher, the only one who established the principles of morality, immortality, loyalty, and reverence upon foundations which no scientific heresy could shake. Neither biology nor physics could, so it seemed, render obsolete his restatement of the great tradition of Western Christendom. And he had the large advantage that he scored this victory without resorting to any authoritative revelation, even while making copious use of the Bible. He seemed to demonstrate the inadequacy of any and every Naturalism to cope with the human predicament, yet to find in the predicament itself a resolution for anguish and doubt. He could afford to give cards and spades to the Devil, for he was adroit enough at the dialectical game to win back from evil every trick, for the truth of God's eternity.

III

One reason for the immense appeal of Idealism to Americans—especially to the cultivated classes—was that it did supply a methodology for resisting the threat to traditional morality, to the very conception of humanity, emanating from *The Origin of Species*. Idealism advertised itself as better equipped for the task than dogmatic theology, Catholic or Protestant, because it could incorporate evolution itself into an ideal scheme, and so enlist it on the side of righteousness, without having to thunder hysterical anathemas. If the Absolute is seen as reproducing Himself through man in the form of an aspiration to perfection, and if prophets of the Absolute can prove even out of Darwin that the discipline of life calls for a "thwarting" of baser impulses, then the process of evolution can be shown (after the first shock is over) to be nothing more than a crude version of the ideal. Hence Idealists could still insist that the spiritual categories—the transcendent forms of the mind—are not the results of evolution, but that the laws of evolution are concepts imposed upon nature by these same spiritual or mental powers. Idealists were prepared—as the theologians were not—to turn to pious and moral ends Darwin's blasting of the doctrine of eternally fixed species. Thus they managed to declare that, in spite of Darwin, man is man, the most exalted being in the scale of being, not the miserable and accidental consequence of a haphazard squabble.

However, they had their work cut out for them. For one thing, as "The Problem of Job" reveals, they were put fatally upon the defensive. They were compelled, as Santayana said at the time, to protect a vested interest: "they know they are defending prisoners suspected by the world, and perhaps by their own good sense, of falsification." Hence many of their students rebelled against the enchantment, coming to suspect that Idealist professors did not covet truth but only victory. Some, like Dewey (who started as a disciple of Morris), were obliged to ask whether it was after all a proper use of philosophy to make it a substitute for theology, whether this was the reason why philosophy in America was acquiring an unction, was "rarely without a tone of edification, as if feeling itself the patron of man's spiritual interests in contrast to the supposed crudeness and insensitiveness of naturalism and empiricism." Certain temperaments—Sumner and Holmes are cases in point—became so disgusted with this uplifting exhortation that they turned with vehement relief to Darwin, stoically preferring, as they felt, to face the grimmest of reality rather than to drape it with resounding verbiage.

If these recalcitrants were temperamentally unsuited to Idealism, they did not have to rest their rebellion only upon their emotions. Within a few years—or even months—after *The Origin of Species* shattered Victorian complacency, acute minds began to see that the least of its revolutionary meanings was its substantive denial of fixed species, or even its implied discrediting of Christian morality; what struck them was its unprecedented method of investigation. To those who caught this vision—whether or not Darwin himself intended it—the book opened both for thought and for action an illimitable future. Neither Hegel nor Royce could, these dissidents were assured, offer humanity anything like so intoxicating a prospect.

Hegel taught the Idealists that history is reason and reason history, that the actual course of things has been rational, and that the rational is consequently the actual. This pattern of rationality might be stated in Hegel's triad of thesis, antithesis, and synthesis, or in any variation of the theme that Royce or Howison could devise, but the basic contention was the same: just as nature is so linked to mind that the two always correspond, so likewise the historical record must conform to a coherent program of ideas. Royce said that evolution, as comprehended by ordinary Darwinians, was "too ambiguous a process to admit of any one assured metaphysical interpretation." Actually, certain scientists of repute also supported this charge—the greatest being Louis Agassiz at Harvard—and they were equally scandalized by the incoherence of the Darwinian account. They too denounced it, refusing to believe that humanity's conceptions of the self, of God, and of the universe were products of an aimless working of such vulgar principles as natural selection and survival of the fittest.

Yet there were other scientists—at first a minority—and a few speculative minds that had mastered the scientific point of view who countered Agassiz and the Idealists by contending that, while on the surface the story told by Darwin might seem irrational, the configuration of forces operating beneath the play of phenomena was held together in a fashion which might indeed be called illogical but which was definitely not opposed to reason. This system of explanation might not correspond to the categories of intellect as unscientific philosophers had defined them, and not to the traditional rules of morality, but in its own terms it was coherent. If the human intellect would abdicate its pretense of knowing intuitively the innermost logic of things, it could learn to conform itself to the figure hidden in the carpet. That in the course of fulfilling itself this figure had slaughtered myriads of individuals and ruthlessly exterminated whole species or cultures would be, for those who beheld the perfection of the drama, a footnote. Here, they could say, is the true secret of change, of progress. Here, they were prepared to argue, is at last revealed the hitherto incomprehensible way in which God governs the universe, here is the only really satisfactory answer to the problem of Job. To accept it, to live with it, would require courage, but men like Sumner and Ward, like Wright, Peirce, and James, were, whatever their failings, not deficient in that virtue.

Dewey's essay, here reprinted (pages 214–224), is a superb summary of the impact of Darwin upon nineteenth-century America. Dewey was close enough to share the emotions, yet sufficiently remote to see them in perspective. No heresy of the past—no matter how naturalistic or atheistic—had so much as suggested that the hierarchy of species was accidental. Not the most devastating of sceptics, not Montaigne or Hume, had deprived man of his assurance that he is separated by an impassable gulf from the animal kingdom, even though several misanthropes had expressed a preference for the animal rather than for the man. Now Darwin was saying that all life is originally one stuff, that species might have become any conceivable form as well as any other, that the forms they have stumbled into are explicable because the stuff has been pushed or pulled in this or that direction. Matter blindly moves because it is driven by the struggle for existence; the reason why one organization rather than another survives is accident. The over-all law is only a statistical average. The root of evil (only, of course, it is not truly "evil") is over-population, so that the sacred instinct of parenthood is, in biological fact, a fiendish contrivance for strife and for killing. Destruction is salutary, and the only slim consolation left to trembling sensitivity is Darwin's reflection "that the war of nature is not incessant, that no fear is felt, that death is generally prompt, and that the vigorous, the healthy and the happy survive and multiply."

This might be hard on the sentiments, but to the intellect it gave infinite consolation. For when the several principles which Darwin took from earlier pessimists—such as Malthus' law that population outruns subsistence—were combined into his amalgam, his judicious union of variation, struggle for existence, natural selection made the story of life intelligible. The effect was not pessimism but adventure—a costly adventure, a brutal, extravagant one, but nevertheless exuberant. Behind the shimmer of bloodshed and death was a reign of law—not law in the conventional sense, not what theologians had meant by law or what Newtonian physicists had supposed, but a code infinitely more concrete and explicable than any "law of nature" men had yet imagined. Truth at last was found, and found in nature itself, not in the fallible mind of fallible man. The lofty conclusion of later editions of *The Origin of Species* must be studied in every word if the student is to make sense out of the selections in this volume:

It is interesting to contemplate a tangled bank, clothed with many plants of many kinds, with birds singing on the bushes, with various insects flitting about, and with worms crawling through the damp earth, and to reflect that these elaborately constructed forms, so different from each other, and dependent upon each other in so complex a manner, have all been produced by laws acting around us. These laws, taken in the largest sense, being Growth with reproduction: Inheritance which is almost implied by reproduction; Variability from the indirect and direct action of the conditions of life, and from use and disuse; a Ratio of Increase so high as to lead to a Struggle for Life, and as a consequence to Natural Selection, entailing Divergence of Character and the Extinction of less improved forms. Thus, from the war of nature, from famine and death, the most exalted object which we are capable of conceiving, namely, the production of the higher animals, directly follows. There is grandeur in this view of life, with its several powers, having been originally breathed by the Creator into a few forms or into one; and that, while this planet has gone circling on according to the fixed law of gravity, from so simple a beginning endless forms most beautiful and most wonderful have been, and are being evolved.

The modern mind—including that mind in America that had been trained by Locke and the Scots—had long since accustomed itself to the idea that behind the appearances of the heavens and the solar system were at work the Newtonian laws of motion, "the fixed law of gravity." But this system of law had been identified with the content of "reason"; it was mathematical, simple, and logical. The laws which, by combining to form a pattern of biological evolution, so excited Darwin's admiration that he put them in capitals—Inheritance, Variability, Struggle for Life, Natural Selection, and Extinction—seemed of a different order from the physical. They seemed hardly to be laws at all, and the total picture they gave was only a deadly madness. Yet for hardy spirits Darwin's paragraph was exhilarating precisely because his complex was a triumph of mind greater than the Hegelian dialectic. And then, because it was the secret of nature as well as of mind, it put into the hands of comprehending man absolute control over the instruments which up until 1859 had controlled him.

IV

Almost as soon as thoughtful Americans began to grasp these implications in *The Origin of Species,* even amid the distractions of the Civil War and Reconstruction, a number recovered from their initial dismay and, taking their cue from Darwin himself, bravely determined to appropriate evolution, with the "grandeur" of its view of life, for an enlarged religious purpose. Darwin was anything but an irreligious man, and took pride in quoting a clerical friend that it was as noble a conception of the Deity "to believe that He created a few original forms capable of self-development into other and needful forms, as to believe that He required a fresh act of creation to supply the voids caused by the action of His laws." Some of these Americans were professing Christians, others were merely "theists"; some were scientists, others only sentimentalists; some wrote on scholarly levels, others for the Sunday supplements. The pioneer was Asa Gray, Professor of Botany at Harvard and antagonist of Agassiz; he was the first to argue that, far from rushing into atheism, Darwinism established the proof of design in the universe by separating that proof from the no longer tenable hypothesis of the immutability and isolated creation of species. The literature of this school—except that it was never an organized "school"—is voluminous, and includes such disparate figures as Joseph Le Conte, Henry Ward Beecher (whose *Evolution and Religion* in 1885 was vapid, but quieted the fears of multitudes of Protestants), George Harris (whose *Moral Evo-*

lution in 1896 is still a cogent book), and Lyman Abbott (*The Theology of an Evolutionist*, 1896). The victory seemed complete in 1888 when even old James McCosh, after considerable search of soul, published *The Religious Aspects of Evolution*. Popular acceptance was further facilitated by the eloquent English lecturer, Henry Drummond, whose *Natural Law in the Spiritual World* (1890) and *The Ascent of Man* (1894) went through innumerable editions.

The most conspicuous of these optimistic Darwinians was John Fiske (1842–1901). Were this anthology designed to give the full historical spectrum, it would run to several volumes, and would include much of Fiske. However, although Fiske figured prominently in the period, his thought (along with that of his allies) has worn thin; he and they can claim no more than a historical consideration. For this reason I have omitted Fiske, but the student must bear in mind that the lines of thought here represented were worked out in a society of which a large group, mostly of solid and respectable citizens, had persuaded themselves that the true meaning of Darwinism was an infinite and eternal power of God operating through nature up to man. Armed with that conviction, they were as little touched by the harshness of Sumner as by the humanitarianism of George and Ward; by the same token, they were obtuse to the questions raised by Peirce and James, were dumbly amazed by Holmes, indifferent to the Adamses, and outraged by Veblen (if they so much as noticed him) and by Brandeis (who forced them to pay him attention). They rested relatively secure in the belief that the brutality and waste of the process were minor episodes, and that these were justified by the emergence of the end product, the decent, moral man.

Theistic evolutionists were not Idealists; indeed, the latter considered them betrayers of the citadel. They did not derive their program of ascent from an a priori concept, but professed to find it incarnated in biology itself. Fiske, for example, saw in prolonged infancy a contrivance for making man the one species capable of social organization. However various their interpretations—some were highly ingenious—they all converted evolution into a doctrine of progress, and on the whole believed that progress in society would be continued by the evolutionary method of free and un-regulated competition. All insisted that their thought was molded by nature and that they imposed no ideas, metaphysical or eco-nomic, upon reality. All abandoned their allegiance to older theo-logical conceptions only after they were persuaded that Darwin demonstrated a cosmic teleology in which all is for the best.

The number of Americans (or, for that matter, of Europeans) who could face Darwinism as a purely scientific statement, without having to placate religious or moral qualms, was small. Of these Chauncey Wright (1830–1875) was the first to speak. Graduated from Harvard in 1852, he lived in Cambridge as a free-lance journalist, holding an academic post only in his last year. He was the pivotal figure in a group that gathered for occasional talk and that included Peirce, James, and Holmes. He was well read in science, was humorous, critical, detached, and born disillusioned. He published little, and that little in long, discursive essays which were difficult even for his friends to grasp. The most important of these, "Evolution of Self-Consciousness," appeared in *The North American Review;* I have taken the liberty of extracting the sub-stantial portions and giving them titles of my own devising. Be-cause the original piece is so meandering, it never had upon the country the arresting effect it would indubitably have had could it have been understood. But for the few who were capable of following it, the experience was unforgettable.

Wright here took the step few could bring themselves even to contemplate: if man is the creation of evolution, then all the attributes which formerly were supposed to be badges of his spiritual estate have also been developed by material means out of matter itself. The last stronghold of Idealists and theists alike was "self-consciousness." The body and its organs might have come out of some primal stuff, but self-consciousness could not have evolved; like the Christian "soul," for which it was the psychological sub-stitute, it must have been inserted, somewhere along the way, by supernatural intervention. Wright asserted, calmly and devastat-ingly, that philosophy, did it care to preserve its self-respect, must cease to be concerned with final causes, must limit itself to analyz-ing particular phenomena, and make no absolute pronouncements.

Introduction

He welcomed *The Origin of Species* as soon as did Asa Gray, but he had an equal contempt for the Hegelians and for the optimistic Darwinians. In this essay he dared to treat man as a purely natural organism, and to account for the origin of self-consciousness in wholly biological terms, hinging his explanation upon the organism's response to words as signs. Self-consciousness thus becomes a comprehensible extension of the animal powers of sensation and memory. With intellectual activity conceived as being precisely like the bodily, a part of the complex interaction of things, the famous epistemological problem of modern philosophy, the discrepancy between idea and object, simply disappears. To add insult to injury, Wright turned upon Idealists and theists the accusation that, by defending loyalty and reverence as ends-in-themselves, they showed only that they were barbarians, or at best "partially civilized." (His scorn of the barbarian is worth comparing with Veblen's; see pages 306–329.) He is among the first, if not the very first, in our culture to assert that agnostics and naturalists can be as devoted to the aims of civilization as the righteous.

Wright had his differences with Darwin, though Darwin always respected him. His early death deprived America of a tough intelligence it sorely needed. He would never have become popular, but he could have challenged those who did. Had he lived longer, he might have made as tremendous an impression upon the nation as he made on his associates. As it was, he pointed the way to Pragmatism by saying that all ideas—including even those of mathematics—are "finders, not merely summaries of truth." The territory Wright thus opened up for exploration beckoned especially to the pioneering mind of Charles Sanders Peirce.

V

Meanwhile, during the years when Wright was composing his abstruse meditations, the attention of a large portion of the American populace—a greater body, numerically, even than that which followed the evolutionary theists—was enraptured by yet another interpreter of Darwin, one who purported to be as naturalistic as Wright but who expressed himself in a language which, in spite of a semblance of profundity, could in fact be readily absorbed by the half-educated, the self-educated, and even the ignorant. The popularity of Herbert Spencer (1820–1903) in America between the Civil War and the end of the century is a phenomenon that has frequently been described, but remains for all that staggering. Not only village agnostics, but scientists, many theologians, and most captains of industry paid him as great homage as the Revolutionary generation paid to Locke. It would hardly be too much to say that the bulk of American "thought" in this period, measured solely by the weight of printed paper, was not thought at all, but only a recapitulation of Spencer. When Justice Holmes said, in his memorable dissent of 1906, in *Lochner* v. *New York,* that "the fourteenth Amendment does not enact Mr. Herbert Spencer's Social Statics," he was not only trying to get back to the original meaning of the amendment, but was blurting out his irritation with the decades in which Spencer had permeated the minds of businessmen and lawyers.

Spencer, we know, had already started work upon his gigantic system, utilizing Malthus' doctrine of population outrunning subsistence and Ricardo's of wages being inexorably fixed by the supply of food, when Darwin supplied him the keystone. He organized his conception around the conservation of energy—or, as he liked to phrase it, "the persistence of force." This meant that the simplest forms of existence are steadily propelled by force (behind the propulsive power Spencer posited "the Unknowable," thus excusing himself and his disciples from further concern about God or the Absolute) until they are pushed into complexity. After they have attained the full degree of complexity, they hang in a state of equilibrium, and it seemed in general that the nineteenth century embodied this final triumph. Undoubtedly the main reason for the appeal of Spencer to so many Americans was the economic theory which followed as an indisputable corollary from these premises: the self-operating order. Such "laws" as supply and demand, or survival of the strong at the expense of the laggards, were demonstrated to be so competent to conduct the business of mankind that the only thing left for the businessman was to conform to them. Above all, no "artificial" interference—especially by the state—was to be tolerated. In economics this meant unlimited laissez faire. Nature is a state of ruthless competition in which the weak are eliminated, and nature supplies the sum and substance of what Spencer (borrowing the term from Auguste Comte) called "sociology." In short, the clear injunction of the Spencerian cosmology was that the competitive America of the 1870's should continue to be just what it was, and nobody should complain. According to Spencer, this economy was the highest stage yet attained in the battle of evolution.

Nevertheless, against the domination of Spencer there were raised successive voices of protest, most of them strident, a few violent. They came out of distress and poverty, out of the agrarian crisis, or else out of moral indignation and the Christian conscience. A complete anthology of American "thought" between the Civil War and World War I would include the orators, agitators, pamphleteers who were Grangers, Greenbackers, Knights of Labor, Populists, Liberals, Socialists, Muckrakers, Social Gospelers, and a few scattered Marxists. Passages would be reprinted from Edward Bellamy, Howells, Henry Demarest Lloyd, Jane Addams, John P. Altgeld, Terence Powderly, Samuel Gompers, Daniel De Leon, Ignatius Donnelley, Eugene Debs, and a hundred others. However, the story of these "progressive" movements has been extensively told; furthermore, although the leaders of these protests often uttered words that still echo, most of them were addressed to particular grievances. Few had either the leisure or the ability to speculate about the reasons for their activity. Their thoughts were attached to specific causes, now lost or won, such as the free coinage of silver or the direct election of senators. In the strenuous competition among ideas for survival within the rigid environmental confines of this small volume, there is room for only one representative of the immense ferment; obviously if there is to be only the most important (although to leave out Lloyd and Walter Rauschenbusch costs the editor a pang), then it must be Henry George.

All these agitators had in common a refusal to lie down supinely before the Spencerian juggernaut. Yet, curiously enough, they were generally Darwinians. That is, they did not take issue with Darwin concerning the origin of man, but tried to find, with the help of Darwin, some way of arguing that a naturally evolved species could still demand ordinary justice. In this respect, Henry George (1839–1897) is indeed the pre-eminent spokesman for what has come to be called "reforming Darwinism." His strategy was to contend that since intelligence itself is a product of evolution, it can be employed, now that it is here, in so modifying the environment that the conditions for survival shall be humanized. The joys and prerogatives of the strong shall thus be extended to the weak. The enormous waste of natural evolution need no longer, under intelligent control, be squandered. The highest reach of mind—as Spencer was insisting—is the social order. Why not, then, utilize evolution *consciously* in order to attain prosperity for the whole society? For Henry George, this prospect reconciled science with his deep religious conviction: would not a reign of economic morality be also the application to society of the Gospel of Christ?

Henry George made his mark upon the age with *Progress and Poverty* in 1879; within twenty-five years it went through over a hundred editions and was read by thousands with a veneration second only to that bestowed upon the Bible. It proposed, as an infallible remedy for economic ills, a single tax upon all increments in the value of land. In the cold light of history, it seems clear that this ingenious device is impracticable, and one can only lament the time and energy George expended in trying to prove it feasible. Despite the commotion he made, despite the crusading spirit of his "Single Tax Clubs," George had no effect upon the actual economy; including his deliberate sacrifice of himself in the New York mayoralty campaign of 1897, his work must be rated, in these regards, a failure.

What is worth remembering about Henry George is not the intricacies of his single-tax argument, but the larger assumptions on which he based it. He came from a California that was still frontier; the spectacle of such crowded and dirty cities as London, Philadelphia, and New York outraged his conception of the American hope. George was a child both of nature and of the

Protestant conscience; he simply could not endure the thought that the American dream should be crushed by a civilization which heartlessly eliminated his sort of people. He could not refute Darwin, but he could see the doom threatening a civilization that loses its spiritual integrity. After 1879 he was endlessly engaged in propagandizing for the single tax, yet somehow he also found time to write more philosophically. *Progress and Poverty* contains, no doubt, his most moving passages, but the book he published in 1883, *Social Problems,* is his best attempt to think clearly about his reasons for feeling as he did. The three chapters here reprinted are fair samples of his warmth and nobility, as well as of his way of transforming Darwinism into a program of social melioration.

VI

The opposing directions of the two philosophies legitimately derived from Darwin and yet irreconcilably opposed to each other were articulated in America by William Graham Sumner (1840–1910) and Lester Ward (1841–1910). Two contemporaries could hardly be more incompatible in every respect, except (significantly) that they both commenced from humble beginnings. Sumner's father was a worker on the railroad, but the son managed to get to Yale, where a rich friend helped him, bought him a substitute for the Army, and financed a trip to Europe. Sumner became an ordained minister in the Episcopal Church, but returned to Yale in 1872 as Professor of Political and Social Science. Years later he said that he put his religious beliefs in a drawer and turned the lock, that upon unlocking it, he found the drawer empty. Possibly this points up the real cleavage between him and George, for whom, as these selections show, he had nothing but contempt.

Sumner staged a famous fight with President Noah Porter over the right to use as the textbook for his course Spencer's *Principles of Sociology.* He published articles in all sorts of journals, popular or scholarly, and eventually made himself known as the one above all others who would ruthlessly, rigorously, apply to society the most dismal of the principles Spencer had deduced out of Darwin.

Actually, Sumner was no slavish follower of Spencer; his individualism was so rugged that he was never accepted by the business community. He was, for example, flatly opposed to protectionism and imperialism; he said that in 1898 America was conquered by Spain! His America was the old one that offered a free field to energetic men wanting to get ahead; he fought to keep it intact. Darwin gave him a "scientific" language for his patriotism, so he followed Spencer and became a "sociologist." What the concept meant to Sumner, his essay of 1881 reveals: it was not really an objective study of society, it was a militant defense of his creed in the language of Darwin. Self-seeking is the primary instinct; it is folly for sentimentalists to imagine that they can care for those they do not personally love. Reformers, by tampering with self-operating laws, only make things worse. Sumner coined the phrase "Forgotten Man," but he did not use it as did Franklin Roosevelt: he meant the ordinary, hard-working, law-abiding citizen who pays his taxes and who consequently "is the only one for whom there is no provision in the great scramble and big divide." He had as great a hatred for corrupt politicians and unscrupulous businessmen as for starry-eyed idealists. Today he is often called a conservative; if he be that, then conservatism means an obstinate belief that only in a society where the struggle for survival is allowed to work itself out can there be freedom. If "progress" is taken to mean delimiting the battlefield, it is illusory and pernicious.

Sumner was not a metaphysician, and so never admitted that he had an epistemology; nevertheless, he did have one, and in this respect stands at the opposite pole from the Idealists. He in effect maintained that the mind is entirely molded by circumstances and that it should resign itself to that fact, abandoning every pretense either that it has innate ideas or that it can remodel the world. For him, sociology became the science of dispelling the false notions by which man fools himself. His major book, *Folkways* (1906), argues that the psychic factors—the abstractions we pretend to live by, such as "honor," "common sense," "eternal truth," "justice," "law of nature"—are created by the situation; they follow changes and fluctuations, are shaped and reshaped, but never do they shape or alter the situation. We are guided by them only because they are symbolic renderings of the physical surroundings, because they are "ways" in which folk decipher their desires, and they become obsolete the moment they prove ineffective. They are substantially what modern parlance calls rationalizations, and the true drama of life is to be found, by the method of Darwin's final paragraph, in the play of power and force behind the shimmer of surface phenomena. The laws are universal, irreversible, inexorable; wherefore any effort to make the world over, especially if it would use the government for bettering the lot of the poor and shiftless, is patently absurd.

Pragmatists, as can readily be seen by comparing Sumner's pieces with those of James and Dewey, had a great deal in common with Sumner's method, but nothing at all with his temper and conclusions; hence they ignored him. Upon his sometime student, Thorstein Veblen, he made a deep impression, although Veblen was to make use of Sumner in an oblique fashion that contrasts strangely with Sumner's bluntness. As for Sumner himself, at the end of his life he lost hope for America. "I have lived through the best period of this country's history. The next generations are going to see war and social calamities. I am glad I don't have to live on into them." We may shudder at the bleakness of a mind that could die with this conclusion, but, as the Adamses were further to testify, there is in the thought of this period a certain strain of realistic appraisal which is entirely out of tune with the prevalent optimism and which beholds in the fabulous material progress of the age only a looming horror.

But over against Sumner stands Lester Ward, who never lost the vision of an increasing purpose working through evolution toward the intelligent achievement of the good society. Born in poverty, he was entirely self-educated; unlike Sumner, he fought and bled in the Civil War. He worked at government jobs in Washington, went to night school, took several degrees, learned ten or twelve languages, read omnivorously, and set out to rival Spencer as the modern Aristotle by taking all knowledge to be his province. Not until 1906, when Brown University made him Professor of Sociology, did he have the leisure of an academic position. In the year of his death, 1913, sociology had won a place in the university curricula, and much of the credit is Ward's, although social scientists, like natural scientists, quickly lose all memory of their forebears. Ward has fallen into oblivion, except as works like this keep something of him alive; yet in the constellation of American thought during the time he was attacking Sumner, his role was important. He was the most reasonable exponent of the argument that evolution has devised, in the natural course of events, the instruments whereby man can direct and improve his future; the principal engine for this control of destiny, he frankly announced, is government. It is not fantastic to see in him the forgotten prophet of the New Freedom and the New Deal.

Ward was as much a Darwinian as Sumner, as much a naturalistic monist. But as he read the struggle for survival he found matter led by brute desire, by the lust for pleasure, into forming highly complex organizations, until at last it devised intelligence as a weapon for acquiring the greatest possible gratification. In society this goal becomes the greatest good not merely of the greatest number but of *all* the number. Ward first spelled out this recasting of Darwin in *Dynamic Sociology* (1883) and finally in *Applied Sociology* (1906). His most readable book (although many of the essays collected in *Glimpses of the Cosmos* [1918] are delightful) is *The Psychic Factors of Civilization,* published in 1893, of which I reproduce the last chapter. His thesis is that the "psychic factors" took shape in the midst of the Darwinian struggle, but that instead of being merely hieroglyphic renderings of surrounding pressures, as were Sumner's "folkways," they are functional, instrumental, and can be used for purposes other than their original intention. They so radically alter the equation that Darwin's laws, applicable as they once were to raw nature and primitive man, have entirely different implications when set to work in modern society. Mind, which at first was the servant of desire, has become the master of nature, and now directs the quest for welfare toward a collectivist state. Art has taken over direction of the drama; psychic factors supplant material urges, and "if we call biologic processes natural, we must call social processes artificial." Hence the artificial interference of government with the natural forces of free enterprise, which seemed to Sumner a blasphemy and an idiocy, becomes for

Ward the end of human existence. "My chief purpose has been to emphasize the fact that sociology is a science, that it is a domain of natural forces of which man may take advantage precisely as he has taken advantage of the physical forces of nature."

Whether or not politicians and theorists of the last generation or of today ever heard about Sumner and Ward, they have been all the while (and at this writing still are) ranged in the camp of the one or the other. Sociologists and anthropologists find the works of both men crude; however, even if their books be obsolete as scientific treatises, the nation has yet to decide for one against the other, a fact which may cause us to suspect that the debate will continue. Consequently there is good reason why students should give careful scrutiny to these two opposing interpreters of .the American spirit.

VII

It was indeed discouraging for those who had real insight into the intellectual problems of the day, who were ready and qualified to think for themselves, to have on all sides the multitude (including such competent scientists as Edward Livingston Youmans) hailing Spencer as the master philosopher of all times. Few paid attention when Charles Sanders Peirce (1839–1914) referred to Spencer's *First Principles* as "antiquated and ignorant," or when he insisted that Darwinian theory was primarily statistical in nature and so should not be regarded as definitive. The Idealistic critique of Darwinism had an audience, at least in circles where both Sumner and Ward were thought too materialistic, but the Pragmatists had to fight for a hearing against both the Spencerians and the Idealists.

Pragmatism is a large subject; with the details and conflicting interpretations this volume cannot be concerned. Neither is there space to set forth the differences among the three major champions, Peirce, James, and Dewey, let alone to settle the much-vexed question of whether Holmes is or is not to be accounted a Pragmatist. Peirce is customarily said to be the founder of the school, but we are always obliged to note that the word is principally associated with James, and that Peirce, once he saw what James was doing with the method, renounced all property in it, and changed the name of his philosophy to "Pragmaticism."

Peirce is a complicated, a difficult mind. He published no philosophical book in his lifetime, only a series of articles which his ardent admirers often found incomprehensible. He lived a rather shoddy existence, never was considered respectable enough to be offered a chair of philosophy, got such income as he could by working for the Geodetic Survey or receiving alms from friends. He was cantankerous and isolated, and only in recent years, when his scattered pieces and manuscripts are at last being printed, has he come into his own. In fact, there already exists something that may be called a Peirce cult, and possibly the danger is no longer that he be neglected, but that too much be made of him.

This book need not attempt to expound his far-ranging metaphysical system. In 1877–1878 he published in *The Popular Science Monthly* six papers under the general title, "Illustrations of the Logic of Science." The second of these, "How to Make Our Ideas Clear," with its injunction, "Consider what effects, which might conceivably have practical bearings, we conceive the object of our conception to have," and then its conclusion, that "our conception of these effects is the whole of our conception of the object," became famous when to it James attributed the beginning of Pragmatism. It is indeed one of the few pieces in our literature which, like Emerson's *Nature,* deserve the adjective "seminal." Yet its importance is greater for the history of logic than for general ideas. Besides, it is available in several reprints; wherefore I have elected to give the first in this remarkable series. I am all the more drawn toward "The Fixation of Belief" because it furnishes a dramatic and (I hope the student will agree) fascinating comparison with James's "The Will to Believe."

Peirce's point, which is the starting point for all his thinking, and in a sense for all varieties of Pragmatism, is that thinking of any kind, logical, scientific, religious, does not come naturally to man but is forced upon him. If man could remain comfortable with a ready-made set of opinions, he would never bestir himself to ask questions; but life is puzzling and disturbing, and causes even the least intellectual to doubt. Now doubt is uncomfortable, and profound doubt is agony. The organism tries to escape, and belief is to be defined as whatever will administer relief. Though Peirce later worked out more circumspect analyses of the mechanism of conviction, in this essay he is saying, as indeed he always was to say, that the real question about a belief is not whether it be "true" but whether because of it the patient passes, as they say in hospitals, a comfortable night. Or as Peirce took delight in saying (Peirce was not, like James and Holmes, a playful man, but there is always in Pragmatic thinking an element of deliberate naughtiness) that a belief is to be tested not by arguing that its content corresponds to the facts of the universe, but by its ability to serve as a "habit." Habits are the ways in which we get along; if they are not disrupted, we are content with our world and with ourselves. When we come to believe something, we settle down. Thinking, Peirce might have said, is a kind of sowing of wild oats.

Peirce's essay is so short, and of such disarming simplicity, that the load of dynamite it carries may not at once be evident. The detonation becomes audible, however, when we remind ourselves that for centuries philosophy and theology were supposed to construct systems, and that the problem of belief was presented as making a choice of one or another—or of building one yourself. As Peirce surveys them through cold, calm eyes, they shrink. "The demonstrations of metaphysicians," he says (even though he himself was a metaphysician), "are all moonshine." They are no longer blueprints of the universe, as if philosophers could read the mind of God—they are habits. In a single gesture, Peirce reduced the lofty structures of the past and, more importantly, the two structures competing for the allegiance of Americans, Idealism and Spencerian Naturalism, to this mundane level. With the path thus cleared before him, he proposed to lead those who would not be lulled by shallow demonstrations into a rigorous investigation of the actual nature of thought.

Partisans of the two systems—who, as James never tired of pointing out, had a vested interest in their mysteries, either as regarded their professorships or their public—accused Peirce of vulgarizing the life of the mind into a way of satisfying animal appetites or anxieties. They took Peirce to mean that he was liberating himself from the necessity of being either an Idealist or a Spencerian, like the proverbial ostrich, by hiding his head in sand. They would not listen to the final portion of his paper, or to his later discussions—when, for instance, he attacked Dewey's logical theory as being merely a "natural history of thought" and insufficiently "normative"—but insisted that he pleaded for nothing more than that anybody could believe anything so long as he felt good. This charge continues to be levied against the pragmatic tradition, and has lately been taken up not so much by opposing philosophers as by a reinvigorated theology. Pragmatism did seem, about the time of James's death, to be the wave of the future, at least in American thought; that prospect is not so certain today, but assuredly all enemies of Pragmatism acknowledge that it is a peculiarly American invention. From the beginning Pragmatists had to contend against the charge that they preached intellectual irresponsibility; Peirce concludes with what essentially is always the Pragmatist's reply. Whether it in turn is "satisfactory" to all students is of less moment than that they understand how much rigor of mind Peirce brought to the definition of belief. At bottom, Peirce's analysis of thought and of what constitutes valid grounds for belief is a declaration of intellectual freedom.

The one work above all his other writings by which William James (1842–1910) is known outside psychological laboratories and the closed circle of professional philosophers is "The Will to Believe." It may not represent his most profound thought; several of the essays collected in 1897 in the volume to which this gives the title (particularly, in my opinion, "The Dilemma of Determinism," 1884) are deeper speculation. Still, this address, first delivered at a "Summer School for Ethics" sponsored by Felix Adler in Plymouth, Massachusetts, in 1895, and repeated the next year at Yale and Brown, is assuredly James's most appealing as well as most popular utterance.

Much of its pre-eminence results from the fact that it was in its day, and is now, taken by critics of Pragmatism to be a reckless apology for willfulness and capriciousness in belief. James did not take even the modicum of care that Peirce did to protect himself. Indeed, it was over this essay that Peirce (to whom the volume is dedicated) made emphatic his parting with James. He commented that he too had a high regard for the individual deed as that which gives life to an idea, but that if belief were to be described as a plan of procedure (as one might say that Lester Ward was then doing), it would work more harm than good. Tenacity, yes, as he had said in "The Fixation of Belief"; but if that "means you are not going to be alert for indications that the moment has come to change your tactics, I think it ruinous in practice." James contended against his critics, and largely in vain, that he had not intended to justify a belief in nonsense, but to justify belief itself. He did not suppose for a moment that the believer should pay no heed to motives and reasons; what he did want to establish was the point that belief is volitional—and therefore free. He later said that he should have entitled the article "The Right to Believe"; in that light, his argument may be said to pertain more to theology than to philosophy.

James delivered this essay after he had exhausted himself writing *The Principles of Psychology* and had suffered from a prolonged spell of depression. His assertion can be seen to spring from a resolution to cherish the spontaneity of the mind against, on the one side, Idealism (which he called "Gnosticism") and, on the other, Spencerian Naturalism (which he called "Agnosticism"). He tried to keep thought from being pulverized by either "block universe." Writing as a psychologist, a wit, a gentleman, James saw nothing to make one of these systems better than the other; he called them both "idealisms" in that they set up some hypothetical scheme and then demanded that it be translated directly into action by the nervous organization of mankind. They would chain the psyche to an inhuman mechanism. Whether the stimulus of the reflex was said to originate from a transcendent idea or from a material environment was a mere quibble as long as one held that the impulse goes through the brain and emerges as behavior without there being any power at the center of the personality capable of turning it this way or that. James hated what he and

Dewey called "the spectator theory of knowledge," the notion that man is passive and impotent until prodded or jerked. Where Royce thought he could vindicate freedom by showing it to be conformity to the Absolute, and where Ward found it in the mastery of an evolved intelligence, James saw both solutions as ways of disguising a surrender of the intellect. As for Herbert Spencer, James scored his point by burlesquing Spencer's famous definition of evolution. It is, Spencer had said, "an integration of matter and concomitant dissipation of motion; during which matter passes from an indefinite, incoherent homogeneity to a definite, coherent heterogeneity; and during which the retained motion undergoes a parallel transformation." What this amounts to, said James, is "a change from a no-howish untalkaboutable all-alikeness to a somehowish and in general talkaboutable not-all-alikeness by continuous sticktogetherations and somethingelseifications."

Peirce and James, we must perceive, would not have been so ready to confront the problem of belief in these vital terms, to rescue ideas from the imprimatur of a system, and to give them a chance to discover their meanings in action, had not Darwin supplied them with a technique for appreciating the logic of life rather than of the syllogism. Primarily because of him—although they were anything but meek Darwinians—they could formulate this logic in a language utterly different from that of logicians. Hence they were not so afraid of Darwin as were the Idealists, nor so overwhelmed by him as were George, Sumner, and Ward. Peirce and James fought against what most in the age took to be this Hobson's choice by crying a plague on both the houses. They maintained that mind need not abdicate unconditionally. They disagreed with each other, but the last thing either of them would ever do was to surrender.

Out of this effort to mediate between extremes came James's classic statement, growing out of lectures given in 1905–1907, his *Pragmatism*, published May, 1907. It is acknowledged, even by those who regard it as an unmitigated evil, to be the most readable piece of philosophizing yet written in this country; for this very reason, not to mention others, it has been assaulted. The more it is criticized, the more its great qualities emerge. There is no need to add to James's own exposition, to the lucid second chapter which is here reproduced. James's differences from Peirce stand out in every sentence; if Peirce is the sounder thinker, James is the more lovable man. He could not be content with an organon for the clarification of meaning; he had to go further, to contend that mind engenders truth upon reality, and thus to assert a faith in man's nature that gives human significance to an evolutionary process which otherwise would be monstrous. "Our minds," says William James, "are not here simply to copy a reality that is already complete."

Oliver Wendell Holmes (1841–1935) is usually called the Pragmatic theorist of the law. Yet, though he was a friend, or at least an associate, of James, he was a very different sort of man; his cynicism, his admiration for the military virtues, his distrust of human nature, and his hatred of self-deception gave him a considerable contempt for "The Will to Believe." While he read widely in modern philosophy, the sources of his thinking were rather historical, legal, and literary. Yet he too had imbibed, along with Chauncey Wright and Peirce, the spirit of Darwin. Like other members of the Metaphysical Club, he early learned to reject ideas which claim to be copies of a completed reality; instinctively he turned to the sort of analysis which, conceiving them as manifestations of the organism's adaptation to environment, throws out the window all historic abstractions. He may not actually be a Pragmatist in philosophy, but he most dramatically poses the question of finding the meaning of a concept in its practical consequences.

As a judge on the Supreme Court of Massachusetts from 1882 to 1902 and on the Supreme Court of the United States from 1902 to 1932 he wrote many famous decisions, some of them before the terminal limit of this volume. His monumental study, *The Common Law* (1881), is fairly technical, yet is the first and possibly still the most impressive application to the façade of the law of that method of ascertaining the forces at work which is the essential method of Darwin; the book is as much an essay in anthropology and cultural history as a treatise on jurisprudence. For general readers, Holmes's occasional pieces, usually given as addresses, are the most enjoyable as well as the more precise statements of his philosophy. There is universal agreement that "The Path of the

Law" in 1897 is the most successful; therefore it becomes the inevitable choice. Like "The Will to Believe," Holmes's discourse has become a battleground; his critics have decried it as making an unreal and pernicious separation between law and morality. In recent years the reaction against so hard-boiled and ruthless an objectivity has become considerable; wherever one's sympathies may lie, the fact remains that his reduction of the toplofty platitudes of textbooks to the simple assertion that a law is nothing more, in actual fact, than a prediction of what the judge will do is in the spirit of Wright, Peirce, and James. In order that he may further and clearly stand in the light to which his opponents most object, but in which he would most wish to appear, I have reached forward as far as 1918 to include his "Natural Law." The debate as to whether Holmes's doctrine is no more than polite brutality continues, just as students are never entirely sure that this "liberal" was not in reality a rock-bound "conservative." It should, however, be said that in the opinion of those best acquainted with him personally, as also in the opinion of this editor, the charge that Holmes had no concern for "values" and that he took the side of the "bad man" as easily as that of the good is nonsense. "Natural Law" shocks those who want to "believe" that the universe is governed by an ideal and universal justice, who need such consolation in the face of "The Problem of Job." Too often they do not stop to read, or to sound the depths of, the conclusion of the essay, where the deeply religious dedication which carried Holmes through his amazingly productive and serviceable life comes into the open. The mixture in him of scepticism and belief, of frivolity and high seriousness, along with his prodigious open-mindedness, his hospitality to all ideas, makes him indeed an authentic spokesman for one of the profound traits of the American mind.

The writings by which John Dewey (1859–1952) is best known, commencing with *Democracy and Education* in 1916, come after the concluding date of this collection. Before 1916 he had attracted attention as an educational reformer and made contributions to logic; as a publicist he was chiefly occupied, during the first decade of the century, in working out a version of Pragmatism that started with Peirce and James (especially with James's *Psychology*), but was more elaborately integrated with the concept of evolution. Born in Vermont, and always something of the shy countryman, Dewey did not have Peirce's demonic drive nor James's brilliance; yet he had a patience and thoroughness they conspicuously lacked. Commencing as a student of Morris, he went through a Hegelian phase, from which he extricated himself with difficulty, and which left permanent marks upon his thinking. More than either Peirce or James he was disposed to comprehend ideas in a framework of process and development, to push to the utmost the *genetic* method. The differences between his and James's Pragmatism steadily increased, although in the years before 1910 Dewey became as much of an influence on James as James had originally been on him. His "Instrumentalism" became a Pragmatism with a much greater social orientation than either of the founders had conceived. He could have a much greater sympathy with Henry George, and a much warmer understanding of Lester Ward.

Just as Holmes (who felt himself intellectually closer to Dewey than to James) found the life of the law in experience and not in logic, and therefore presented the Common Law not as a rigid structure but as a growth entirely conditioned by historical circumstances, Dewey sought to define the words involved in any philosophical problem, particularly in the venerable ones of traditional metaphysics, within a historical perspective. He was much perturbed by the essay Thomas Huxley published in 1893, which reverberated throughout Christendom, "Evolution and Ethics." Huxley roundly asserted that the practices which this culture considers ethically best—those of goodness and virture—are in all respects "opposed to that which leads to success in the cosmic struggle for existence." In 1910 Dewey collected his several pieces on this theme in *The Influence of Darwin on Philosophy*, which has been neglected by comparison with his more famous works, but which has a literary charm he seldom thereafter equaled and which is indispensable for comprehending the climate of opinion at the turn of the century. The titular essay was delivered in a course of public lectures by which Columbia University observed the fiftieth anniversary of *The Origin of Species*—published in the year, as has been frequently remarked, in which Dewey himself was born. His discussion of 1909 might well stand as preface to this entire collection, except that Dewey holds the effect of Darwin upon science, philosophy, and ethics (he was little concerned with the effect on religion) to be salutary only when viewed through Pragmatic eyes. Peirce and James relieved him of the burden that weighed upon—indeed crushed—Lester Ward: he did not have to tell precisely how and where in the course of evolution the psychic factor was generated out of matter. Like his masters, Dewey could argue that the peculiar function of the human species which we call intelligence, once it has divined the secret of nature, is in a position to apply the method to every problem. It need no longer devise systematic transcripts of the objective universe. Thought has become an active transformer of the situation, introducing new elements; hence it never was designed to unearth a single, pre-existing answer. In this spirit Dewey sought to resolve the ethical dilemma presented by Huxley: "Intelligence and Morals," a lecture given in an earlier series at Columbia, in March 1908, is a work of art, not only for its concise exemplification of the method, but also for the way it indicates how, in Dewey's view, Pragmatism must come out on the side of that social idea we call democracy. It is a first draft of the larger book called *Reconstruction in Philosophy* that was to appear in 1920 and that still remains, to friends and foes alike, one of the central works of our time. Politically Dewey is on the side of George and Ward, but he does not have to enter the lists against Sumner. Having behind him the sophistication of Peirce and James, he can perfect a more subtle and more complex, a less strident but actually more revolutionary, investigation into the intellectual implications of Darwinism.

VIII

The two brothers Adams, Henry (1838–1918) and Brooks (1848–1927), inherited a family disposition as well as a tradition. If this imparted a rugged sense of independence, a refusal to truckle to any man or to go with any tide, it also manifested itself as crotchetiness and even downright perversity. If history and society would not employ them on their own terms, so much the worse for history and society; they would get their revenge by dissecting the idiocies of both until the essential rightness of all Adamses was remorselessly vindicated. Because so many of their dire predictions, which before 1914 sounded fantastic, have been confirmed by grim events, they are rated as major prophets unhonored by their country or their contemporaries. Assuredly they belong in any collection of the thinkers of the epoch, but they are not representative. As against Ward and Sumner, no less than against James and Dewey, they stand in the opposition.

This dissidence was a result, fundamentally, of their refusal to bow to Darwin. They used the terminology of *The Origin of Species,* but only for their private purposes. Neither of them had any true comprehension of biology or of the experimental method. They were cosmologically minded. They thought (and rethought their thought) in order to manufacture some grand conception of the universe upon which judgment could then be pronounced. They regarded intelligence not in the Pragmatic spirit, as a method of testing the meanings of words and slogans, but as a dogmatic faculty which expounds the analogies between things and concepts. At Harvard, Henry was on the side of Agassiz, and to the end harbored Aggasiz's hatred for Darwin. He and Brooks got, as all their writings show, a positive glee from every evidence that could be turned into a refutation of Darwin, if only what to them was the obvious de-volution from Washington to President Grant. Because they did think in terms of cosmologies rather than of growth, they set up to be not historians put philosophers of history. They discovered, or at least arrayed in patterns, the immense forces unleashed in modern times, especially those of the machine, the dynamo, and the factory. They saw in the America of their old age a crisis not so much of the spirit as of pure force. The deeper they pressed their analysis, the more they could foresee for this industrial society only catastrophe. They were obliged by the succession of events to keep revising their prevision—repeatedly they become ridiculous as they reinterpret the sweep of history in order to account for an American election. They seem predetermined that every occurrence shall be made to prove that destruction is on its way.

To their Olympian view, the pattern persisted and accelerated, and both of them ended as prophets of doom.

Despite his subjectivity and general grumpiness, and despite his spectacular changes of course, Brooks Adams stands out in retrospect as the most coherent philosopher in his day of conservatism, imperialism, and concentration of power. It is true that he seldom bothered to train his barrage upon liberals and reformers; instead he concentrated it upon those groups who are customarily called conservative, that is, upon bankers, manufacturers, and businessmen. He expended himself in a lifelong campaign to convince the economic rulers of America that they were stupid, shortsighted, and ignorant of their true interest.

In part, Brooks Adams' strategy was a prolongation of his family's feud with "State Street." But in greater part, he was convinced that the business community was funking its opportunity and its responsibility by accepting, as its reason for being, a shallow and facile Darwinian argument for free competition and for opposition to governmental regulation. Adams may have exerted influence upon Theodore Roosevelt when the latter formulated that vague program of control in the name of social justice which became the "New Nationalism," and which, at the end of our period, was aligned against the "New Freedom" of Woodrow Wilson. At any rate, Brooks Adams did everything he could to encourage such nationalist tendencies.

Actually, the New Nationalism owed more to Arthur Thayer Mahan's (1840–1914) *The Influence of Sea Power upon History* (1890) and, in its later—its "Progressive"—phase, to Herbert Croly's (1869–1930) *The Promise of American Life* (1909). (Both these works, needless to say, would be represented in this collection were there space enough.) Mahan presented the brute weight of sea power as the decisive factor in the conflict of nations; behind him was a kind of Darwinian sanction, but he was not conceiving of sea power as a creation of evolutionary intelligence nor as a concept to be tested in experience, but simply as the supreme instrument of a national policy. A navy wins victories, but in order to maintain it, society must be regimented to that end. Otherwise defeat is inescapable. Croly's work had a larger objective: the conquest of the entire government for the comprehensive aims of a vigorous nationalism. Croly was disgusted by the disruptive uprisings of the reformers and the incompetence of liberals; he declared that, in order to survive, a society must become consolidated under the leadership of the strong and the capable. He repudiated alike the Jeffersonian ideal of equality, the capitalist's worship of free competition, and the reformer's dream of civil service. He found the meaning of democracy in the doctrine of a collective action directed by a qualified elite. Croly had only scorn for the naïve Darwinism of Sumner: that was much too moralistic and too recalcitrantly individualistic for so monolithic a power as industrialized America had become.

Even though Brooks Adams probably had less effect on Theodore Roosevelt than legend supposes, and though his books were not so widely read as those of Mahan and Croly—though he died in the belief that his country had paid no heed and was headed for the abyss—he brought to the formulation of this implacable nationalism a range of historical reference which makes him today the most formidable of the superconservatives. Divining the momentum of the argument, and untrammeled by the scruples which Darwinism curiously imposed upon its most militant adherents (novelists like Frank Norris and Theodore Dreiser are cases in point), Adams leaped ahead of his contemporaries, and anticipated conclusions to which less imaginative and more timorous conservatives found their way, if at all, slowly. If they have dallied along the road, it is, we may be sure, not because Brooks Adams failed to make the prospect clear before them.

One might say that he out-Darwinizes the Darwinians. In his view, *The Origin of Species* becomes an academic exercise. The real actors in the struggle for survival have always been not species but avatars of force. The pattern of prehistoric conflict is carried over into historical times as a successive gathering of vitalities around particular centers—Rome, Constantinople, Venice, Flanders, London, New York—one after another going down in defeat before the rise of a stronger and more efficient conqueror. Through every rephrasing of his evidence, Adams' idea is that America, having become the latest incarnation of power, will, unless it lives up to the occasion, unless it can dominate the world, go the way of Carthage, Macedon, and Imperial Rome.

We have got to start something new, and use our facts to some practical purpose, or we shall go ashore—and neither Phoenician, nor Greek, nor Roman, nor anyone else has any particular interest for us at this moment, unless we can extract from his experience something which may aid us in protecting our lives against our enemies.

Because he felt that the situation was becoming desperate, he scandalized (where he did not merely bewilder) his fellow conservatives by telling them that they must save themselves by becoming conservative with a vengeance. He demanded that they undertake a reorganization of the state which seemed to them, in their simplicity, extreme socialism.

Brooks Adams first tried to become a participant in politics by agitating for Populism and for Bryan, who, he hoped, would bring the "gold bugs" to their senses. In 1894 he published *The Gold Standard,* and in 1895 *The Law of Civilization and Decay,* which put the cosmic rule in one sentence: "The theory proposed is based upon the accepted scientific principle, that the law of force and energy is of universal application in nature, and animal life is one of the outlets through which solar energy is dissipated." This energy manifests itself in instinct, not in conscious thought; intelligence, far from being a shaper of the environment, is only that which amusedly registers the process. Mind is not inside the process; it is at best an impotent by-product.

When the agrarian insurgency failed, Adams went over to McKinley and the Republicans, declaring imperialism a substitute for silver coinage, and wrote *America's Economic Supremacy* (1900), which contains the startling prediction that shortly there will be left only two nations to contend for world mastery: the United States and Russia. In 1902 came *The New Empire,* his most strident effort to rouse America to an understanding of its destiny. In 1912 Adams supported the Roosevelt campaign, and after the defeat, in 1913, published *The Theory of Social Revolutions.* I give the opening chapter of *The New Empire* as a fair sample of Adams' hortatory vein, and the conclusion of *Social Revolutions* as the form in which his despairing admonition settled toward the end of his life.

Along with his frank acceptance of brutality, his intense nationalism, and his extravagant admiration for the soldierly virtues, Adams' principal contention was the necessity in modern society for "administration." He preached the need for training superior minds to conduct the national policy, and demanded that this bureaucracy be given dictatorial authority: "Everything is to be cured by the concentration of power in some one who really will protect the whole community." Because these dictators would have to be educated in the art of "generalization," he attacked the universities, which, under the misguided sponsoring of capitalists, were rushing into specialization. He called for social planning and the forcible curbing of all individualism, whether radical, liberal, or commercial. He utterly repudiated any notion that economic life can be left to the "guiding hand" of either a divine or a Darwinian providence, and told the men with power that if they did not promptly show that they could wield it, power would be taken from them. Thus it may be perceived that Adams, by declaring war to the death not only upon George as well as upon Sumner but also upon the entire tribe of Pragmatists, becomes the supreme advocate in America of absolute authoritarianism.

Henry Adams, unlike his brother, early gave up any hope of playing a part in practical politics. He preferred to stand aside (or let himself be pushed aside), and contented himself with the role of spectator, seeking (or posing as seeking) a comprehensive philosophy to explain the tragic course of a history which consigned him to futility. In American literature the results of his meditations are two books of indubitable merit, long since established as literary classics: *Mont-Saint-Michel and Chartres* and *The Education of Henry Adams*. These enjoyed no great audience before Adams' death, but today they spread his thesis broadcast. In the thirteenth century, it goes, men achieved a unified culture (symbolized by the Virgin) through a mastery of all the lines of force to which they were then exposed; but in the twentieth, the race is bombarded by an augmenting multiplicity of forces (symbolized by the dynamo), and the problem is whether its brain can keep up with the shattering complexity. If the brain cannot, chaos will come again. Adams died in the conviction (or should one say the hope?) that the end was not far off.

In 1910 he addressed *A Letter to American Teachers of History* (to which the teachers paid no attention) in an effort, beyond that of the *Education,* to convey his conception of history; the year before he had attempted a shorter statement, *The Rule of Phase Applied to History,* which he later somewhat rewrote, but which was published only after his death, in 1919, by his brother Brooks. Adams said of the *Letter* what he might well have said of the *Rule,* that it was a "joke" of which only he could get the point. Both writings incarnate those elements of perversity, affectation, parade of erudition, assumption of intellectual superiority, and downright irresponsibility which make Adams both fascinating and exasperating. The student must handle them warily, but both (especially the *Rule,* here reprinted) constitute the furthest any American in the period went toward erecting against the evolutionary and Pragmatic idea a rigid system within which the heavens themselves might be confined. Part of the "joke" is that in order to construct his cage Adams had to pretend to employ a historical method, but as his little diagrams reveal, the scheme itself is static and (in Dewey's terms) unhistorical.

Critics competent to judge his use of the scientific materials say that Adams wantonly or mischievously misused them, that he capriciously extracted from the work of Gibbs, Lord Kelvin, and other physicists whatever pleased him, and ignored the rest. For this volume, the question is not relevant; for us the important things are the passion Adams poured into his consuming quest for "unity," his determination to achieve it even if unification was to be found only in universal calamity, and his sly persistence in a method of thinking which, having discovered (or claiming to have discovered) the design of the cosmos in the second law of thermodynamics, applied this law and all its consequences to the plight of mankind. The *Rule* is less judicious and less scientific than the *Letter,* but for that reason alone, if not for others (including its brevity), is a better expression of the demon that preyed upon Henry Adams. We should remember when dealing with so tricky a mind that his lack of caution may be calculated, that he is fully capable of employing physics (particularly that comet!) as a metaphor while pretending to treat it as a science. The intention of the *Rule* is to demolish the overeasy optimism which lies at the heart of most varieties of Darwinism. The psychological depths of Adams' thinking are probably impenetrable, for by an ostentatious candor he concealed them; but the methodological result amounts to a complete contradiction of the dominant tendencies of the age. Since those tendencies have subsequently been subjected to several critiques, Adams' amateur scientism, with its imagery of accelerating degradation, demands a respect which has little concern with the correctness of his physics. The dying William James, to his last breath the vibrant Pragmatist, simply was not impressed by the *Rule* and wrote in protest, "The 'second law' is wholly irrelevant to 'history.'" If James is right, the essay is, of course, "unsound." However, I think it fair to say that the *Rule* is not a treatise or an argument: it is an eschatological vision, an apocalyptical lament over the approaching (and simultaneous) extinction of both solar and historical energy. In Adams' view, mankind, by its inept fumbling with nature, has brought itself to the point where it can blow itself to pieces; he could not contemplate this eventuality without insisting that the entire universe would commit suicide at the same time.

IX

The career of Thorstein Veblen (1851–1929) demonstrates at least one fact: a man does not need to be born an Adams or to be descended from a line of Puritans in order to become a master of perversity, of the art of mystifying even while alluring his audience. Through his long life Veblen displayed such an independence of manner and morals as cost him his marriage, his friends, and a series of jobs, and such an independence of mind as leaves him a social theorist who defies classification and who, more than any figure of recent times, has deeply influenced a variety of followers, hardly one of whom agrees with any other. Born on a

frontier farm in Wisconsin, the fourth son of Norwegian immigrants, he learned English in such a manner as to make his writings
appear to be translated from some weird and forgotten tongue. Many
critics believed flatly that he just could not cope with the language;
lately the suspicion has dawned that he maliciously cultivated his
gawky mannerisms in order to conceal, behind a deliberate clumsi-
ness, a deadly satirical purpose. To the end he remained an alien
in this culture, not so much racially as spiritually; yet in the
freedom with which he manipulated the concepts of the era, in
the originality of his revision of the Darwinian laws, in the very
idiosyncrasy of his combinations of principles, there speaks something which could have been uttered in no land but America.

After being graduated from Carleton College, Veblen studied
at Johns Hopkins, Yale, and Cornell. He read everything, but especially Kant, Hegel, Spencer—and Marx. He also attended lectures
by Peirce and Sumner, and was a friend of Lester Ward. Having
grown up in the area, he knew at firsthand the Populist mood, and
had an equally comprehensive appreciation of Henry George.
Some sardonic trait in his make-up kept him from becoming in the
slightest a crusader. In 1892 he reached the new University of
Chicago, and there in the next decade produced a series of articles,
and in 1899 *The Theory of the Leisure Class,* which seemed to
his colleagues in the nascent social sciences the flights of a lawless
fancy designed, one of them said, to bring sociology into "disrepute
among careful and scientific thinkers." Today the book and the
articles are recognized as profound and fruitful analyses of twentieth-century society; to some extent Veblen's propositions have
entered into everybody's thinking and his catch phrases have become common property. Still, it would be rash to say that his
full meaning has been exposed.

To amputate portions of the *Leisure Class* (which is now available in several reprints) is to spoil a work of art. Its thesis, that
in a capitalist society the creation of waste is an index of success, is
in effect a standing of Herbert Spencer on his head. The mingling
of serious and satiric tones make the book doubly effective, since
no reader knows exactly when his leg is being pulled or whether
the moral of the book should be moral indignation against an

improvident society or a Pascalian compliance with folly. Veblen has inspired New Dealers and reassured reactionaries. He understood the meaning of Darwinism as thoroughly as did Chauncey Wright, but he drew upon a more sophisticated anthropology and psychology to give his own ironic twist to the Darwinian workings of modern civilization. He translated the profligacy of natural selection into the lust for conspicuous waste, and replaced the restrictive pressure of adaptation by "the instinct of workmanship," while he found a more vital version of the law of variation in the principle of "emulation." Prosaic sociologists found this list of substitutes for the Darwinian concepts too bizarre to be taken seriously, but Veblen, armed with such revisions, went the Darwinians one better. He constructed a pattern of illogical rationality behind the false front of formality which made the Pragmatists, both James and Dewey, look like apostles of a utilitarian rationalism still rooted in the eighteenth century. They could, by contrast with Veblen, be made to sound as systematic, as little aware of how life is actually lived, as Royce himself.

The full panoply of Veblen's dialectic does not explicitly appear in the article he published in *The American Journal of Sociology* for March, 1906, "The Place of Science in Modern Civilization"; yet his basic scheme is there by implication. More importantly, it is a good sample of his style (he himself thought it his best article), and so I choose it to represent him. Ostensibly it is a justification of human irrationality against the pretensions of exact science, a *cri de cœur* of humanity; it looks like an attack upon Pragmatists for not taking sufficient account of the ineradicable propensity of the human animal for self-delusion, and so, by providing facile formulas for the fixation of belief or the will to believe, aiding that mechanization of society against which the primordial instincts revolt. But on a deeper level, the essay is, if carefully read, a criticism of Veblen's colleagues—one of whom had been John Dewey—for not understanding just how strong and how deep is the desire to survive. There is a manifestation which comes from the center of life itself, that "idle curiosity" which, in defiance of immediate interests or practicability, produces science. But at the same time, there is a compulsion at work among the masses which can make extremely short work, should they be alarmed, of the applications of scientific theorems to their daily lives. Mankind loves to tell stories about the sun and stars, and pure science is thus one with mythmaking; but it is not happy with the results of "applied science," all Pragmatists to the contrary notwithstanding.

Veblen continues to be a disturbing figure to economists (Spencerian or Marxist) as well as to all proponents of an ideal (whether Royce or Brooks Adams) because he proceeds upon an apparently inhuman, an "anthropological," approach to humanity. He thus recognizes all that Ward meant by the "psychic factors" without committing himself to Ward's gentle belief that these are now equipped to take over direction of the protoplasm. Likewise, Veblen excuses himself from the duty of investing the term "intelligence" with the creative power ascribed to it by Dewey; the engineers in whom he hoped society would find saviors would not be so much intelligent as artistic, carried by an instinct of workmanship into a love of art for art's sake. Veblen founds his sociology upon the more primitive, upon atavistic, hungers. He could not have formulated them had not Darwin been a predecessor, but the concluding paragraph of *The Origin of Species* could not possibly have foreseen that the nonrational exposure of formalities would be carried to such lengths of irony as Veblen employed. In his tortured and angry prose, the impersonality of a pure scientist joins forces with the bard of savagery in an alliance against the perversion of human dignity perpetrated by a profit-seeking, "barbarian" civilization. The ultra-Darwinian emerges as the partisan of Hegel, who is "romantic," against a Darwinism that had let itself become too "realistic," and thus endeavors to save the mind from enslavement to the "passionless matter-of-fact."

The Brandeis of the great decisions handed down after 1916 (the best known of them being dissents!) from the bench of the Supreme Court can hardly be accused of perversity. Yet at the moment President Wilson nominated him, there were many who felt that Louis Dembitz Brandeis (1856–1941) was the most perverse man in the country. A brilliant corporation lawyer, who made millions by defending special interests, inexplicably began in the 1890's, and continued at an accelerating rate, to bite the hand that had fed him. According to his own account, he did so because he had become persuaded that somebody had to take it upon himself to act as attorney for the people. When he took a case, he noted that his opponent had a lawyer, but he further observed that in disputes involving the public interest nobody represented the masses. So he, declining in these affairs to accept a retainer, selected his client, that amorphous patron who could hire nobody and who was too befuddled to comprehend that his welfare was at stake. Brandeis outraged corporations, railroads, and banks, and was reputed a dangerous radical; all the time he called himself a conservative, which is precisely what he was. Not, of course, in the sense in which Brooks Adams was a conservative; he simply wanted justice done in the light of the facts. He had no use for cosmological doctrines, and we can hardly say he was motivated by any abstract idealism beyond a profound love for his country and for freedom. He had little sympathy with ideological reformers like Henry George, was little affected by either Darwin or Spencer. He had a clear, efficient mind; he liked to grasp the total situation, and he saw nothing either incongruous or heroic in acting according to the most accurate information.

It is a striking fact that Brandeis, like Veblen, was the son of immigrants, that he too was born outside the pale that includes every other figure, from Royce to the Adamses, in this collection. History is often more symbolic than historians bargain for, and just possibly the ultimate comment to be made upon the America of this period is that, with all its imperfections and confusions, it allows me to present as the concluding contributors two children of new Americans, coming from races that had to fight to gain recognition from the dominant "Anglo-Saxon" respectability.

Brandeis figures in American social thought and in jurisprudence as the champion of "small business," as the defender of little men and little institutions. In this respect, he is indeed the arch-opponent of Brooks Adams. Yet in the pattern of the American mind, he has a still deeper significance: "It has been one of the rules of my life," he said in 1916, "that no one shall ever trip me on a question of fact." What he most incarnates is a method of investigation, of drawing conclusions from *all* the evidence. In 1908, he first made an impression upon the nation at large (after he had for over a decade been disturbing the serenity of Boston) when defending before the Supreme Court a law of the state of Oregon limiting the working day for women to ten hours; he presented a brief of 104 pages, only two of which dealt with the precedents while the rest comprised an exhaustive sociological study of the health and morals of the mothers of the future. By the time Wilson named him, January 28, 1916, he had, as self-appointed attorney for the people, fought a series of bitter legal battles against traction interests, railroads, and combines; he had won victories for public conservation, and acquired a multitude of enemies. In 1913–1914 he had published *Other People's Money,* a devastating attack upon investment trusts.

Ideally, a portion of that book ought to close this anthology, but most of Brandeis' writings, before the Supreme Court obliged him to cultivate a literary style, are so factual, legalistic, argumentative as to be unreadable to any but lawyers and economists. However, in 1905, when he was steadily gaining in fame and notoriety, a society of Harvard students invited him to speak, and for once Brandeis had no occasion to prepare a brief. "The Opportunity in the Law" is as compact as was his mind, and deliberately avoids the purple patches an ordinary speaker—or an Oliver Wendell Holmes—would permit himself; yet it is, in every seemingly placid sentence, full of that steely determination which is the essence of Brandeis.

In 1915, with the war already raging in Europe and the part that America should or should not play in it becoming the topic of furious discussion, his friends persuaded the municipal authorities to select him as the Independence Day orator for the civic observance in Faneuil Hall. His enemies were horrified, and the atmosphere was tense. "True Americanism" is not one of the more stirring pieces of American oratory, and characteristically plays down the forensic opportunities; it is a measured, resonant statement of that liberalism which he, the clear-eyed conservative, believed to be the meaning of this republic. The international ideal he outlined has, of course, come to be associated with the name of Wilson. Hence his nomination to the Court and the confirmation that was won on June 1, 1916, form an appropriate ending for this book.

By April of the next year, with the declaration of war, the era closed which had opened when the mind of America was first aroused and challenged by the twin invasions of Hegel and Darwin. It is not, perhaps, one of the most luminous epochs in the record of human intelligence; in creative literature it is nothing like so brilliant as the one that followed, but in speculation it was indeed one of bold adventure. As this very limited excerption from the vast body of the publications will, I hope, make clear, it was a period in which the American mind was intensively active—or at least many minds in America were—in which the issues of the national consciousness were, for better or worse, and for a long time yet to come, discovered and defined. Here they were set in that array of battle, not just of one against another but of each against all the others, which is the supreme expression of vitality among a free people.

PERRY MILLER

Princeton, New Jersey
January, 1954

BIBLIOGRAPHY

I. GENERAL WORKS

The bibliography of the social history of the period from the Civil War to 1917 is, naturally, immense, and is every year increasing. I am listing here only the works which, in whole or in part, deal with the life of the mind. Many of them touch only incidentally upon the major themes of this volume, and several of them make heroes or villains out of persons not cited in my collection. I have appended comments only to those I feel worth singling out. The student can see, from this bibliography if not from my selections, how rich and complicated an era it was.

Aaron, Daniel
　　Men of Good Hope, New York, 1951.
Beard, Charles A., and Mary R. Beard
　　The Rise of American Civilization, New York, 1927.
Buck, Paul H.
　　The Road to Reunion, 1865–1900 Boston, 1937.
Cargill, Oscar
　　Intellectual America, New York, 1941.
Chamberlain, John
　　Farewell to Reform, New York, 1932.
Cochran, Thomas C., and William Miller
　　The Age of Enterprise, New York, 1942.
Cohen, I. Bernard
　　Science, Servant of Man, Boston, 1948.
Commager, Henry S.
　　The American Mind, New Haven, 1950.
Commons, John R.
　　History of Labour in the United States, New York, 1918.
Curti, Merle
　　The Growth of American Thought, New York, 1943.

Bibliography

Destler, Chester M.
   American Radicalism, 1865–1901, New London, 1946.
Dorfman, Joseph
   The Economic Mind in American Civilization, New York, 1946.
Egbert, Donald D., and Stow Persons
   Socialism and American Life, Princeton, 1952.
Faulkner, Harold U.
   The Quest for Social Justice, 1898–1914, New York, 1931.
Filler, Louis
   Crusaders for American Liberalism, New York, 1939.
Foster, Frank Hugh
   The Modern Movement in America Theology, New York, 1939.
Gabriel, Ralph
   The Course of American Democratic Thought, New York, 1940.
Goldman, Eric F.
   Rendezvous with Destiny, New York, 1952. (A clever, often perceptive, often glib, on the whole superficial survey of the period.)
Handlin, Oscar
   The Uprooted, Boston, 1951.
Hicks, Granville
   The Great Tradition, New York, 1933.
Hicks, John D.
   The Populist Revolt, Minneapolis, 1931.
Hofstadter, Richard
   Social Darwinism in American Thought, 1860–1915, Philadelphia, 1944. (A basic work for any student of the period.)
Hofstadter, Richard
   The American Political Tradition, New York, 1948.
Hopkins, Charles H.
   The Rise of the Social Gospel in American Protestantism, 1865–1915, New Haven, 1940.
Josephson, Matthew
   The Politicos, 1865–1896, New York, 1938.
Josephson, Matthew
   The Robber Barons, New York, 1934.

Kazin, Alfred
On Native Grounds, New York, 1942.

Lovejoy, Arthur O.
The Revolt against Dualism, New York, 1930.

Lowenberg, Bert James
"Darwinism Comes to America, 1859–1900," *Mississippi Valley Historical Review,* XXVIII (1941) 339–368.

Lowenberg, Bert James
"The Reaction of American Scientists to Darwinism," *American Historical Review,* XXXVIII (1932–1933) 687–701.

Lundberg, George A.
Trends in American Sociology, New York, 1929.

McCloskey, Robert G.
American Conservatism in the Age of Enterprise, Cambridge, 1951.

May, Henry F.
Protestant Churches and Industrial America, New York, 1949.

Mumford, Lewis
The Brown Decades, New York, 1931.

Nevins, Allan
The Emergence of Modern America, 1865–1878, New York, 1927.

Parrington, Vernon L.
Main Currents in American Thought; Vol. III: *The Beginnings of Critical Realism in America, 1860–1920* (completed to 1900 only), New York, 1930.

Perry, Ralph Barton
Philosophy of the Recent Past, New York, 1926.

Perry, Ralph Barton
The Present Conflict of Ideals, New York, 1918.

Persons, Stow, ed.
Evolutionary Thought in America, New Haven, 1950.

Riley, I. Woodbridge
American Thought from Puritanism to Pragmatism, New York, 1907.

Santayana, George
Character and Opinion in the United States, New York, 1920.

Schlesinger, Arthur M.
The Rise of the City, 1878–1898, New York, 1933.
Schneider, Herbert W.
A History of American Philosophy, New York, 1946.
Smith, Henry Nash
Virgin Land; The American West as Symbol and Myth, Cambridge, 1950.
Townsend, Harvey G.
Philosophical Ideas in the United States, New York, 1934.
Werkmeister, William H.
A History of Philosophical Ideas in America, New York, 1949.
White, Morton G.
Social Thought in America, New York, 1949. (The most important study on the revolt against "formalism" that runs deeply through the period.)
Wiener, Philip P.
Evolution and the Founders of Pragmatism, Cambridge, 1949.

II. WORKS ON PARTICULAR WRITERS

On each of these writers there are many discussions. I have disregarded magazine articles however cogent, and for the sake of brevity have offered the student a minimum list of books.

1. Josiah Royce
Brown, Stuart Gerry, ed.
The Religious Philosophy of Josiah Royce, Syracuse, 1952.
Brown, Stuart Gerry, ed.
The Social Philosophy of Josiah Royce, Syracuse, 1950.
Papers in Honor of Josiah Royce; Philosophical Review, XXV (May, 1916) No. 3.

2. Chauncey Wright
Fiske, John
"Chauncey Wright," *Darwinism, and Other Essays*, New York, 1879.

James, William
"Chauncey Wright," *Collected Essays and Reviews,* New York, 1920.
Thayer, James B.
Letters of Chauncey Wright, Cambridge, 1878.

3. Henry George
De Mille, Anna
Henry George, Chapel Hill, 1950.
George, Henry, Jr.
The Life of Henry George, New York, 1900.
Nock, Albert J.
Henry George, New York, 1939.

4. William Graham Sumner
Keller, Albert G.
Reminiscences (Mainly Personal) of William Graham Sumner, New Haven, 1933.
Starr, Harris E.
William Graham Sumner, New York, 1925.

5. Lester Ward
Cape, Emily Palmer
Lester F. Ward; A Personal Sketch, New York, 1922.
Chugerman, Samuel
Lester F. Ward, The American Aristotle, Durham, 1939.

6. Charles Sanders Peirce
Buchler, Justus, ed.
The Philosophy of Peirce, New York, 1940.
Cohen, Morris R.
"Introduction," Charles S. Peirce, *Chance, Love and Logic,* New York, 1923.
Feibleman, James
An Introduction to Peirce's Philosophy, New York, 1946.
Gallie, Walter Bryce
Peirce and Pragmatism, Penguin Books, 1952.

Goudge, Thomas A.
The Thought of C. S. Peirce, Toronto, 1950.
Thompson, Manley H.
The Pragmatic Philosophy of C. S. Peirce, Chicago, 1945.
Wiener, Philip P., and Frederick H. Young, eds.
Studies in the Philosophy of Charles Sanders Peirce, Cambridge, 1952.

7. William James
In Commemoration of William James, 1842–1942, New York, 1942.
Perry, Ralph Barton
The Thought and Character of William James, Boston, 1935.

8. Oliver Wendell Holmes
Howe, Mark De Wolfe, ed.
Holmes-Laski Letters, Cambridge, 1953.
Howe, Mark De Wolfe, ed.
Holmes-Pollock Letters, Cambridge, 1941.
Lerner, Max, ed.
The Mind and Faith of Justice Holmes, Boston, 1943.
Shriver, Harry C., ed.
Justice Oliver Wendell Holmes: His Book Notices and Uncollected Letters and Papers, New York, 1936.

9. John Dewey
Hook, Sidney
John Dewey, New York, 1939.
Hook, Sidney, ed.
John Dewey, Philosopher of Science and Freedom: a Symposium, New York, 1950.
Schilpp, Paul A., ed.
The Philosophy of John Dewey, Evanston, 1939.
Thomas, Milton H., and Herbert W. Schneider
A Bibliography of John Dewey, 1882–1939, New York, 1939.
White, Morton G.
The Origin of Dewey's Instrumentalism, New York, 1943.

10. Brooks Adams
    Anderson, Thornton
        Brooks Adams, Constructive Conservative, Ithaca, 1951.

11. Henry Adams
    Jordy, William H.
        Henry Adams: Scientific Historian, New Haven, 1952.

12. Thorstein Veblen
    Dorfman, Joseph
        Thorstein Veblen and His America, New York, 1934.
    Duffus, Robert L.
        The Innocents at Cedro; a Memoir of Thorstein Veblen and Some Others, New York, 1944.
    Schneider, Louis
        The Freudian Psychology and Veblen's Social Theory, New York, 1948.

13. Louis Dembitz Brandeis
    Fraenkel, Osmond K.
        The Curse of Bigness, New York, 1935.
    Mason, Alpheus T.
        Brandeis; A Free Man's Life, New York, 1946.

TABLE OF CONTENTS

Table of Contents

·I·

JOSIAH ROYCE

[1 8 5 5 - 1 9 1 6]

THE PROBLEM OF JOB

THE PROBLEM OF JOB

I

Job's world, as he sees it, is organized in a fashion extremely familiar to us all. The main ideas of this cosmology are easy to be reviewed. The very simplicity of the scheme of the universe here involved serves to bring into clearer view the mystery and horror of the problem that besets Job himself. The world, for Job, is the work of a being who, in the very nature of the case, ought to be intelligible (since he is wise), and friendly to the righteous, since, according to tradition, and by virtue of his divine wisdom itself, this God must know the value of a righteous man. But—here is the mystery—this God, as his works get known through our human experiences of evil, appears to us not friendly, but hopelessly foreign and hostile in his plans and his doings. The more, too, we study his ways with man, the less intelligible seems his nature. Tradition has dwelt upon his righteousness, has called him merciful, has magnified his love towards his servants, has described his justice in bringing to naught the wicked. One has learned to trust all these things, to conceive God in these terms, and to expect all this righteous government from him. Moreover, tradition joins with the pious observation of nature in assuring us of the omnipotence of God. Job himself pathetically insists that he never doubts, for an instant, God's power to do whatever in heaven or earth he may please to do. Nothing hinders God. No blind faith thwarts him. Sheol is naked before him. The abyss has no covering. The earth hangs over chaos because he orders it to do so. His power shatters the monsters and pierces the dragons. He can, then, do with evil precisely what he does with Rahab or with the shades, with the clouds or with the light or with the

From *Studies of Good and Evil*, pp. 1-28, by Josiah Royce. Copyright, 1898, D. Appleton & Company; reprinted by permission of the publishers, Appleton-Century-Crofts, Inc.

sea, namely, exactly what he chooses. Moreover, since he knows everything, and since the actual value of a righteous man is, for Job, an unquestionable and objective fact, God cannot fail to know this real worth of righteousness in his servants, as well as the real hatefulness and mischief of the wicked. God knows worth, and cannot be blind to it, since it is as real a fact as heaven and earth themselves.

Yet despite all these unquestioned facts, this God, who can do just what he chooses, "deprives of right" the righteous man, in Job's own case, and "vexes his soul," becomes towards him as a "tyrant," "persecutes" him "with strong hand," "dissolves" him "into storm," makes him a "byword" for outcasts, "casts" him "into the mire," renders him "a brother to jackals," deprives him of the poor joy of his "one day as a hireling," of the little delight that might come to him as a man before he descends hopelessly to the dark world of the shades, "watches over" him by day to oppress, by night to "terrify" him "with dreams and with visions"— in brief, acts as his enemy, "tears" him "in anger," "gnashes upon" him "with his teeth." All these are the expressions of Job himself. On the other hand, as, with equal wonder and horror the righteous Job reports, God on occasion does just the reverse of all this to the notoriously and deliberately wicked, who "grow old," "wax mighty in power," "see their offspring established," and their homes "secure from fear." If one turns from this view of God's especially unjust dealings with righteous and with wicked individuals to a general survey of his providential government of the world, one sees vast processes going on, as ingenious as they are merciless, as full of hints of a majestic wisdom as they are of indifference to every individual right.

> *A mountain that falleth is shattered,*
> *And a rock is removed from its place;*
> *The waters do wear away stones,*
> *Its floods sweep the earth's dust away;*
> *And the hope of frail man thou destroyest.*
> *Thou subdu'st him for aye, and he goes;*
> *Marring his face thou rejectest him.*

3

Here is a mere outline of the divine government as Job sees it. To express himself thus is for Job no momentary outburst of passion. Long days and nights he has brooded over these bitter facts of experience, before he has spoken at all. Unweariedly, in presence of his friends' objections, he reiterates his charges. He has the right of the sufferer to speak, and he uses it. He reports the facts that he sees. Of the paradox involved in all this he can make nothing. What is clear to him, however, is that this paradox is a matter for reasoning, not for blind authority. God ought to meet him face to face, and have the matter out in plain words. Job fears not to face his judge, or to demand his answer from God. God knows that Job has done nothing to deserve this fury. The question at issue between maker and creature is therefore one that demands a direct statement and a clear decision. "Why, since you can do precisely as you choose, and since you know, as all-knower, the value of a righteous servant, do you choose, as enemy, to persecute the righteous with this fury and persistence of hate?" Here is the problem.

The human interest of the issue thus so clearly stated by Job lies, of course, in the universality of just such experiences of undeserved ill here upon earth. What Job saw of evil we can see ourselves to-day whenever we choose. Witness Armenia. Witness the tornadoes and earthquakes. Less interesting to us is the thesis mentioned by Job's friends, in the antiquated form in which they state it, although to be sure, a similar thesis, in altered forms, is prevalent among us still. And of dramatic significance only is the earnestness with which Job defends his own personal righteousness. So naïve a self-assurance as is his is not in accordance with our modern conscience, and it is seldom indeed that our day would see any man sincerely using this phraseology of Job regarding his own consciousness of rectitude. But what is to-day as fresh and real to us as it was to our poet is the fact that all about us, say in every child born with an unearned heredity of misery, or in every pang of the oppressed, or in every arbitrary coming of ill-fortune, some form of innocence is beset with an evil that the sufferer has not deserved. Job wins dramatic sympathy as an extreme, but for the purpose all the more typical, case of this universal experience of unearned ill-fortune. In every such case we therefore still have the interest that Job had in demanding the solution of this central problem of evil. Herein, I need not say, lies the permanent significance of the problem of Job,—a problem that wholly outlasts any ancient Jewish controversy as to the question whether the divine justice always does or does not act as Job's friends, in their devotion to tradition, declare that it acts. Here, then, is the point where our poem touches a question, not merely of an older religion, but of philosophy, and of all time.

II

The general problem of evil has received, as is well known, a great deal of attention from the philosophers. Few of them, at least in European thought, have been as fearless in stating the issue as was the original author of Job. The solutions offered have, however, been very numerous. For our purposes they may be reduced to a few.

First, then, one may escape Job's paradox by declining altogether to view the world in teleological terms. Evils, such as death, disease, tempests, enemies, fires, are not, so one may declare, the works of God or of Satan, but are natural phenomena. Natural, too, are the phenomena of our desires, of our pains, sorrows and failures. No divine purpose rules or overrules any of these things. That happens to us, at any time, which must happen, in view of our natural limitations and of our ignorance. The way to better things is to understand nature better than we now do. For this view—a view often maintained in our day—there is no problem of evil, in Job's sense, at all. Evil there indeed is, but the only rational problems are those of natural laws. I need not here further consider this method, not of solving but of abolishing the problem before us, since my intent is, in this paper, to suggest the possibility of some genuinely teleological answer to Job's question. I mention this first view only to recognize, historically, its existence.

In the second place, one may deal with our problem by attempting any one, or a number, of those familiar and popular compromises between the belief in a world of natural law and the belief in a teleological order, which are all, as compromises, reducible to the assertion that the presence of evil in the creation is a relatively insignificant, and an inevitable, incident of a plan that produces sentient creatures subject to law. Writers who expound such compromises have to point out that, since a burnt child dreads the fire, pain is, on the whole, useful as a warning. Evil is a transient discipline, whereby finite creatures learn their place in the system of things. Again, a sentient world cannot get on without some experience of suffering, since sentience means tenderness. Take away pain (so one still again often insists), take away pain, and we should not learn our share of natural truth. Pain is the pedagogue to teach us natural science. The contagious diseases, for instance, are useful in so far as they lead us in the end to study Bacteriology, and thus to get an insight into the life of certain beautiful creatures of God whose presence in the world we should otherwise blindly overlook! Moreover (to pass to still another variation of this sort of explanation), created beings obviously grow from less to more. First the lower, then the higher. Otherwise there could be no Evolution. And were there no evolution, how much of edifying natural science we should miss! But if one is evolved, if one grows from less to more, there must be something to make the stages of growth. Now evil is useful to mark the lower stages of evolution. If you are to be, first an infant, then a man, or first a savage, then a civilized being, there must be evils attendant upon the earlier stages of your life—evils that make growth welcome and conscious. Thus, were there no colic and croup, were there no tumbles and crying-spells in infancy, there would be no sufficient incentives to loving parents to hasten the growing robustness of their children, and no motives to impel the children to long to grow big! Just so, cannibalism is valuable as a mark of a lower grade of evolution. Had there been no cannibalism, we should realize less joyously than we do what a respectable thing it is to have become civilized! In brief, evil is, as it were, the dirt of the natural order, whose value is that, when you wash it off, you thereby learn the charm of the bath of evolution.

The foregoing are mere hints of familiar methods of playing about the edges of our problem, as children play barefoot in the shallowest reaches of the foam of the sea. In our poem, . . . the speeches ascribed to Elihu contain the most hints of some such way of defining evil, as a merely transient incident of the discipline of the individual. With many writers explanations of this sort fill much space. They are even not without their proper place in popular discussion. But they have no interest for whoever has once come into the presence of Job's problem as it is in itself. A moment's thought reminds us of their superficiality. Pain is useful as a warning of danger. If we did not suffer, we should burn our hands off. Yes, but this explanation of one evil presupposes another, and a still unexplained and greater evil, namely, the existence of the danger of which we need to be thus warned. No doubt it is well that the past sufferings of the Armenians should teach the survivors, say the defenseless women and children, to have a wholesome fear in future of Turks. Does that explain, however, the need for the existence, or for the murderous doings of the Turks? If I can only reach a given goal by passing over a given road, say of evolution, it may be well for me to consent to the toilsome journey. Does that explain why I was created so far from my goal? Discipline, toil, penalty, surgery, are all explicable as means to ends, if only it be presupposed that there exists, and that there is quite otherwise explicable, the necessity for the situations which involve such fearful expenses. One justifies the surgery, but not the disease; the toil, but not the existence of the need for the toil; the penalty, but not the situation which has made the penalty necessary, when one points out that evil is in so many cases medicinal or disciplinary or prophylactic—an incident of imperfect stages of evolution, or the price of a distant good attained through misery. All such explanations, I insist, trade upon borrowed capital. But God, by hypothesis, is no borrower. He produces his own capital of ends and means. Every evil is explained on the foregoing plan only by presupposing at least an equal, and often a greater and a preëxistent evil, namely, the very state of things which renders the first evil the only physically possible way of reaching a given goal. But what Job wants his judge to explain is not that evil A is a physical means of warding off some other greater evil B, in this cruel world where the waters wear away even the stones, and where hopes of man are so much frailer than the stones; but why a God who can do whatever he wishes chooses situations where such a heaped-up mass of evil means become what we should call physical necessities to the ends now physically possible.

No real explanation of the presence of evil can succeed which declares evil to be a merely physical necessity for one who desires, in this present world, to reach a given goal. Job's business is not with physical accidents, but with the God who chose to make this present nature; and an answer to Job must show that evil is not a physical but a logical necessity—something whose non-existence would simply contradict the very essence, the very perfection of God's own nature and power. This talk of medicinal and disciplinary evil, perfectly fair when applied to our poor fate-bound human surgeons, judges, jailors, or teachers, becomes cruelly, even cynically trivial when applied to explain the ways of a God who is to choose, not only the physical means to an end, but the very *Physis* itself in which path and goal are to exist together. I confess, as a layman, that whenever, at a funeral, in the company of mourners who are immediately facing Job's own personal problem, and who are sometimes, to say the least, wide enough awake to desire not to be stayed with relative comforts, but to ask that terrible and uttermost question of God himself, and to require the direct answer—that whenever, I say, in such company I have to listen to these half-way answers, to these superficial plashes in the wavelets at the water's edge of sorrow, while the black, unfathomed ocean of finite evil spreads out before our wide-opened eyes—well, at such times this trivial speech about useful burns and salutary medicines makes me, and I fancy others, simply and wearily heartsick. Some words are due to children at school, to peevish paitents in the sick-room who need a little temporary quieting. But quite other speech is due to men and women when they are wakened to the higher reason of Job by the fierce anguish of our mortal life's ultimate facts. They deserve either our simple silence, or, if we are ready to speak, the speech of people who ourselves inquire as Job inquired.

III

A third method of dealing with our problem is in essence identical with the course which, in a very antiquated form, the friends of Job adopt. This method takes its best known expression in the doctrine that the presence of evil in the world is explained by the fact that the value of free will in moral agents logically involves, and so explains and justifies, the divine permission of the evil deeds of those finite beings who freely choose to sin, as well as the inevitable fruits of the sins. God creates agents with free will. He does so because the existence of such agents has of itself an infinite worth. Were there no free agents, the highest good could not be. But such agents, because they are free, can offend. The divine justice of necessity pursues such offenses with attendant evils. These evils, the result of sin, must, logically speaking, be permitted to exist, if God once creates the agents who have free will, and himself remains, as he must logically do, a just God. How much ill thus results depends upon the choice of the free agents, not upon God, who wills to have only good chosen, but of necessity must leave his free creatures to their own devices, so far as concerns their power to sin.

This view has the advantage of undertaking to regard evil as a logically necessary part of a perfect moral order, and not as a mere incident of an imperfectly adjusted physical mechanism. So dignified a doctrine, by virtue of its long history and its high theological reputation, needs here no extended exposition. I assume it as familiar, and pass at once to its difficulties. It has its share of truth. There is, I doubt not, moral free will in the universe. But the presence of evil in the world simply cannot be explained by free will alone. This is easy to show. One who maintains this view asserts, in substance, "All real evils are the results of the acts of free and finite moral agents." These agents may be angels or men. If there is evil in the city, the Lord has *not* done it, except in so far as his justice has acted in readjusting wrongs already done. Such ill is due to the deeds of his creatures. But hereupon one asks at once, in presence of any ill, "Who did this?" Job's friends answer: "The sufferer himself; his deed wrought his own undoing. God punishes only the sinner. Every one suffers for his own wrongdoing. Your ill is the result of your crime."

But Job, and all his defenders of innocence, must at once reply: "Empirically speaking, this is obviously, in our visible world, simply not true. The sufferer may suffer innocently. The ill is often undeserved. The fathers sin; the child, diseased from birth, degraded, or a born wretch, may pay the penalty. The Turk or the active rebel sins. Armenia's helpless women and babes cry in vain unto God for help."

Hereupon the reply comes, although not indeed from Job's friends: "Alas! it is so. Sin means suffering; but the innocent may suffer *for* the guilty. This, to be sure, is God's way. One cannot help it. It is so." But therewith the whole effort to explain evil as a logically necessary result of free will and of divine justice alone is simply abandoned. The unearned ills are not justly due to the free will that indeed partly caused them, but to God who declines to protect the innocent. God owes the Turk and the rebel their due. He also owes to his innocent creatures, the babes and the women, his shelter. He owes to the sinning father his penalty, but to the son, born in our visible world a lost soul from the womb, God owes the shelter of his almighty wing, and no penalty. Thus Job's cry is once more in place. The ways of God are not thus justified.

But the partisan of free will as the true explanation of ill may reiterate his view in a new form. He may insist that we see but a fragment. Perhaps the soul born here as if lost, or the wretch doomed to pangs now unearned, sinned of old, in some previous state of existence. Perhaps Karma is to blame. You expiate to-day the sins of your own former existences. Thus the Hindoos varied the theme of our familiar doctrine. This is what Hindoo friends might have said to Job. Well, admit even that, if you like; and what then follows? Admit that here or in former ages the free deed of every present sufferer earned as its penalty every ill, physical or moral, that appears as besetting just this sufferer to-day. Admit that, and what logically follows? It follows, so I must insist, that the moral world itself, which this free-will theory of the source of evil, thus abstractly stated, was to save, is destroyed in its very heart and center.

For consider. A suffers ill. B sees A suffering. Can B, the onlooker, help his suffering neighbor, A? Can he comfort him in any true way? No, a miserable comforter must B prove, like Job's friends, so long as B, believing in our present hypothesis, clings strictly to the logic of this abstract free-will explanation of the origin of evil. To A he says: "Well, you suffer for your own ill-doing. I therefore simply cannot relieve you. This is God's world of justice. If I tried to hinder God's justice from working in your case, I should at best only postpone your evil day. It would come, for God is just. You are hungry, thirsty, naked, sick, in prison. What can I do about it? All this is your own deed come back to you. God himself, although justly punishing, is not the author of this evil. You are the sole originator of the ill." "Ah!" so A may cry out, "but can you not give me light, insight, instruction, sympathy? Can you not at least teach me to become good?" "No," B must reply, if he is a logical believer in the sole efficacy of the private free will of each finite agent as the one source, under the divine justice, of that agent's ill: "No, if you deserved light or any other comfort, God, being just, would enlighten you himself, even if I absolutely refused. But if you do not deserve light, I should preach to you in vain, for God's justice would harden your heart against any such good fortune as I could offer you from without, even if I spoke with the tongues of men and of angels. Your free will is yours. No deed of mine could give you a good free will, for what I gave you from without would not be *your* free will at all. Nor can any one but you cause your free will to be this or that. A great gulf is fixed between us. You and I, as sovereign free agents, live in God's holy world in sin-tight compartments and in evil-tight compartments too. I cannot hurt you, nor you me. You are damned for your own sins, while all that I can do is to look out for my own salvation." This, I say, is the logically inevitable result of asserting that every ill, physical or moral, that can happen to any agent, is solely the result of that agent's own free will acting under the government of the divine justice. The only possible consequence would indeed be that we live, every soul of us, in separate, as it were absolutely fire-proof, free-will compartments, so that real coöperation as to good and ill is excluded. What more cynical denial of the reality of any sort of moral world could be imagined than is involved in this horrible thesis, which no sane partisan of the abstract and traditional free-will explanation of the source of evil will to-day maintain, precisely because no such partisan really knows or can know what his doctrine logically means, while still continuing to maintain it. Yet whenever one asserts with pious obscurity that "No harm can come to the righteous," one in fact implies, with logical necessity, just this cynical consequence.

IV

There remains a fourth doctrine as to our problem. This doctrine is in essence the thesis of philosophical idealism, a thesis which I myself feel bound to maintain, and, so far as space here permits, to explain. The theoretical basis of this view, the philosophical reasons for the notion of the divine nature which it implies, I cannot here explain. That is another argument. But I desire to indicate how the view in question deals with Job's problem.

This view first frankly admits that Job's problem is, upon Job's presuppositions, simply and absolutely insoluble. Grant Job's own presupposition that God is a being other than this world, that he is its external creator and ruler, and then all solutions fail. God is then either cruel or helpless, as regards all real finite ill of the sort that Job endures. Job, moreover, is right in demanding a reasonable answer to his question. The only possible answer is, however, one that undertakes to develop what I hold to be the immortal soul of the doctrine of the divine atonement. The answer to Job is: God is not in ultimate essence another being than yourself. He is the Absolute Being. You truly are one with God, part of his life. He is the very soul of your soul. And so, here is the first truth: When you suffer, *your sufferings are God's sufferings,* not his external work, not his external penalty, not the fruit of his neglect, but identically his own personal woe. In you God himself suffers, precisely as you do, and has all your concern in overcoming this grief.

The true question then is: Why does God thus suffer? The sole possible, necessary, and sufficient answer is, Because without suffering, without ill, without woe, evil, tragedy, God's life could not be perfected. This grief is not a physical means to an external end. It is a logically necessary and eternal constituent of the divine life. It is logically necessary that the Captain of your salvation should be perfect through suffering. No outer nature compels him. He chooses this because he chooses his own perfect selfhood. He is perfect. His world is the best possible world. Yet all its finite regions know not only of joy but of defeat and sorrow, for thus alone, in the completeness of his eternity, can God in his wholeness be triumphantly perfect.

This I say, is my thesis. In the absolute oneness of God with the sufferer, in the concept of the suffering and therefore triumphant God, lies the logical solution of the problem of evil. The doctrine of philosophical idealism is, as regards its purely theoretical aspects, a fairly familiar metaphysical theory at the present time. One may, then, presuppose here as known the fact that, for reasons which I have not now to expound, the idealist maintains that there is in the universe but one perfectly real being, namely, the Absolute, that the Absolute is self-conscious, and that his world is essentially in its wholeness the fulfillment *in actu* of an all-perfect ideal. We ourselves exist as fragments of the absolute life, or better, as partial functions in the unity of the absolute and conscious process of the world. On the other hand, our existence and our individuality are not illusory, but are what they are in an organic unity with the whole life of the Absolute Being. This

13

doctrine once presupposed, our present task is to inquire what case idealism can make for the thesis just indicated as its answer to Job's problem.

In endeavoring to grapple with the theoretical problem of the place of evil in a world that, on the whole, is to be conceived, not only as good, but as perfect, there is happily one essentially decisive consideration concerning good and evil which falls directly within the scope of our own human experience, and which concerns matters at once familiar and momentous as well as too much neglected in philosophy. When we use such words as good, evil, perfect, we easily deceive ourselves by the merely abstract meanings which we associate with each of the terms taken apart from the other. We forget the experiences from which the words have been abstracted. To these experiences we must return whenever we want really to comprehend the words. If we take the mere words, in their abstraction, it is easy to say, for instance, that if life has any evil in it at all, it must needs not be so perfect as life would be were there no evil in it whatever. Just so, speaking abstractly, it is easy to say that, in estimating life, one has to set the good over against the evil, and to compare their respective sums. It is easy to declare that, since we hate evil, wherever and just so far as we recognize it, our sole human interest in the world must be furthered by the removal of evil from the world. And thus viewing the case, one readily comes to say that if God views as not only good but perfect a world in which we find so much evil, the divine point of view must be very foreign to ours, so that Job's rebellious pessimism seems well in order, and Prometheus appears to defy the world-ruler in a genuinely humane spirit. Shocked, however, by the apparent impiety of this result, some teachers, considering divine matters, still misled by the same one-sided use of words, have opposed one falsely abstract view by another, and have strangely asserted that the solution must be in proclaiming that since God's world, the real world, in order to be perfect, must be without evil, what we men call evil must be a mere illusion—a mirage of the human point of view—a dark vision which God, who sees all truth, sees not at all. To God, so this view asserts, the eternal world in its wholeness is not only perfect, but has merely the perfection of an utterly transparent crystal, unstained by any color of ill. Only mortal error imagines that there is any evil. There is no evil but only good in the real world, and that is why God finds the world perfect, whatever mortals dream.

Now neither of these abstract views is my view. I consider them both the result of a thoughtless trust in abstract words. I regard evil as a distinctly real fact, a fact just as real as the most helpless and hopeless sufferer finds it to be when he is in pain. Furthermore, I hold that God's point of view is not foreign to ours. I hold that God willingly, freely, and consciously suffers in us when we suffer, and that our grief is his. And despite all this I maintain that the world from God's point of view fulfills the divine ideal and is perfect. And I hold that when we abandon the one-sided abstract ideas which the words good, evil, and perfect suggest, and when we go back to the concrete experiences upon which these very words are founded, we can see, even within the limits of our own experience, facts which make these very paradoxes perfectly intelligible, and even commonplace.

As for that essentially pernicious view, nowadays somewhat current amongst a certain class of gentle but inconsequent people—the view that all evil is *merely* an illusion and that there is no such thing in God's world—I can say of it only in passing that it is often advanced as an idealistic view, but that, in my opinion, it is false idealism. Good idealism it is to regard all finite experience as an appearance, a hint, often a very poor hint, of deeper truth. Good idealism it is to admit that man can err about truth that lies beyond his finite range of experience. And very good idealism it is to assert that all truth, and so all finite experience, exists in and for the mind of God, and nowhere outside of or apart from God. But it is not good idealism to assert that any facts which fall within the range of finite experience are, even while they are experienced, mere illusions. God's truth is inclusive, not exclusive. What you experience God experiences. The difference lies only in this, that God sees in unity what you see in fragments. For the rest, if one said, "The source and seat of evil is only the error of mortal mind," one would but have changed the name of one's problem. If the evil were but the error, the error would still be the evil, and altering the name would not have diminished the horror of the evil of this finite world.

V

But I hasten from the false idealism to the true; from the abstractions to the enlightening insights of our life. As a fact, idealism does not say: The finite world is, as such, a mere illusion. A sound idealism says, whatever we experience is a fragment, and, as far as it goes, a genuine fragment of the truth of the divine mind. With this principle before us, let us consider directly our own experiences of good and of evil, to see whether they are as abstractly opposed to each other as the mere words often suggest. We must begin with the elementary and even trivial facts. We shall soon come to something deeper.

By good, as we mortals experience it, we mean something that, when it comes or is expected, we actively welcome, try to attain or keep, and regard with content. By evil in general, as it is in our experience, we mean whatever we find in any sense repugnant and intolerable. I use the words repugnant and intolerable because I wish to indicate that words for evil frequently, like the words for good, directly refer to our actions as such. Commonly and rightly, when we speak of evil, we make reference to acts of resistance, of struggle, of shrinking, of flight, of removal of ourselves from a source of mischief—acts which not only follow upon the experience of evil, but which serve to define in a useful fashion what we mean by evil. The opposing acts of pursuit and of welcome define what we mean by good. By the evil which we experience we mean precisely whatever we regard as something to be gotten rid of, shrunken from, put out of sight, of hearing, or of memory, eschewed, expelled, assailed, or otherwise directly or indirectly resisted. By good we mean whatever we regard as something to be welcomed, pursued, won, grasped, held, persisted in, preserved. And we show all this in our acts in presence of any grade of good or evil, sensuous, aesthetic, ideal, moral. To shun, to flee, to resist, to destroy, these are our primary attitudes towards ill; the opposing acts are our primary attitudes towards the good; and whether you regard us as animals or as moralists, whether it is a sweet taste, a poem, a virtue, or God that we look to as good, and whether it is a burn or a temptation, an outward physical fore, or a stealthy, inward, ideal enemy, that we regard as evil. In all our organs of voluntary movement, in all our deeds, in a turn of the eye, in a sigh, a groan, in a hostile gesture, in an act of silent contempt, we can show in endlessly varied ways the same general attitude of repugnance.

But man is a very complex creature. He has many organs. He performs many acts at once, and he experiences his performance of these acts in one highly complex life of consciousness. As the next feature of his life we all observe that he can at the same time shun one object and grasp at another. In this way he can have at once present to him a consciousness of good and a consciousness of ill. But so far in our account these sorts of experience appear merely as facts side by side. Man loves, and he *also* hates, loves this, and hates that, assumes an attitude of repugnance towards one object, while he welcomes another. So far the usual theory follows man's life, and calls it an experience of good and ill as mingled but exclusively and abstractly opposed facts. For such a view the final question as to the worth of a man's life is merely the question whether there are more intense acts of satisfaction and of welcome than of repugnance and disdain in his conscious life.

But this is by no means an adequate notion of the complexity of man's life, even as an animal. If every conscious act of hindrance, of thwarting, of repugnance, means just in so far an awareness of some evil, it is noteworthy that men can have and can show just such tendencies, not only towards external experiences, but towards their own acts. That is, men can be seen trying to thwart and to hinder even their own acts themselves, at the very moment when they note the occurrence of these acts. One can consciously have an impulse to do something, and at that very moment a conscious disposition to hinder or to thwart as an evil that very impulse. If, on the other hand, every conscious act of attainment, of pursuit, of reinforcement, involves the awareness of some good, it is equally obvious that one can show by one's acts a disposition to reinforce or to emphasize or to increase, not only the externally present gifts of fortune, but also one's own deeds, in so far as one observes them. And in our complex lives it is common enough to find ourselves actually trying to reinforce and to insist upon a situation which involves for us, even at the moment of its occurrence, a great deal of repugnance. In such cases we often act as if we felt the very thwarting of our own primary impulses to be so much of a conscious good that we persist in pursuing and reinforcing the very situation in which this thwarting and hindering of our own impulses is sure to arise.

In brief, as phenomena of this kind show, man is a being who can to a very great extent find a sort of secondary satisfaction in the very act of thwarting his own desires, and thus of assuring for the time his own dissatisfactions. On the other hand, man can to an indefinite degree find himself dissatisfied with his satisfaction and disposed to thwart, not merely his external enemies, but his own inmost impulses themselves. But I now affirm that in all such cases you cannot simply say that man is preferring the less of two evils, or the greater of two goods, as if the good and evil stood merely side by side in his experience. On the contrary, in such cases, man is not merely setting his acts or his estimates of good and evil side by side and taking the sum of each; but he is making his own relatively primary acts, impulses, desires, the objects of all sorts of secondary impulses, desires, and reflective observations. His whole inner state is one of tension: and he is either making a secondary experience of evil out of his estimate of a primary experience of good, as is the case when he at once finds himself disposed to pursue a given good and to thwart this pursuit as being an evil pursuit; or else he is making a secondary experience of good out of his primary experience of evil, as when he is primarily dissatisfied with his situation, but yet secondarily regards this very dissatisfaction as itself a desirable state. In this way man comes not only to love some things and also to hate other things, he comes to love his own hates and to hate his own loves in an endlessly complex hierarchy of superposed interests in his own interests.

Now it is easy to say that such states of inner tension, where our conscious lives are full of a warfare of the self with itself, are contradictory or absurd states. But it is easy to say this only when you dwell on the words and fail to observe the facts of experience. As a fact, not only our lowest but our highest states of activity are the ones which are fullest of this crossing, conflict, and complex interrelation of loves and hates, of attractions and repugnances. As a merely physiological fact, we begin no muscular act without at the same time initiating acts which involve the innervation of opposing sets of muscles, and these opposing sets of muscles hinder each other's freedom. Every sort of control of movement means the conflicting play of opposed muscular impulses. We do nothing simple, and we will no complex act without willing what involves a certain measure of opposition between the impulses or partial acts which go to make up the whole act. If one passes from single acts to long series of acts, one finds only the more obviously this interweaving of repugnance and of acceptance, of pursuit and of flight, upon which every complex type of conduct depends.

One could easily at this point spend time by dwelling upon numerous and relatively trivial instances of this interweaving of conflicting motives as it appears in all our life. I prefer to pass such instances over with a mere mention. There is, for instance, the whole marvelous consciousness of play, in its benign and in its evil forms. In any game that fascinates, one loves victory and shuns defeat, and yet as a loyal supporter of the game scorns anything that makes victory certain in advance; thus as a lover of fair play preferring to risk the defeat that he all the while shuns, and partly thwarting the very love of victory that from moment to moment fires his hopes. There are, again, the numerous cases in which we prefer to go to places where we are sure to be in a considerable measure dissatisfied; to engage, for instance, in social functions that absorbingly fascinate us despite or even in view of the very fact that, as long as they continue, they keep us in a state of tension which makes us, amongst other things, long to have the whole occasion over. Taking a wider view, one may observe that the greater part of the freest products of the activity of civilization, in ceremonies, in formalities, in the long social drama of flight, of pursuit, of repartee, of contest and of courtesy, involve an elaborate and systematic delaying and hindering of elemental human desires, which we continually outwit, postpone and thwart, even while we nourish them. When students of human nature assert that hunger and love rule the social world, they recognize that the elemental in human nature is trained by civilization into the service of the highest demands of the Spirit. But such students have to recognize that the elemental rules the higher world only in so far as the elemental is not only cultivated, but endlessly thwarted, delayed, outwitted, like a constitutional monarch, who is said to be a sovereign, but who, while he rules, must not govern.

But I pass from such instances, which in all their universality are still, I admit, philosophically speaking trivial, because they depend upon the accidents of human nature. I pass from these instances to point out what must be the law, not only of human nature, but of every broader form of life as well. I maintain that this organization of life by virtue of the tension of manifold impulses and interests is not a mere accident of our imperfect human nature, but must be a type of the organization of every rational life. There are good and bad states of tension, there are conflicts that can only be justified when resolved into some higher form of harmony. But I insist that, in general, the only harmony that can exist in the realm of the spirit is the harmony that we possess when we thwart the present but more elemental impulse for the sake of the higher unity of experience; as when we rejoice in the endurance of the tragedies of life, because they show us the depth of life, or when we know that it is better to have loved and lost than never to have loved at all, or when we possess a virtue in the moment of victory over the tempter. And the reason why this is true lies in the fact that the more one's experience fulfills ideals, the more that experience presents to one, not of ignorance, but of triumphantly wealthy acquaintance with the facts of manifold, varied and tragic life, full of tension and thereby of unity. Now this is an universal and not merely human law. It is not those innocent of evil who are fullest of the life of God, but those who in their own case have experienced the triumph over evil. It is not those naturally ignorant of fear, or those who, like Siegfried, have never shivered, who possess the genuine experience of courage; but the brave are those who have fears, but control their fears. Such know the genuine virtues of the hero. Were it otherwise, only the stupid could be perfect heroes.

To be sure it is quite false to say, as the foolish do, that the object of life is merely that we may "know life" as an irrational chaos of experiences of good and evil. But knowing the good in life is a matter which concerns the form, rather than the mere content of life. One who knows life wisely knows indeed much of the content of life; but he knows the good of life in so far as, in the unity of his experience, he finds the evil of his experience not abolished, but subordinated, and in so far relatively thwarted by a control which annuls its triumph even while experiencing its existence.

VI

Generalizing the lesson of experience we may then say: It is logically impossible that a complete knower of truth should fail to know, to experience, to have present to his insight, the fact of actually existing evil. On the other hand, it is equally impossible for one to know a higher good than comes from the subordination of evil to good in a total experience. When one first loving, in an elemental way, whatever you please, himself hinders, delays, thwarts his elemental interest in the interest of some larger whole of experience, he not only knows more fact, but he possesses a higher good than would or could be present to one who was aware neither of the elemental impulse, nor of the thwarting of it in the tension of a richer life. The knowing of the good, in the higher sense, depends upon contemplating the overcoming and subordination of a less significant impulse, which survives even in order that it should be subordinated. Now this law, this form of the knowledge of the good, applies as well to the existence of moral as to that of sensuous ill. If moral evil were simply destroyed and wiped away from the external world, the knowledge of moral goodness would also be destroyed. For the love of moral good is the thwarting of lower loves for the sake of the higher organization. What is needed, then, for the definition of the divine knowledge of a world that in its wholeness is perfect, is not a divine knowledge that shall ignore, wipe out and utterly make naught the existence of any ill, whether physical or moral, but a divine knowledge to which shall be present that love of the world as a whole which is fulfilled in the endurance of physical ill, in the subordination of moral ill, in the thwarting of impulses which survive even when subordinated, in the acceptance of repugnances which are still eternal, in the triumph over an enemy that endures even through its eternal defeat, and in the discovery that the endless tension of the finite world is included in the contemplative consciousness of the repose and harmony of eternity. To view God's nature thus is to view his nature as the whole idealistic theory views him, not as the Infinite One beyond the finite imperfections, but as the being whose unity determines the very constitution, the lack, the tension, and relative disharmony of the finite world.

The existence of evil, then, is not only consistent with the perfection of the universe, but is necessary for the very existence of that perfection. This is what we see when we no longer permit ourselves to be deceived by the abstract meanings of the words good and evil into thinking that these two opponents exist merely as mutually exclusive facts side by side in experience, but when we go back to the facts of life and perceive that all relatively higher good, in the trivial as in the more truly spiritual realm, is known only in so far as, from some higher reflective point of view, we accept as good the thwarting of an existent interest that is even thereby declared to be a relative ill, and love a tension of various impulses which even thereby involves, as the object of our love, the existence of what gives us aversion or grief. Now if the love of God is more inclusive than the love of man, even as the divine world of experience is richer than the human world, we can simply set no human limit to the intensity of conflict, to the tragedies of existence, to the pangs of finitude, to the degree of moral ill, which in the end is included in the life that God not only loves, but finds the fulfillment of the perfect ideal. If peace means satisfaction, acceptance of the whole of an experience as good, and if even we, in our weakness, can frequently find rest in the very presence of conflict and of tension, in the very endurance of ill in a good cause, in the hero's triumph over temptation, or in the mourner's tearless refusal to accept the lower comforts of forgetfulness, or to wish that the lost one's preciousness had been less painfully revealed by death—well, if even we know our little share of this harmony in the midst of the wrecks and disorders of life, what limit shall we set to the divine power to face this world of his own sorrows, and to find peace in the victory over all its ills.

But in the last expression I have pronounced the word that serves to link this theory as to the place of evil in a good world with the practical problem of every sufferer. Job's rebellion came from the thought that God, as a sovereign, is far off, and that, for his pleasure, his creature suffers. Our own theory comes to the mourner with the assurance: "Your suffering, just as it is in you, is God's suffering. No chasm divides you from God. He is not remote from you even in his eternity. He is here. His eternity means merely the completeness of his experience. But that completeness is inclusive. Your sorrow is one of the included facts." I do not say: "God sympathizes with you from without, would spare you if he could, pities you with helpless external pity merely as a father pities his children." I say: "God here sorrows, not *with* but *in* your sorrow. Your grief is identically his grief, and what you know as your loss, God knows as his loss, just in and through the very moment when you grieve."

But hereupon the sufferer perchance responds: "If this is God's loss, could he not have prevented it? To him are present in unity all the worlds; and yet he must lack just this for which I grieve." I respond: "He suffers here that he may triumph. For the triumph of the wise is no easy thing. Their lives are not light, but sorrowful. Yet they rejoice in their sorrow, not, to be sure, because it is mere experience, but because, for them, it becomes part of a strenuous whole of life. They wander and find their home even in wandering. They long, and attain through their very love of longing. Peace they find in triumphant warfare. Contentment they have most of all in endurance. Sovereignty they win in endless service. The eternal world contains Gethsemane."

Yet the mourners may still insist: "If my sorrow is God's, his triumph is not mine. Mine is the woe. His is the peace." But my theory is a philosophy. It proposes to be coherent. I must persist: "It is your fault that you are thus sundered from God's triumph. His experience in its wholeness cannot now be yours, for you just as you—this individual—are now but a fragment, and see his truth as through a glass darkly. But if you see his truth at all, through even the dimmest light of a glimmering reason, remember, that truth is in fact your own truth, your own fulfillment, the whole from which your life cannot be divorced, the reality that you mean even when you most doubt, the desire of your heart even when you are most blind, the perfection that you unconsciously strove for even when you were an infant, the complete Self apart from whom you mean nothing, the very life that gives your life the only value which it can have. In thought, if not in the fulfillment of thought, in aim if not in attainment of aim, in aspiration if not in the presence of the revealed fact, you can view God's triumph and peace as your triumph and peace. Your defeat will be no less real than it is, nor will you falsely call your evil a mere illusion. But you will see not only the grief but the truth, your truth, your rescue, your triumph."

Well, to what ill-fortune does not just such reasoning apply? I insist: our conclusion is essentially universal. It discounts any evil that experience may contain. All the horrors of the natural order, all the concealments of the divine plan by our natural ignorance, find their general relation to the unity of the divine experience indicated in advance by this account of the problem of evil.

"Yes," one may continue, "ill-fortune you have discovered, but how about moral evil? What if the sinner now triumphantly retorts: 'Aha! So my will is God's will. All then is well with me.'" I reply: What I have said disposes of moral ill precisely as definitely as of physical ill. What the evil will is to the good man, whose goodness depends upon its existence, but also upon the thwarting and the condemnation of its aim, just such is the sinner's will to the divine plan. God's will, we say to the sinner, is your will. Yes, but it is your will thwarted, scorned, over-come, defeated. In the eternal world you are seen, possessed, present, but your damnation is also seen including and thwarting you. Your apparent victory in this world stands simply for the vigor of your impulses. God wills you not to triumph. And that is the use of you in the world—the use of evil generally—to be hated but endured, to be triumphed over through the very fact of your presence, to be willed down even in the very life of which you are a part.

But to the serious moral agent we say: What you mean when you say that evil in this temporal world ought not to exist, and ought to be suppressed, is simply what God means by seeing that evil ought to be and is endlessly thwarted, endured, but subordinated. In the natural world you are the minister of God's triumph. Your deed is his. You can never clean the world of evil: but you can subordinate evil. The justification of the presence in the world of the morally evil becomes apparent to us mortals only in so far as this evil is overcome and condemned. It exists only that it may be cast down. Courage, then, for God works in you. In the order of time you embody in outer acts what is for him the truth of his eternity.

·II·

CHAUNCEY WRIGHT

[1 8 3 0 - 1 8 7 5]

EVOLUTION OF
SELF-CONSCIOUSNESS

EVOLUTION OF
SELF-CONSCIOUSNESS

I

The True Method of Scientific Evolution

It has come to be understood, and very generally allowed, that the conception of the origin of man as an animal race, as well as the origin of individual men within it, in accordance with the continuity of organic development maintained in the theory of evolution, does not involve any very serious difficulties, or difficulties so great as are presented by any other hypothesis of this origin, not excepting that of "special creation"—if that can be properly called a hypothesis, which is, in fact, a resumption of all the difficulties of natural explanation, assuming them to be insuperable and summarizing them under a single positive name. Yet in this evolution, the birth of self-consciousness is still thought by many to be a step not following from antecedent conditions in "nature," except in an incidental manner, or in so far only as "natural" antecedents have prepared the way for the "supernatural" advent of the self-conscious soul.

Independently of the form of expression, and of the false sentiment which is the motive of the antithesis in this familiar conception, or independently of its mystical interest, which has given to the words "natural" and "supernatural" their commonly accepted meanings, there is a foundation of scientific truth in the conception. For the word "evolution" conveys a false impression to the imagination, not really intended in the scientific use of it. It misleads by suggesting a continuity in the *kinds* of powers and

---

From *The North American Review* (April, 1873). Reprinted in *Philosophical Discussions*, pp. 199-266, ed. Charles Eliot Norton (New York: Henry Holt and Company, Inc., 1877). Titles of sections supplied by the editor.

functions in living beings, that is, by suggesting transition by insensible steps from one *kind* to another, as well as in the *degrees* of their importance and exercise at different stages of development. The truth is, on the contrary, that according to the theory of evolution, new uses of old powers arise discontinuously both in the bodily and mental natures of the animal, and in its individual developments, as well as in the development of its race, although, at their rise, these uses are small and of the smallest importance to life. They seem merged in the powers to which they are incident, and seem also merged in the special purposes or functions in which, however, they really have no part, and which are no parts of them. Their services or functions in life, though realized only incidentally at first, and in the feeblest degree, are just as distinct as they afterwards come to appear in their fullest development. The new uses are related to older powers only as *accidents,* so far as the special services of the older powers are concerned, although from the more general point of view of natural law, their relations to older uses have not the character of accidents, since these relations are, for the most part, determined by universal properties and laws, which are not especially related to the needs and conditions of living beings. Thus the uses of limbs for swimming, crawling, walking, leaping, climbing, and flying are distinct uses, and are related to each other only through the general mechanical principles of locomotion, through which some one use, in its first exercise, may be incident to some other, though, in its full exercise and perfection of special service, it is independent of the other, or has only a common dependence with the other or more general conditions. . . .

To make any event or power supernatural in the mystic's regard requires not merely that it shall be isolated and unparalleled in nature, but that it shall have more than an ordinary, or merely scientific, interest to the mystic's or to the *human* mind. The distinctively human or self-conscious interest, or sentiment, of self-consciousness gives an emphasis to the contrast named "natural and supernatural," through which mysticism is led to its speculations or assumptions of correspondingly emphatic contrasts in real existences. For mysticism is a speculation interpreting as matters of fact, or real existences outside of consciousness, impressions which are only determined within it by emphasis of attention or feeling. It is for the purpose of deepening still more, or to the utmost that its interest suggests, the really profound distinction between human and animal consciousness, or for the purpose of making the distinction *absolute,* of deepening this gulf into an unfathomable and impassable one, that mysticism appears to be moved to its speculations, and has imbued most philosophy and polite learning with its conceptions. Mental philosophy, or metaphysics, has, consequently, come down to us from ancient times least affected by the speculative interests and methods of modern science. Mysticism still reigns over the science of the mind, though its theory in general, or what is common to all theories called mystical, is very vague, and obscure even in the exclusively religious applications of the term. This vagueness has given rise to the more extended use and understanding of the term as it is here employed, which indicates little else than the generally apprehended *motive* of its speculations, or the feelings allied to all its forms of conception. These center in the feeling of absolute worthiness in self-consciousness, as the source, and at the same time the perfection of existence and power. The naturalist's observations on the minds of men and animals are impertinences of the least possible interest to this sense of worth, very much as the geologist's observations are generally to the speculator who seeks in the earth for hidden mineral treasures. . . .

The terms "science" and "scientific" have come, in modern times, to have so wide a range of application, and so vague a meaning that (like many other terms, not only in common speech, but also in philosophy and in various branches of learning, which have come down to us through varying usages) they would oppose great difficulties to any attempts at defining them by *genus* and difference, or otherwise than by enumerating the branches of knowledge and the facts, or relations of the facts, to which usage has affixed them as names. Precision in proper definition being then impossible, it is yet possible to give these terms so general a meaning as to cover all the knowledge to which they are usually applied, and still to exclude much besides. As the terms thus defined coincide with what I propose to show as the character of the knowledge peculiar to men, or which distinguishes the minds of men from those of other animals, I will begin with this definition. In science and in scientific facts there is implied a conscious purpose of including particular facts under general facts, and the less general under the more general ones. Science, in the modern use of the term, consists, essentially, of a knowledge of things and events either as effects of general causes, or as instances of general classes, rules, or laws; or even as isolated facts of which the class, law, rule, or cause is sought. The conscious purpose of arriving at general facts and at an adequate statement of them in language, or of bringing particular facts under explicit general ones, determines for any knowledge a scientific character.

II

How Consciousness Is a Natural *Result of Evolution*

Language, strictly so called, which some of these animals also have, or signs *purposely* used for communication, is not only required for scientific knowledge, but a second step of generalization is needed, and is made through reflection, by which this use of a sign is itself made an object of attention, and the sign is recognized in its general relations to what it signifies, and to what it has signified in the past, and will signify in the future. It is highly improbable that such a knowledge of knowledge, or such a *re*-cognition, belongs in any considerable, or effective, degree to even the most intelligent of the lower animals, or even to the lowest of the human race. This is what is properly meant by being "rational" or being a "rational animal." It is what I have preferred to call "scientific" knowledge. . . .

This knowledge comes from reflecting on what we know in the common-sense, or semi-instinctive form, or making what we know a field of renewed research, observation, and analysis in the generalization of major premises. The line of distinction between such results of reflection, or between scientific knowledge and the common-sense form of knowledge, is not simply the dividing line between the minds of men and those of other animals; but is that which divides the knowledge produced by outward attention from that which is further produced by reflective attention. The former, throughout a considerable range of the higher intelligent animals, involves veritable judgments of a complex sort. It involves combinations of minor premises leading to conclusions through implicit major premises in the enthymematic reasonings, commonly employed in inferences from signs and likelihoods, as in prognostications of the weather, or in orientations with many animals. This knowledge belongs both to men and to the animals next to men in intelligence, though in unequal degrees.

So far as logicians are correct in regarding an enthymeme as a reasoning, independently of its statement in words, . . . so far, I say, as this can be regarded as a reasoning, or a rational process, so far observation shows that the more intelligent dumb animals reason, or are rational. But this involves great vagueness or want of that precision in the use of signs which the antitheses of essential and accidental attributes and that of proper predication secure. There is little, or no, evidence to show that the animals which learn, to some extent, to comprehend human speech have an analytical comprehension of real general propositions, or of propositions in which both subject and predicate are general terms and differ in meaning. A merely verbal general proposition, declaring only the equivalence of two general names, might be comprehended by such minds, if it could be made of sufficient interest to attract their attention. But this is extremely doubtful, and it would not be as a *proposition,* with its contrasts of essential and added elements of conception that it would be comprehended. It would be, in effect, only repeating in succession two general names of the same class of objects. Such minds could, doubtless, comprehend a single class of objects, or an indefinite number of resembling things by several names:—that is, several signs of such a class would recall it to their thoughts, or revive a representative image of it; and they would thus be aware of the equivalence of these signs; but they would not attach precision of meaning and different degrees of generality to them, or regard one name as the name or sign of another name; as when we define a triangle to be a rectilinear figure, and a figure of three sides.

Only one degree of generality is, however, essential to inference from signs, or in enthymematic reasoning. Moreover, language in its relation to thought does not consist exclusively of spoken, or written, or imagined words, but of signs in general, and, essentially, of internal images or successions of images, which are the representative imaginations of objects and their relations; imaginations which severally stand for each and all of the particular objects or relations of a *kind*. Such are the visual imaginations called up by spoken or written concrete general names of visible objects, as "dog" or "tree"; which are vague and feeble as images, but effective as notative, directive, or guiding elements in thought. These are the internal signs of things and events, and are instruments of thought in judgment and reasoning, not only with dumb animals but also with men, in whom they are supplemented, rather than supplanted, by names.

But being of feeble intensity, and little under the influence of distinct attention or control of the will, compared to actual perceptions and to the voluntary movements of utterance and gesture, their nature has been but dimly understood even by metaphysicians, who are still divided into two schools in logic:— the conceptualists and the nominalists. The "concepts" of the former are really composed of these vague and feeble notative images, or groups of images, to which clearness and distinctness of attention are given by their associations with outward (usually vocal) signs. Hence a second degree of observation and generalization upon these images, as objects in reflective thought, cannot be readily realized independently of what would be the results of such observations, namely, their associations with outward signs. Even in the most intelligent dumb animal they are probably so feeble that they cannot be associated with outward signs in such a manner as to make these distinctly appear as substitutes, or signs equivalent to them.

So far as images act in governing trains of thought and reasoning, they act as signs; but, with reference to the more vivid outward signs, they are, in the animal mind, merged in the things signified, like stars in the light of the sun. Hence language, in its narrower sense, as the instrument of reflective thought, appears to depend directly on the intensity of significant, or representative, images; since the power to attend to these and intensify them still further, at the same time that an equivalent outward sign is an object of attention, would appear to depend solely on the relative intensities of the two states, or on the relations of intensity in perception and imagination, or in original and revived impressions. The direct power of attention to intensify a revived impression in imagination does not appear to be different in kind from the power of attention in perception, or in outward impressions generally. But this direct power would be obviously aided by the indirect action of attention when fixed by an outward sign, provided attention could be directed to both at the same time: as a single glance may comprehend in one field of view the moon or the brighter planets and the sun, since the moon or planet is not hidden like the stars, by the glare of day.

As soon, then, as the progress of animal intelligence through an extension of the range in its powers of memory, or in revived impressions, together with a corresponding increase in the vividness of these impressions, has reached a certain point—a progress in itself useful, and therefore likely to be secured in some part of nature, as one among its numerous grounds of selection, or lines of advantage—it becomes possible for such an intelligence to fix its attention on a vivid outward sign, without losing sight of, or dropping out of distinct attention, an image or revived impression; which latter would only serve, in case of its spontaneous revival in imagination, as a sign of the same thing, or the same event. Whether the vivid outward sign be a real object or event (of which the revived image is the counterpart), or whether it be a sign in a stricter meaning of the term,—that is, some action, figure, or utterance, associated either naturally or artificially with all similar objects or events, and, consequently, with the revived and representative image of them,—whatever the character of this outward sign may be, provided the representative image or inward sign still retains, in distinct consciousness, its power as such, then the outward sign may be consciously recognized as a substitute for the inward one, and a consciousness of simultaneous internal and external suggestion or significance might be realized. And the contrast of thoughts and things, at least in their power of suggesting that of which they may be coincident signs, could, for the first time be perceptible. This would plant the germ of the distinctively human form of self-consciousness. . . .

To exemplify this somewhat abstruse analysis, let us examine what, according to it, would be the mental movements in a man —let him be a sportsman—and a domestic animal—let it be his dog—on hearing a name—let it be the name of some game, as "fox." The general character of the phenomena in both would be the same on the actual first hearing of this word. The word would suggest a mental image of the fox, then its movements of escape from its hunters, and the thought would pass on and dwell, through the absorbing interest of it, on the hunter's movements of pursuit, or pass on even to the capture and destruction of the game. This would, doubtless, recall to the minds of the hunter and his hound one or more real and distinctly remembered incidents of the sort. Now if we suppose this train of thought to be revived (as undoubtedly it is capable of being, both in the man and the dog), it will be the same in the man's mind as on its first production. Except that the name "fox" will be thought of as an auditory, or else a vocal image, instead of being heard; and the visual image of the fox will be recalled by it with all the succeeding parts of the repeated train. But in the dog, either the auditory image of the name will not be recalled, since the vocal image does not exist in his mind to aid the recall (his voluntary vocal powers not being capable of forming it even in the first instance); or, if such an auditory image arises, the representative visual or olfactory one will not appear in distinct consciousness. His attention will pass at once from either of these signs, but on only to the more intense and interesting parts of the train—to the pursuit and capture of the game, or to actually remembered incidents of the kind. Either the first or the immediate sign will remain in oblivion. . . .

When a thought, or an outward expression, acts in an animal's mind or in a man's, in the capacity of a sign, it carries forward the movements of a train, and directs attention away from itself to what it signifies or suggests; and consciousness is concentrated on the latter. But being sufficiently vivid in itself to engage distinct attention, it determines a new kind of action, and a new faculty of observation, of which the cerebral hemispheres appear to be the organs. From the action of these, in their more essential powers in memory and imagination, the objects or materials of reflection are also derived. Reflection would thus be—not what most metaphysicians appear to regard it—a fundamentally new faculty in man, as elementary and primordial as memory itself, or the power of abstractive attention, or the function of signs and representative images in generalization. But it would be determined in its contrasts with other mental faculties by the nature of its objects.

On its subjective side it would be composed of the same mental faculties—namely, memory, attention, abstraction—as those which are employed in the primary use of the senses. It would be engaged upon what these senses have furnished to memory; but would act as independently of any order of grouping and succession presented by them, as the several senses do of one another. To this extent, reflection is a distinct faculty, and though, perhaps, not peculiar to man, is in him so prominent and marked in its effects on the development of the individual mind, that it may be regarded as his most essential and elementary mental distinction in kind. For differences of degrees in causes may make differences of kinds in effects. . . .

That a dumb animal should not know itself to be a thinking being, is hardly more surprising than that it should not be aware of the circulation of its blood and other physiological functions; or that it should not know the anatomy of its frame or that of its nervous system, or the seat of its mental faculties, or the fact that the brain is much smaller in it, in proportion to the size of its body, than in man. Its reflective observation may be as limited in respect to the phenomena of thought as the outward observation of most men is in respect to these results of scientific research. And, on the other hand, the boasted intellectual self-consciousness of man is a knowledge of a subject, not through all its attributes and phenomena, but only through enough of them in general to determine and distinguish it from outward objects, and make it serve as the subject of further attributions or predications, as reflective observation makes them known. The abstract forms of this knowledge—the laws of logic and grammar, and the categories of the understanding, which are forms of all scientific knowledge—are all referable to the action of a *purpose* to know and to fix knowledge by precise generalization: just as the mechanical conditions of flight are referable to the purpose to fly and to secure the requisite means. Generalization already exists, however, with particular acts of inquisitiveness in the animal mind; and there is required only the proper degree of attention to signs in order to make it act in accordance with laws which, *if they are universal and necessary laws of the mind,* are equally laws of the animal intelligence, though not actually exemplified in it; just as the laws of locomotion are not actually exemplified in the bodies of plants, but are still potential in them.

The inferior and savage races of men, whose languages do not include any abstract terms like truth, goodness, and sweetness, but only concrete ones, like true, good, and sweet, would hardly be able to form a conception, even a vague and obscure one, of the mystic's research of omniscience in the profundities of self-consciousness. They ought on this account, perhaps, to be regarded as races distinct from that of these philosophers, at least mentally; and to be classed, in spite of their powers of speech and limited vocabularies, with the dumb but still intelligent animals. If, however, the theory above propounded be true, this greatest of human qualities, intelligent self-consciousness, understood in its actual and proper limits, would follow as a consequence of a greater brain, a greater or more powerful and vivid memory and imagination, bringing to light, as it were, and into distinct consciousness, phenomena of thought which reflective observation refers to the subject, already known in the dumb animal, or distinguished as an active cause from the forces of outward nature and from the wills of other animals.

The degrees of abstraction and the successively higher and higher steps of generalization—the process which, in scientific knowledge, brings not only the particulars of experience under general designation, but, with a conscious purpose, brings the less general under the more general; or gives common names not only to each and all resembling objects and relation, but also more general common names to what is denoted by these names, thus grouping them under higher categories—this process brings together the several forms of self-consciousness. Willing, desiring, feeling, and lastly thinking, also, are seen in thought to belong together, or to the same subject; and by thinking they are brought under a common view and receive a common name, or several common names: to wit, "my mind," "me," "I," "my mental states."

III

The Opposition of Scientific Evolution to All Forms of Religion, Philosophical Idealism, or Simple Materialism

Truths independent of all experience are not known to exist, unless we exclude from what we mean by "experience" that experience which we have in learning the meanings of words and in agreeing to definitions and conventions of language, on the ground that they depend solely, or may be considered as depending solely, on a lexical authority, from which a kind of necessity proceeds, independent of reality in the relations and connections of the facts denoted by the words. It is possible that laws exist absolutely universal, binding fate and infinite power as well as speech and the intelligible use of words; but it is not possible that the analytical processes of any finite intellect should discover what particular laws these are. Such an intellect may legislate with absolute freedom in the realm of definition and word-making, provided it limits itself to its autonomy, and does not demand of other intellects that they shall be governed by such laws, as if they were of universal application in the world of common experience.

It is also possible that beliefs, or convictions, exist, supposed by the mystic to be independent of all ordinary forms of particular experience, "which no amount of experience could produce." But it is not true that there are any universal or scientific beliefs of this kind. The effects of inherited aptitudes, and of early, long-continued, and constantly repeated experiences in the individual, together with the implications of language itself, in fixing and in giving force and certainty to an idea or a belief, have, probably, not been sufficiently considered by those metaphysicians who claim a preternatural and absolute origin for certain of our cognitions; and also, perhaps, the more dogmatic among these thinkers over-estimate the force and certainty of the beliefs, or mistake the *kind* of necessity they have. The essential importance, the necessity and universality in language, of pronominal words or signs, should not be mistaken for a real *a priori* necessity in the relations expressed by them. Metaphysicians should consider that *ego* and *non-ego,* as real existences, are not individual phenomena, but groups with demonstrative names the least possible determined in meaning; or are the most abstract subjects of the phenomena of experience, though determined, doubtless, in their applications partly by spontaneous, instinctive, or natural and inherited tendencies to their formation. . . .

Our volitions, desires, and feelings are in general so obscure in respect to the particular causes which precede them and are anterior to their immediate determination or production, that introspective observation in reflection can penetrate only a little way, and is commonly quite unable to trace them back to remote causes in our characters, organizations, and circumstances. Hence, the conception of the causes of our own inward volitions, or our desires and intentions, as being of an inscrutable, nonphenomenal nature, would naturally arise. But this conception would probably be made much more prominent in the unreflective barbarian's mind, by his association of it with the obscurity to him of inward, or personal, causes of outward actions and expressions in others.

Darkness is seen where light is looked for and does not appear. Causes are missed where research is made without success. We are conscious of minds in other men and in other animals only through their outward expressions. The inward causes are not apparent or directly known to us as phenomena; and though the inference of their existence is not in all cases, even with men, made through analogy, or from an observation of their connections with similar outward actions and expressions in ourselves, but is grounded, doubtless, in many cases on an instinctive connection between these expressions in other and *feelings,* at least, in ourselves, yet we do not think of them as really inscrutable in their natures, but only as imperceptible to our outward senses. They have their representatives in the phenomena of our imaginations. These would be but vaguely conceived, however, in many cases. Even reverence in the barbarian's mind might prevent him, as an obedient subject, from attempting to fathom or reproduce in his own imagination the thoughts and intentions of his majesty the king. Reverence is not, however, in any case, an unreflective or thoughtless feeling. It would not be like the feelings of the sheep, which, not being able to comprehend through its own experience the savage feelings of the wolf, would only interpret his threatening movements as something fearful, or would connect in an instinctive judgment these outward movements only with anticipated painful consequences. Reverence in the loyal barbarian subject would not go so far as to make his king appear a mere automaton, as the wolf might seem to the sheep. The commands of his king, or of his deity, would be to him rather the voice of a wisdom and authority inscrutable, the outward manifestation of mysterious *power,* the type of metaphysical causation. Accordingly, we find that a capacity for strong, unappropriated feelings of loyalty and reverence, demanding an object for their satisfaction, have also descended to those thinkers who have inherited "the ontological passion." It would, therefore, appear most probably, that the metaphysician's invincible belief in the conception of the will as a mysterious power behind the inward phenomena of volition, and as incapable of analysis into the determinations of character, organization, and circumstances, arises also from inherited feelings about the will of other men rather than from attentive observation of the phenomena of his own.

Science and scientific studies have led a portion of the human race a long way aside from the guidance of these inherited intellectual instincts, and have also appeared able to conquer them in many minds to which in youth they seemed invincible. Positivists, unlike poets, become—are not born—such thinkers. The conception of the causes of phenomena, with which these studies render them familiar, had small beginnings in the least noble occupations and necessities of life, and in the need of knowing the future and judging of it from present signs. From this grew up gradually a knowledge of natural phenomena, and phenomena of mind also, both in their outward and combined orders or laws and in their intimate and elementary succession, or the "laws of nature." The latter are involved in the relations of effects to their "physical" causes, so called because metaphysicians have discovered that they are not the same sort of powers as those which the invincible instincts look for as ultimate and absolute in nature. But this is not a new or modern meaning of the word "cause." It was always its practical, common-sense, every-day meaning:—in the relations of means to ends; in rational explanations and anticipations of natural events; in the familiar processes and observation of common human life; in short, in the relations of phenomena to phenomena, as apparent causes and effects. This meaning was not well defined, it is true; nor is it now easily made clear, save by examples; yet it is by examples, rather than by a distinct abstraction of what is common to them, that the use of many other words, capable of clear definition, is determined in common language. The relations of invariable succession in phenomena do not, except in ultimate laws where the phenomena are simple or elementary, define the relation of phenomenal cause and effect; for, as it has been observed, night follows day, and day follows night invariably, yet neither is the cause of the other. These relations belong to the *genus* of natural successions.

41

The relation of cause and effect is a *species* of this *genus*. It means an *unconditional,* invariable succession; *independence* of other orders of succession, or of all orders not involved in it.

The day illuminates objects; the night obscures them; the sun and fires warm them; the clouds shed rain upon them; the savage animal attacks and hurts others: these facts involve natural orders, in which relations of cause and effect are apparent, and are indicated in the antitheses of their terms as the subjects and objects of transitive propositions. But these relations are only indicated; they are not explicitly set forth. Metaphysics undertakes their explication by referring the illumination, obscurity, warmth, rain, and hurt to *powers* in the day, the sun and fires, the clouds, and the animal. Modern metaphysics would not go so far as to maintain, in the light of science, that the powers in these examples are inscrutable, or incapable of further analysis. Nevertheless, when the analysis is made, and the vision of objects, for example, is understood to arise from the incidence of the light of the sun on the air and on objects, and thence from reflections on all surfaces of objects, and thence again from diffused reflections falling partly on our eyes, and so on to the full realization of vision in the brain, all according to determinate laws of succession—an analysis which sets forth these *elementary* invariable orders, or *ultimate* and independent laws of succession in phenomena, to which, in their independent combinations, science refers the relations of cause and effect;—when this analysis has been made, then metaphysics interposes, and, from its ancient habits of thought, ascribes to the elementary antecedent a *power* to produce the elementary consequent. Or when the effect, as in vision, follows from the ultimate properties and elementary laws of great numbers of beings and arrangement,—the sun, the medium of light, the air, the illuminated objects, the eye, its nerves and the brain,—and follows through a long series of steps, however rapid, from the earliest to the latest essential antecedent, metaphysics still regards the whole process, with the elementary powers involved, as explicated only in its *outward* features. There is still the mystery inherent in the being of each elementary antecedent, of its power to produce its elementary consequent;

and these mysterious powers, combined and referred to the most conspicuous essential conditions of the effect (like the existence of the sun and the eye), make in the whole a mystery as great as if science had never inquired into the process.

Metaphysics demands, in the interest of mystery, *why* an elementary antecedent is followed by its elementary consequent. But this question does not arise from that inquisitiveness which inspires scientific research. It is asked to show that it cannot be answered, and hence that all science rests on mystery. It is asked from the feelings that in the barbarian or child forbid or check inquiry. But, being a question, it is open to answer; or it makes legitimate, at least, the counter question: "When can a question be properly asked?" or, "What is the purpose of asking a question?" Is it not to discover the causes, classes, laws, or rules that determine the existence, properties, or production of a thing or event? And when these are discovered, is there any further occasion for inquiry, except in the interest of feelings which would have checked inquiry at the outset? The feelings of loyalty and reverence, instinctive in our natures, and of the utmost value in the history of our race, as the mediums of co-operation, discipline, and instruction, are instincts more powerful in some minds than in others, and, like all instincts, demand their proper satisfaction. From the will, or our active powers, they demand devotion; from the intellect, submission to authority and mystery. But, like all instincts, they may demand too much; too much for their proper satisfaction, and even for their most energetic and useful service to the race, or to the individual man. Whether it is possible for any one to have too much loyalty, reverence, love, or devotion, is, therefore, a question which the metaphysical spirit and mode of thought suggest. For in the mystic's mind these feelings have set themselves up as absolute excellencies, as money sets itself up in the mind of the miser. And it is clear that, under these absolute forms, it is difficult to deny the demand. It is only in respect to *what* is reverenced, loved, or worshipped, or *what* claims our allegiance, that questions of how much of them is due can be rationally asked.

To demand the submission of the intellect to the mystery of

the simplest and most elementary relations of cause and effect in phenomena, or the restraint of its inquisitiveness on reaching an ultimate law of nature, is asking too much, in that it is a superfluous demand. The intellect in itself has no disposition to go any further, and, on the other hand, no impulse to kneel before its completed triumph. The highest generality, or universality, in the elements or connections of elements in phenomena, is the utmost reach both in the power and the desire of the scientific intellect. Explanation cannot go, and does not rationally seek to go, beyond such facts. The invention of *noumena* to account for ultimate and universal properties and relations in phenomena arises from no other necessity than the action of a desire urged beyond the normal promptings of its power. To demand of the scientific intellect that it shall pause in the interest of mystery at the movements of a falling body or at the laws of these movements, is a misappropriation of the quality of mystery. For mystery still has its uses; and, in its useful action, is an ally of inquisitiveness, inciting and guiding it, giving it steadiness and seriousness, opposing only its waywardness and idleness. It fixes attention, even inquisitive attention, on its objects, and in its active form of wonder "is a highly philosophical affection." So also devotion, independently of its intrinsic worth in the mystic's regard, has its uses; and these determine its rational measure, or how much of it is due to any object. In its active forms of usefulness and duty, it is an ally of freedom in action, opposing this freedom only in respect to what would limit it still more, or injuriously and on the whole.

The metaphysical modes of thought and feeling foster, on the other hand, the sentiments of mystery and devotion in their passive forms, and as attitudes of the intellect and will, rather than as their inciting and guiding motives. These attitudes, which are symbolized in the forms of religious worship, were no doubt needed to fix the attention of the barbarian, as they are still required to fix the attention of the child upon serious contemplations and purposes. Obedience and absolute submission are, at one stage of intellectual and moral development, both in a race and in the individual, required as the conditions of discipline for effecting the more directly serviceable and freer action of the mind and character under the guidance of rational loyalty and reverence. The metaphysical modes of thought and feeling retain these early habits in relations in which they have ceased to be serviceable to the race, or to the useful development of the individual, especially when in the mystic's regard obedience has acquired an intrinsic worth, and submission has become a beatitude. The scientific habit of thought, though emancipated from any such outward supports and constraints, is yet not wanting in earnestness of purpose and serious interests, and is not without the motives of devotion and mystery, or their active guidance in the directions of usefulness and duty, and in the investigations of truth. It does not stand in awe before the unknown, as if life itself depended on a mysterious and capricious will in that unknown; for awe is habitual only with the barbarian, and is a useful motive only in that severe instruction which is exacted by the wants, insecurities, and necessities of his life, while among the partially civilized it often constrains the thoughtless by a present fear to avoid or resist evils really greater than what is feared, though less obvious to the imagination.

·III·

HENRY GEORGE

[1 8 3 9 - 1 8 9 7]

SOCIAL PROBLEMS

SOCIAL PROBLEMS

I

The Increasing Importance of Social Questions

There come moments in our lives that summon all our powers—when we feel that, casting away illusions, we must decide and act with our utmost intelligence and energy. So in the lives of peoples come periods specially calling for earnestness and intelligence.

We seem to have entered one of these periods. Over and again have nations and civilizations been confronted with problems which, like the riddle of the Sphinx, not to answer was to be destroyed; but never before have problems so vast and intricate been presented. This is not strange. That the closing years of this century must bring up momentous social questions follows from the material and intellectual progress that has marked its course.

Between the development of society and the development of species there is a close analogy. In the lowest forms of animal life there is little difference of parts; both wants and powers are few and simple; movement seems automatic; and instincts are scarcely distinguishable from those of the vegetable. So homogeneous are some of these living things, that if cut in pieces, each piece still lives. But as life rises into higher manifestations, simplicity gives way to complexity, the parts develop into organs having separate functions and reciprocal relations, new wants and powers arise, and a greater and greater degree of intelligence is needed to secure food and avoid danger. Did fish, bird or beast possess no higher intelligence than the polyp, nature could bring them forth only to die.

From *Social Problems,* pp. 1-9, 70-80, 241-245, by Henry George (New York: Doubleday & Co., Inc., 1930). Reprinted with the permission of Miss Agnes De Mille.

This law—that the increasing complexity and delicacy of organization which give higher capacity and increased power are accompanied by increased wants and dangers, and require, therefore, increased intelligence—runs through nature. In the ascending scale of life at last comes man, the most highly and delicately organized of animals. Yet not only do his higher powers require for their use a higher intelligence than exists in other animals, but without higher intelligence he could not live. His skin is too thin; his nails too brittle; he is too poorly adapted for running, climbing, swimming or burrowing. Were he not gifted with intelligence greater than that of any beast, he would perish from cold, starve from inability to get food, or be exterminated by animals better equipped for the struggle in which brute instinct suffices.

In man, however, the intelligence which increases all through nature's rising scale passes at one bound into an intelligence so superior, that the difference seems of kind rather than degree. In him, that narrow and seemingly unconscious intelligence that we call instinct becomes conscious reason, and the godlike power of adaptation and invention makes feeble man nature's king.

But with man the ascending line stops. Animal life assumes no higher form; nor can we affirm that, in all his generations, man, as an animal has a whit improved. But progression in another line begins. Where the development of species ends, social development commences, and that advance of society that we call civilization so increases human powers, that between savage and civilized man there is a gulf so vast as to suggest the gulf between the highly organized animal and the oyster glued to the rocks. And with every advance upon this line new vistas open. When we try to think what knowledge and power progressive civilization may give to the men of the future, imagination fails.

In this progression which begins with man, as in that which leads up to him, the same law holds. Each advance makes a demand for higher and higher intelligence. With the beginnings of society arises the need for social intelligence—for that consensus of individual intelligence which forms a public opinion, a public conscience, a public will, and is manifested in law, institutions and administration. As society develops, a higher and higher degree of this social intelligence is required, for the relation of individuals to each other becomes more intimate and important, and the increasing complexity of the social organization brings liability to new dangers.

In the rude beginning, each family produces its own food, makes its own clothes, builds its own house, and, when it moves, furnishes its own transportation. Compare with this independence the intricate independence of the denizens of a modern city. They may supply themselves with greater certainty, and in much greater variety and abundance, than the savage; but it is by the coöperation of thousands. Even the water they drink, and the artificial light they use, are brought to them by elaborate machinery, requiring the constant labor and watchfulness of many men. They may travel at a speed incredible to the savage; but in doing so resign life and limb to the care of others. A broken rail, a drunken engineer, a careless switchman, may hurl them to eternity. And the power of applying labor to the satisfaction of desire passes, in the same way, beyond the direct control of the individual. The laborer becomes but part of a great machine, which may at any time be paralyzed by causes beyond his power, or even his foresight. Thus does the well-being of each become more and more dependent upon the well-being of all—the individual more and more subordinate to society.

And so come new dangers. The rude society resembles the creatures that though cut into pieces will live; the highly civilized society is like a highly organized animal: a stab in a vital part, the suppression of a single function, is death. A savage village may be burned and its people driven off—but, used to direct recourse to nature, they can maintain themselves. Highly civilized man, however, accustomed to capital, to machinery, to the minute division of labor, becomes helpless when suddenly deprived of these and thrown upon nature. Under the factory system, some sixty persons, with the aid of much costly machinery cooperate to the making of a pair of shoes. But, of the sixty, not one could make a whole shoe. This is the tendency in all branches of production, even in agriculture. How many farmers of the new generation can use the flail? How many farmers' wives can now make a coat from the wool? Many of our farmers do not even make their own butter or raise their own vegetables! There is an enormous gain in productive power from this division of labor, which assigns to the individual the production of but a few of the things, or even but a small part of one of the things, he needs, and makes each dependent upon others with whom he never comes in contact; but the social organization becomes more sensitive. A primitive village community may pursue the even tenor of its life without feeling disasters which overtake other villages but a few miles off; but in the closely knit civilization to which we have attained, a war, a scarcity, a commercial crisis, in one hemisphere produces powerful effects in the other, while shocks and jars from which a primitive community easily recovers would to a highly civilized community mean wreck.

It is startling to think how destructive in a civilization like ours would be such fierce conflicts as fill the history of the past. The wars of highly civilized countries, since the opening of the era of steam and machinery, have been duels of armies rather than conflicts of peoples or classes. Our only glimpse of what might happen, were passion fully aroused, was in the struggle of the Paris Commune. And, since 1870, to the knowledge of petroleum has been added that of even more destructive agents. The explosion of a little nitro-glycerin under a few water-mains would make a great city uninhabitable; the blowing up of a few railroad bridges and tunnels would bring famine quicker than the wall of circumvallation that Titus drew around Jerusalem; the pumping of atmospheric air into the gas-mains, and the application of a match, would tear up every street and level every house. The Thirty Years' War set back civilization in Germany; so fierce a war now would all but destroy it. Not merely have destructive powers vastly increased, but the whole social organization has become vastly more delicate.

In a simpler state master and man, neighbor and neighbor, know each other, and there is that touch of the elbow which, in times of danger, enables society to rally. But present tendencies are to the loss of this. In London, dwellers in one house do not know those in the next; the tenants of adjoining rooms are utter strangers to each other. Let civil conflict break or paralyze the authority that preserves order and the vast population would become a terror-stricken mob, without point of rally or principle of cohesion, and your London would be sacked and burned by an army of thieves. London is only the greatest of great cities. What is true of London is true of New York, and in the same measure true of the many cities whose hundreds of thousands are steadily growing toward millions. These vast aggregations of humanity, where he who seeks isolation may find it more truly than in the desert; where wealth and poverty touch and jostle; where one revels and another starves within a few feet of each other, yet separated by as great a gulf as that fixed between Dives in Hell and Lazarus in Abraham's bosom—they are centers and types of our civilization. Let jar or shock dislocate the complex and delicate organization, let the policeman's club be thrown down or wrested from him, and the fountains of the great deep are opened, and quicker than ever before chaos comes again. Strong as it may seem, our civilization is evolving destructive forces. Not desert and forest, but city slums and country roadsides are nursing the barbarians who may be to the new what Hun and Vandal were to the old.

Nor should we forget that in civilized man still lurks the savage. The men who, in past times, oppressed or revolted, who fought to the death in petty quarrels and drunk fury with blood, who burned cities and rent empires, were men essentially such as those we daily meet. Social progress has accumulated knowledge, softened manners, refined tastes and extended sympathies, but man is yet capable of as blind a rage as when, clothed in skins, he fought wild beasts with a flint. And present tendencies, in some respects at least, threaten to kindle passions that have so often before flamed in destructive fury.

There is in all the past nothing to compare with the rapid changes now going on in the civilized world. It seems as though in the European race, and in the nineteenth century, man was just beginning to live—just grasping his tools and becoming conscious of his powers. The snail's pace of crawling ages has suddenly become the headlong rush of the locomotive, speeding faster and faster. This rapid progress is primarily in industrial methods and material powers. But industrial changes imply social changes and necessitate political changes. Progressive societies outgrow institutions as children outgrow clothes. Social progress always requires greater intelligence in the management of public affairs; but this the more as progress is rapid and change quicker.

And that the rapid changes now going on are bringing up problems that demand most earnest attention may be seen on every hand. Symptoms of danger, premonitions of violence, are appearing all over the civilized world. Creeds are dying, beliefs are changing; the old forces of conservatism are melting away. Political institutions are failing, as clearly in democratic America as in monarchical Europe. There is growing unrest and bitterness among the masses, whatever be the form of government, a blind groping for escape from conditions becoming intolerable. To attribute all this to the teachings of demagogues is like attributing the fever to the quickened pulse. It is the new wine beginning to ferment in old bottles. To put into a sailing-ship the powerful engines of a first-class ocean steamer would be to tear her to pieces with their play. So the new powers rapidly changing all the relations of society must shatter social and political organizations not adapted to meet their strain.

To adjust our institutions to growing needs and changing conditions is the task which devolves upon us. Prudence, patriotism, human sympathy, and religious sentiment, alike call upon us to undertake it. There is danger in reckless change; but greater danger in blind conservatism. The problems beginning to confront us are grave—so grave that there is fear they may not be solved in time to prevent great catastrophes. But their gravity comes from indisposition to recognize frankly and grapple boldly with them.

These dangers, which menace not one country alone, but modern civilization itself, do but show that a higher civilization is struggling to be born—that the needs and the aspirations of men have outgrown conditions and institutions that before sufficed.

A civilization which tends to concentrate wealth and power in the hands of a fortunate few, and to make of others mere human machines, must inevitably evolve anarchy and bring destruction. But a civilization is possible in which the poorest could have all the comforts and conveniences now enjoyed by the rich; in which prisons and almshouses would be needless, and charitable societies unthought of. Such a civilization waits only for the social intelligence that will adapt means to ends. Powers that might give plenty to all are already in our hands. Though there is poverty and want, there is, yet, seeming embarrassment from the very excess of wealth-producing forces. "Give us but a market," says the manufacturers, "and we will supply goods without end!" "Give us but work!" cry idle men.

The evils that begin to appear spring from the fact that the application of intelligence to social affairs has not kept pace with the application of intelligence to individual needs and material ends. Natural science strides forward, but political science lags. With all our progress in the arts which produce wealth, we have made no progress in securing its equitable distribution. Knowledge has vastly increased; industry and commerce have been revolutionized; but whether free trade or protection is best for a nation we are not yet agreed. We have brought machinery to a pitch of perfection that, fifty years ago, could not have been imagined; but, in the presence of political corruption, we seem as helpless as idiots. The East River bridge is a crowning triumph of mechanical skill; but to get it built a leading citizen of Brooklyn had to carry to New York sixty thousand dollars in a carpet-bag to bribe New York aldermen. The human soul that thought out the great bridge is prisoned in a crazed and broken body that lies bedfast, and could watch it grow only by peering through a telescope. Nevertheless, the weight of the immense mass is estimated and adjusted for every inch. But the skill of the engineer could not prevent condemned wire being smuggled into the cable.

The progress of civilization requires that more and more intelligence be devoted to social affairs, and this not the intelligence of the few, but that of the many. We cannot safely leave politics to politicians, or political economy to college professors. The people themselves must think, because the people alone can act.

In a "journal of civilization" a professed teacher declares the saving word for society to be that each shall mind his own business. This is the gospel of selfishness, soothing as soft flutes to those who, having fared well themselves, think everybody should be satisfied. But the salvation of society, the hope for the free, full development of humanity, is in the gospel of brotherhood—the gospel of Christ. Social progress makes the well-being of all more and more the business of each; it binds all closer and closer together in bonds from which none can escape. He who observes the law and the proprieties, and cares for his family, yet takes no interest in the general weal, and gives no thought to those who are trodden under foot, save now and then to bestow alms, is not a true Christian. Nor is he a good citizen. The duty of the citizen is more and harder than this.

The intelligence required for the solving of social problems is not a thing of the mere intellect. It must be animated with the religious sentiment and warm with sympathy for human suffering. It must stretch out beyond self-interest, whether it be the self-interest of the few or of the many. It must seek justice. For at the bottom of every social problem we will find a social wrong.

II

That We All Might Be Rich

The terms rich and poor are of course frequently used in a relative sense. Among Irish peasants, kept on the verge of starvation by the tribute wrung from them to maintain the luxury of absentee landlords in London or Paris, "the woman of three cows" will be looked on as rich, while in the society of millionaires a man with only $500,000 will be regarded as poor. Now, we cannot, of course, all be rich in the sense of having more than others; but when people say, as they so often do, that we cannot all be rich, or when they say that we must always have the poor with us, they do not use the words in this comparative sense. They mean by the rich those who have enough, or more than enough, wealth to gratify all reasonable wants, and by the poor those who have not.

Now, using the words in this sense, I join issue with those who say that we cannot all be rich; with those who declare that in human society the poor must always exist. I do not, of course, mean that we all might have an array of servants; that we all might outshine each other in dress, in equipage, in the lavishness of our balls or dinners, in the magnificence of our houses. That would be a contradiction in terms. What I mean is, that we all might have leisure, comfort and abundance, not merely of the necessaries, but even of what are now esteemed the elegancies and luxuries of life. I do not mean to say that absolute equality could be had, or would be desirable. I do not mean to say that we could all have, or would want, the same quantity of all the different forms of wealth. But I do mean to say that we might all have enough wealth to satisfy reasonable desires; that we might all have so much of the material things we now struggle for, that no one would want to rob or swindle his neighbor; that no one would worry all day, or lie awake at nights, fearing he might be brought to poverty, or thinking how he might acquire wealth.

Does this seem an utopian dream? What would people of fifty years ago have thought of one who would have told them that it was possible to sew by steam-power; to cross the Atlantic in six days, or the continent in three; to have a message sent from London at noon delivered in Boston three hours before noon; to hear in New York the voice of a man talking in Chicago?

Did you ever see a pail of swill given to a pen of hungry hogs? That is human society as it is.

Did you ever see a company of well-bred men and women sitting down to a good dinner, without scrambling, or jostling, or gluttony, each, knowing that his own appetite will be satisfied, deferring to and helping the others? That is human society as it might be.

"Devil catch the hindmost" is the motto of our so-called civilized society to-day. We learn early to "take care of No. 1," lest No. 1 should suffer; we learn early to grasp from others that we may not want ourselves. The fear of poverty makes us admire great wealth; and so habits of greed are formed, and we behold the pitiable spectacle of men who have already more than they can by any possibility use, toiling, striving, grasping to add to their store up to the very verge of the grave—that grave which, whatever else it may mean, does certainly mean the parting with all earthly possessions however great they be.

In vain, in gorgeous churches, on the appointed Sunday, is the parable of Dives and Lazarus read. What can it mean in churches where Dives would be welcomed and Lazarus shown the door? In vain may the preacher preach of the vanity of riches, while poverty engulfs the hindmost. But the mad struggle would cease when the fear of poverty had vanished. Then, and not till then, will a truly Christian civilization become possible.

And may not this be?

We are so accustomed to poverty that even in the most advanced countries we regard it as the natural lot of the great masses of the people; that we take it as a matter of course that even in our highest civilization large classes should want the necessaries of healthful life, and the vast majority should only get a poor and pinched living by the hardest toil. There are professors of political economy who teach that this condition of things is the result of social laws of which it is idle to complain! There are ministers of religion who preach that this is the condition which an all-wise, all-powerful Creator intended for his children! If an architect were to build a theater so that not more than one-tenth of the audience could see and hear, we would call him a bungler and a botch. If a man were to give a feast and provide so little food that nine-tenths of his guests must go away hungry, we would call him a fool, or worse. Yet so accustomed are we to poverty, that even the preachers of what passes for Christianity tell us that the great Architect of the Universe, to whose infinite skill all nature testifies, has made such a botch job of this world that the vast majority of the human creatures whom he has called into it are condemned by the conditions he has imposed to want, suffering, and brutalizing toil that gives no opportunity for the development of mental powers—must pass their lives in a hard struggle to merely live!

Yet who can look about him without seeing that to whatever cause poverty may be due, it is not due to the niggardliness of nature; without seeing that it is blindness or blasphemy to assume that the Creator has condemned the masses of men to hard toil for a bare living?

If some men have not enough to live decently, do not others have far more than they really need? If there is not wealth sufficient to go around, giving every one abundance, is it because we have reached the limit of the production of wealth? Is our land all in use? is our labor all employed? is our capital all utilized? On the contrary, in whatever direction we look we see the most stupendous waste of productive forces—of productive forces so potent that were they permitted to play freely the production of wealth would be so enormous that there would be more than a sufficiency for all. What branch of production is there in which the limit of production has been reached? What single article of wealth is there of which we might not produce enormously more?

If the mass of the population of New York are jammed into the fever-breeding rooms of tenement-houses, it is not because there are not vacant lots enough in and around New York to give each family space for a separate home. If settlers are going into Montana and Dakota and Manitoba, it is not because there are not vast areas of untilled land much nearer the centers of population. If farmers are paying one-fourth, one-third, or even one-half of their crops for the privilege of getting land to cultivate, it is not because there are not, even in our oldest States, great quantities of land which no one is cultivating.

So true is it that poverty does not come from the inability to produce more wealth that from every side we hear that the power to produce is in excess of the ability to find a market; that the constant fear seems to be not that too little, but that too much, will be produced! Do we not maintain a high tariff, and keep at every port a horde of Custom-House officers, for fear the people of other countries will overwhelm us with their goods? Is not a great part of our machinery constantly idle? Are there not, even in what we call good times, an immense number of unemployed men who would gladly be at work producing wealth if they could only get the opportunity? Do we not, even now, hear, from every side, of embarrassment from the very excess of productive power, and of combinations to reduce production? Coal operators band together to limit their output; iron-works have shut down, or are running on half-time; distillers have agreed to limit their production to one-half their capacity, and sugar-refiners to sixty per cent.; paper-mills are suspending for one, two or three days a week; the gunny-cloth manufacturers, at a recent meeting, agreed to close their mills until the present overstock on the market is greatly reduced; many other manufacturers have done the same thing. The shoemaking machinery of New England can, in six months' full running, it is said, supply the whole demand of the United States for twelve months; the machinery for making rubber goods can turn out twice as much as the market will take.

This seeming glut of production, this seeming excess of productive power, runs through all branches of industry, and is evident all over the civilized world. From blackberries, bananas or apples, to ocean steamships or plate-glass mirrors, there is scarcely an article of human comfort or convenience that could not be produced in very much greater quantities than now without lessening the production of anything else.

So evident is this that many people think and talk and write as though the trouble is that there is not *work* enough to go around. We are in constant fear that other nations may do for us some of the work we might do for ourselves, and, to prevent them, guard ourselves with a tariff. We laud as public benefactors those who, as we say, "furnish employment." We are constantly talking as though this "furnishing of employment," this "giving of work," were the greatest boon that could be conferred upon society. To listen to much that is talked and much that is written, one would think that the cause of poverty is that there is not work enough for so many people, and that if the Creator had made the rock harder, the soil less fertile, iron as scarce as gold, and gold as diamonds; or if ships would sink and cities burn down oftener, there would be less poverty, because there would be more work to do.

The Lord Mayor of London tells a deputation of unemployed

workingmen that there is no demand for their labor, and that the only resource for them is to go to the poor house or emigrate. The English government is shipping from Ireland able-bodied men and women to avoid maintaining them as paupers. Even in our own land there are at all times large numbers, and in hard times vast numbers, earnestly seeking work—the opportunity to give labor for the things produced by labor.

Perhaps nothing shows more clearly the enormous forces of production constantly going to waste than the fact that the most prosperous time in all branches of business that this country has known was during the Civil War, when we were maintaining great fleets and armies, and millions of our industrial population were engaged in supplying them with wealth for unproductive consumption or for reckless destruction. It is idle to talk about the fictitious prosperity of those "flush" times. The masses of the people lived better, dressed better, found it easier to get a living, and had more luxuries and amusements than in normal times. There was more real, tangible wealth in the North at the close than at the beginning of the war. Nor was it the great issue of paper money, nor the creation of the debt, which caused this prosperity. The government presses struck off promises to pay; they could not print ships, cannon, arms, tools, food and clothing. Nor did we borrow these things from other countries or "from posterity." Our bonds did not begin to go to Europe until the close of the war, and the people of one generation can no more borrow from the people of a subsequent generation than we who live on this planet can borrow from the inhabitants of another planet or another solar system. The wealth consumed and destroyed by our fleets and armies came from the then existing stock of wealth. We could have carried on the war without the issue of a single bond, if, when we did not shrink from taking from wife and children their only bread-winner, we had not shrunk from taking the wealth of the rich.

Our armies and fleets were maintained, the enormous unproductive and destructive use of wealth was kept up, by the labor and capital then and there engaged in production. And it was that the demand caused by the war stimulated productive forces into activity that the enormous drain of the war was not only supplied, but that the North grew richer. The waste of labor in marching and countermarching, in digging trenches, throwing up earthworks, and fighting battles, the waste of wealth consumed or destroyed by our armies and fleets, did not amount to as much as the waste constantly going on from unemployed labor and idle or partially used machinery.

It is evident that this enormous waste of productive power is due, not to defects in the laws of nature, but to social maladjustments which deny to labor access to the natural opportunities of labor and rob the laborer of his just reward. Evidently the glut of markets does not really come from over-production when there are so many who want the things which are said to be over-produced, and would gladly exchange their labor for them did they have opportunity. Every day passed in enforced idleness by a laborer who would gladly be at work could he find opportunity, means so much less in the fund which creates the effective demand for other labor; every time wages are screwed down means so much reduction in the purchasing power of the workmen whose incomes are thus reduced. The paralysis which at all times wastes productive power, and which in times of industrial depression causes more loss than a great war, springs from the difficulty which those who would gladly satisfy their wants by their labor find in doing so. It cannot come from any natural limitation, so long as human desires remain unsatisfied, and nature yet offers to man the raw material of wealth. It must come from social maladjustments which permit the monopolization of these natural opportunities, and which rob labor of its fair reward. . . .

What these maladjustments are I shall in subsequent chapters endeavor to show. In this I wish simply to call attention to the fact that productive power in such a state of civilization as ours is sufficient, did we give it play, to so enormously increase the production of wealth as to give abundance to all—to point out that the cause of poverty is not in natural limitations, which we cannot alter, but in inequalities and injustices of distribution entirely within our control.

The passenger who leaves New York on a trans-Atlantic steamer does not fear that the provisions will give out. The men who run these steamers do not send them to sea without provisions enough for all they carry. Did he who made this whirling planet for our sojourn lack the forethought of man? Not so. In soil and sunshine, in vegetable and animal life, in veins of minerals, and in pulsing forces which we are only beginning to use, are capabilities which we cannot exhaust—materials and powers from which human effort, guided by intelligence, may gratify every material want of every human creature. There is in nature no reason for poverty—not even for the poverty of the crippled or the decrepit. For man is by nature a social animal, and the family affections and the social sympathies would, where chronic poverty did not distort and embrute, amply provide for those who could not provide for themselves.

But if we will not use the intelligence with which we have been gifted to adapt social organization to natural laws—if we allow dogs in the manger to monopolize what they cannot use; if we allow strength and cunning to rob honest labor, we must have chronic poverty, and all the social evils it inevitably brings. Under such conditions there would be poverty in paradise.

"The poor ye have always with you." If ever a scripture has been wrested to the devil's service, this is that scripture. How often have these words been distorted from their obvious meaning to soothe conscience into acquiescence in human misery and degradation—to bolster that blasphemy, the very negation and denial of Christ's teachings, that the All-Wise and Most Merciful, the Infinite Father, has decreed that so many of his creatures must be poor in order that others of his creatures to whom he wills the good things of life should enjoy the pleasure and virtue of doling out alms! "The poor ye have always with you," said Christ; but all his teachings supply the limitation, "until the coming of the Kingdom." In that kingdom of God *on earth,* that kingdom of justice and love for which he taught his followers to strive and pray, there will be no poor. But though the faith and the hope and the striving for this kingdom are of the very essence of Christ's teaching, the stanchest disbelievers and revilers of its possibility are found among those who call themselves Christians. Queer ideas of the Divinity have some of these Christians who hold themselves orthodox and contribute to the conversion of the heathen. A very rich orthodox Christian said to a newspaper reporter, awhile ago, on the completion of a large work out of which he is said to have made millions: "We have been peculiarly favored by Divine Providence; iron never was so cheap before, and labor has been a drug in the market."

That in spite of all our great advances we have yet with us the poor, those who, without fault of their own, cannot get healthful and wholesome conditions of life, is *our* fault and *our* shame. Who that looks about him can fail to see that it is only the injustice that denies natural opportunities to labor, and robs the producer of the fruits of his toil, that prevents us all from being rich? Consider the enormous powers of production now going to waste; consider the great number of unproductive consumers maintained at the expense of producers—the rich men and dudes, the worse than useless government officials, the pickpockets, burglars and confidence men; the highly respectable thieves who carry on their operations inside the law; the great army of lawyers; the beggars and paupers, and inmates of prisons; the monopolists and cornerers and gamblers of every kind and grade. Consider how much brains and energy and capital are devoted, not to the production of wealth, but to the grabbing of wealth. Consider the waste caused by competition which does not increase wealth; by laws which restrict production and exchange. Consider how human power is lessened by insufficient food, by unwholesome lodgings, by work done under conditions that produce disease and shorten life. Consider how intemperance and unthrift follow poverty. Consider how the ignorance bred of poverty lessens production, and how the vice bred of poverty causes destruction, and who can doubt that under conditions of social justice all might be rich?

The wealth-producing powers that would be evoked in a social state based on justice, where wealth went to the producers of wealth, and the banishment of poverty had banished the fear and greed and lusts that spring from it, we now can only faintly imagine. Wonderful as have been the discoveries and inventions of this century, it is evident that we have only begun to grasp that dominion which it is given to mind to obtain over matter. Discovery and invention are born of leisure, of material comfort, of freedom. These secured to all, and who shall say to what command over nature man may not attain?

It is not necessary that any one should be condemned to monotonous toil; it is not necessary that any one should lack the wealth and the leisure which permit the development of the faculties that raise man above the animal. Mind, not muscle, is the motor of progress, the force which compels nature and produces wealth. In turning men into machines we are wasting the highest powers. Already in our society there is a favored class who need take no thought for the morrow—what they shall eat, or what they shall drink, or wherewithal they shall be clothed. And may it not be that Christ was more than a dreamer when he told his disciples that in that kingdom of justice for which he taught them to work and pray this might be the condition of all?

III

What We Must Do

At the risk of repetition let me recapitulate:

The main source of the difficulties that menace us is the growing inequality in the distribution of wealth. To this all modern inventions seem to contribute, and the movement is hastened by political corruption, and by special monopolies established by abuse of legislative power. But the primary cause lies evidently in fundamental social adjustments—in the relations which we have established between labor and the natural material and means of labor—between man and the planet which is his dwelling-place, workshop and storehouse. As the earth must be the foundation of every material structure, so institutions which regulate the use of land constitute the foundation of every social organization, and must affect the whole character and development of that organization. In a society where the equality of natural rights is recognized, it is manifest that there can be no great disparity in fortunes. None except the physically incapacitated will be dependent on others; none will be forced to sell their labor to others. There will be differences in wealth, for there are differences among men as to energy, skill, prudency, foresight and industry; but there can be no very rich class, and no very poor class; and, as each generation becomes possessed of equal natural opportunities, whatever differences in fortune grow up in one generation will not tend to perpetuate themselves. In such a community, whatever may be its form, the political organization must be essentially democratic.

But, in a community where the soil is treated as the property of but a portion of the people, some of these people from the very day of their birth must be at a disadvantage, and some will have an enormous advantage. Those who have no rights in the land will be forced to sell their labor to the landholders for what they can get; and, in fact, cannot live without the landlord's permission. Such a community must inevitably develop a class of masters and a class of serfs—a class possessing great wealth, and a class having nothing; and its political organization, no matter what its form, must become a virtual despotism.

Our fundamental mistake is in treating land as private property. On this false basis modern civilization everywhere rests, and hence, as material progress goes on, is everywhere developing such monstrous inequalities in condition as must ultimately destroy it. As without land man cannot exist; as his very physical substance, and all that he can acquire or make, must be drawn from the land, the ownership of the land of a country is necessarily the ownership of the people of that country—involving their industrial, social and political subjection. Here is the great reason why the labor-saving inventions, of which our century has been so strikingly prolific, have signally failed to improve the condition of laborers. Labor-saving inventions primarily increase the power of labor, and should therefore increase wages and improve the condition of the laboring-classes. But this only where land is free to labor; for labor cannot exert itself without land. No labor-saving inventions can enable us to make something out of nothing, or in any wise lessen our dependence upon land. They can merely add to the efficiency of labor in working up the raw materials drawn from land. Therefore, wherever land has been subjected to private ownership, the ultimate effect of labor-saving inventions, and of all improved processes and discoveries, is to enable landowners to demand, and labor to pay, more for the use of land. Land becomes more valuable, but the wages of labor do not increase; on the contrary, if there is any margin for possible reductions, they may be absolutely reduced.

This we already see, and that in spite of the fact that a very important part of the effect of modern invention has been, by the improvement of transportation, to open up new land. What will be the effect of continued improvement in industrial processes when the land of this continent is all "fenced in," as in a few more years it will be, we may imagine if we consider what would have been the effect of labor-saving inventions upon Europe had no New World been opened.

But it may be said that, in asserting that where land is private property the benefit of industrial improvements goes ultimately to landowners, I ignore facts, and attribute to one principle more importance than is its due, since it is clear that a great deal of the increased wealth arising from modern improvements has not gone to the owners of land, but to capitalists, manufacturers, speculators, railroad-owners, and the holders of other monopolies than that of land. It may be pointed out that the richest family in Europe are the Rothschilds, who are more loan-jobbers and bankers than landowners; that the richest in America are the Vanderbilts, and not the Astors; that Jay Gould got his money, not by securing land, but by bulling and bearing the stock-market, by robbing people with hired lawyers and purchased judges and corrupted legislatures. I may be asked if I attach no importance to the jobbery and robbery of the tariff, under pretense of "protecting American labor;" to the jugglery with the monetary system, from the wildcat State banks and national banking system down to the trade-dollar swindle? . . .

In previous chapters I have given answers to all such objections; but to repeat in concise form, my reply is, that I do not ignore any of these things, but that they in no wise invalidate the self-evident principle that land being private property, the ultimate benefit of all improvements in production must go to the landowners. To say that if a man continues to play at rondo the table will ultimately get his money, is not to say that in the meantime he may not have his pocket picked. Let me illustrate:

Suppose an island, the soil of which is conceded to be the property of a few of the inhabitants. The rest of the inhabitants of this island must either hire land of these landowners, paying rent for it, or sell their labor to them, receiving wages. As population increases, the competition between the non-landowners for employment or the means of employment must increase rent and decrease wages until the non-landowners get merely a bare living, and the landholders get all the rest of the produce of the island. Now, suppose any improvement or invention made which will increase the efficiency of labor, it is manifest that, as soon as it becomes general, the competition between the non-landholders must give to the landholders all the benefit. No matter how great the improvement be, it can have but this ultimate result. If the improvements are so great that all the wealth the island can produce or that the landowners care for can be obtained with one-half the labor, they can let the other half of the laborers starve or evict them into the sea; or if they are pious people of the conventional sort, who believe that God Almighty intended these laborers to live, though he did not provide any land for them to live on, they may support them as paupers or ship them off to some other country as the English government is shipping the "surplus" Irishmen. But whether they let them die or keep them alive, they would have no use for them, and, if improvement still went on, they would have use for less and less of them.

This is the general principle.

But in addition to this population of landowners and their tenants and laborers, let us suppose there are on the island a storekeeper, an inventor, a gambler and a pirate. To make our supposition conform to modern fashions, we will suppose a highly respectable gambler—one of the kind who endows colleges and subscribes to the conversion of the heathen—and a very gentlemanly pirate, who flies on his swift cruiser the ensign of a yacht club instead of the old rawhead and bloody-bones, but who, even more regularly and efficiently than the old-fashioned pirate, levies his toll.

Let us suppose the storekeeper, the gambler and the pirate well established in business and making money. Along comes the inventor, and says: "I have an invention which will greatly add to the efficiency of labor and enable you greatly to increase the produce of this island, so that there will be very much more to divide among you all; but, as a condition for telling you of it, I want you to agree that I shall have a royalty upon its use." This is agreed to, the invention is adopted, and does greatly increase the production of wealth. But it does not benefit the laborers. The competition between them still forces them to pay such high rent or take such low wages that they are no better off than before. They still barely live. But the whole benefit of the invention does not in this case go to the landowners. The inventor's royalty gives him a great income, while the storekeeper, the gambler and the pirate all find their incomes much increased. The incomes of each one of these four, we may readily suppose, are larger than any single one of the landowners, and their gains offer the most striking contrast to the poverty of the laborers, who are bitterly disappointed at not getting any share of the increased wealth that followed the improvement. Something they feel is wrong, and some among them even begin to murmur that the Creator of the island surely did not make it for the benefit of only a few of its inhabitants, and that, as the common creatures of the Creator, they, too, have some rights to the use of the soil of the island.

Suppose then some one to arise and say: "What is the use of discussing such abstractions as the land question, that cannot come into practical politics for many a day, and that can only excite dissension and general unpleasantness, and that, moreover, savor of communism, which as you laborers, who have nothing but your few rags, very well know is a highly wicked and dangerous thing, meaning the robbery of widow women and orphans, and being opposed to religion? Let us be practical. You laborers are poor and can scarcely get a living, because you are swindled by the storekeeper, taxed by the inventor, gouged by the gambler and robbed by the pirate. Landholders and non-landholders, our interests are in common as against these vampires. Let us unite to stop their exactions. The storekeeper makes a profit of from ten to fifty per cent. on all that he sells. Let us form a cooperative society, which will sell everything at cost and enable laborers to get rich by saving the storekeeper's profit on all that they use. As for the inventor, he has been already well enough paid. Let us stop his royalty, and there will be so much more to divide between the landowners and the non-landowners. As for the gambler and the pirate, let us put a summary end to their proceedings and drive them off the island!"

Let us imagine a roar of applause, and these propositions carried out. What then? Then the landowners would become so much the richer. The laborers would gain nothing, unless it might be in a clearer apprehension of the ultimate cause of their poverty. For although, by getting rid of the storekeeper, the laborers might be able to live cheaper, the competition between them would soon force them to give up this advantage to the landowners by taking lower wages or giving higher rents. And so the elimination of the inventor's royalty, and of the pickings and stealings of the gambler and pirate, would only make land more valuable and increase the incomes of the landholders. The saving made by getting rid of the storekeeper, inventor, gambler and pirate would accrue to their benefit, as did the increase in production from the application of the invention.

That all this is true we may see, as I have shown. The growth of the railroad system has, for instance, resulted in putting almost the whole transportation business of the country in the hands of giant monopolies, who, for the most part, charge "what the traffic will bear," and who frequently discriminate in the most outrageous way against localities. The effect where this is done, as is alleged in the complaints that are made, is to reduce the price of land. And all this might be remedied, without raising wages or improving the condition of labor. It would only make land more valuable—that is to say, in consideration of the saving effected in transportation, labor would have to pay a higher premium for land.

So with all monopolies, and their name is legion. If all monopolies, save the monopoly of land, were abolished; if, even, by means of coöperative societies, or other devices, the profits of exchange were saved, and goods passed from producer to consumer at the minimum of cost; if government were reformed to the point of absolute purity and economy, nothing whatever would be done toward equalization in the distribution of wealth. The competition between laborers, who, having no rights in the land, cannot work without some one else's permission, would increase the value of land, and force wages to the point of bare subsistence.

Let me not be misunderstood. I do not say that in the recognition of the equal and unalienable right of each human being to the natural elements from which life must be supported and wants satisfied, lies the solution of all social problems. I fully recognize the fact that even after we do this, much will remain to do. We might recognize the equal right to land, and yet tyranny and spoliation be continued. But whatever else we do, so long as we fail to recognize the equal right to the elements of nature, nothing will avail to remedy that unnatural inequality in the distribution of wealth which is fraught with so much evil and danger. Reform as we may, until we make this fundamental reform our material progress can but tend to differentiate our people into the monstrously rich and the frightfully poor. Whatever be the increase of wealth, the masses will still be ground toward the point of bare subsistence—we must still have our great criminal classes, our paupers and our tramps, men and women driven to degradation and desperation from inability to make an honest living.

·IV·

WILLIAM GRAHAM SUMNER

[1 8 4 0 - 1 9 1 0]

SOCIOLOGY

THE ABSURD EFFORT TO
MAKE THE WORLD OVER

SOCIOLOGY

Each of the sciences which, by giving to man greater knowledge of the laws of nature, has enabled him to cope more intelligently with the ills of life, has had to fight for its independence of metaphysics. We have still lectures on metaphysical biology in some of our colleges and in some of our public courses, but biology has substantially won its independence. Anthropology is more likely to give laws to metaphysics than to accept laws from that authority. Sociology, however, the latest of this series of sciences, is rather entering upon the struggle than emerging from it. Sociology threatens to withdraw an immense range of subjects of the first importance from the dominion of *a priori* speculation and arbitrary dogmatism, and the struggle will be severe in proportion to the dignity and importance of the subject. The struggle, however, is best carried forward indirectly, by simply defining the scope of sociology and by vindicating its position amongst the sciences, while leaving its relations to the other sciences and other pursuits of men to adjust themselves according to the facts. I know of nothing more amusing in these days than to see an old-fashioned metaphysician applying his tests to the results of scientific investigation, and screaming with rage because men of scientific training do not care whether the results satisfy those tests or not.

Sociology is the science of life in society. It investigates the forces which come into action wherever a human society exists. It studies the structure and functions of the organs of human society, and its aim is to find out the laws in subordination to which human society takes its various forms and social institutions grow and change. Its practical utility consists in deriving the rules of right social living from the facts and laws which prevail by nature in the constitution and functions of society. It must, without doubt, come into collision with all other theories of right living

---

From *Collected Essays in Political and Social Science,* by William Graham Sumner. Copyright, 1885, Henry Holt and Company, Inc.; reprinted by permission. The essay first appeared in 1881.

which are founded on authority, tradition, arbitrary invention, or poetic imagination.

Sociology is perhaps the most complicated of all the sciences, yet there is no domain of human interest the details of which are treated ordinarily with greater facility. Various religions have various theories of social living, which they offer as authoritative and final. It has never, so far as I know, been asserted by anybody that a man of religious faith, in any religion, could not study sociology or recognize the existence of any such science; but it is incontestably plain that a man who accepts the dogmas about social living which are imposed by the authority of any religion must regard the subject of right social living as settled and closed, and he cannot enter on any investigation the first groundwork of which would be doubt of the authority which he recognizes as final. Hence social problems and social phenomena present no difficulty to him who has only to cite an authority or obey a prescription.

Then again the novelists set forth "views" about social matters. To write and read novels is perhaps the most royal road to teaching and learning which has ever been devised. The proceeding of the novelists is kaleidoscopic. They turn the same old bits of colored glass over and over again into new combinations. There is no limit, no sequence, no bond of consistency. The romance-writing social philosopher always proves his case, just as a man always wins who plays chess with himself.

Then again the utopians and socialists make easy work of the complicated phenomena with which sociology has to deal. These persons, vexed with the intricacies of social problems and revolting against the facts of the social order, take upon themselves the task of inventing a new and better world. They brush away all which troubles us men and create a world free from annoying limitations and conditions—in their imagination. In ancient times, and now in half-civilized countries, these persons have been founders of religions. Something of that type always lingers around them still and among us, and is to be seen amongst the reformers and philanthropists, who never contribute much to the improvement of society in any actual detail, but find a key principle for making the world anew and regenerating society. I have even seen faint signs of the same mysticism in social matters in some of the green-backers who have "thought out" in bed, as they relate, a scheme of wealth by paper money, as Mahomet would have received a surah or Joe Smith a revelation about polygamy. Still there are limits to this resemblance, because in our nineteenth century American life a sense of humor, even if defective, answers some of the purposes of common sense.

Then again all the whimsical people who have hobbies of one sort or another come forward with projects which are the result of a strong impression, an individual misfortune, or an unregulated benevolent desire, and which are therefore the product of a facile emotion, not of a laborious investigation.

Then again the *dilettanti* make light work of social questions. Everyone, by the fact of living in society, gathers some observations of social phenomena. The belief grows up, as it was expressed some time ago by a professor of mathematics, that everybody knows about the topics of sociology. Those topics have a broad and generous character. They lend themselves easily to generalizations. There are as yet no sharp tests formulated. Above all, and worst lack of all as yet, we have no competent criticism. Hence it is easy for the aspirant after culture to venture on this field without great danger of being brought to account, as he would be if he attempted geology, or physics, or biology. Even a scientific man of high attainments in some other science, in which he well understands what special care, skill, and training are required, will not hesitate to dogmatize about a topic of sociology. A group of half-educated men may be relied upon to attack a social question and to hammer it dead in a few minutes with a couple of commonplaces and a sweeping *a priori* assumption. Above all other topics, social topics lend themselves to the purposes of the diner-out.

Two facts, however, in regard to social phenomena need only be mentioned to be recognized as true. (1) Social phenomena always present themselves to us in very complex combinations, and (2) it is by no means easy to interpret the phenomena. The phenomena are aften at three or four removes from their causes.

Tradition, prejudice, fashion, habit, and other similar obstacles continually warp and deflect the social forces, and they constitute interferences whose magnitude is to be ascertained separately for each case. It is also impossible for us to set up a social experiment. To do that we should need to dispose of the time and liberty of a certain number of men. It follows that sociology requires a special method, and that probably no science requires such peculiar skill and sagacity in the observer and interpreter of the phenomena which are to be studied. One peculiarity may be especially noted because it shows a very common error of students of social science. A sociologist needs to arrange his facts before he has obtained them; that is to say, he must make a previous classification so as to take up the facts in a certain order. If he does not do this he may be overwhelmed in the mass of his material so that he never can master it. How shall anyone know how to classify until the science itself has made some progress? Statistics furnish us the best illustration at the present time of the difficulty here referred to.

When, now, we take into account these difficulties and requirements, it is evident that the task of sociology is one which will call for especial and long training, and that it will probably be a long time yet before we can train up any body of special students who will be so well trained in the theory and science of society as to be able to form valuable opinions on points of social disease and social remedy. But it is a fact of familiar observation that all popular discussions of social questions seize directly upon points of social disease and social remedies. The diagnosis of some asserted social ill and the prescription of the remedy are undertaken offhand by the first comer, and without reflecting that the diagnosis of a social disease is many times harder than that of a disease in an individual, and that to prescribe for a society is to prescribe for an organism which is immortal. To err in prescribing for a man is at worst to kill him; to err in prescribing for a society is to set in operation injurious forces which extend, ramify, and multiply their effects in ever new combinations throughout an indefinite future. It may pay to experiment with an individual, because he cannot wait for medical science to be perfected; it cannot pay to experiment with a society, because the society does not die and can afford to wait.

If we have to consider the need of sociology, innumerable reasons for studying it present themselves. In spite of all our acquisitions in natural science, the conception of a natural law—which is the most important good to be won from studying natural science—is yet exceedingly vague in the minds of ordinary intelligent people, and is very imperfect even amongst the educated. That conception is hardly yet applied by anybody to social facts and problems. Social questions force themselves upon us in multitudes every year as our civilization advances and our society becomes complex. When such questions arise they are wrangled over and tossed about without any orderly discussion, but as if they were only the sport of arbitrary whims. Is it not then necessary that we enable ourselves, by study of the facts and laws of society, to take up such questions from the correct point of view, and to proceed with the examination of them in such order and method that we can reach solid results, and thus obtain command of an increasing mass of knowledge about social phenomena? The assumption which underlies almost all discussion of social topics is that we men need only to make up our minds what kind of a society we want to have, and that then we can devise means for calling that society into existence. It is assumed that we can decide to live on one spot of the earth's surface or another, and to pursue there one industry or another, and then that we can, by our devices, make that industry as productive as any other could be in that place. People believe that we have only to choose whether we will have aristocratic institutions or democratic institutions. It is believed that statesmen can, if they will, put a people in the way of material prosperity. It is believed that rent on land can be abolished if it is not thought expedient to have it. It is assumed that peasant proprietors can be brought into existence anywhere where it is thought that it would be an advantage to have them. These illustrations might be multiplied indefinitely. They show the need of sociology, and if we should go on to notice the general conceptions of society, its ills and their remedies, which are held by various religious, political, and social sects, we should find ample further evidence of this need.

Let us then endeavor to define the field of sociology. Life in society is the life of a human society on this earth. Its elementary conditions are set by the nature of human beings and the nature of the earth. We have already become familiar, in biology, with the transcendent importance of the fact that life on earth must be maintained by a struggle against nature, and also by a competition with other forms of life. In the latter fact biology and sociology touch. Sociology is a science which deals with one range of phenomena produced by the struggle for existence, while biology deals with another. The forces are the same, acting on different fields and under different conditions. The sciences are truly cognate. Nature contains certain materials which are capable of satisfying human needs, but those materials must, with rare and mean exceptions, be won by labor, and must be fitted to human use by more labor. As soon as any number of human beings are struggling each to win from nature the material goods necessary to support life, and are carrying on this struggle side by side, certain social forces come into operation. The prime condition of this society will lie in the ratio of its numbers to the supply of materials within its reach. For the supply at any moment attainable is an exact quantity, and the number of persons who can be supplied is arithmetically limited. If the actual number present is very much less than the number who might be supported, the condition of all must be ample and easy. Freedom and facility mark all social relations under such a state of things. If the number is larger than that which can be supplied, the condition of all must be one of want and distress, or else a few must be well provided, the others being proportionately still worse off. Constraint, anxiety, possibly tyranny and repression, mark social relations. It is when the social pressure due to an unfavorable ratio of population to land becomes intense that the social forces develop increased activity. Division of labor, exchange, higher social organization, emigration, advance in the arts, spring from the necessity of contending against

77

the harsher conditions of existence which are continually reproduced as the population surpasses the means of existence on any given status.

The society with which we have to deal does not consist of any number of men. An army is not a society. A man with his wife and his children constitutes a society, for its essential parts are all present, and the number more or less is immaterial. A certain division of labor between the sexes is imposed by nature. The family as a whole maintains itself better under an organization with division of labor than it could if the functions were shared so far as possible. From this germ the development of society goes on by the regular steps of advancement to higher organization, accompanied and sustained by improvements in the arts. The increase of population goes on according to biological laws which are capable of multiplying the species beyond any assignable limits, so that the number to be provided for steadily advances and the status of ease and abundance gives way to a status of want and constraint. Emigration is the first and simplest remedy. By winning more land the ratio of population to land is once more rendered favorable. It is to be noticed, however, that emigration is painful to all men. To the uncivilized man, to emigrate means to abandon a mass of experiences and traditions which have been won by suffering, and to go out to confront new hardships and perils. To the civilized man migration means cutting off old ties of kin and country. The earth has been peopled by man at the cost of this suffering.

On the side of the land also stands the law of the diminishing return as a limitation. More labor gets more from the land, but not proportionately more, hence, if more men are to be supported, there is need not of a proportionate increase of labor, but of a disproportionate increase of labor. The law of population, therefore, combined with the law of the diminishing returns, constitutes the great underlying condition of society. Emigration, improvements in the arts, in morals, in education, in political organization, are only stages in the struggle of man to meet these conditions, to break their force for a time, and to win room under them for ease and enlargement. Ease and enlargement mean either power to support more men on a given stage of comfort or power to advance the comfort of a given number of men. Progress is a word which has no meaning save in view of the laws of population and the diminishing return, and it is quite natural that anyone who fails to understand those laws should fall into doubt which way progress points, whether towards wealth or poverty. The laws of population and the diminishing return, in their combination, are the iron spur which has driven the race on to all which it has ever achieved, and the fact that population ever advances, yet advances against a barrier which resists more stubbornly at every step of advance, unless it is removed to a new distance by some conquest of man over nature, is the guarantee that the task of civilization will never be ended, but that the need for more energy, more intelligence, and more virtue will never cease while the race lasts. If it were possible for an increasing population to be sustained by proportionate increments of labor, we should all still be living in the original home of the race on the spontaneous products of the earth. Let him, therefore, who desires to study social phenomena first learn the transcendent importance for the whole social organization, industrial, political, and civil, of the ratio of population to land.

We have noticed that the relations involved in the struggle for existence are twofold. There is first the struggle of individuals to win the means of subsistence from nature, and secondly there is the competition of man with man in the effort to win a limited supply. The radical error of the socialists and sentimentalists is that they never distinguish these two relations from each other. They bring forward complaints which are really to be made, if at all, against the author of the universe for the hardships which man has to endure in his struggle with nature. The complaints are addressed, however, to society; that is, to other men under the same hardships. The only social element, however, is the competition of life, and when society is blamed for the ills which belong to the human lot, it is only burdening those who have successfully contended with those ills with the further task of conquering the same ills over again for somebody else. Hence liberty perishes in all socialistic schemes, and the tendency of such schemes is to the deterioration of society by burdening the good members and relieving the bad ones. The law of the survival of the fittest was not made by man and cannot be abrogated by man. We can only, by interfering with it, produce the survival of the unfittest. If a man comes forward with any grievance against the order of society so far as this is shaped by human agency, he must have patient hearing and full redress; but if he addresses a demand to society for relief from the hardships of life, he asks simply that somebody else should get his living for him. In that case he ought to be left to find out his error from hard experience.

The sentimental philosophy starts from the first principle that nothing is true which is disagreeable, and that we must not believe anything which is "shocking," no matter what the evidence may be. There are various stages of this philosophy. It touches on one side the intuitional philosophy which proves that certain things must exist by proving that man needs them, and it touches on the other side the vulgar socialism which affirms that the individual has a right to whatever he needs, and that this right is good against his fellow men. To this philosophy in all its grades the laws of population and the diminishing return have always been very distasteful. The laws which entail upon mankind an inheritance of labor cannot be acceptable to any philosophy which maintains that man comes into the world endowed with natural rights and an inheritor of freedom. It is a death-blow to any intuitional philosophy to find out, as an historical fact, what diverse thoughts, beliefs, and actions man has manifested, and it requires but little actual knowledge of human history to show that the human race has never had any ease which it did not earn, or any freedom which it did not conquer. Sociology, therefore, by the investigations which it pursues, dispels illusions about what society is or may be, and gives instead knowledge of facts which are the basis of intelligent effort by man to make the best of his circumstances on earth. Sociology, therefore, which can never accomplish anything more than to enable us to make the best of our situation, will never be able to reconcile itself with those philosophies which are trying to find out how we may arrange things so as so satisfy any ideal of society.

The competition of life has taken the form, historically, of a struggle for the possession of the soil. In the simpler states of society the possession of the soil is tribal, and the struggles take place between groups, producing the wars and feuds which constitute almost the whole of early history. On the agricultural stage the tribal or communal possession of land exists as a survival, but it gives way to private property in land whenever the community advances and the institutions are free to mold themselves. The agricultural stage breaks up tribal relations and encourages individualization. This is one of the reasons why it is such an immeasurable advance over the lower forms of civilization. It sets free individual energy, and while the social bond gains in scope and variety, it also gains in elasticity, for the solidarity of the group is broken up and the individual may work out his own ends by his own means, subject only to the social ties which lie in the natural conditions of human life. It is only on the agricultural stage that liberty as civilized men understand it exists at all. The poets and sentimentalists, untaught to recognize the grand and world-wide cooperation which is secured by the free play of individual energy under the great laws of the social order, bewail the decay of early communal relations and exalt the liberty of the primitive stages of civilization. These notions all perish at the first touch of actual investigation. The whole retrospect of human history runs downwards towards beast-like misery and slavery to the destructive forces of nature. The whole history has been one series of toilsome, painful, and bloody struggles, first to find out where we were and what were the conditions of greater ease, and then to devise means to get relief. Most of the way the motives of advance have been experience of suffering and instinct. It is only in the most recent years that science has undertaken to teach without and in advance of suffering, and as yet science has to fight so hard against tradition that its authority is only slowly winning recognition. The institutions whose growth constitutes the advance of civilization have their guarantee in the very fact that they grew and became established. They suited man's purpose better than what went before. They are all imperfect, and all carry with them incidental ills, but each came to be because it was better than what went before, and each of which has perished, perished because a better one supplanted it.

It follows once and for all that to turn back to any defunct institution or organization because existing institutions are imperfect is to turn away from advance and is to retrograde. The path of improvement lies forwards. Private property in land, for instance, is an institution which has been developed in the most direct and legitimate manner. It may give way at a future time to some other institution which will grow up by imperceptible stages out of the efforts of men to contend successfully with existing evils, but the grounds for private property in land are easily perceived, and it is safe to say that no *a priori* scheme of state ownership or other tenure invented *en bloc* by any philosopher and adopted by legislative act will ever supplant it. To talk of any such thing is to manifest a total misconception of the facts and laws which it is the province of sociology to investigate. The case is less in magnitude but scarcely less out of joint with all correct principle when it is proposed to adopt a unique tax on land, in a country where the rent of land is so low that any important tax on land exceeds it, and therefore becomes indirect, and where also political power is in the hands of small landowners, who hold, without ever having formulated it, a doctrine of absolute property in the soil such as is not held by any other landowners in the world.

Sociology must exert a most important influence on political economy. Political economy is the science which investigates the laws of the material welfare of human societies. It is not its province to teach individuals how to get rich. It is a social science. It was the first branch of sociology which was pursued by man as a science. It is not strange that when the industrial organization of society was studied apart from the organism of which it forms a part it was largely dominated over by arbitrary dogmatism, and that it should have fallen into disrepute as a mere field of opinion, and of endless wrangling about opinions for which no guarantees could be given. The rise of a school of "historical" economists is itself a sign of a struggle towards a positive and scientific study of political economy, in its due relations to other social sciences, and this sign loses none of its significance in spite of the crudeness and extravagance of the opinions of the historical economists, and in spite of their very marked tendency to fall into dogmatism and hobby-riding. Political economy is thrown overboard by all groups and persons whenever it becomes troublesome. When it got in the way of Mr. Gladstone's land-bill he relegated it, by implication, to the planet Saturn, to the great delight of all the fair-traders, protectionists, soft-money men, and others who had found it in the way of their devices. What political economy needs in order to emerge from the tangle in which it is now involved, and to win a dignified and orderly development, is to find its field and its relations to other sciences fairly defined within the wider scope of sociology. Its laws will then take their place not as arbitrary or broken fragments, but in due relation to other laws. Those laws will win proof and establishment from this relation.

For instance, we have plenty of books, some of them by able writers, in which the old-fashioned Malthusian doctrine of population and the Ricardian law of rent are disputed because emigration, advance in the arts, etc., can offset the action of those laws or because those laws are not seen in action in the United States. Obviously no such objections ever could have been raised if the laws in question had been understood or had been put in their proper bearings. The Malthusian law of population and the Ricardian law of rent are cases in which by rare and most admirable acumen powerful thinkers perceived two great laws in particular phases of their action. With wider information it now appears that the law of population breaks the barriers of Malthus' narrower formulæ and appears as a great law of biology. The Ricardian law of rent is only a particular application of one of the great conditions of production. We have before us not special dogmas of political economy, but facts of the widest significance for the whole social development of the race. To object that these facts may be set aside by migration or advance in the arts is nothing to the purpose, for this is only altering the constants in the equation, which does not alter the form of the curve, but only its position relatively to some standard line. Furthermore, the laws themselves indicate that they have a maximum point for any society, or any given stage of the arts, and a condition of under-population, or of an extractive industry below its maximum, is just as consistent with the law as a condition of over-population and increasing distress. Hence inferences as to the law of population drawn from the status of an under-populated country are sure to be fallacious. In like manner arguments drawn from American phenomena in regard to rent and wages, when rent and wages are as yet only very imperfectly developed here, lead to erroneous conclusions. It only illustrates the unsatisfactory condition of political economy, and the want of strong criticism in it, that such arguments can find admission to its discussions and disturb its growth.

It is to the pursuit of sociology and the study of the industrial organization in combination with the other organizations of society that we must look for the more fruitful development of political economy. We are already in such a position with sociology that a person who has gained what we now possess of that science will bring to bear upon economic problems a sounder judgment and a more correct conception of all social relations than a person who may have read a library of the existing treatises on political economy. The essential elements of political economy are only corollaries or special cases of sociological principles. One who has command of the law of the conservation of energy as it manifests itself in society is armed at once against socialism, protectionism, paper money, and a score of other economic fallacies. The sociological view of political economy also includes whatever is sound in the dogmas of the "historical school" and furnishes what that school is apparently groping after.

As an illustration of the light which sociology throws on a great number of political and social phenomena which are constantly misconstrued, we may notice the differences in the industrial, political, and civil organizations which are produced all along at different stages of the ratio of population to land.

When a country is under-populated newcomers are not competitors, but assistants. If more come they may produce not only new quotas, but a surplus besides, to be divided between themselves and all who were present before. In such a state of things land is abundant and cheap. The possession of it confers no power or privilege. No one will work for another for wages when he can take up new land and be his own master. Hence it will pay no one to own more land than he can cultivate by his own labor, or with such aid as his own family supplies. Hence, again, land bears little or no rent; there will be no landlords living on rent and no laborers living on wages, but only a middle class of yeoman farmers. All are substantially on an equality, and democracy becomes the political form, because this is the only state of society in which the dogmatic assumption of equality, on which democracy is based, is realized as a fact. The same effects are powerfully reenforced by other facts. In a new and under-populated country the industries which are most profitable are the extractive industries. The characteristic of these, with the exception of some kinds of mining, is that they call for only a low organization of labor and small amount of capital. Hence they allow the workman to become speedily his own master, and they educate him to freedom, independence, and self-reliance. At the same time, the social groups being only vaguely marked off from each other, it is easy to pass from one class of occupations, and consequently from one social grade, to another. Finally, under the same circumstances education, skill, and superior training have but inferior value compared with what they have in densely populated countries. The advantages lie, in an under-populated country, with the coarser, unskilled, manual occupations, and not with the highest developments of science, literature, and art.

If now we turn for comparison to cases of over-population we see that the struggle for existence and the competition of life are intense where the pressure of population is great. This competition draws out the highest achievements. It makes the advantages of capital, education, talent, skill, and training tell to the utmost. It draws out the social scale upwards and downwards to great extremes and produces aristocratic social organizations in spite of all dogmas of equality. Landlords, tenants (*i.e.,* capitalist employers), and laborers are the three primary divisions of any aristocratic order, and they are sure to be developed whenever land bears rent and whenever tillage requires the application of large capital. At the same time liberty has to undergo curtailment. A man who has a square mile to himself can easily do as he likes, but a man who walks Broadway at noon or lives in a tenement-house finds his power to do as he likes limited by scores of considerations for the rights and feelings of his fellowmen. Furthermore, organization with subordination and discipline is essential in order that the society as a whole may win a support from the land. In an over-populated country the extremes of wealth and luxury are presented side by side with the extremes of poverty and distress. They are equally the products of an intense social pressure. The achievements of power are highest, the rewards of prudence, energy, enterprise, foresight, sagacity, and all other industrial virtues is greatest; on the other hand, the penalties of folly, weakness, error, and vice are most terrible. Pauperism, prostitution, and crime are the attendants of a state of society in which science, art, and literature reach their highest developments. Now it is evident that over-population and under-population are only relative terms. Hence as time goes on any under-populated nation is surely moving forward towards the other status, and is speedily losing its natural advantages which are absolute, and also that relative advantage which belongs to it if it is in neighborly relations with nations of dense population and high civilization; *viz.*, the chance to borrow and assimilate from them the products, in arts and science, of high civilization without enduring the penalties of intense social pressure.

We have seen that if we should try by any measures of arbitrary interference and assistance to relieve the victims of social pressure from the calamity of their position we should only offer premiums to folly and vice and extend them further. We have also seen that we must go forward and meet our problems. We cannot escape them by running away. If then it be asked what the wit and effort of man can do to struggle with the problems offered by social pressure, the answer is that he can do only what his instinct has correctly and surely led him to do without any artificial social organization of any kind, and that is, by improvements in the arts, in science, in morals, in political institutions, to widen and strengthen the power of man over nature. The task of dealing with social ills is not a new task. People set about it and discuss it as if the human race had hitherto neglected it, and as if the solution of the problem was to be something new in form and substance, different from the solution of all problems which have hitherto engaged human effort. In truth, the human race has never done anything else but struggle with the problem of social welfare. That struggle constitutes history, or the life of the human race on earth. That struggle embraces all minor problems which occupy attention here, save those of religion, which reaches beyond this world and finds its objects beyond this life. Every successful effort to widen the power of man over nature is a real victory over poverty, vice, and misery, taking things in general and in the long run. It would be hard to find a single instance of a direct assault by positive effort upon poverty, vice, and misery which has not either failed or, if it has not failed directly and entirely, has not entailed other evils greater than the one which it removed. The only two things which really tell on the welfare of man on earth are hard work and self-denial (in technical language, labor and capital), and these tell most when they are brought to bear directly upon the effort to earn an honest living, to accumulate capital, and to bring up a family of children to be industrious and self-denying in their turn. I repeat that this is the way to work for the welfare of man on earth; and what I mean to say is that the common notion that when we are going to work for the social welfare of man we must adopt a great dogma, organize for the realization of some great scheme, have before us an abstract ideal, or otherwise do anything but live honest and industrious lives, is a great mistake. From the standpoint of the sociologist pessimism and optimism are alike impertinent. To be an optimist one must forget the frightful sanctions which are attached to the laws of right living. To be a pessimist one must overlook the education and growth which are the product of effort and self-denial. In either case one is passing judgment on what is inevitably fixed, and on which the approval or condemnation of man can produce no effect. The facts and laws are, once and for all, so, and for us men that is the end of the matter. The only persons for whom there would be any sense in the question whether life is worth living are primarily the yet unborn children, and secondarily the persons who are proposing to found families. For these latter the question would take a somewhat modified form: Will life be worth living for children born of me? This question is, unfortunately, not put to themselves by the appropriate persons as it would be if they had been taught sociology. The sociologist is often asked if he wants to kill off certain classes of troublesome and burdensome persons. No such inference follows from any sound sociological doctrine, but it is allowed to infer, as to a great many persons and classes, that it would have been better for society, and would have involved no pain to them, if they had never been born.

In further illustration of the interpretation which sociology offers of phenomena which are often obscure, we may note the world-wide effects of the advances in the arts and sciences which have been made during the last hundred years. These improvements have especially affected transportation and communication; that is, they have lessened the obstacles of time and space which separate the groups of mankind from each other and have tended to make the whole human race a single unit. The distinction between over-populated and under-populated countries loses its sharpness, and all are brought to an average. Every person who migrates from Europe to America affects the comparative status of the two continents. He lessens the pressure in the country he leaves and increases it in the country to which he goes. If he goes to Minnesota and raises wheat there, which is carried back to the country he left as cheap food for those who have not emigrated, it is evident that the bearing upon social pressure is twofold. It is evident, also, that the problem of social pressure can no longer be correctly studied if the view is confined either to the country of immigration or the country of emigration, but that it must embrace both. It is easy to see, therefore, that the ratio of population to land with which we have to deal is only in peculiar and limited cases that ratio as it exists in England, Germany, or the United States. It is the ratio as it exists in the civilized world, and every year that passes, as our improved arts break down the barriers between different parts of the earth, brings us nearer to the state of things where all the population of Europe, America, Australasia, and South Africa must be considered in relation to all the land of the same territories, for all that territory will be available for all that population, no matter what the proportion may be in which the population is distributed over the various portions of the territory. The British Islands may become one great manufacturing city. Minnesota, Texas, and Australia may not have five persons to the square mile. Yet all will eat the meat of Texas and the wheat of Minnesota and wear the wool of Australia manufactured on the looms of England. That all will enjoy the maximum of food and raiment under that state of things is as clear as anything possibly can be which is not yet an accomplished fact. We are working towards it by all our instincts of profit and improvement. The greatest obstacles are those which come from prejudices, traditions, and dogmas, which are held independently of any observation of facts or any correct reasoning, and which set the right hand working against the left. For instance, the Mississippi Valley was, a century ago, as unavailable to support the population of France and Germany as if it had been in the moon. The Mississippi Valley is now nearer to France and Germany than the British Islands were a century ago, reckoning distance by the only true standard; *viz.*, difficulty of communication. It is a fair way of stating it to say that the improvements in transportation of the last fifty years have added to France and Germany respectively a tract of land of the very highest fertility, equal in area to the territory of those states, and available for the support of their population. The public men of those countries are now declaring that this is a calamity, and are devising means to counteract it.

The social and political effects of the improvements which have been made must be very great. It follows from what we have said about the effects of intense social pressure and high competition that the effect of thus bringing to bear on the great centers of population the new land of outlying countries must be to relieve the pressure in the oldest countries and at the densest centers. Then the extremes of wealth and poverty, culture and brutality, will be contracted and there will follow a general tendency towards an average equality which, however, must be understood only within very broad limits. Such is no doubt the meaning of the general tendency towards equality, the decline of aristocratic institutions, the rise of the proletariat, and the ambitious expansion, in short, which is characteristic of modern civilized society. It would lead me too far to follow out this line of speculation as to the future, but two things ought to be noticed in passing. (1) There are important offsets to the brilliant promise which there is for mankind in a period during which, for the whole civilized world, there will be a wide margin of ease between the existing population and the supporting power of the available land. These offsets consist in the effects of ignorance, error, and folly—the same forces which have always robbed mankind of half what they might have enjoyed on earth. Extravagant governments, abuses of public credit, wasteful taxation, legislative monopolies and special privileges, juggling with currency, restrictions on trade, wasteful armaments on land and sea, and other follies in economy and statecraft, are capable of wasting and nullifying all the gains of civilization. (2) The old classical civilization fell under an irruption of barbarians from without. It is possible that our new civilization may perish by an explosion from within. The sentimentalists have been preaching for a century notions of rights and equality, of the dignity, wisdom, and power of the proletariat, which have filled the minds of ignorant men with impossible dreams. The thirst for luxurious enjoyment has taken possession of us all. It is the dark side of the power to foresee a possible future good with such distinctness as to make it a motive of energy and persevering industry—a power which is distinctly modern. Now the thirst for luxurious enjoyment, when brought into connection with the notions of rights, of power, and of equality, and dissociated from the notions of industry and economy, produces the notion that a man is robbed of his rights if he has not everything that he wants, and that he is deprived of equality if he sees anyone have more than he has, and that he is a fool if, having the power of the State in his hands, he allows this state of things to last. Then we have socialism, communism, and nihilism; and the fairest conquests of civilization, with all their promise of solid good to man, on the sole conditions of virtue and wisdom, may be scattered to the winds in a war of classes, or trampled underfoot by a mob which can only hate what it cannot enjoy.

It must be confessed that sociology is yet in a tentative and inchoate state. All that we can affirm with certainty is that social phenomena are subject to law, and that the natural laws of the social order are in their entire character like the laws of physics. We can draw in grand outline the field of sociology and foresee the shape that it will take and the relations it will bear to other sciences. We can also already find the standpoint which it will occupy, and, if a figure may be allowed, although we still look over a wide landscape largely enveloped in mist, we can see where the mist lies and define the general features of the landscape, subject to further corrections. To deride or contemn a science in this state would certainly be a most unscientific proceeding. We confess, however, that so soon as we go beyond the broadest principles of the science we have not yet succeeded in discovering social laws, so as to be able to formulate them. A great amount of labor yet remains to be done in the stages of preparation. There are, however, not more than two or three other sciences which are making as rapid progress as sociology, and there is no other which is as full of promise for the welfare of man. That sociology has an immense department of human interests to control is beyond dispute. Hitherto this department has been included in moral science, and it has not only been confused and entangled by dogmas no two of which are consistent with each other, but also it has been without any growth, so that at this moment our knowledge of social science is behind the demands which existing social questions make upon us. We are face to face with an issue no less grand than this: Shall we, in our general social policy, pursue the effort to realize more completely that constitutional liberty for which we have been struggling throughout modern history, or shall we return to the mediæval device of functionaries to regulate procedure and to adjust interests? Shall we try to connect with liberty an equal and appropriate responsibility as its essential complement and corrective, so that a man who gets his own way shall accept his own consequences, or shall we yield to the sentimentalism which, after preaching an unlimited liberty, robs those who have been wise out of pity for those who have been foolish? Shall we accept the inequalities which follow upon free competition as the definition of justice, or shall we suppress free competition in the interest of equality and to satisfy a baseless dogma of justice? Shall we try to solve the social entanglements which arise in a society where social ties are constantly becoming more numerous and more subtle, and where contract has only partly superseded custom and status, by returning to the latter, only hastening a more complete development of the former? These certainly are practical questions, and their scope is such that they embrace a great number of minor questions which are before us and which are coming up. It is to the science of society, which will derive true conceptions of society from the facts and laws of the social order,[1] studied without prejudice or bias of any sort, that we must look for the correct answer to these questions. By this observation the field of sociology and the work which it is to do for society are sufficiently defined.

---

[1] It has been objected that no proof is offered that social laws exist in the order of nature. By what demonstration could any such proof be given *a priori*? If a man of scientific training finds his attention arrested, in some group of phenomena, by these sequences, relations, and recurrences which he has learned to note as signs of action of law, he seeks to discover the law. If it exists, he finds it. What other proof of its existences could there be?

THE ABSURD EFFORT TO MAKE THE WORLD OVER

It will not probably be denied that the burden of proof is on those who affirm that our social condititon is utterly diseased and in need of radical regeneration. My task at present, therefore,

---

From *War and Other Essays*, by William Graham Sumner (New Haven: Yale University Press, 1911); originally published in the *Forum*, 1894.

is entirely negative and critical: to examine the allegations of fact and the doctrines which are put forward to prove the correctness of the diagnosis and to warrant the use of the remedies proposed.

The propositions put forward by social reformers nowadays are chiefly of two kinds. There are assertions in historical form, chiefly in regard to the comparison of existing with earlier social states, whch are plainly based on defective historical knowledge, or at most on current stock historical dicta which are uncritical and incorrect. Writers very often assert that something never existed before because they do not know that it ever existed before, or that something is worse than ever before because they are not possessed of detailed information about what has existed before. The other class of propositions consists of dogmatic statements which, whether true or not, are unverifiable. This class of propositions is the pest and bane of current economic and social discussion. Upon a more or less superficial view of some phenomenon a suggestion arises which is embodied in a philosophical proposition and promulgated as a truth. From the form and nature of such propositions they can always be brought under the head of "ethics." This word at least gives them an air of elevated sentiment and purpose, which is the only warrant they possess. It is impossible to test or verify them by any investigation or logical process whatsoever. It is therefore very difficult for anyone who feels a high responsibility for historical statements, and who absolutely rejects any statement which is unverifiable, to find a common platform for discussion or to join issue satisfactorily in taking the negative.

When anyone asserts that the class of skilled and unskilled manual laborers of the United States is worse off now in respect to diet, clothing, lodgings, furniture, fuel, and lights; in respect to the age at which they can marry; the number of children they can provide for; the start in life which they can give to their children, and their chances of accumulating capital, than they ever have been at any former time, he makes a reckless assertion for which no facts have been offered in proof. Upon an appeal to facts, the contrary of this assertion would be clearly established.

It suffices, therefore, to challenge those who are responsible for the assertion to make it good.

If it is said that the employed class are under much more stringent discipline than they were thirty years ago or earlier, it is true. It is not true that there has been any qualitative change in this respect within thirty years, but it is true that a movement which began at the first settlement of the country has been advancing with constant acceleration and has become a noticeable feature within our time. This movement is the advance in the industrial organization. The first settlement was made by agriculturists, and for a long time there was scarcely any organization. There were scattered farmers, each working for himself, and some small towns with only rudimentary commerce and handicrafts. As the country has filled up, the arts and professions have been differentiated and the industrial organization has been advancing. This fact and its significance has hardly been noticed at all; but the stage of the industrial organization existing at any time, and the rate of advance in its development, are the absolutely controlling social facts. Nine-tenths of the socialistic and semi-socialistic, and sentimental or ethical, suggestions by which we are overwhelmed come from failure to understand the phenomena of the industrial organization and its expansion. It controls us all because we are all in it. It creates the conditions of our existence, sets the limits of our social activity, regulates the bonds of our social relations, determines our conceptions of good and evil, suggests our life-philosophy, molds our inherited political institutions, and reforms the oldest and toughest customs, like marriage and property. I repeat that the turmoil of heterogeneous and antagonistic social whims and speculations in which we live is due to the failure to understand what the industrial organization is and its all-pervading control over human life, while the traditions of our school of philosophy lead us always to approach the industrial organization, not from the side of objective study, but from that of philosophical doctrine. Hence it is that we find that the method of measuring what we see happening by what are called ethical standards, and of proposing to attack the phenomena by methods thence deduced, is so popular.

The Absurd Effort to Make the World Over

The advance of a new country from the very simplest social coordination up to the highest organization is a most interesting and instructive chance to study the development of the organization. It has of course been attended all the way along by stricter subordination and higher discipline. All organization implies restriction of liberty. The gain of power is won by narrowing individual range. The methods of business in colonial days were loose and slack to an inconceivable degree. The movement of industry has been all the time toward promptitude, punctuality, and reliability. It has been attended all the way by lamentations about the good old times; about the decline of small industries; about the lost spirit of comradeship between employer and employee; about the narrowing of the interests of the workman; about his conversion into a machine or into a "ware," and about industrial war. These lamentations have all had reference to unquestionable phenomena attendant on advancing organization. In all occupations the same movement is discernible—in the learned professions, in schools, in trade, commerce, and transportation. It is to go on faster than ever, now that the continent is filled up by the first superficial layer of population over its whole extent and the intensification of industry has begun. The great inventions both make the intension of the organization possible and make it inevitable, with all its consequences, whatever they may be. I must expect to be told here, according to the current fashions of thinking, that we ought to control the development of the organization. The first instinct of the modern man is to get a law passed to forbid or prevent what, in his wisdom, he disapproves. A thing which is inevitable, however, is one which we cannot control. We have to make up our minds to it, adjust ourselves to it, and sit down to live with it. Its inevitableness may be disputed, in which case we must re-examine it; but if our analysis is correct, when we reach what is inevitable we reach the end, and our regulations must apply to ourselves, not to the social facts.

Now the intensification of the social organization is what gives us greater social power. It is to it that we owe our increased comfort and abundance. We are none of us ready to sacrifice this. On the contrary, we want more of it. We would not return to the colonial simplicity and the colonial exiguity if we could. If not, then we must pay the price. Our life is bounded on every side by conditions. We can have this if we will agree to submit to that. In the case of industrial power and product the great condition is combination of force under discipline and strict coordination. Hence the wild language about wage-slavery and capitalistic tyranny.

In any state of society no great achievements can be produced without great force. Formerly great force was attainable only by slavery aggregating the power of great numbers of men. Roman civilization was built on this. Ours has been built on steam. It is to be built on electricity. Then we are all forced into an organization around these natural forces and adapted to the methods or their application; and although we indulge in rhetoric about political liberty, nevertheless we find ourselves bound tight in a new set of conditions, which control the modes of our existence and determine the directions in which alone economic and social liberty can go.

If it is said that there are some persons in our time who have become rapidly and in a great degree rich, it is true; if it is said that large aggregations of wealth in the control of individuals is a social danger, it is not true.

The movement of the industrial organization which has just been described has brought out a great demand for men capable of managing great enterprises. Such have been called "captains of industry." The analogy with military leaders suggested by this name is not misleading. The great leaders in the development of the industrial organization need those talents of executive and administrative skill, power to command, courage, and fortitude, which were formerly called for in military affairs and scarcely anywhere else. The industrial army is also as dependent on its captains as a military body is on its generals. One of the worst features of the existing system is that the employees have a constant risk in their employer. If he is not competent to manage the business with success, they suffer with him. Capital also is dependent on the skill of the captain of industry for the certainty and magnitude of its profits. Under these circumstances there has been a great demand for men having the requisite ability for this function. As the organization has advanced, with more impersonal bonds of coherence and wider scope of operations, the value of this functionary has rapidly increased. The possession of the requisite ability is a natural monopoly. Consequently, all the conditions have concurred to give to those who possessed this monopoly excessive and constantly advancing rates of remuneration.

Another social function of the first importance in an intense organization is the solution of those crises in the operation of it which are called the conjuncture of the market. It is through the market that the lines of relation run which preserve the system in harmonious and rhythmical operation. The conjuncture is the momentary sharper misadjudgment of supply and demand which indicates that a redistribution of productive effort is called for. The industrial organization needs to be insured against these conjunctures, which, if neglected, produce a crisis and catastrophe; and it needs that they shall be anticipated and guarded against as far as skill and foresight can do it. The rewards of this function for the bankers and capitalists who perform it are very great. The captains of industry and the capitalists who operate on the conjuncture, therefore, if they are successful, win, in these days, great fortunes in a short time. There are no earnings which are more legitimate or for which greater services are rendered to the whole industrial body. The popular notions about this matter really assume that all the wealth accumulated by these classes of persons would be here just the same if they had not existed. They are supposed to have appropriated it out of the common stock. This is so far from being true that, on the contrary, their own wealth would not be but for themselves; and besides that, millions more of wealth, many-fold greater than their own, scattered in the hands of thousands, would not exist but for them.

Within the last two years I have traveled from end to end of the German Empire several times on all kinds of trains. I reached the conviction, looking at the matter from the passenger's standpoint, that, if the Germans could find a Vanderbilt and put their railroads in his hands for twenty-five years, letting him reorganize the system and make twenty-five million dollars out of it for himself in that period, they would make an excellent bargain.

But it is repeated until it has become a commonplace which people are afraid to question, that there is some social danger in the possession of large amounts of wealth by individuals. I ask, Why? I heard a lecture two years ago by a man who holds perhaps the first chair of political economy in the world. He said, among other things, that there was great danger in our day from great accumulations; that this danger ought to be met by taxation, and he referred to the fortune of the Rothschilds and to the great fortunes made in America to prove his point. He omitted, however, to state in what the danger consisted or to specify what harm has ever been done by the Rothschild fortunes or by the great fortunes accumulated in America. It seemed to me that the assertions he was making, and the measures he was recommending, ex-cathedra, were very serious to be thrown out so recklessly. It is hardly to be expected that novelists, popular magazinists, amateur economists, and politicians will be more responsible. It would be easy, however, to show what good is done by accumulations of capital in a few hands—that is, under close and direct management, permitting prompt and accurate application; also to tell what harm is done by loose and unfounded denunciations of any social component or any social group. In the recent debates on the income tax the assumption that great accumulations of wealth are socially harmful and ought to be broken down by taxation was treated as an axiom, and we had direct proof how dangerous it is to fit out the average politician with such unverified and unverifiable dogmas as his warrant for his modes of handling the direful tool of taxation.

Great figures are set out as to the magnitude of certain fortunes and the proportionate amount of the national wealth held by a fraction of the population, and eloquent exclamation-points are set against them. If the figures were beyond criticism, what would they prove? Where is the rich man who is oppressing anybody? If there was one, the newspapers would ring with it. The facts about the accumulation of wealth do not constitute a plutocracy, as I will show below. Wealth, in itself considered, is only power, like steam, or electricity, or knowledge. The question of its good or ill turns on the question how it will be used. To prove any harm in aggregations of wealth it must be shown that great wealth is, as a rule, in the ordinary course of social affairs, put to a mischievous use. This cannot be shown beyond the very slightest degree, if at all.

Therefore, all the allegations of general mischief, social corruption, wrong, and evil in our society must be referred back to those who make them for particulars and specifications. As they are offered to us we cannot allow them to stand, because we discern in them faulty observation of facts, or incorrect interpretation of facts, or a construction of facts according to some philosophy, or misunderstanding of phenomena and their relations, or incorrect inferences, or crooked deductions.

Assuming, however, that the charges against the existing "capitalistic"—that is, industrial—order of things are established, it is proposed to remedy the ill by reconstructing the industrial system on the principles of democracy. Once more we must untangle the snarl of half ideas and muddled facts.

Democracy is, of course, a word to conjure with. We have a democratic-republican political system, and we like it so well that we are prone to take any new step which can be recommended as "democratic" or which will round some "principle" of democracy to a fuller fulfillment. Everything connected with this domain of political thought is crusted over with false historical traditions, cheap philosophy, and undefined terms, but it is useless to try to criticize it. The whole drift of the world for five hundred years has been toward democracy. That drift, produced by great discoveries and inventions, and by the discovery of a new continent, has raised the middle class out of the servile class. In alliance with the crown they crushed the feudal classes. They made the crown absolute in order to do it. Then they turned against the crown and, with the aid of the handicraftsmen and peasants, conquered it. Now the next conflict which must inevitably come is that between the middle capitalist class and the proletariat, as the word has come to be used. If a certain construction is put on this conflict, it may be called that between democracy and plutocracy, for it seems that industrialism must be developed into plutocracy by the conflict itself. That is the conflict which stands before civilized society to-day. All the signs of the times indicate its commencement, and it is big with fate to mankind and to civilization.

Although we cannot criticize democracy profitably, it may be said of it, with reference to our present subject, that up to this time democracy never has done anything, either in politics, social affairs, or industry, to prove its power to bless mankind. If we confine our attention to the United States, there are three difficulties with regard to its alleged achievements, and they all have the most serious bearing on the proposed democratization of industry.

1. The time during which democracy has been tried in the United States is too short to warrant any inferences. A century or two is a very short time in the life of political institutions, and if the circumstances change rapidly during the period the experiment is vitiated.

2. The greatest question of all about American democracy is whether it is a cause or a consequence. It is popularly assumed to be a cause, and we ascribe to its beneficent action all the political vitality, all the easiness of social relations, all the industrial activity and enterprise which we experience and which we value and enjoy. I submit, however, that, on a more thorough examination of the matter, we shall find that democracy is a consequence. There are economic and sociological causes for our political vitality and vigor, for the ease and elasticity of our social relations, and for our industrial power and success. Those causes have also produced democracy, given it success, and have made its faults and errors innocuous. Indeed, in any true philosophy, it must be held that in the economic forces which control the material prosperity of a population lie the real causes of its political institutions, its social class-adjustments, its industrial prosperity, its moral code, and its world-philosophy. If democracy and the industrial system are both products of the economic conditions which exist, it is plainly absurd to set democracy to defeat those conditions in the control of industry. If, however, it is not

true that democracy is a consequence, and I am well aware that very few people believe it, then we must go back to the view that democracy is a cause. That being so, it is difficult to see how democracy, which has had a clear field here in America, is not responsible for the ills which Mr. Bellamy and his comrades in opinion see in our present social state, and it is difficult to see the grounds of asking us to intrust it also with industry. The first and chief proof of success of political measures and systems is that, under them, society advances in health and vigor and that industry develops without causing social disease. If this has not been the case in America, American democracy has not succeeded. Neither is it easy to see how the masses, if they have undertaken to rule, can escape the responsibilities of ruling, especially so far as the consequences affect themselves. If, then, they have brought all this distress upon themselves under the present system, what becomes of the argument for extending the system to a direct and complete control of industry?

3. It is by no means certain that democracy in the United States has not, up to this time, been living on a capital inherited from aristocracy and industrialism. We have no pure democracy. Our democracy is limited at every turn by institutions which were developed in England in connection with industrialism and aristocracy, and these institutions are of the essence of our system. While our people are passionately democratic in temper and will not tolerate a doctrine that one man is not as good as another, they have common sense enough to know that he is not; and it seems that they love and cling to the conservative institutions quite as strongly as they do to the democratic philosophy. They are, therefore, ruled by men who talk philosophy and govern by the institutions. Now it is open to Mr. Bellamy to say that the reason why democracy in America seems to be open to the charge made in the last paragraph, of responsibility for all the ill which he now finds in our society, is because it has been infected with industrialism (capitalism); but in that case he must widen the scope of his proposition and undertake to purify democracy before turning industry over to it. The socialists generally seem to think that they make their undertakings easier when they widen

their scope, and make them easiest when they propose to remake everything; but in truth social tasks increase in difficulty in an enormous ratio as they are widened in scope.

The question, therefore, arises, if it is proposed to reorganize the social system on the principles of American democracy, whether the institutions of industrialism are to be retained. If so, all the virus of capitalism will be retained. It is forgotten, in many schemes of social reformation in which it is proposed to mix what we like with what we do not like, in order to extirpate the latter, that each must undergo a reaction from the other, and that what we like may be extirpated by what we do not like. We may find that instead of democratizing capitalism we have capitalized democracy—that is, have brought in plutocracy. Plutocracy is a political system in which the ruling force is wealth. The denunciation of capital which we hear from all the reformers is the most eloquent proof that the greatest power in the world to-day is capital. They know that it is, and confess it most when they deny it most strenuously. At present the power of capital is social and industrial, and only in a small degree political. So far as capital is political, it is on account of political abuses, such as tariffs and special legislation on the one hand and legislative strikes on the other. These conditions exist in the democracy to which it is proposed to transfer the industries. What does that mean except bringing all the power of capital once for all into the political arena and precipitating the conflict of democracy and plutocracy at once? Can anyone imagine that the masterfulness, the overbearing disposition, the greed of gain, and the ruthlessness in methods, which are the faults of the master of industry at his worst, would cease when he was a functionary of the State, which had relieved him of risk and endowed him with authority? Can anyone imagine that politicians would no longer be corruptly fond of money, intriguing, and crafty when they were charged, not only with patronage and government contracts, but also with factories, stores, ships, and railroads? Could we expect anything except that, when the politician and the master of industry were joined in one, we should have the vices of both unchecked by the restraints of either? In any socialistic state there will be one set of positions which will offer chances of wealth beyond the wildest dreams of avarice; *viz.,* on the governing committees. Then there will be rich men whose wealth will indeed be a menace to social interests, and instead of industrial peace there will be such war as no one has dreamed of yet: the war between the political ins and outs—that is, between those who are on the committee and those who want to get on it.

We must not drop the subject of democracy without one word more. The Greeks already had occasion to notice a most serious distinction between two principles of democracy which lie at its roots. Plutarch says that Solon got the archonship in part by promising equality, which some understood of esteem and dignity, others of measure and number. There is one democratic principle which means that each man should be esteemed for his merit and worth, for just what he is, without regard to birth, wealth, rank, or other adventitious circumstances. The other principle is that each one of us ought to be equal to all the others in what he gets and enjoys. The first principle is only partially realizable, but, so far as it goes, it is elevating and socially progressive and profitable. The second is not capable of an intelligible statement. The first is a principle of industrialism. It proceeds from and is intelligible only in a society built on the industrial virtues, free endeavor, security of property, and repression of the baser vices; that is, in a society whose industrial system is built on labor and exchange. The other is only a rule of division for robbers who have to divide plunder or monks who have to divide gifts. If, therefore, we want to democratize industry in the sense of the first principle, we need only perfect what we have now, especially on its political side. If we try to democratize it in the sense of the other principle, we corrupt politics at one stroke; we enter upon an industrial enterprise which will waste capital and bring us all to poverty, and we set loose greed and envy as ruling social passions.

If this poor old world is as bad as they say, one more reflection may check the zeal of the headlong reformer. It is at any rate a tough old world. It has taken its trend and curvature and all its twists and tangles from a long course of formation. All its wry and crooked gnarls and knobs are therefore stiff and stubborn. If we puny men by our arts can do anything at all to straighten them, it will only be by modifying the tendencies of some of the forces at work, so that, after a sufficient time, their action may be changed a little and slowly the lines of movement may be modified. This effort, however, can at most be only slight, and it will take a long time. In the meantime spontaneous forces will be at work, compared with which our efforts are like those of a man trying to deflect a river, and these forces will have changed the whole problem before our interferences have time to make themselves felt. The great stream of time and earthly things will sweep on just the same in spite of us. It bears with it now all the errors and follies of the past, the wreckage of all the philosophies, the fragments of all the civilizations, the wisdom of all the abandoned ethical systems, the debris of all the institutions, and the penalties of all the mistakes. It is only in imagination that we stand by and look at and criticize it and plan to change it. Everyone of us is a child of his age and cannot get out of it. He is in the stream and is swept along with it. All his sciences and philosophy come to him out of it. Therefore the tide will not be changed by us. It will swallow up both us and our experiments. It will absorb the efforts at change and take them into itself as new but trivial components, and the great movement of tradition and work will go on unchanged by our fads and schemes. The things which will change it are the great discoveries and inventions, the new reactions inside the social organism, and the changes in the earth itself on account of changes in the cosmical forces. These causes will make of it just what, in fidelity to them, it ought to be. The men will be carried along with it and be made by it. The utmost they can do by their cleverness will be to note and record their course as they are carried along, which is what we do now, and is that which leads us to the vain fancy that we can make or guide the movement. That is why it is the greatest folly of which a man can be capable, to sit down with a slate and pencil to plan out a new social world.

·V·

LESTER WARD

[1 8 4 1 - 1 9 1 3]

SOCIOCRACY

SOCIOCRACY

Every applied science has its corresponding art. And although the social art is none other than this same government of which it has already been necessary to say so much, still, our social synthesis would be incomplete without some more special inquiry into the essential character of that art as a product of the combined consciousness, will, and intellect of society. Existing governments, it must be confessed, after all that can be said in their favor, realize this only to a very feeble extent. The social consciousness is as yet exceedingly faint, corresponding more nearly to that of a *coenobium*, as in the *Flagellata* and *Ciliata*, than to any of the developed animal forms. The social will is, therefore, merely a mass of conflicting desires which largely neutralize one another and result in little advance movement in one settled direction. The social intellect proves a poor guide, not because it is not sufficiently vigorous, but because knowledge of those matters which principally concern society is so limited, while that which exists is chiefly lodged in the minds of those individuals who are allowed no voice in the affairs of state.

In *Dynamic Sociology* I have pointed out what I regard as the one certain correction possible to apply to this state of things, and have entered into a logically arranged demonstration of this point. "The universal diffusion of the maximum amount of the most important knowledge" was the formula reached for the expression of the result, and it was shown that its attainment is not only practicable but easy and simple whenever the social intelligence shall reach the stage at which its importance is distinctly recognized. It is only after the mind of society, as embodied in its consciousness, will, and intellect, shall, through the application of this formula for a sufficiently prolonged period to produce the required result, come to stand to the social

From *The Psychic Factors of Civilization*, pp. 315-331, by Lester Ward (Boston: Ginn & Company, 1893).

organism in somewhat the relation that the individual mind stands to the individual organism, that any fully developed art of government can be expected to appear. Such an art will partake of the nature of all other arts. It will be the product of the inventive faculty perfected through the inventive genius, and systematized by scientific discovery under the influence of the scientific method and spirit.

Contrasted with this the governments of the past and present may be regarded as empirical. Useful, as is all empirical art, necessary, and adapted in a manner to their age and country, they have served and are serving a purpose in social development and civilization. They have taken on a number of different forms, of which the principal ones are called either monarchies or democracies. These terms, however, never very precise, have now become in most cases wholly misleading. The monarchies of Europe, with perhaps two exceptions, are now all democracies, if there are any such, and some of those that still prefer to be called monarchies are more democratic than some that call themselves republics. And in America, where none of the governments have the monarchical form, some of them are decidedly autocratic and elections are either a signal for revolution or else a mere farce. So that the names by which governments are known are wholly inadequate indexes to their true character. A more exact classification would be into *autocracies, aristocracies,* and *democracies.* By aristocracy would then be meant a ruling class, not necessarily superior, but held to be so. Most monarchies belong to this class. The aristocracy consists not merely of the royal family or dynasty, but of the nobles, clergy, and other privileged persons, for all such really belong to the ruling class. Most European countries have passed through the first two of these stages into the third. Some may be considered as still in the second, while most half-civilized, barbarous, or savage nations have not emerged from the first. . . .

The intellect was developed as an aid to the will in furthering the personal ends of the individual; . . . among the many modes of acquisition government played a leading part. This is more especially the case in the stages of autocracy and aristocracy. It becomes less so in that of democracy, where it is confined to the professional politician and the "legal fraternity." Most of the attacks upon government that it is now so fashionable to make are based upon the vivid manner in which history portrays the doings of the ruling class during the stages of autocracy and aristocracy, and those who make them seem to forget that in all fully enlightened nations this stage has been passed and that of democracy has been fairly reached. But the fear and dread of government still lingers, and its ghost still perpetually rises and will not down. Although modern governments, chiefly on account of the known odium in which they are held, scarcely dare carry out the emphatically declared will of those who create them, and hesitate to take a step forward for fear of being forthwith overthrown by a sweeping plebiscite, still they are the objects of the most jealous vigilance and violent denunciation. Their power for usefulness is thus greatly weakened, and social progress and reform are slow.

It must not, however, be inferred that human nature has been changed by the transition from autocracy and aristocracy to democracy. The spirit of self-agrandizement is undiminished, but the methods of accomplishing it have been changed. Just as society by the establishment of the institution of government put an end to the internecine strifes that threatened its existence, so also by the overthrow of autocracy and aristocracy it wrested from the autocrat and the aristocrat his power to subsist upon the masses. But the keen egoism of the astute individual immediately sought other means to better his condition at the expense of those less gifted with this irrepressible mental power or less favorably circumstanced for its exercise. What could not be secured through statecraft must be gained through some other species of craft. And soon was found in the very weakness of government the means of accomplishing far more than could ever be accomplished by the aid of the strongest form of government. What could no longer be attained through the universal or complete social organization has become easy of attainment through some one or other of the many kinds of partial or incomplete social organizations. With the rigid system which has grown up for the protection of the individual in his legal vested rights there is nothing in the way of advancing to almost any length in this direction.

The reaction in the direction of democracy, obeying the rhythmic law of social progress, aimed at, and to a large extent attained, a fourth stage which may be appropriately called *physiocracy*. Indeed, it may be said to consist of little else than that which was demanded by the French school of political economists who styled themselves Physiocrats. Neglecting some of their special tenets arising out of local conditions in France, this movement was not essentially different from that which was soon after introduced into England and made such rapid progress that it took complete possession of the public mind and has furnished the foundation of the political philosophy of that country and of the social and economic science taught from the high chairs of learning wherever the English language is spoken. This physiocracy, as a habit of thought rather than a form of government, now goes by the name of individualism, and is carried so far by many as to amount to a practical anarchism,[1] reducing all government to the action of so-called natural laws.

The general result is that the world, having passed through the stages of autocracy and aristocracy into the stage of democracy, has, by a natural reaction against personal power, so far minimized the governmental influence that the same spirit which formerly used government to advance self is now ushering in a fifth stage, viz., that of *plutocracy*, which thrives well in connection with a weak democracy or physiocracy, and aims to supersede it entirely. Its strongest hold is the widespread distrust of all government, and it leaves no stone unturned to fan the flame of misarchy. Instead of demanding more and stronger government it demands less and feebler. Shrewdly clamoring for individual liberty, it perpetually holds up the outrages committed by governments in their autocratic and aristocratic stages, and falsely insists that there is imminent danger of their reënactment. *Laissez faire* and the most extreme individualism, bordering on practical anarchy in all except the enforcement of existing proprietary rights, are loudly

---

[1] *Acracy* would be the word necessary to harmonize the terminology.

advocated, and the public mind is thus blinded to the real condition of things. The system of political economy that sprang up in France and England at the close of the aristocratic stage in those countries is still taught in the higher institutions of learning. It is highly favorable to the spread of plutocracy, and is pointed to by those who are to profit by that system of government as the invincible scientific foundation upon which it rests. Many honest political economists are still lured by the specious claims of this system and continue to uphold it, and at least one important treatise on social science, that of Herbert Spencer, defends it to the most extreme length. Thus firmly intrenched, it will require a titanic effort on the part of a society to dislodge this baseless prejudice, and rescue itself once more from the rapacious jaws of human egoism under the crafty leadership of a developed and instructed rational faculty.

Under the system as it now exists the wealth of the world, however created, and irrespective of the claims of the producer, is made to flow toward certain centers of accumulation, to be enjoyed by those holding the keys to such situations. The world appears to be approaching a stage at which those who labor, no matter how skilled, how industrious, or how frugal, will receive, according to the "iron law" formulated by Ricardo, only so much for their services as will enable them "to subsist and to perpetuate their race." The rest finds its way into the hands of a comparatively few, usually non-producing, individuals, whom the usages and laws of all counties permit to claim that they own the very sources of all wealth and the right to allow or forbid its production.

These are great and serious evils, compared with which all the crimes, recognized as such, that would be committed if no government existed, would be as trifles. The underpaid labor, the prolonged and groveling drudgery, the wasted strength, the misery and squalor, the diseases resulting, and the premature deaths that would be prevented by a just distribution of the products of labor, would in a single year outweigh all the so-called crime of a century, for the prevention of which, it is said, government alone exists. This vast theater of woe is regarded as wholly outside the jurisdiction of government, while the most strenuous efforts are put forth to detect and punish the perpetrators of the least of the ordinary recognized crimes. This ignoring of great evils while so violently striking at small ones is the mark of an effete civilization, and warns us of the approaching dotage of the race.

Against the legitimate action of government in the protection of society from these worst of its evils, the instinctive hostility to government, or misarchy, above described, powerfully militates. In the face of it the government hesitates to take action, however clear the right or the method. But, as already remarked, this groundless over-caution against an impossible occurrence would not, in and of itself, have sufficed to prevent government from redressing such palpable wrongs. It has been nursed and kept alive for a specific purpose. It has formed the chief argument of those whose interests require the maintenance of the existing social order in relation to the distribution of wealth. Indeed, it is doubtful whether, without the incessant reiteration given to it by this class, it could have persisted to the present time. This inequitable economic system has itself been the product of centuries of astute management on the part of the shrewdest heads, with a view to securing by legal devices that undue share of the world's products which was formerly the reward of superior physical strength. It is clear to this class that their interest require a policy of strict non-interference on the part of government in what they call the natural laws of political economy, and they are quick to see that the old odium that still lingers among the people can be made a bulwark of strength for their position. They therefore never lose an opportunity to appeal to it in the most effective manner. Through the constant use of this *argumentum ad populum* the anti-government sentiment, which would naturally have smoldered and died out after its cause ceased to exist, is kept perpetually alive.

The great evils under which society now labors have grown up during the progress of intellectual supremacy. They have crept in stealthily during the gradual encroachment of organized cunning upon the domain of brute force. Over that vanishing domain, government retains its power, but it is still powerless in the expanding and now all-embracing field of psychic influence. No one ever claimed that in the trial of physical strength the booty should fall to the strongest. In all such cases the arm of government is stretched out and justice is enforced. But in those manifold, and far more unequal struggles now going on between mind and mind, or rather between the individual and an organized system, the product of ages of thought, it is customary to say that such matters must be left to regulate themselves, and that the fittest must be allowed to survive. Yet, to anyone who will candidly consider the matter, it must be clear that the first and principal acts of government openly and avowedly prevented, through forcible interference, the natural results of all trials of physical strength. These much-talked-of laws of nature are violated every time the highway robber is arrested and sent to jail.

Primitive government, when only brute force was employed, was strong enough to secure the just and equitable distribution of wealth. To-day, when mental force is everything, and physical force is nothing, it is powerless to accomplish this. This alone proves that government needs to be strengthened in its primary quality—the protection of society. There is no reasoning that applies to one kind of protection that does not apply equally to the other. It is utterly illogical to say that aggrandizement by physical force should be forbidden while aggrandizement by mental force or legal fiction should be permitted. It is absurd to claim that injustice committed by muscle should be regulated, while that committed by brain should be unrestrained.

While the modern plutocracy is not a form of government in the same sense that the other forms mentioned are, it is, nevertheless, easy to see that its power is as great as any government has ever wielded. The test of governmental power is usually the manner in which it taxes the people, and the strongest indictments ever drawn up against the worst forms of tyranny have been those which recited their oppressive methods of extorting tribute. But tithes are regarded as oppressive, and a fourth part of the yield of any industry would justify a revolt. Yet to-day there are many commodities for which the people pay two and three times as much as would cover the cost of production, transportation, and exchange at fair wages and fair profits. The monopolies in many lines actually tax the consumer from 25 to 75 per cent of the real value of the goods. Imagine an excise tax that should approach these figures! Under the operation of either monopoly or aggressive competition the price of everything is pushed up to the maximum limit that will be paid for the commodity in profitable quantities, and this wholly irrespective of the cost of production. No government in the world has now, or ever had, the power to enforce such an extortion as this. It is a governing power in the interest of favored individuals, which exceeds that of the most powerful monarch or despot that ever wielded a scepter.

What then is the remedy? How can society escape this last conquest of power by the egoistic intellect? It has overthrown the rule of brute force by the establishment of government. It has supplanted autocracy by aristocracy and this by democracy, and now it finds itself in the coils of plutocracy. Can it escape? Must it go back to autocracy for a power sufficient to cope with plutocracy? No autocrat ever had a tithe of that power. Shall it then let itself be crushed? It need not. There is one power and only one that is greater than that which now chiefly rules society. That power is society itself. There is one form of government that is stronger than autocracy or aristocracy or democracy, or even plutocracy, and that is *sociocracy*.

The individual has reigned long enough. The day has come for society to take its affairs into its own hands and shape its own destinies. The individual has acted as best he could. He has acted in the only way he could. With a consciousness, will, and intellect of his own he could do nothing else than pursue his natural ends. He should not be denounced nor called any names. He should not even be blamed. Nay, he should be praised, and even *imitated*. Society should learn its great lesson from him, should follow the path he has so clearly laid out that leads to success. It should imagine itself an individual, with all the interests of an individual, and becoming fully *conscious* of these interests it should pursue them with the same indomitable *will* with which the individual pursues his interests. Not only this, it must be guided, as he is guided, by the social *intellect*, armed with all the knowledge that all individuals combined, with so great labor, zeal, and talent have placed in its possession, constituting the social intelligence.

Sociocracy will differ from all other forms of government that have been devised, and yet that difference will not be so radical as to require a revolution. Just as absolute monarchy passed imperceptibly into limited monarchy, and this, in many states without even a change of name has passed into more or less pure democracy, so democracy is capable of passing as smoothly into sociocracy, and without taking on this unfamiliar name or changing that by which it is now known. For, though paradoxical, democracy, which is now the weakest of all forms of government, at least in the control of its own internal elements, is capable of becoming the strongest. Indeed, none of the other forms of government would be capable of passing directly into a government by society. Democracy is a phase through which they must first pass on any route that leads to the ultimate social stage which all governments must eventually attain if they persist.

How then, it may be asked, do democracy and sociocracy differ? How does society differ from the people? If the phrase "the people" really meant the people, the difference would be less. But that shibboleth of democratic states, where it means anything at all that can be described or defined, stands simply for the majority of qualified electors, no matter how small that majority may be. There is a sense in which the action of a majority may be looked upon as the action of society. At least, there is no denying the right of the majority to act for society, for to do this would involve either the denial of the right of government to act at all, or the admission of the right of a minority to act for society. But a majority acting for society is a different thing from society acting for itself, even though, as must always be the case, it acts through an agency chosen by its members. All democratic governments are largely party governments. The electors range themselves on one side or the other of some party line, the winning side considers itself the state as much as Louis the Fourteenth did. The losing party usually then regards the government as something alien to it and hostile, like an invader, and thinks of nothing but to gain strength enough to overthrow it at the next opportunity. While various issues are always brought forward and defended or attacked, it is obvious to the looker-on that the contestants care nothing for these, and merely use them to gain an advantage and win an election.

From the standpoint of society this is child's play. A very slight awakening of the social consciousness will banish it and substitute something more business-like. Once get rid of this puerile gaming spirit and have attention drawn to the real interests of society, and it will be seen that upon nearly all important questions all parties and all citizens are agreed, and that there is no need of this partisan strain upon the public energies. This is clearly shown at every change in the party complexion of the government. The victorious party which has been denouncing the government merely because it was in the hands of its political opponents boasts that it is going to revolutionize the country in the interest of good government, but the moment it comes into power and feels the weight of national responsibility it finds that it has little to do but carry out the laws in the same way that its predecessors had been doing.

There is a vast difference between all this outward show of partisanship and advocacy of so-called principles, and attention to the real interests and necessary business of the nation, which latter is what the government must do. It is a social duty. The pressure which is brought to enforce it is the power of the social will. But in the factitious excitement of partisan struggles where professional politicians and demagogues on the one hand, and the agents of plutocracy on the other, are shouting discordantly in the ears of the people, the real interests of society are, temporarily at least, lost sight of, clouded and obscured, and men lose their grasp on the real issues, forget even their own best interest, which, however selfish, would be a far safer guide, and the general result usually is that these are neglected and nations continue in the hands of mere politicians who are easily managed by the shrewd representatives of wealth.

Sociocracy will change all this. Irrelevant issues will be laid aside. The important objects upon which all but an interested few are agreed will receive their proper degree of attention, and measures will be considered in a non-partisan spirit with the sole purpose of securing these objects. Take as an illustration the postal telegraph question. No one not a stockholder in an existing telegraph company would prefer to pay twenty-five cents for a message if he could send it for ten cents. Where is the room for discussing a question of this nature? What society wants is the cheapest possible system. It wants to know with certainty whether a national postal telegraph system would secure this universally desired object. It is to be expected that the agents of the present telegraph companies would try to show that it would not succeed. This is according to the known laws of psychology as set forth in this work. But why be influenced by the interests of such a small number of persons, however worthy, when all the rest of mankind are interested in the opposite solution? The investigation should be a disinterested and strictly scientific one, and should actually settle the question in one way or the other. If it was found to be a real benefit, the system should be adopted. There are to-day a great number of these strictly social questions before the American people, questions which concern every citizen in the country, and whose solution would doubtless profoundly affect the state of civilization attainable on this continent. Not only is it impossible to secure this, but it is impossible to secure an investigation of them on their real merits. The same is true of other countries, and in general the prevailing democracies of the world are incompetent to deal with problems of social welfare.

The more extreme and important case referred to a few pages back may make the distinction still more clear. It was shown, and is known to all political economists, that the prices of most of the staple commodities consumed by mankind have no necessary relation to the cost of producing them and placing them in the hands of the consumer. It is always the highest price that the consumer will pay rather than do without. Let us suppose that price to be on an average double what it would cost to produce, transport, exchange, and deliver the goods, allowing in each of these transactions a fair compensation for all services rendered. Is there any member of society who would prefer to pay two dollars for what is thus fairly worth only one? Is there any sane ground for arguing such a question? Certainly not. The individual cannot correct this state of things. No democracy can correct it. But a government that really represented the interests of society would no more tolerate it than an individual would tolerate a continual extortion of money on the part of another without an equivalent.

And so it would be throughout. Society would inquire in a business way without fear, favor, or bias, into everything that concerned its welfare, and if it found obstacles it would remove them, and if it found opportunities it would improve them. In a word, society would do under the same circumstances just what an intelligent individual would do. It would further, in all possible ways, its own interests.

I anticipate the objection that this is an ideal state of things, and that it has never been attained by any people, and to all appearances never can be. No fair-minded critic will, however, add the customary objection that is raised, not wholly without truth, to all socialistic schemes, that they presuppose a change in "human nature." Because in the transformation here foreshadowed the permanence of all the mental attributes is postulated, and I have not only refrained from dwelling upon the moral progress of the world, but have not even enumerated among the social forces the power of sympathy as a factor in civilization. I recognize this factor as one of the derivative ones, destined to perform an important part, but I have preferred to rest the case upon the primary and original egoistic influences, believing that neither meliorism nor sociocracy is dependent upon any sentiment, or upon altruistic props for its support. At least the proofs will be stronger if none of these aids are called in, and if they can be shown to have a legitimate influence, this is only so much added to the weight of evidence.

To the other charge the answer is that ideals are necessary, and also that no ideal is ever fully realized. If it can be shown that society is actually moving toward any ideal the ultimate substantial realization of that ideal is as good as proved. The proofs of such a movement in society to-day are abundant. In many countries the encroachments of egoistic individualism have been checked at a number of important points. In this country alarm has been taken in good earnest at the march of plutocracy under the protection of democracy. Party lines are giving way and there are unmistakable indications that a large proportion of the people are becoming seriously interested in social progress of the country. For the first time in the history of political parties there has been formed a distinctively industrial party[1] which possesses all the elements of permanence and may soon be a controlling factor in American politics. Though this may not as yet presage a great social revolution, still it is precisely the way in which a reform in the direction indicated should be expected to originate. But whether the present movement prove enduring or ephemeral, the seeds of reform have been sown broadcast throughout the land, and sooner or later they must spring up, grow, and bear their fruit.

For a long time to come social action must be chiefly negative and be confined to the removal of evils that exist, but a positive stage will ultimately be reached in which society will consider and adopt measures for its own advancement. The question of the

---

[1] For the last ten years or more there have been indications in this country that a deep undercurrent of public sentiment was setting in toward the formation of such a political party, and while I claim for myself no special gift of prophecy, I was able to foresee this some years before it took any definite form. In the *Forum* for June, 1887, or about four years before the Cincinnati convention was called, at the close of an article on False Notions of Government, some parts of which I have reproduced in this chapter, occurs the following paragraph which may be said to foreshadow events that followed, and which is as true and salutary now as it was at that date:

"The true solution of the great social problem of this age is to be found in the ultimate establishment of a genuine *people's government*, with ample power to protect society against all forms of injustice, from whatever source, coupled with a warm and dutiful regard for the true interests of each and all, the poor as well as the rich. If this be what is meant by the oft-repeated phrase 'paternal government,' then were this certainly a consummation devoutly to be wished. But in this conception of government there is nothing paternal. It gets rid entirely of the paternal, the patriarchal, the personal element, and becomes nothing more nor less than the effective expression of the public will, the active agency by which society consciously and intelligently governs its own conduct."

respective provinces of social action and individual action cannot be entered into here at length, but it is certain that the former will continue to encroach upon the latter so long as such encroachment is a public benefit. There is one large field in which there is no question on this point, viz., the field covered by what, in modern economic parlance, is called "natural monopoly." The arguments are too familiar to demand restatement here, and the movement is already so well under way that there is little need of further argument. As to what lies beyond this, however, there is room for much discussion and honest difference of opinion. This is because there has been so little induction. It is the special characteristic of the form of government that I have called sociocracy, resting as it does directly upon the science of sociology, to investigate the facts bearing on every subject, not for the purpose of depriving any class of citizens of the opportunity to benefit themselves, but purely and solely for the purpose of ascertaining what is for the best interests of society at large.

The socialistic arguments in favor of society taking upon itself the entire industrial operations of the world have never seemed to me conclusive, chiefly because they have consisted so largely of pure theory and *a priori* deductions. Any one who has become imbued by the pursuit of some special branch of science with the nature of scientific evidence requires the presentation of such evidence before he can accept conclusions in any other department. And this should be the attitude of all in relation to these broader questions of social phenomena. The true economist can scarcely go farther than to say that a given question is an open one, and that he will be ready to accept the logic of facts when these are brought forward. I do not mean that we must not go into the water until we have learned to swim. This, however, suggests the true method of solving such questions. One learns to swim by a series of trials, and society can well afford to try experiments in certain directions and note the results. There are, however, other methods, such as careful estimates of the costs and accurate calculations of the effect based on the uniform laws of social phenomena. Trial is the ultimate test of scientific theory thus formed, and may, in social as in physical science, either establish or overthrow hypotheses. But in social science, no less than in other branches of science, the working hypothesis must always be the chief instrument of successful research.

Until the scientific stage is reached, and as a necessary introduction to it, social problems may properly be clearly stated and such general considerations brought forward as have a direct bearing upon them. I know of no attempts of this nature which I can more warmly recommend than those made by John Stuart Mill in his little work on Liberty,[1] and in his Chapters on Socialism, of which the latter appeared posthumously. They are in marked contrast, by their all-sided wisdom, with the intensely one-sided writings of Herbert Spencer on substantially the same subject; and yet the two authors are obviously at one on the main points discussed. This candid statement of the true claims of the *laissez faire* school is perfectly legitimate. Equally so are like candid presentations of the opposite side of the question. The more light that can be shed on all sides the better, but in order really to elucidate social problems it must be the dry light of science, as little influenced by feeling as though it were the inhabitants of Jupiter's moons, instead of those of this planet, that were under the field of the intellectual telescope.

---

[1] Even despotism does not produce its worst effects, so long as Individuality exists under it; and whatever crushes individuality is despotism, by whatever name it may be called.—John Stuart Mill: *On Liberty*, pp. 122-123.

Neither one person, nor any number of persons, is warranted in saying to another human creature of ripe years, that he shall not do with his life for his own benefit what he chooses to do with it.—John Stuart Mill: *Ibid.*, p. 147.

The strongest of all the arguments against the interference of the public with purely personal conduct, is that when it does interfere, the odds are that it interferes wrongly, and in the wrong place.—John Stuart Mill: *Ibid.*, p. 161.

·VI·

CHARLES SANDERS PEIRCE

[1 8 3 9 - 1 9 1 4]

THE FIXATION OF BELIEF

THE FIXATION OF BELIEF

I

Few persons care to study logic, because everybody conceives himself to be proficient enough in the art of reasoning already. But I observe that this satisfaction is limited to one's own ratiocination, and does not extend to that of other men.

We come to the full possession of our power of drawing inferences the last of all our faculties, for it is not so much a natural gift as a long and difficult art. The history of its practice would make a grand subject for a book. The medieval schoolman, following the Romans, made logic the earliest of a boy's studies after grammar, as being very easy. So it was as they understood it. Its fundamental principle, according to them, was, that all knowledge rests on either authority or reason; but that whatever is deduced by reason depends ultimately on a premise derived from authority. Accordingly, as soon as a boy was perfect in the syllogistic procedure, his intellectual kit of tools was held to be complete.

To Roger Bacon, that remarkable mind who in the middle of the thirteenth century was almost a scientific man, the schoolmen's conception of reasoning appeared only an obstacle to truth. He saw that experience alone teaches anything—a proposition which to us seems easy to understand, because a distinct conception of experience has been handed down to us from former generations; which to him also seemed perfectly clear, because its difficulties had not yet unfolded themselves. Of all kinds of experience, the best, he thought, was interior illumination, which teaches many things about Nature which the external senses could never discover, such as the transubstantiation of bread.

From *Chance, Love, and Logic,* by Charles Sanders Peirce. Copyright, 1923, Harcourt, Brace and Company, Inc.; reprinted with the permission of Routledge and Kegan Paul, Ltd. The article first appeared in *Popular Science Monthly,* November, 1877.

Four centuries later, the more celebrated Bacon, in the first book of his "Novum Organum," gave his clear account of experience as something which must be open to verification and re-examination. But, superior as Lord Bacon's conception is to earlier notions, a modern reader who is not in awe of his grandiloquence is chiefly struck by the inadequacy of his view of scientific procedure. That we have only to make some crude experiments, to draw up briefs of the results in certain blank forms, to go through these by rule, checking off everything disproved and setting down the alternatives, and that thus in a few years physical science would be finished up—what an idea! "He wrote on science like a Lord Chancellor," indeed.

The early scientists, Copernicus, Tycho, Brahe, Kepler, Galileo, and Gilbert, had methods more like those of their modern brethren. Kepler undertook to draw a curve through the places of Mars; and his greatest service to science was in impressing on men's minds that this was the thing to be done if they wished to improve astronomy; that they were not to content themselves with inquiring whether one system of epicycles was better than another but that they were to sit down by the figures and find out what the curve, in truth, was. He accomplished this by his incomparable energy and courage, blundering along in the most inconceivable way (to us), from one irrational hypothesis to another, until, after trying twenty-two of these, he fell, by the mere exhaustion of his invention, upon the orbit which a mind well furnished with the weapons of modern logic would have tried almost at the outset.

In the same way, every work of science great enough to be remembered for a few generations affords some exemplification of the defective state of the art of reasoning of the time when it was written; and each chief step in science has been a lesson in logic. It was so when Lavoisier and his contemporaries took up the study of Chemistry. The old chemist's maxim had been, "Lege, lege, lege, labora, ora, et relege." Lavoisier's method was not to read and pray, not to dream that some long and complicated chemical process would have a certain effect, to put it into practice with dull patience, after its inevitable failure to dream that with some modification it would have another result, and to end by publishing the last dream as a fact: his way was to carry his mind into his laboratory, and to make of his alembics and cucurbits instruments of thought, giving a new conception of reasoning as something which was to be done with one's eyes open, by manipulating real things instead of words and fancies.

The Darwinian controversy is, in large part, a question of logic. Mr. Darwin proposed to apply the statistical method to biology. The same thing has been done in a widely different branch of science, the theory of gases. Though unable to say what the movement of any particular molecule of gas would be on a certain hypothesis regarding the constitution of this class of bodies, Clausius and Maxwell were yet able, by the application of the doctrine of probabilities, to predict that in the long run such and such a proportion of the molecules would, under given circumstances, acquire such and such velocities; that there would take place, every second, such and such a number of collisions, etc.; and from these propositions they were able to deduce certain properties of gases, especially in regard to their heat-relations. In like manner, Darwin, while unable to say what the operation of variation and natural selection in every individual case will be, demonstrates that in the long run they will adapt animals to their circumstances. Whether or not existing animal forms are due to such action, or what position the theory ought to take, forms the subject of a discussion in which questions of fact and questions of logic are curiously interlaced.

II

The object of reasoning is to find out, from the consideration of what we already know, something else which we do not know. Consequently, reasoning is good if it be such as to give a true conclusion from true premises, and not otherwise. Thus, the question of validity is purely one of fact and not of thinking. A being the premises and B being the conclusion, the question is, whether these facts are really so related that if A is B is. If so, the inference is valid; if not, not. It is not in the least the question whether, when the premises are accepted by the mind, we feel an impulse to accept the conclusion also. It is true that we do generally reason correctly by nature. But that is an accident; the true conclusion would remain true if we had no impulse to accept it; and the false one would remain false, though we could not resist the tendency to believe in it.

We are, doubtless, in the main logical animals, but we are not perfectly so. Most of us, for example, are naturally more sanguine and hopeful than logic would justify. We seem to be so constituted that in the absence of any facts to go upon we are happy and self-satisfied; so that the effect of experience is continually to counteract our hopes and aspirations. Yet a lifetime of the application of this corrective does not usually eradicate our sanguine disposition. Where hope is unchecked by any experience, it is likely that our optimism is extravagant. Logicality in regard to practical matters is the most useful quality an animal can possess, and might, therefore, result from the action of natural selection; but outside of these it is probably of more advantage to the animal to have his mind filled with pleasing and encouraging visions, independently of their truth; and thus, upon unpractical subjects, natural selection might occasion a fallacious tendency of thought.

That which determines us, from given premises, to draw one inference rather than another, is some habit of mind, whether it be constitutional or acquired. The habit is good or otherwise, according as it produces true conclusions from true premises or not; and an inference is regarded as valid or not, without reference to the truth or falsity of its conclusion specially, but according as the habit which determines it is such as to produce true conclusions in general or not. The particular habit of mind which governs this or that inference may be formulated in a proposition whose truth depends on the validity of the inferences which the habit determines; and such a formula is called a *guiding principle of inference*. Suppose, for example, that we observe that a rotating disk of copper quickly comes to rest when placed between the poles of a magnet, and we infer that this will happen with every disk of copper. The guiding principle is, that what is true of one piece of copper is true of another. Such a guiding principle with regard to copper would be much safer than with regard to many other substances—brass, for example.

A book might be written to signalize all the most important of these guiding principles of reasoning. It would probably be, we must confess, of no service to a person whose thought is directed wholly to practical subjects, and whose activity moves along thoroughly beaten paths. The problems which present themselves to such a mind are matters of routine which he has learned once for all to handle in learning his business. But let a man venture into an unfamiliar field, or where his results are not continually checked by experience, and all history shows that the most masculine intellect will ofttimes lose his orientation and waste his efforts in directions which bring him no nearer to his goal, or even carry him entirely astray. He is like a ship on the open sea, with no one on board who understands the rules of navigation. And in such a case some general study of the guiding principles of reasoning would be sure to be found useful.

The subject could hardly be treated, however, without being first limited; since almost any fact may serve as a guiding principle. But it so happens that there exists a division among facts, such that in one class are all those which are absolutely essential as guiding principles, while in the other are all those which have any other interest as objects of research. This division is between those which are necessarily taken for granted in asking whether a certain conclusion follows from certain premises, and those which are not implied in that question. A moment's thought will show that a variety of facts are already assumed when the logical question is first asked. It is implied, for instance, that there are such states of mind as doubt and belief—that a passage from one to the other is possible, the object of thought remaining the same, and that this transition is subject to some rules which all minds are alike bound by. As these are facts which we must already know before we can have any clear conception of reasoning at all, it cannot be supposed to be any longer of much interest to inquire into their truth or falsity. On the other hand, it is easy to believe that those rules of reasoning which are deduced from the very idea of the process are the ones which are the most essential; and, indeed, that so long as it conforms to these it will, at least, not lead to false conclusions from true premises. In point of fact, the importance of what may be deduced from the assumptions involved in the logical question turns out to be greater than might be supposed, and this for reasons which it is difficult to exhibit at the outset. The only one which I shall here mention is, that conceptions which are really products of logical reflections, without being readily seen to be so, mingle with our ordinary thoughts, and are frequently the causes of great confusion. This is the case, for example, with the conception of quality. A quality as such is never an object of observation. We can see that a thing is blue or green, but the quality of being blue and the quality of being green are not things which we see; they are products of logical reflections. The truth is, that common-sense, or thought as it first emerges above the level of the narrowly practical, is deeply imbued with that bad logical quality to which the epithet *metaphysical* is commonly applied; and nothing can clear it up but a severe course of logic.

III

We generally know when we wish to ask a question and when we wish to pronounce a judgment, for there is a dissimilarity between the sensation of doubting and that of believing.

But this is not all which distinguishes doubt from belief. There is a practical difference. Our beliefs guide our desires and shape our actions. The Assassins, or followers of the Old Man of the Mountain, used to rush into death at his least command, because they believed that obedience to him would insure everlasting felicity. Had they doubted this, they would not have acted as they did. So it is with every belief, according to its degree. The feeling of believing is a more or less sure indication of there being established in our nature some habit which will determine our actions. Doubt never has such an effect.

Nor must we overlook a third point of difference. Doubt is an uneasy and dissatisfied state from which we struggle to free our-selves and pass into the state of belief; while the latter is a calm and satisfactory state which we do not wish to avoid, or to change to a belief in anything else. On the contrary, we cling tenaciously, not merely to believing, but to believing just what we do believe.

Thus, both doubt and belief have positive effects upon us, though very different ones. Belief does not make us act at once, but puts us into such a condition that we shall behave in a certain way, when the occasion arises. Doubt has not the least effect of this sort, but stimulates us to action until it is destroyed. This re-minds us of the irritation of a nerve and the reflex action produced thereby; while for the analogue of belief, in the nervous system, we must look to what are called nervous associations—for example, to that habit of the nerves in consequence of which the smell of a peach will make the mouth water.

IV

The irritation of doubt causes a struggle to attain a state of belief. I shall term this struggle *inquiry,* though it must be admitted that this is sometimes not a very apt designation.

The irritation of doubt is the only immediate motive for the struggle to attain belief. It is certainly best for us that our beliefs should be such as may truly guide our actions so as to satisfy our desires; and this reflection will make us reject any belief which does not seem to have been so formed as to insure this result. But it will only do so by creating a doubt in the place of that belief. With the doubt, therefore, the struggle begins, and with the ces-sation of doubt it ends. Hence, the sole object of inquiry is the settlement of opinion. We may fancy that this is not enough for us, and that we seek not merely an opinion, but a true opinion. But put this fancy to the test, and it proves groundless; for as soon as a firm belief is reached we are entirely satisfied, whether the belief be false or true. And it is clear that nothing out of the sphere of our knowledge can be our object, for nothing which does not affect the mind can be a motive for a mental effort. The most that can be maintained is, that we seek for a belief that we shall *think* to be true. But we think each one of our beliefs to be true, and, indeed, it is mere tautology to say so.

That the settlement of opinion is the sole end of inquiry is a very important proposition. It sweeps away, at once, various vague and erroneous conceptions of proof. A few of these may be noticed here.

1. Some philosophers have imagined that to start an inquiry it was only necessary to utter or question or set it down on paper, and have even recommended us to begin our studies with questioning everything! But the mere putting of a proposition into the interrogative form does not stimulate the mind to any struggle after belief. There must be a real and living doubt, and without all this discussion is idle.

2. It is a very common idea that a demonstration must rest on some ultimate and absolutely indubitable propositions. These, according to one school, are first principles of a general nature; according to another, are first sensations. But, in point of fact, an inquiry, to have that completely satisfactory result called demonstration, has only to start with propositions perfectly free from all actual doubt. If the premises are not in fact doubted at all, they cannot be more satisfactory than they are.

3. Some people seem to love to argue a point after all the world is fully convinced of it. But no further advance can be made. When doubt ceases, mental action on the subject comes to an end; and, if it did go on, it would be without a purpose.

V

If the settlement of opinion is the sole object of inquiry, and if belief is of the nature of a habit, why should we not attain the desired end, by taking any answer to a question, which we may fancy, and constantly reiterating it to ourselves, dwelling on all which may conduce to that belief, and learning to turn with contempt and hatred from anything which might disturb it? This simple and direct method is really pursued by many men. I remember once being entreated not to read a certain newspaper lest it might change my opinion upon free-trade. "Lest I might be entrapped by its fallacies and misstatements," was the form of expression. "You are not," my friend said, "a special student of political economy. You might, therefore, easily be deceived by fallacious arguments upon the subject. You might, then, if you read this paper, be led to believe in protection. But you admit that free-trade is the true doctrine; and you do not wish to believe what is not true." I have often known this system to be deliberately adopted. Still oftener, the instinctive dislike of an undecided state of mind, exaggerated into a vague dread of doubt, makes men cling spasmodically to the views they already take. The man feels that, if he only holds to his belief without wavering, it will be entirely satisfactory. Nor can it be denied that a steady and immovable faith yields great peace of mind. It may, indeed, give rise to inconveniences, as if a man should resolutely continue to believe that fire would not burn him, or that he would be eternally damned if he received his *ingesta* otherwise than through a stomach-pump. But then the man who adopts this method will not allow that its inconveniences are greater than its advantages. He will say, "I hold steadfastly to the truth and the truth is always wholesome." And in many cases it may very well be that the pleasure he derives from his calm faith overbalances any inconveniences resulting from its deceptive character. Thus, if it be true that death is annihilation, then the man who believes that he will certainly go straight to heaven when he dies, provided he have fulfilled certain simple observances in this life, has a cheap pleasure which will not be followed by the least disappointment. A similar consideration seems to have weight with many persons in religious topics, for we frequently hear it said, "Oh, I could not believe so-and-so, because I should be wretched if I did." When an ostrich buries its head in the sand as danger approaches, it very likely takes the happiest course. It hides the danger, and then calmly says there is no danger; and, it feels perfectly sure there is none, why should it raise its head to see? A man may go through life, systematically keeping out of view all that might cause a change in his opinions, and if he only succeeds—basing his method, as he does, on two fundamental psychological laws—I do not see what can be said against his doing so. It would be an egotistical impertinence to object that his procedure is irrational, for that only amounts to saying that his method of settling belief is not ours. He does not propose to himself to be rational, and indeed, will often talk with scorn of man's weak and illusive reason. So let him think as he pleases.

But this method of fixing belief, which may be called the method of tenacity, will be unable to hold its ground in practice. The social impulse is against it. The man who adopts it will find that other men think differently from him, and it will be apt to occur to him in some saner moment that their opinions are quite as good as his own, and this will shake his confidence in his belief. This conception, that another man's thought or sentiment may be equivalent to one's own, is a distinctly new step, and a highly important one. It arises from an impulse too strong in man to be suppressed, without danger of destroying the human species. Unless we make ourselves hermits, we shall necessarily influence each other's opinions; so that the problem becomes how to fix belief, not in the individual merely, but in the community.

Let the will of the state act, then, instead of that of the individual. Let an institution be created which shall have for its object to keep correct doctrines before the attention of the people, to reiterate them perpetually, and to teach them to the young; having at the same time power to prevent contrary doctrines from being taught, advocated, or expressed. Let all possible causes of a change of mind be removed from men's apprehensions. Let them be kept ignorant, lest they should learn of some reason to think otherwise than they do. Let their passions be enlisted, so that they may regard private and unusual opinions with hatred and horror. Then, let all men who reject the established belief be terrified into silence. Let the people turn out and tar-and-feather such men, or let inquisitions be made into the manner of thinking of suspected persons, and, when they are found guilty of forbidden beliefs, let them be subjected to some signal punishment. When complete agreement could not otherwise be reached, a general massacre of all who have not thought in a certain way has proved a very effective means of settling opinion in a country. If the power to do this be wanting, let a list of opinions be drawn up, to which no man of the least independence of thought can assent, and let the faithful be required to accept all these propositions, in order to segregate them as radically as possible from the influence of the rest of the world.

This method has, from the earliest times, been one of the chief means of upholding correct theological and political doctrines, and of preserving their universal or catholic character. In Rome, especially, it has been practiced from the days of Numa Pompilius to those of Pius Nonus. This is the most perfect example in history; but wherever there is a priesthood—and no religion has been without one—this method has been more or less made use of. Wherever there is aristocracy, or a guild, or any association of a class of men whose interests depend or are supposed to depend on certain propositions, there will be inevitably found some traces of this natural product of social feeling. Cruelties always accompany this system; and when it is consistently carried out, they become atrocities of the most horrible kind in the eyes of any rational man. Nor should this occasion surprise, for the officer of a society does not feel justified in surrendering the interests of that society for the sake of mercy, as he might his own private interests. It is natural, therefore, that sympathy and fellowship should thus produce a most ruthless power.

In judging this method of fixing belief, which may be called the method of authority, we must, in the first place, allow its immeasurable mental and moral superiority to the method of tenacity. Its success is proportionally greater; and in fact it has over and over again worked the most majestic results. The mere structures of stone which it has caused to be put together—in Siam, for example, in Egypt, and in Europe—have many of them a sublimity hardly more than rivaled by the greatest works of Nature. And, except the geological epochs, there are no periods of time so vast as those which are measured by some of these organized faiths. If we scrutinize the matter closely, we shall find that there has not been one of their creeds which has remained always the same; yet the change is so slow as to be imperceptible during one person's life, so that individual belief remains sensibly fixed. For the mass of mankind, then, there is perhaps no better method than this. If it is their highest impulse to be intellectual slaves, then slaves they ought to remain.

But no institution can undertake to regulate opinions upon every subject. Only the most important ones can be attended to, and on the rest men's minds must be left to the action of natural causes. This imperfection will be no source of weakness so long as men are in such a state of culture that one opinion does not influence another—that is, so long as they cannot put two and two together. But in the most priest-ridden states some individuals will be found who are raised above that condition. These men possess a wider sort of social feeling; they see that men in other countries and in other ages have held to very different doctrines from those which they themselves have been brought up to believe; and they cannot help seeing that it is the mere accident of their having been taught as they have, and of their having been surrounded with the manners and associations they have, that has caused them to believe as they do and not far differently. And their candor cannot resist the reflection that there is no reason to rate their own views at a higher value than those of other nations and other centuries; and this gives rise to doubts in their minds.

They will further perceive that such doubts as these must exist in their minds with reference to every belief which seems to be determined by the caprice either of themselves or of those who originated the popular opinions. The willful adherence to a belief, and the arbitrary forcing of it upon others, must, therefore, both be given up and a new method of settling opinions must be adopted, which shall not only produce an impulse to believe, but shall also decide what proposition it is which is to be believed. Let the action of natural preferences be unimpeded, then, and under their influence let men conversing together and regarding matters in different lights, gradually develop beliefs in harmony with natural causes. This method resembles that by which conceptions of art have been brought to maturity. The most perfect example of it is to be found in the history of metaphysical philosophy. Systems of this sort have not usually rested upon observed facts, at least not in any great degree. They have been chiefly adopted because their fundamental propositions seemed "agreeable to reason." This is an apt expression; it does not mean that which agrees with experience, but that which we find ourselves inclined to believe. Plato, for example, finds it agreeable to reason that the distances of the celestial spheres from one another should be proportional to the different lengths of strings which produce harmonious chords. Many philosophers have been led to their main conclusions by considerations like this; but this is the lowest and least developed form which the method takes, for it is clear that another man might find Kepler's [earlier] theory, that the celestial spheres are proportional to the inscribed and circumscribed spheres of the different regular solids, more agreeable to *his* reason. But the shock of opinions will soon lead men to rest on preferences of a far more universal nature. Take, for example, the doctrine that man only acts selfishly—that is, from the consideration that acting in one way will afford him more pleasure than acting in another. This rests on no fact in the world, but it has had a wide acceptance as being the only reasonable theory.

This method is far more intellectual and respectable from the point of view of reason than either of the others which we have noticed. But its failure has been the most manifest. It makes of inquiry something similar to the development of taste; but taste, unfortunately, is always more or less a matter of fashion, and accordingly, metaphysicians have never come to any fixed agreement, but the pendulum has swung backward and forward between a more material and a more spiritual philosophy, from the earliest times to the latest. And so from this, which has been called the *a priori* method, we are driven, in Lord Bacon's phrase, to a true induction. We have examined into this *a priori* method as something which promised to deliver our opinions from their accidental and capricious element. But development, while it is a process which eliminates the effect of some casual circumstances, only magnifies that of others. This method, therefore, does not differ in a very essential way from that of authority. The government may not have lifted its finger to influence my convictions; I may have been left outwardly quite free to choose, we will say, between monogamy and polygamy, and appealing to my conscience only, may have concluded that the latter practice is in itself licentious. But when I come to see that the chief obstacle to the spread of Christianity among a people of as high culture as the Hindoos has been a conviction of the immorality of our way of treating women, I cannot help seeing that, though governments do not interfere, sentiments in their development will be very greatly determined by accidental causes. Now, there are some people, among whom I must suppose that my reader is to be found, who, when they see that any belief of theirs is determined by any circumstance extraneous to the facts, will from that moment not merely admit in words that that belief is doubtful, but will experience a real doubt of it, so that it ceases to be a belief.

To satisfy our doubts, therefore, it is necessary that a method should be found by which our beliefs may be caused by nothing human, but by some external permanency—by something upon which our thinking has no effect. Some mystics imagine that they have such a method in a private inspiration from on high. But that is only a form of the method of tenacity, in which the conception of truth as something public is not yet developed. Our external permanency would not be external, in our sense, if it was restricted in its influence to one individual. It must be something which affects, or might affect, every man. And, though these affections are necessarily as various as are individual conditions, yet the method must be such that the ultimate conclusion of every man shall be the same. Such is the method of science. Its fundamental hypothesis, restated in more familiar language, is this: There are real things, whose characters are entirely independent of our opinions about them; whose realities affect our senses according to regular laws, and, though our sensations are as different as our relations to the objects, yet, by taking advantage of the laws of perception, we can ascertain by reasoning how things really are, and any man, if he have sufficient experience and reason enough about it, will be led to the one true conclusion. The new conception here involved is that of reality. It may be asked how I know that there are any realities. If this hypothesis is the sole support of my method of inquiry, my method of inquiry must not be used to support my hypothesis. The reply is this: 1. If investigation cannot be regarded as proving that there are real things, it at least does not lead to a contrary conclusion; but the method and the conception on which it is based remain ever in harmony. No doubts of the method, therefore, necessarily arise from its practice, as is the case with all the others. 2. The feeling which gives rise to any method of fixing belief is a dissatisfaction at two repugnant propositions. But here already is a vague concession that there is some *one* thing to which a proposition should conform. Nobody, therefore, can really doubt that there are realities, or, if he did doubt would not be a source of dissatisfaction. The hypothesis, therefore, is one which every mind admits. So that the social impulse does not cause me to doubt it. 3. Everybody uses the scientific method about a great many things, and only ceases to use it when he does not know how to apply it. 4. Experience of the method has not led me to doubt it, but, on the contrary, scientific investigation has had the most wonderful triumphs in the way of settling opinion. These afford the explanation of my not doubting the method or the hypothesis which it supposes; and not having any doubt, nor believing that anybody else whom I could influence has, it would be the merest babble for me to say more about it. If there be anybody with a living doubt upon the subject, let him consider it.

To describe the method of scientific investigation is the object of this series of papers. At present I have only room to notice some points of contrast between it and other methods of fixing belief.

This is the only one of the four methods which presents any distinction of a right and a wrong way. If I adopt the method of tenacity and shut myself out from all influences, whatever I think necessary to doing this is necessary according to that method. So with the method of authority: the state may try to put down heresy by means which, from a scientific point of view, seems very ill-calculated to accomplish its purposes; but the only test *on that method* is what the state thinks, so that it cannot pursue the method wrongly. So with the *a priori* method. The very essence of it is to think as one is inclined to think. All metaphysicians will be sure to do that, however they may be inclined to judge each other to be perversely wrong. The Hegelian system recognizes every natural tendency of thought as logical, although it is certain to be abolished by counter-tendencies. Hegel thinks there is a regular system in the succession of these tendencies, in consequence of which, after drifting one way and the other for a long time, opinion will at last go right. And it is true that metaphysicians get the right ideas at last; Hegel's system of Nature represents tolerably the science of that day; and one may be sure that whatever scientific investigation has put out of doubt will presently receive *a priori* demonstration on the part of the metaphysicians. But with the scientific method the case is different. I may start with known and observed facts to proceed to the unknown; and yet the rules which I follow in doing so may not be such as investigation would approve. The test of whether I am truly following the method is not an immediate appeal to my feelings and purposes, but, on the contrary, itself involves the application of the method. Hence it is that bad reasoning as well as good reasoning is possible; and this fact is the foundation of the practical side of logic.

It is not to be supposed that the first three methods of settling opinion present no advantage whatever over the scientific method. On the contrary, each has some peculiar convenience of its own. The *a priori* method is distinguished for its comfortable conclusions. It is the nature of the process to adopt whatever belief we are inclined to, and there are certain flatteries to one's vanities which we all believe by nature, until we are awakened from our pleasing dream by rough facts. The method of authority will always govern the mass of mankind; and those who wield the various forms of organized force in the state will never be convinced that dangerous reasoning ought not to be suppressed in some way. If liberty of speech is to be untrammeled from the grosser forms of constraint, then uniformity of opinion will be secured by a moral terrorism to which the respectability of society will give its thorough approval. Following the method of authority is the path of peace. Certain non-conformities are permitted; certain others (considered unsafe) are forbidden. These are different in different countries and in different ages; but, wherever you are let it be known that you seriously hold a tabooed belief, and you may be perfectly sure of being treated with a cruelty no less brutal but more refined than hunting you like a wolf. Thus, the greatest intellectual benefactors of mankind have never dared, and dare not now, to utter the whole of their thought; and thus a shade of *prima facie* doubt is cast upon every proposition which is considered essential to the security of society. Singularly enough, the persecution does not all come from without; but a man torments himself and is oftentimes most distressed at finding himself believing propositions which he has been brought up to regard with aversion. The peaceful and sympathetic man will, therefore, find it hard to resist the temptation to submit his opinions to authority. But most of all I admire the method of tenacity for its strength, simplicity, and directness. Men who pursue it are distinguished for their decision of character, which becomes very easy with such a mental rule. They do not waste time in trying to make up their minds to what they want, but, fastening like lightning upon whatever alternative comes first, they hold to it to the end, whatever happens, without an instant's irresolution. This is one of the splendid qualities which generally accompany brilliant, unlasting success. It is impossible not to envy the man who can dismiss reason, although we know how it must turn out at last.

Such are the advantages which the other methods of settling opinions have over scientific investigation. A man should consider well of them; and then he should consider that, after all, he wishes his opinions to coincide with the fact, and that there is no reason why the results of these three methods should do so. To bring about this effect is the prerogative of the method of science. Upon such considerations he has to make his choice—a choice which is far more than the adoption of any intellectual opinion, which is one of the ruling decisions of his life, to which when once made he is bound to adhere. The force of habit will sometimes cause a man to hold on to old beliefs, after he is in a condition to see that they have no sound basis. But reflection upon the state of the case will overcome these habits, and he ought to allow reflection full weight. People sometimes shrink from doing this, having an idea that beliefs are wholesome which they cannot help feeling rest on nothing. But let such persons suppose an analogous though different case from their own. Let them ask themselves what they would say to a reformed Mussulman who should hesitate to give up his old notions in regard to the relations of the sexes; or to a reformed Catholic who should still shrink from the Bible. Would they not say that these persons ought to consider the matter fully, and clearly understand the new doctrine, and then ought to embrace it in its entirety? But, above all, let it be considered that what is more wholesome than any particular belief, is integrity of belief; and that to avoid looking into the support of any belief from a fear that it may turn out rotten is quite as immoral as it is disadvantageous. The person who confesses that there is such a thing as truth, which is distinguished from falsehood simply by this, that if acted on it will carry us to the point we aim at and not astray, and then though convinced of this, dares not know the truth and seeks to avoid it, is in a sorry state of mind, indeed.

Yes, the other methods do have their merits: a clear logical conscience does cost something—just as any virtue, just as all that we cherish, costs us dear. But, we should not desire it to be otherwise. The genius of a man's logical method should be loved and reverenced as his bride, whom he has chosen from all the world. He need not condemn the others; on the contrary, he may honor them deeply, and in doing so he only honors her the more. But she is the one that he has chosen, and he knows that he was right in making that choice. And having made it, he will work and fight for her, and will not complain that there are blows to take, hoping that there may be as many and as hard to give, and will strive to be the worthy knight and champion of her from the blaze of whose splendors he draws his inspiration and his courage.

·VII·

WILLIAM JAMES

[1 8 4 2 - 1 9 1 0]

THE WILL TO BELIEVE

WHAT PRAGMATISM MEANS

THE WILL TO BELIEVE

In the recently published Life by Leslie Stephen of his brother, Fitz-James, there is an account of a school to which the latter went when he was a boy. The teacher, a certain Mr. Guest, used to converse with his pupils in this wise: "Gurney, what is the difference between justification and sanctification?—Stephen, prove the omnipotence of God!" etc. In the midst of our Harvard freethinking and indifference we are prone to imagine that here at your good old orthodox College conversation continues to be somewhat upon this order; and to show you that we at Harvard have not lost all interest in these vital subjects, I have brought with me to-night something like a sermon on justification by faith to read to you, —I mean an essay in justification *of* faith, a defence of our right to adopt a believing attitude in religious matters, in spite of the fact that our merely logical intellect may not have been coerced. 'The Will to Believe,' accordingly, is the title of my paper.

I have long defended to my own students the lawfulness of voluntarily adopted faith; but as soon as they have got well imbued with the logical spirit, they have as a rule refused to admit my contention to be lawful philosophically, even though in point of fact they were personally all the time chock-full of some faith or other themselves. I am all the while, however, so profoundly convinced that my own position is correct, that your invitation has seemed to me a good occasion to make my statements more clear. Perhaps your minds will be more open than those with which I have hitherto had to deal. I will be as little technical as I can, though I must begin by setting up some technical distinctions that will help us in the end.

I

Let us give the name of *hypothesis* to anything that may be proposed to our belief; and just as the electricians speak of live and dead wires, let us speak of any hypothesis as either *live* or *dead*. A live hypothesis is one which appeals as a real possibility to him to whom it is proposed. If I ask you to believe in the Mahdi, the notion makes no electric connection with your nature,—it refuses to scintillate with any credibility at all. As an hypothesis it is completely dead. To an Arab, however (even if he be not one of the Mahdi's followers), the hypothesis is among the mind's possibilities: it is alive. This shows that deadness and liveness in an hypothesis are not intrinsic properties, but relations to the individual thinker. They are measured by his willingness to act. The maximum of liveness in an hypothesis means willingness to act irrevocably. Practically, that means belief; but there is some believing tendency wherever there is willingness to act at all.

Next, let us call the decision between two hypotheses an *option*. Options may be of several kinds. They may be—1, *living* or *dead*; 2, *forced* or *avoidable*; 3, *momentous* or *trivial*; and for our purposes we may call an option a *genuine* option when it is of the forced, living, and momentous kind.

1. A living option is one in which both hypotheses are live ones. If I say to you: "Be a theosophist or be a Mohammedan," it is probably a dead option, because for you neither hypothesis is likely to be alive. But if I say: "Be an agnostic or be a Christian," it is otherwise: trained as you are, each hypothesis makes some appeal, however small, to your belief.

2. Next, if I say to you: "Choose between going out with your umbrella or without it," I do not offer you a genuine option, for it is not forced. You can easily avoid it by not going out at all. Similarly, if I say, "Either love me or hate me," "Either call my theory true or call it false," your option is avoidable. You may remain indifferent to me, neither loving nor hating, and you may decline to offer any judgment as to my theory. But if I say, "Either accept

this truth or go without it," I put on you a forced option, for there is no standing place outside of the alternative. Every dilemma based on a complete logical disjunction, with no possibility of not choosing, is an option of this forced kind.

3. Finally, if I were Dr. Nansen and proposed to you to join my North Pole expedition, your option would be momentous; for this would probably be your only similar opportunity, and your choice now would either exclude you from the North Pole sort of immortality altogether or put at least the chance of it into your hands. He who refuses to embrace a unique opportunity loses the prize as surely as if he tried and failed. *Per contra,* the option is trivial when the opportunity is not unique, when the stake is insignificant, or when the decision is reversible if it later prove unwise. Such trivial options abound in the scientific life. A chemist finds an hypothesis live enough to spend a year in its verification: he believes in it to that extent. But if his experiments prove inconclusive either way, he is quit for his loss of time, no vital harm being done.

It will facilitate our discussion if we keep all these distinctions well in mind.

II

The next matter to consider is the actual psychology of human opinion. When we look at certain facts, it seems as if our passional and volitional nature lay at the root of all our convictions. When we look at others, it seems as if they could no nothing when the intellect had once said its say. Let us take the latter facts up first.

Does it not seem preposterous on the very face of it to talk of our opinions being modifiable at will? Can our will either help or hinder our intellect in its perceptions of truth? Can we, by just willing it, believe that Abraham Lincoln's existence is a myth, and that the portraits of him in McClure's Magazine are all of some one else? Can we, by any effort of our will, or by any strength of wish that it were true, believe ourselves well and about when we are roaring with rheumatism in bed, or feel certain that the sum of the two one-dollar bills in our pocket must be a hundred dollars? We can *say* any of these things, but we are absolutely impotent to believe them; and of just such things is the whole fabric of the truths that we do believe in made up,—matters of fact, immediate or remote, as Hume said, and relations between ideas, which are either there or not there for us if we see them so, and which if not there cannot be put there by any action of our own.

In Pascal's Thoughts there is a celebrated passage known in literature as Pascal's wager. In it he tries to force us into Christianity by reasoning as if our concern with truth resembled our concern with the stakes in a game of chance. Translated freely his words are these: You must either believe or not believe what God is—which will you do? Your human reason cannot say. A game is going on between you and the nature of things which at the day of judgment will bring out either heads or tails. Weigh what your gains and your losses would be if you should stake all you have on heads, or God's existence: if you win in such case, you gain eternal beatitude; if you lose, you lose nothing at all. If there were an infinity of chances, and only one for God in this wager, still you ought to stake your all on God; for though you surely risk a finite loss by this procedure, any finite loss is reasonable, even a certain one is reasonable, if there is but the possibility of infinite gain. Go, then, and take holy water, and have masses said; belief will come and stupefy your scruples,—*Cela vous fera croire et vous abêtira*. Why should you not? At bottom, what have you to lose?

You probably feel that when religious faith expresses itself thus, in the language of the gaming-table, it is put to its last trumps. Surely Pascal's own personal belief in masses and holy water had far other springs; and this celebrated page of his is but an argument for others, a last desperate snatch at a weapon against the hardness of the unbelieving heart. We feel that a faith in masses and holy water adopted willfully after such a mechanical calculation would lack the inner soul of faith's reality; and if we were ourselves in the place of the Deity, we should probably take particular pleasure in cutting off believers of this pattern from their infinite reward. It is evident that unless there be some pre-existing tendency to believe in masses and holy water, the option offered to the will by Pascal is not a living option. Certainly no Turk ever took to masses and holy water on its account; and even to us Protestants these means of salvation seem such foregone impossibilities that Pascal's logic, invoked for them specifically, leaves us unmoved. As well might the Mahdi write to us, saying, "I am the Expected One whom God has created in his effulgence. You shall be infinitely happy if you confess me; otherwise you shall be cut off from the light of the sun. Weigh, then, your infinite gain if I am genuine against your finite sacrifice if I am not!" His logic would be that of Pascal; but he would vainly use it on us, for the hypothesis he offers us is dead. No tendency to act on it exists in us to any degree.

The talk of believing by our volition seems, then, from one point of view, simply silly. From another point of view it is worse than silly, it is vile. When one turns to the magnificent edifice of the physical sciences, and sees how it was reared; what thousands of disinterested moral lives of men lie buried in its mere foundations; what patience and postponement, what choking down of preference, what submission to the icy laws of outer fact are wrought into its very stones and mortar; how absolutely impersonal it stands in its vast augustness,—then how besotted and contemptible seems every little sentimentalist who comes blowing his voluntary smoke-wreaths, and pretending to decide things from out of his private dream! Can we wonder if those bred in the rugged and manly school of science should feel like spewing such subjectivism out of their mouths? The whole system of loyalties which grow up in the schools of science go dead against its toleration; so that it is only natural that those who have caught the scientific fever should pass over to the opposite extreme, and write sometimes as if the incorruptibly truthful intellect ought positively to prefer bitterness and unacceptableness to the heart in its cup.

> *It fortifies my soul to know*
> *That, though I perish, Truth is so—*

sings Clough, while Huxley exclaims: "My only consolation lies in the reflection that, however bad our posterity may become, so far as they hold by the plain rule of not pretending to believe what they have no reason to believe, because it may be to their advantage so to pretend [the word 'pretend' is surely here redundant], they will not have reached the lowest depth of immorality." And that delicious *enfant terrible* Clifford writes: "Belief is desecrated when given to unproved and unquestioned statements for the solace and private pleasure of the believer. . . . Whoso would deserve well of his fellows in this matter will guard the purity of his belief with a very fanaticism of jealous care, lest at any time it should rest on an unworthy object, and catch a stain which can never be wiped away. . . . If [a] belief has been accepted on insufficient evidence [even though the belief be true, as Clifford on the same page explains] the pleasure is a stolen one. . . . It is sinful because it is stolen in defiance of our duty to mankind. That duty is to guard ourselves from such beliefs as from a pestilence which may shortly master our own body and then spread to the rest of the town. . . . It is wrong always, everywhere, and for every one, to believe anything upon insufficient evidence."

III

All this strikes one as healthy, even when expressed, as by Clifford, with somewhat too much of robustious pathos in the voice. Free-will and simple wishing do seem, in the matter of our credences, to be only fifth wheels to the coach. Yet if any one should thereupon assume that intellectual insight is what remains after wish and will and sentimental preference have taken wing, or that pure reason is what then settles our opinions, he would fly quite as directly in the teeth of the facts.

It is only our already dead hypotheses that our willing nature is unable to bring to life again. But what has made them dead for us is for the most part a previous action of our willing nature of an antagonistic kind. When I say 'willing nature,' I do not mean only such deliberate volitions as may have set up habits of belief that we cannot now escape from,—I mean all such factors of belief as fear and hope, prejudice and passion, imitation and partisanship, the circumpressure of our caste and set. As a matter of fact we find ourselves believing, we hardly know how or why. Mr. Balfour gives the name of 'authority' to all those influences, born of the intellectual climate, that make hypotheses possible or impossible for us, alive or dead. Here in this room, we all of us believe in molecules and the conservation of energy, in democracy and necessary progress, in Protestant Christianity and the duty of fighting for 'the doctrine of the immortal Monroe,' all for no reasons worthy of the name. We see into these matters with no more inner clearness, and probably with much less, than any disbeliever in them might possess. His unconventionality would probably have some grounds to show for its conclusions; but for us, not insight, but the *prestige* of the opinions, is what makes the spark shoot from them and light up our sleeping magazines of faith. Our reason is quite satisfied, in nine hundred and ninety-nine cases out of every thousand of us, if it can find a few arguments that will do to recite in case our credulity is criticised by some one else. Our faith is faith in some one else's faith, and in the greatest matters this is most the case. Our belief in truth itself, for instance, that there is a truth, and that our minds and it are made for each other,—what is it but a passionate affirmation of desire, in which our social system backs us up? We want to have a truth; we want to believe that our experiments and studies and discussions must put us in a continually better and better position towards it; and on this line we agree to fight out our thinking lives. But if a pyrrhonistic sceptic asks us *how we know* all this, can our logic find a reply? No! certainly it cannot. It is just one volition against another,—we willing to go in for life upon a trust or assumption which he, for his part, does not care to make.

As a rule we disbelieve all facts and theories for which we have no use. Clifford's cosmic emotions find no use for Christian feelings. Huxley belabors the bishops because there is no use for sacerdotalism in his scheme of life. Newman, on the contrary, goes over to Romanism, and finds all sorts of reasons good for staying there, because a priestly system is for him an organic need and delight. Why do so few 'scientists' even look at the evidence for telepathy, so called? Because they think, as a leading biologist, now dead, once said to me, that even if such a thing were true, scientists ought to band together to keep it suppressed and concealed. It would undo the uniformity of Nature and all sorts of other things without which scientists cannot carry on their pursuits. But if this very man had been shown something which as a scientist he might *do* with telepathy, he might not only have examined the evidence, but even have found it good enough. This very law which the logicians would impose upon us—if I may give the name of logicians to those who would rule out our willing nature here—is based on nothing but their own natural wish to exclude all elements for which they, in their professional quality of logicians, can find no use.

Evidently, then, our non-intellectual nature does influence our convictions. There are passional tendencies and volitions which run before and others which come after belief, and it is only the latter that are too late for the fair; and they are not too late when the previous passional work has been already in their own direction. Pascal's argument, instead of being powerless, then seems a regular clincher, and is the last stroke needed to make our faith in masses and holy water complete. The state of things is evidently far from simple; and pure insight and logic, whatever they might do ideally, are not the only things that really do produce our creeds.

IV

Our next duty, having recognized this mixed-up state of affairs, is to ask whether it be simply reprehensible and pathological, or whether, on the contrary, we must treat it as a normal element in making up our minds. The thesis I defend is, briefly stated, this: *Our passional nature not only lawfully may, but must, decide an option between propositions, whenever it is a genuine option that cannot by its nature be decided on intellectual grounds; for to say, under such circumstances, "Do not decide, but leave the question open," is itself a passional decision,—just like deciding yes or no,—and is attended with the same risk of losing the truth.* The thesis thus abstractly expressed will, I trust, soon become quite clear. But I must first indulge in a bit more of preliminary work.

V

It will be observed that for the purposes of this discussion we are on 'dogmatic ground,—ground, I mean, which leaves systematic philosophical scepticism altogether out of account. The postulate that there is truth, and that it is the destiny of our minds to attain it, we are deliberately resolving to make, though the sceptic will not make it. We part company with him, therefore, absolutely, at this point. But the faith that truth exists, and that our minds can find it, may be held in two ways. We may talk of the *empiricist* way and of the *absolutist* way of believing in truth. The absolutists in this matter say that we not only can attain to knowing truth, but we can *know when* we have attained to knowing it; while the empiricists think that although we may attain it, we cannot infallibly know when. To *know* is one thing, and to know for certain *that* we know is another. One may hold to the first being possible without the second; hence the empiricists and the absolutists, although neither of them is a sceptic in the usual philosophic sense of the term, show very different degrees of dogmatism in their lives.

If we look at the history of opinions, we see that the empiricist tendency has largely prevailed in science, while in philosophy the absolutist tendency has had everything its own way. The characteristic sort of happiness, indeed, which philosophies yield has mainly consisted in the conviction felt by each successive school or system that by it bottom-certitude had been attained. "Other philosophies are collections of opinions, mostly false; *my* philosophy gives standing-ground forever,"—who does not recognize in this the key-note of every system worthy of the name? A system, to be a system at all, must come as a *closed* system, reversible in this or that detail, perchance, but in its essential features never!

Scholastic orthodoxy, to which one must always go when one wishes to find perfectly clear statement, has beautifully elaborated this absolutist conviction in a doctrine which it calls that of 'objective evidence.' If, for example, I am unable to doubt that I now exist before you, that two is less than three, or that if all men are mortal then I am mortal too, it is because these things illumine my intellect irresistibly. The final ground of this objective evidence possessed by certain propositions is the *adæquatio intellectûs nostri cum rê.* The certitude it brings involves an *aptitudinem ad extorquendum certum assensum* on the part of the truth envisaged, and on the side of the subject a *quietem in cognitione,* when once the object is mentally received, that leaves no possibility of doubt behind; and in the whole transaction nothing operates but the *entitas ipsa* of the object and the *entitas ipsa* of the mind. We slouchy modern thinkers dislike to talk in Latin, —indeed, we dislike to talk in set terms at all; but at bottom our own state of mind is very much like this whenever we uncritically abandon ourselves: You believe in objective evidence, and I do. Of some things we feel that we are certain: we know, and we know that we do know. There is something that gives a click inside of us, a bell that strikes twelve, when the hands of our mental clock have swept the dial and meet over the meridian hour. The greatest empiricists among us are only empiricists on reflection: when left to their instincts, they dogmatize like infallible popes. When the Cliffords tell us how sinful it is to be Christians on such 'insufficient evidence,' insufficiency is really the last thing they have in mind. For them the evidence is absolutely sufficient, only it makes the other way. They believe so completely in an anti-christian order of the universe that there is no living option: Christianity is a dead hypothesis from the start.

VI

But now, since we are all such absolutists by instinct, what in our quality of students of philosophy ought we to do about the fact? Shall we espouse and indorse it? Or shall we treat it as a weakness of our nature from which we must free ourselves, if we can?

I sincerely believe that the latter course is the only one we can follow as reflective men. Objective evidence and certitude are doubtless very fine ideals to play with, but where on this moonlit and dream-visited planet are they found? I am, therefore, myself a complete empiricist so far as my theory of human knowledge goes. I live, to be sure, by the practical faith that we must go on experiencing and thinking over our experience, for only thus can our opinions grow more true; but to hold any one of them—I absolutely do not care which—as if it never could be reinterpretable or corrigible, I believe to be a tremendously mistaken attitude, and I think that the whole history of philosophy will bear me out. There is but one indefectibly certain truth, and that is the truth that pyrrhonistic scepticism itself leaves standing,—the truth that the present phenomenon of consciousness exists. That, however, is the bare starting-point of knowledge, the mere admission of a stuff to be philosophized about. The various philosophies are but so many attempts at expressing what this stuff really is. And if we repair to our libraries what disagreement do we discover! Where is a certainly true answer found? Apart from abstract propositions of comparison (such as two and two are the same as four), propositions which tell us nothing by themselves about concrete reality, we find no proposition ever regarded by any one as evidently certain that has not either been called a falsehood, or at least had its truth sincerely questioned by some one else. The transcending of the axioms of geometry, not in play but in earnest, by certain of our contemporaries (as Zöllner and Charles H. Hinton), and the rejection of the whole Aristotelian logic by the Hegelians, are striking instances in point.

No concrete test of what is really true has ever been agreed upon. Some make the criterion external to the moment of perception, putting it either in revelation, the *consensus gentium*, the instincts of the heart, or the systematized experience of the race. Others make the perceptive moment its own test,—Descartes, for instance, with his clear and distinct ideas guaranteed by the veracity of God; Reid with his 'common-sense;' and Kant with his forms of synthetic judgment *a priori*. The inconceivability of the opposite; the capacity to be verified by sense; the possession of complete organic unity or self-relation, realized when a thing is its own other,—are standards which, in turn, have been used. The much lauded objective evidence is never triumphantly there; it is a mere aspiration or *Grenzbegriff*, marking the infinitely remote ideal of our thinking life. To claim that certain truths now possess it, is simply to say that when you think them true and they *are* true, then their evidence is objective, otherwise it is not. But practically one's conviction that the evidence one goes by is of the real objective brand, is only one more subjective opinion added to the lot. For what a contradictory array of opinions have objective evidence and absolute certitude been claimed! The world is rational through and through,—its existence is an ultimate brute fact; there is a personal God,—a personal God is inconceivable; there is an extra-mental physical world immediately known,—the mind can only know its own ideas; a moral imperative exists,—obligation is only the resultant of desires; a permanent spiritual principle is in every one,—there are only shifting states of mind; there is an endless chain of causes,— there is an absolute first cause; an eternal necessity,—a freedom; a purpose,—no purpose; a primal One,—a primal Many; a universal continuity,—an essential discontinuity in things; an infinity, —no infinity. There is this,—there is that; there is indeed nothing which some one has not thought absolutely true, while his neighbor deemed it absolutely false; and not an absolutist among them seems ever to have considered that the trouble may all the time be essential, and that the intellect, even with truth directly in its grasp, may have no infallible signal for knowing whether it be truth or no. When, indeed, one remembers that the most striking practical application to life of the doctrine of objective certitude has been the conscientious labors of the Holy Office of the Inquisition, one feels less tempted than ever to lend the doctrine a respectful ear.

But please observe, now, that when as empiricists we give up the doctrine of objective certitude, we do not thereby give up the quest or hope of truth itself. We still pin our faith on its existence, and still believe that we gain an ever better position towards it by systematically continuing to roll up experiences and think. Our great difference from the scholastic lies in the way we face. The strength of his system lies in the principles, the origin, the *terminus a quo* of his thought; for us the strength is in the outcome, the upshot, the *terminus ad quem*. Not where it comes from but what it leads to is to decide. It matters not to an empiricist from what quarter an hypothesis may come to him: he may have acquired it by fair means or by foul; passion may have whispered or accident suggested it; but if the total drift of thinking continues to confirm it, that is what he means by its being true.

VII

One more point, small but important, and our preliminaries are done. There are two ways of looking at our duty in the matter of opinion,—ways entirely different, and yet ways about whose difference the theory of knowledge seems hitherto to have shown very little concern. *We must know the truth;* and *we must avoid error,*—these are our first and great commandments as would-be knowers; but they are not two ways of stating an identical commandment, they are two separable laws. Although it may indeed happen that when we believe the truth *A,* we escape as an incidental consequence from believing the falsehood *B,* it hardly ever happens that by merely disbelieving *B* we necessarily believe *A.* We may in escaping *B* fall into believing other falsehoods, *C* or *D,* just as bad as *B;* or we may escape *B* by not believing anything at all, not even *A.*

Believe truth! Shun error!—these, we see, are two materially different laws; and by choosing between them we may end by coloring differently our whole intellectual life. We may regard the chase for truth as paramount, and the avoidance of error as secondary; or we may, on the other hand, treat the avoidance of error as more imperative, and let truth take its chance. Clifford, in the instructive passage which I have quoted, exhorts us to the latter course. Believe nothing, he tells us, keep your mind in suspense forever, rather than by closing it on insufficient evidence incur the awful risk of believing lies. You, on the other hand, may think that the risk of being in error is a very small matter when compared with the blessings of real knowledge, and be ready to be duped many times in your investigation rather than postpone indefinitely the chance of guessing true. I myself find it impossible to go with Clifford. We must remember that these feelings of our duty about either truth or error are in any case only expressions of our passional life. Biologically considered, our minds are as ready to grind out falsehood as veracity, and he who says, "Better go without belief forever than believe a lie!" merely shows his own preponderant private horror of becoming a dupe. He may be critical of many of his desires and fears, but this fear he slavishly obeys. He cannot imagine any one questioning its binding force. For my own part, I have also a horror of being duped; but I can believe that worse things than being duped may happen to a man in this world: so Clifford's exhortation has to my ears a thoroughly fantastic sound. It is like a general informing his soldiers that it is better to keep out of battle forever than to risk a single wound. Not so are victories either over enemies or over nature gained. Our errors are surely not such awfully solemn things. In a world where we are so certain to incur them in spite of all our caution, a certain lightness of heart seems healthier than this excessive nervousness on their behalf. At any rate, it seems the fittest thing for the empiricist philosopher.

VIII

And now, after all this introduction, let us go straight at our question. I have said, and now repeat it, that not only as a matter of fact do we find our passional nature influencing us in our opinions, but that there are some options between opinions in which this influence must be regarded both as an inevitable and as a lawful determinant of our choice.

I fear here that some of you my hearers will begin to scent danger, and lend an inhospitable ear. Two first steps of passion you have indeed had to admit as necessary,—we must think so as to avoid dupery, and we must think so as to gain truth; but the surest path to those ideal consummations, you will probably consider, is from now onwards to take no further passional step.

Well, of course, I agree as far as the facts will allow. Wherever the option between losing truth and gaining it is not momentous, we can throw the chance of *gaining truth* away, and at any rate save ourselves from any chance of *believing falsehood*, by not making up our minds at all till objective evidence has come. In scientific questions, this is almost always the case; and even in human affairs in general, the need of acting is seldom so urgent that a false belief to act on is better than no belief at all. Law courts, indeed, have to decide on the best evidence attainable for the moment, because a judge's duty is to make law as well as to ascertain it, and (as a learned judge once said to me) few cases are worth spending much time over: the great thing is to have them decided on *any* acceptable principle, and got out of the way. But in our dealings with objective nature we obviously are re-corders, not makers, of the truth; and decisions for the mere sake of deciding promptly and getting on to the next business would be wholly out of place. Throughout the breadth of physical nature facts are what they are quite independently of us, and seldom is there any such hurry about them that the risks of being duped by believing a premature theory need be faced. The questions here are always trivial options, the hypotheses are hardly living (at any rate not living for us spectators), the choice between believing truth or falsehood is seldom forced. The attitude of sceptical balance is therefore the absolutely wise one if we would escape mistakes. What difference, indeed, does it make to most of us whether we have or have not a theory of the Röntgen rays, whether we believe or not in mind-stuff, or have a conviction about the causality of conscious states? It makes no difference.

Such options are not forced on us. On every account it is better not to make them, but still keep weighing reasons *pro et contra* with an indifferent hand.

I speak, of course, here of the purely judging mind. For purposes of discovery such indifference is to be less highly recommended, and science would be far less advanced than she is if the passionate desires of individuals to get their own faiths confirmed had been kept out of the game. See for example the sagacity which Spencer and Weismann now display. On the other hand, if you want an absolute duffer in an investigation, you must, after all, take the man who has no interest whatever in its results: he is the warranted incapable, the positive fool. The most useful investigator, because the most sensitive observer, is always he whose eager interest in one side of the question is balanced by an equally keen nervousness lest he become deceived. Science has organized this nervousness into a regular *technique,* her so-called method of verification; and she has fallen so deeply in love with the method that one may even say she has ceased to care for truth by itself at all. It is only truth as technically verified that interests her. The truth of truths might come in merely affirmative form, and she would decline to touch it. Such truth as that, she might repeat with Clifford, would be stolen in defiance of her duty to mankind. Human passions, however, are stronger than technical rules. "Le cœur a ses raisons," as Pascal says, "que la raison ne connaît pas;" and however indifferent to all but the bare rules of the game the umpire, the abstract intellect, may be, the concrete players who furnish him the materials to judge of are usually, each one of them, in love with some pet 'live hypothesis' of his own. Let us agree, however, that wherever there is no forced option, the dispassionately judicial intellect with no pet hypothesis, saving us, as it does, from dupery at any rate, ought to be our ideal.

The question next arises: Are there not somewhere forced options in our speculative questions, and can we (as men who may be interested at least as much in positively gaining truth as in merely escaping dupery) always wait with impunity till the coercive evidence shall have arrived? It seems *a priori* improbable that the truth should be so nicely adjusted to our needs and powers as that. In the great boarding-house of nature, the cakes and the butter and the syrup seldom come out so even and leave the plates so clean. Indeed, we should view them with scientific suspicion if they did.

IX

Moral questions immediately present themselves as questions whose solution cannot wait for sensible proof. A moral question is a question not of what sensibly exists, but of what is good, or would be good if it did exist. Science can tell us what exists; but to compare the *worths*, both of what exists and of what does not exist, we must consult not science, but what Pascal calls our heart. Science herself consults her heart when she lays it down that the infinite ascertainment of fact and correction of false belief are the supreme goods for man. Challenge the statement, and science can only repeat it oracularly, or else prove it by showing that such ascertainment and correction bring man all sorts of other goods which man's heart in turn declares. The question of having moral beliefs at all or not having them is decided by our will. Are our moral preferences true or false, or are they only odd biological phenomena, making things good or bad for *us,* but in themselves indifferent? How can your pure intellect decide? If your heart does not *want* a world of moral reality, your head will assuredly never make you believe in one. Mephistophelian scepticism, indeed, will satisfy the head's play-instincts much better than any rigorous idealism can. Some men (even at the student age) are so naturally cool-hearted that the moralistic hypothesis never has for them any pungent life, and in their supercilious presence the hot young moralist always feels strangely ill at ease. The appearance of knowingness is on their side, of *naïveté* and gullibility on his. Yet, in the inarticulate heart of him, he clings to it that he is not a dupe, and that there is a realm in which (as Emerson says) all their wit and intellectual superiority is no better than the cunning of a fox. Moral scepticism can no more be refuted or proved by logic than intellectual scepticism can. When we stick to it that there *is* truth (be it of either kind), we do so with our whole nature, and resolve to stand or fall by the results. The sceptic with his whole nature adopts the doubting attitude; but which of us is the wiser, Omniscience only knows.

Turn now from these wide questions of good to a certain class of questions of fact, questions concerning personal relations, states of mind between one man and another. *Do you like me or not?*— for example. Whether you do or not depends, in countless instances, on whether I meet you half-way, am willing to assume that you must like me, and show you trust and expectation. The previous faith on my part in your liking's existence is in such cases what makes your liking come. But if I stand aloof, and refuse to budge an inch until I have objective evidence, until you shall have done something apt, as the absolutists say, *ad extorquendum assensum meum,* ten to one your liking never comes. How many women's hearts are vanquished by the mere sanguine insistence of some man that they *must* love him! he will not consent to the hypothesis that they cannot. The desire for a certain kind of truth here brings about that special truth's existence; and so it is in innumerable cases of other sorts. Who gains promotions, boons, appointments, but the man in whose life they are seen to play the part of live hypotheses, who discounts them, sacrifices other things for their sake before they have come, and takes risks for them in advance? His faith acts on the powers above him as a claim, and creates its own verification.

A social organism of any sort whatever, large or small, is what it is because each member proceeds to his own duty with a trust that the other members will simultaneously do theirs. Wherever a desired result is achieved by the co-operation of many independent persons, its existence as a fact is a pure consequence of the precursive faith in one another of those immediately concerned. A government, an army, a commercial system, a ship, a college, an athletic team, all exist on this condition, without which not only is nothing achieved, but nothing is even attempted. A whole train of passengers (individually brave enough) will be looted by a few highwaymen, simply because the latter can count on one another, while each passenger fears that if he makes a movement of resistance, he will be shot before any one else backs him up. If we believed that the whole car-full would rise at once with us, we should each severally rise, and train-robbing would never even be attempted. There are, then, cases where a fact cannot come at all unless a preliminary faith exists in its coming. *And where faith in a fact can help create the fact,* that would be an insane logic which should say that faith running ahead of scientific evidence is the 'lowest kind of immorality' into which a thinking being can fall. Yet such is the logic by which our scientific absolutists pretend to regulate our lives!

X

In truths dependent on our personal action, then, faith based on desire is certainly a lawful and possibly an indispensable thing.

But now, it will be said, these are all childish human cases, and have nothing to do with great cosmical matters, like the question of religious faith. Let us then pass on to that. Religions differ so much in their accidents that in discussing the religious question we must make it very generic and broad. What then do we now mean by the religious hypothesis? Science says things are; morality says some things are better than other things; and religion says essentially two things.

First, she says that the best things are the more eternal things, the overlapping things, the things in the universe that throw the last stone, so to speak, and say the final word. "Perfection is eternal,"—this phrase of Charles Secrétan seems a good way of putting this first affirmation of religion, an affirmation which obviously cannot yet be verified scientifically at all.

The second affirmation of religion is that we are better off even now if we believe her first affirmation to be true.

Now, let us consider what the logical elements of this situation are *in case the religious hypothesis in both its branches be really true.* (Of course, we must admit that possibility at the outset. If we are to discuss the question at all, it must involve a living option. If for any of you religion be a hypothesis that cannot, by any living possibility be true, then you need go no farther. (I speak to the 'saving remnant' alone.) So proceeding, we see, first, that religion offers itself as a *momentous* option. We are supposed to gain, even now, by our belief, and to lose by our non-belief, a certain vital good. Secondly, religion is a *forced* option, so far as that good goes. We cannot escape the issue by remaining sceptical and waiting for more light, because, although we do avoid error in that way *if religion be untrue*, we lose the good, *if it be true*, just as certainly as if we positively chose to disbelieve. It is as if a man should hesitate indefinitely to ask a certain woman to marry him because he was not perfectly sure that she would prove an angel after he brought her home. Would he not cut himself off from that particular angel-possibility as decisively as if he went and married some one else? Scepticism, then, is not avoidance of option; it is option of a certain particular kind of risk. *Better risk loss of truth than chance of error,*—that is your faith-vetoer's exact position. He is actively playing his stake as much as the believer is; he is backing the field against the religious hypothesis, just as the believer is backing the religious hypothesis against the field. To preach scepticism to us as a duty until 'sufficient evidence' for religion be found, is tantamount therefore to telling us, when in presence of the religious hypothesis, that to yield to our fear of its being error is wiser and better than to yield to our hope that it may be true. It is not intellect against all passions, then; it is only intellect with one passion laying down its law. And by what, forsooth, is the supreme wisdom of this passion warranted? Dupery for dupery, what proof is there that dupery through hope is so much worse than dupery through fear? I, for one, can see no proof; and I simply refuse obedience to the scientist's command to imitate his kind of option, in a case where my own stake is important enough to give me the right to choose my own form of risk. If religion be true and the evidence for it be still insufficient, I do not wish, by putting your extinguisher upon my nature (which feels to me as if it had after all some business in this matter), to forfeit my sole chance in life of getting upon the winning side,—that chance depending, of course, on my willingness to run the risk of acting as if my passional need of taking the world religiously might be prophetic and right.

All this is on the supposition that it really may be prophetic and right, and that, even to us who are discussing the matter, religion is a live hypothesis which may be true. Now, to most of us religion comes in a still further way that makes a veto on our active faith even more illogical. The more perfect and more eternal aspect of the universe is represented in our religions as having personal form. The universe is no longer a mere *It* to us, but a *Thou*, if we are religious; and any relation that may be possible from person to person might be possible here. For instance, although in one sense we are passive portions of the universe, in another we show a curious autonomy, as if we were small active centres on our own account. We feel, too, as if the appeal of religion to us were made to our own active good-will, as if evidence might be forever withheld from us unless we met the hypothesis half-way. To take a trivial illustration: just as a man who in a company of gentlemen made no advances, asked a warrant for every concession, and believed no one's word without proof, would cut himself off by such churlishness from all the social rewards that a more trusting spirit would earn,—so here, one who should shut himself up in snarling logicality and try to make the gods extort his recognition willy-nilly, or not get it at all, might cut himself off forever from his only opportunity of making the gods' acquaintance. This feeling, forced on us we know not whence, that by obstinately believing that there are gods (although not to do so would be so easy both for our logic and our life) we are doing the universe the deepest service we can, seems part of the living essence of the religious hypothesis. If the hypothesis *were* true in all its parts, including this one, then pure intellectualism, with its veto on our making willing advances, would be an absurdity; and some participation of our sympathetic nature would be logically required. I, therefore, for one, cannot see my way to accepting the agnostic rules for truth-seeking, or wilfully agree to keep my willing nature out of the game. I cannot do so for this plain reason, that *a rule of thinking which would absolutely prevent me from acknowledging certain kinds of truth if those kinds of truth were really there, would be an irrational rule.* That for me is the long and short of the formal logic of the situation, no matter what the kinds of truth might materially be.

I confess I do not see how this logic can be escaped. But sad experience makes me fear that some of you may still shrink from radically saying with me, *in abstracto,* that we have the right to believe at our own risk any hypothesis that is live enough to tempt our will. I suspect, however, that if this is so, it is because you have got away from the abstract logical point of view altogether, and are thinking (perhaps without realizing it) of some particular religious hypothesis which for you is dead. The freedom to 'believe what we will' you apply to the case of some patent superstition; and the faith you think of is the faith defined by the schoolboy when he said, "Faith is when you believe something that you know ain't true." I can only repeat that this is misapprehension. *In concreto,* the freedom to believe can only cover living options which the intellect of the individual cannot by itself resolve; and living options never seem absurdities to him who has them to consider. When I look at the religious question as it really puts itself to concrete men, and when I think of all the possibilities which both practically and theoretically it involves, then this command that we shall put a stopper on our heart, instincts, and courage, and *wait*—acting of course meanwhile more or less as if religion were *not* true[1]—till doomsday,

---

[1] Since belief is measured by action, he who forbids us to believe religion to be true, necessarily also forbids us to act as we should if we did believe it to be true. The whole defence of religious faith hinges upon action. If the action required or inspired by the religious hypothesis is in no way different from that dictated by the naturalistic hypothesis, then religious faith is a pure superfluity, better pruned away, and controversy about its legitimacy is a piece of idle trifling, unworthy of serious minds. I myself believe, of course, that the religious hypothesis gives to the world an expression which specifically determines our reactions, and makes them in a large part unlike what they might be on a purely naturalistic scheme of belief.

or till such time as our intellect and senses working together may have raked in evidence enough,—this command, I say, seems to me the queerest idol ever manufactured in the philosophic cave. Were we scholastic absolutists, there might be more excuse. If we had an infallible intellect with its objective certitudes, we might feel ourselves disloyal to such a perfect organ of knowledge in not trusting to it exclusively, in not waiting for its releasing word. But if we are empiricists, if we believe that no bell in us tolls to let us know for certain when truth is in our grasp, then it seems a piece of idle fantasticality to preach so solemnly our duty of waiting for the bell. Indeed we *may* wait if we will,—I hope you do not think that I am denying that,—but if we do so, we do so at our peril as much as if we believed. In either case we *act,* taking our life in our hands. No one of us ought to issue vetoes to the other, nor should we bandy words of abuse. We ought, on the contrary, delicately and profoundly to respect one another's mental freedom: then only shall we bring about the intellectual republic; then only shall we have that spirit of inner tolerance without which all our outer tolerance is soulless, and which is empiricism's glory; then only shall we live and let live, in speculative as well as in practical things.

I began by a reference to Fitz James Stephen; let me end by a quotation from him. "What do you think of yourself? What do you think of the world? . . . These are questions with which all must deal as it seems good to them. They are riddles of the Sphinx, and in some way or other we must deal with them. . . . In all important transactions of life we have to take a leap in the dark. . . . If we decide to leave the riddles unanswered, that is a choice; if we waver in our answer, that, too, is a choice: but whatever choice we make, we make it at our peril. If a man chooses to turn his back altogether on God and the future, no one can prevent him; no one can show beyond reasonable doubt that he is mistaken. If a man thinks otherwise and acts as he thinks, I do not see that any one can prove that *he* is mistaken. Each must act as he thinks best; and if he is wrong, so much the worse for him. We stand on a mountain pass in the midst of whirling snow and blinding mist, through which we get glimpses

now and then of paths which may be deceptive. If we stand still
we shall be frozen to death. If we take the wrong road we shall
be dashed to pieces. We do not certainly know whether there
is any right one. What must we do? 'Be strong and of a good
courage.' Act for the best, hope for the best, and take what
comes. . . . If death ends all, we cannot meet death better."

WHAT PRAGMATISM MEANS

Some years ago, being with a camping party in the mountains, I
returned from a solitary ramble to find every one engaged in a fero-
cious metaphysical dispute. The *corpus* of the dispute was a squirrel
—a live squirrel supposed to be clinging to one side of a tree-trunk;
while over against the tree's opposite side a human being was imagined to stand. This human witness tries to get sight of the squirrel
by moving rapidly round the tree, but no matter how fast he goes,
the squirrel moves as fast in the opposite direction, and always keeps
the tree between himself and the man, so that never a glimpse of
him is caught. The resultant metaphysical problem is this: *Does the
man go round the squirrel or not?* He goes round the tree, sure
enough, and the squirrel is on the tree; but does he go round the
squirrel? In the unlimited leisure of the wilderness, discussion had
been worn threadbare. Every one had taken sides, and was obstinate;
and the numbers on both sides were even. Each side, when I appeared, therefore appealed to me to make it a majority. Mindful of
the scholastic adage that whenever you meet a contradiction you
must make a distinction, I immediately sought and found one, as
follows: "Which party is right," I said, "depends on what you *practically mean* by 'going round' the squirrel. If you mean passing from
the north of him to the east, then to the south, then to the west, and
then to the north of him again, obviously the man does go round

Lecture II of *Pragmatism: A New Name for Some Old Ways of Thinking,* pp. 43-81, by William James. Copyright, 1907, Longmans, Green
& Co., Inc.; reprinted by permission.

him, for he occupies these successive positions. But if on the contrary you mean being first in front of him, then on the right of him, then behind him, then on his left, and finally in front again, it is quite as obvious that the man fails to go round him, for by the compensating movements the squirrel makes, he keeps his belly turned towards the man all the time, and his back turned away. Make the distinction, and there is no occasion for any further dispute. You are both right and both wrong according as you conceive the verb 'to go round' in one practical fashion or the other."

Although one or two of the hotter disputants called my speech a shuffling evasion, saying they wanted no quibbling or scholastic hair-splitting, but meant just plain honest English "round," the majority seemed to think that the distinction had assuaged the dispute.

I tell this trivial anecdote because it is a peculiarly simple example of what I wish now to speak of as *the pragmatic method*. The pragmatic method is primarily a method of settling metaphysical disputes that otherwise might be interminable. Is the world one or many?—fated or free?—material or spiritual?—here are notions either of which may or may not hold good of the world; and disputes over such notions are unending. The pragmatic method in such cases is to try to interpret each notion by tracing its respective practical consequences. What difference would it practically make to any one if this notion rather than that notion were true? If no practical difference whatever can be traced, then the alternatives mean practically the same thing, and all dispute is idle. Whenever a dispute is serious, we ought to be able to show some practical difference that must follow from one side or the other's being right.

A glance at the history of the idea will show you still better what pragmatism means. The term is derived from the same Greek word πράγμα, meaning action, from which our words "practice" and "practical" come. It was first introduced into philosophy by Mr. Charles Peirce in 1878. In an article entitled "How to Make Our Ideas Clear," in the *Popular Science Monthly* for January of that year Mr. Peirce, after pointing out that our beliefs are really rules for action, said that, to develop a thought's meaning, we need only determine what conduct it is fitted to produce: that conduct is for us its sole significance. And the tangible fact at the root of all our thought-distinctions, however subtle, is that there is no one of them so fine as to consist in anything but a possible difference of practice. To attain perfect clearness in our thoughts of an object, then, we need only consider what conceivable effects of a practical kind the object may involve—what sensations we are to expect from it, and what reactions we must prepare. Our conception of these effects, whether immediate or remote, is then for us the whole of our conception of the object, so far as that conception has positive significance at all.

This is the principle of Peirce, the principle of pragmatism. It lay entirely unnoticed by any one for twenty years, until I, in an address before Professor Howison's Philosophical Union at the University of California, brought it forward again and made a special application of it to religion. By that date (1898) the times seemed ripe for its reception. The word "pragmatism" spread, and at present it fairly spots the pages of the philosophic journals. On all hands we find the "pragmatic movement" spoken of, sometimes with respect, sometimes with contumely, seldom with clear understanding. It is evident that the term applies itself conveniently to a number of tendencies that hitherto have lacked a collective name, and that it has "come to stay."

To take in the importance of Peirce's principle, one must get accustomed to applying it to concrete cases. I found a few years ago that Ostwald, the illustrious Leipzig chemist, had been making perfectly distinct use of the principle of pragmatism in his lectures on the philosophy of science, though he had not called it by that name.

"All realities influence our practice," he wrote me, "and that influence is their meaning for us. I am accustomed to put questions to my classes in this way: In what respects would the world be different if this alternative or that were true? If I can find nothing that would become different, then the alternative has no sense."

That is, the rival views mean practically the same thing, and meaning, other than practical, there is for us none. Ostwald in a published lecture gives this example of what he means. Chemists have long wrangled over the inner constitution of certain bodies called "tautomerous." Their properties seemed equally consistent with the notion that an instable hydrogen atom oscillates inside of them, or that they are instable mixtures of two bodies. Controversy raged, but never was decided. "It would never have begun," says Ostwald, "if the combatants had asked themselves what particular experimental fact could have been made different by one or the other view being correct. For it would then have appeared that no difference of fact could possibly ensue; and the quarrel was as unreal as if, theorizing in primitive times about the raising of dough by yeast, one party should have invoked a 'brownie,' while another insisted on an 'elf' as the true cause of the phenomenon."

It is astonishing to see how many philosophical disputes collapse into insignificance the moment you subject them to this simple test of tracing a concrete consequence. There can *be* no difference anywhere that doesn't *make* a difference elsewhere—no difference in abstract truth that doesn't express itself in a difference in concrete fact and in conduct consequent upon that fact, imposed on somebody, somehow, somewhere, and somewhen. The whole function of philosophy ought to be to find out what definite difference it will make to you and me, at definite instants of our life, if this world-formula or that world-formula be the true one.

There is absolutely nothing new in the pragmatic method. Socrates was an adept at it. Aristotle used it methodically. Locke, Berkeley, and Hume made momentous contributions to truth by its means. Shadworth Hodgson keeps insisting that realities are only what they are "known as." But these forerunners of pragmatism used it in fragments: they were preluders only. Not until in our time has it generalized itself, become conscious of a universal mission, pretended to a conquering destiny. I believe in that destiny, and I hope I may end by inspiring you with my belief.

Pragmatism represents a perfectly familiar attitude in philosophy, the empiricist attitude, but it represents it, as it seems to me, both in a more radical and in a less objectionable form than it has ever yet assumed. A pragmatist turns his back resolutely and once for all upon a lot of inveterate habits dear to professional philosophers. He turns away from abstraction and insufficiency, from verbal solutions, from bad *a priori* reasons, from fixed principles, closed systems, and pretended absolutes and origins. He turns towards concreteness and adequacy, towards facts, towards action and towards power. That means the empiricist temper regnant and the rationalist temper sincerely given up. It means the open air and possibilities of nature, as against dogma, artificiality, and the pretence of finality in truth.

At the same time it does not stand for any special results. It is a method only. But the general triumph of that method would mean an enormous change in what I called in my last lecture the "temperament" of philosophy. Teachers of the ultra-rationalistic type would be frozen out, much as the courtier type is frozen out in republics, as the ultramontane type of priest is frozen out in protestant lands. Science and metaphysics would come much nearer together, would in fact work absolutely hand in hand.

Metaphysics has usually followed a very primitive kind of quest. You know how men have always hankered after unlawful magic, and you know what a great part in magic *words* have always played. If you have his name, or the formula of incantation that binds him, you can control the spirit, genie, afrite, or whatever the power may be. Solomon knew the names of all the spirits, and having their names, he held them subject to his will. So the universe has always appeared to the natural mind as a kind of enigma, of which the key must be sought in the shape of some illuminating or power-bringing word or name. That word names the universe's *principle,* and to possess it is after a fashion to possess the universe itself. "God," "Matter," "Reason," "the Absolute," "Energy," are so many solving names. You can rest when you have them. You are at the end of your metaphysical quest.

But if you follow the pragmatic method, you cannot look on any such word as closing your quest. You must bring out of each word its practical cash-value, set it at work within the stream of your experience. It appears less as a solution, then, than as a program for more work, and more particularly as an indication of the ways in which existing realities may be *changed.*

Theories thus become instruments, not answers to enigmas, in which we can rest. We don't lie back upon them, we move forward, and, on occasion, make nature over again by their aid. Pragmatism unstiffens all our theories, limbers them up and sets each one at work. Being nothing essentially new, it harmonizes with many ancient philosophic tendencies. It agrees with nominalism, for instance, in always appealing to particulars; with utilitarianism in emphasizing practical aspects; with positivism in its disdain for verbal solutions, useless questions and metaphysical abstractions.

All these, you see, are *anti-intellectualist* tendencies. Against rationalism as a pretension and a method pragmatism is fully armed and militant. But, at the outset, at least, it stands for no particular results. It has no dogmas, and no doctrines save its method. As the young Italian pragmatist Papini has well said, it lies in the midst of our theories, like a corridor in a hotel. Innumerable chambers open out of it. In one you may find a man writing an atheistic volume; in the next some one on his knees praying for faith and strength; in a third a chemist investigating a body's properties. In a fourth a system of idealistic metaphysics is being excogitated; in a fifth the impossibility of metaphysics is being shown. But they all own the corridor, and all must pass through it if they want a practicable way of getting into or out of their respective rooms.

No particular results then, so far, but only an attitude of orientation, is what the pragmatic method means. *The attitude of looking away from first things, principles, "categories," supposed necessities; and of looking towards last things, fruits, consequences, facts.*

So much for the pragmatic method! You may say that I have been praising it rather than explaining it to you, but I shall presently explain it abundantly enough by showing how it works on some familiar problems. Meanwhile the word pragmatism has come to be used in a still wider sense, as meaning also a certain *theory of truth*. I mean to give a whole lecture to the statement of that theory, after first paving the way, so I can be very brief now. But brevity is hard to follow, so I ask for your redoubled attention for a quarter of an hour. If much remains obscure, I hope to make it clearer in the later lectures.

One of the most successfully cultivated branches of philosophy in our time is what is called inductive logic, the study of the conditions under which our sciences have evolved. Writers on this subject have begun to show a singular unanimity as to what the laws of nature and elements of fact mean, when formulated by mathematicians, physicists and chemists. When the first mathematical, logical, and natural uniformities, the first *laws*, were discovered, men were so carried away by the clearness, beauty and simplification that resulted, that they believed themselves to have deciphered authentically the eternal thoughts of the Almighty. His mind also thundered and reverberated in syllogisms. He also thought in comic sections, squares and roots and ratios, and geometrized like Euclid. He made Kepler's laws for the planets to follow; he made velocity increase proportionally to the time in falling bodies; he made the law of the sines for light to obey when refracted; he established the classes, orders, families and genera of plants and animals, and fixed the distances between them. He thought the archetypes of all things, and devised their variations; and when we rediscover any one of these his wondrous institutions, we seize his mind in its very literal intention.

But as the sciences have developed further, the notion has gained ground that most, perhaps all, of our laws are only approximations. The laws themselves, moreover, have grown so numerous that there is no counting them; and so many rival formulations are proposed in all the branches of science that investigators have become accustomed to the notion that no theory is absolutely a transcript of reality, but that any one of them may from some point of view be useful. Their great use is to summarize old facts and to lead to new ones. They are only a man-made language, a conceptual shorthand, as some one calls them, in which we write our reports of nature; and languages, as is well known, tolerate much choice of expression and many dialects.

Thus human arbitrariness has driven divine necessity from scientific logic. If I mention the names of Sigwart, Mach, Ostwald, Pearson, Milhaud, Poincaré, Duhem, Ruyssen, those of you who are students will easily identify the tendency I speak of, and will think of additional names.

Riding now on the front of this wave of scientific logic Messrs. Schiller and Dewey appear with their pragmatistic account of what truth everywhere signifies. Everywhere, these teachers say, "truth" in our ideas and beliefs means the same thing that it means in science. It means, they say, nothing but this, *that ideas (which themselves are but parts of our experience) become true just in so far as they help us to get into satisfactory relation with other parts of our experience,* to summarize them and get about among them by conceptual short-cuts instead of following the interminable succession of particular phenomena. Any idea upon which we can ride, so to speak; any idea that will carry us prosperously from any one part of our experience to any other part, linking things satisfactorily, working securely, simplifying, saving labor; is true for just so much, true in so far forth, true *instrumentally.* This is the "instrumental" view of truth taught so successfully at Chicago, the view that truth in our ideas means their power to "work," promulgated so brilliantly at Oxford.

Messrs. Dewey, Schiller, and their allies, in reaching this general conception of all truth, have only followed the example of geologists, biologists and philologists. In the establishment of these other sciences, the successful stroke was always to take some simple process actually observable in operation—as denudation by weather, say, or variation from parental type, or change of dialect by incorporation of new words and pronunciations—and then to generalize it, making it apply to all times, and produce great results by summating its effects through the ages.

The observable process which Schiller and Dewey particularly singled out for generalization is the familiar one by which any individual settles into *new opinions.* The process here is always the same. The individual has a stock of old opinions already, but he meets a new experience that puts them to a strain. Somebody contradicts them; or in a reflective moment he discovers that they contradict each other; or he hears of facts with which they are incompatible; or desires arise in him which they cease to satisfy. The result is an inward trouble to which his mind till then had been a stranger, and from which he seeks to escape by modifying his previous mass of opinions. He saves as much of it as he can, for in this matter of belief we are all extreme conservatives. So he tries to change first this opinion, and then that (for they resist change very variously), until at last some new idea comes up which he can graft upon the ancient stock with a minimum of disturbance of the latter, some idea that mediates between the stock and the new experience and runs them into one another most felicitously and expediently.

This new idea is then adopted as the true one. It preserves the older stock of truths with a minimum of modification, stretching them just enough to make them admit the novelty, but conceiving that in ways as familiar as the case leaves possible. An *outrée* explanation, violating all our preconceptions, would never pass for a true account of a novelty. We should scratch round industriously till we found something less excentric. The most violent revolutions in an individual's beliefs leave most of his old order standing. Time and space, cause and effect, nature and history, and one's own biography remain untouched. New truth is always a go-between, a smoother-over of transitions. It marries old opinion to new fact so as ever to show a minimum of jolt, a maximum of continuity. We hold a theory true just in proportion to its success in solving this "problem of maxima and minima." But success in solving this problem is eminently a matter of approximation. We say this theory solves it on the whole more satisfactorily than that theory; but that means more satisfactorily to ourselves, and individuals will emphasize their points of satisfaction differently. To a certain degree, therefore, everything here is plastic.

The point I now urge you to observe particularly is the part played by the older truths. Failure to take account of it is the source of much of the unjust criticism levelled against pragmatism. Their influence is absolutely controlling. Loyalty to them is the first principle—in most cases it is the only principle; for by far the most usual way of handling phenomena so novel that they would make for a serious rearrangement of our preconception is to ignore them altogether, or to abuse those who bear witness for them.

You doubtless wish examples of this process of truth's growth, and the only trouble is their superabundance. The simplest case of new truth is of course the mere numerical addition of new kinds of facts, or of new single facts of old kinds, to our experience—an addition that involves no alteration in the old beliefs. Day follows day, and its contents are simply added. The new contents themselves are not true, they simply *come* and *are*. Truth is *what we say about* them, and when we say that they have come, truth is satisfied by the plain additive formula.

But often the day's contents oblige a rearrangement. If I should now utter piercing shrieks and act like a maniac on this platform, it would make many of you revise your ideas as to the probable worth of my philosophy. "Radium" came the other day as part of the day's content, and seemed for a moment to contradict our ideas of the whole order of nature, that order having come to be identified with what is called the conservation of energy. The mere sight of radium paying heat away indefinitely out of its own pocket seemed to violate that conservation. What to think? If the radiations from it were nothing but an escape of unsuspected "potential" energy, pre-existent inside of the atoms, the principle of conservation would be saved. The discovery of "helium" as the radiation's outcome, opened a way to this belief. So Ramsay's view is generally held to be true, because, although it extends our old ideas of energy, it causes a minimum of alteration in their nature.

I need not multiply instances. A new opinion counts as "true" just in proportion as it gratifies the individual's desire to assimilate the novel in his experience to his beliefs in stock. It must both lean on old truth and grasp new fact; and its success (as I said a moment ago) in doing this, is a matter for the individual's appreciation. When old truth grows, then, by new truth's addition, it is for subjective reasons. We are in the process and obey the reasons. That new idea is truest which performs most felicitously its function of satisfying our double urgency. It makes itself true, gets itself classed as true, by the way it works; grafting itself then upon the ancient body of truth, which thus grows much as a tree grows by the activity of a new layer of cambium.

Now Dewey and Schiller proceed to generalize this observation and to apply it to the most ancient parts of truth. They also once were plastic. They also were called true for human reasons. They also mediated between still earlier truths and what in those days were novel observations. Purely objective truth, truth in whose establishment the function of giving human satisfaction in marrying previous parts of experience with newer parts played no rôle whatever, is nowhere to be found. The reasons why we call things true is the reason why they *are* true, for "to be true" *means* only to perform this marriage-function.

The trail of the human serpent is thus over everything. Truth independent; truth that we *find* merely; truth no longer malleable to human need; truth incorrigible, in a word; such truth exists indeed superabundantly—or is supposed to exist by rationalistically minded thinkers; but then it means only the dead heart of the living tree, and its being there means only that truth also has its paleontology, and its "prescription," and may grow stiff with years of veteran service and petrified in men's regard by sheer antiquity. But how plastic even the oldest truths nevertheless really are has been vividly shown in our day by the transformation of logical and mathematical ideas, a transformation which seems even to be invading physics. The ancient formulas are reinterpreted as special expressions of much wider principles, principles that our ancestors never got a glimpse of in their present shape and formulation.

Mr. Schiller still gives to all this view of truth the name of "Humanism," but, for this doctrine too, the name of pragmatism seems fairly to be in the ascendant, so I will treat it under the name of pragmatism in these lectures.

Such then would be the scope of pragmatism—first, a method; and second, a genetic theory of what is meant by truth. And these two things must be our future topics.

What I have said of the theory of truth will, I am sure, have appeared obscure and unsatisfactory to most of you by reason of its brevity. I shall make amends for that hereafter. In a lecture on "common sense" I shall try to show what I mean by truths grown petrified by antiquity. In another lecture I shall expatiate on the idea that our thoughts become true in proportion as they successfully exert their go-between function. In a third I shall show how hard it is to discriminate subjective from objective factors in Truth's development. You may not follow me wholly in these lectures; and if you do, you may not wholly agree with me. But you will, I know, regard me at least as serious, and treat my effort with respectful consideration.

You will probably be surprised to learn, then, that Messrs. Schiller's and Dewey's theories have suffered a hailstorm of contempt and ridicule. All rationalism has risen against them. In influential quarters Mr. Schiller, in particular, has been treated like an impudent schoolboy who deserves a spanking. I should not mention this but for the fact that it throws so much sidelight upon that rationalistic temper to which I have opposed the temper of pragmatism. Pragmatism is uncomfortable away from facts. Rationalism is comfortable only in the presence of abstractions. This pragmatist talk about truths in the plural, about their utility and satisfactoriness, about the success with which they "work," etc., suggests to the typical intellectualist mind a sort of coarse lame second-rate makeshift article of truth. Such truths are not real truth. Such tests are merely subjective. As against this, objective truth must be something non-utilitarian, haughty, refined, remote, august, exalted. It must be an absolute correspondence of our thoughts with an equally absolute reality. It must be what we *ought* to think unconditionally. The conditioned ways in which we *do* think are so much irrelevance and matter for psychology. Down with psychology, up with logic, in all this question!

See the exquisite contrast of the types of mind! The pragmatist clings to facts and concreteness, observes truth at its work in particular cases, and generalizes. Truth, for him, becomes a class-name for all sorts of definite working-values in experience. For the rationalist it remains a pure abstraction, to the bare name of which we must defer. When the pragmatist undertakes to show in detail just *why* we must defer, the rationalist is unable to recognize the concretes from which his own abstraction is taken. He accuses us of *denying* truth; whereas we have only sought to trace exactly why people follow it and always ought to follow it. Your typical ultra-abstractionist fairly shudders at concreteness: other things equal, he positively prefers the pale and spectral. If the two universes were offered, he would always choose the skinny outline rather than the rich thicket of reality. It is so much purer, clearer, nobler.

I hope that as these lectures go on, the concreteness and closeness to facts of the pragmatism which they advocate may be what approves itself to you as its most satisfactory peculiarity. It only follows here the example of the sister-sciences, interpreting the unobserved by the observed. It brings old and new harmoniously together. It converts the absolutely empty notion of a static relation of "correspondence" (what that may mean we must ask later) between our minds and reality, into that of a rich and active commerce (that any one may follow in detail and understand) between particular thoughts of ours, and the great universe of other experiences in which they play their parts and have their uses.

But enough of this at present. The justification of what I say must be postponed. I wish now to add a word in further explanation of the claim I made at our last meeting, that pragmatism may be a happy harmonizer of empiricist ways of thinking with the more religious demands of human beings.

Men who are strongly of the fact-loving temperament, you may remember me to have said, are liable to be kept at a distance by the small sympathy with facts which that philosophy from the present-day fashion of idealism offers them. It is far too intellectualistic. Old fashioned theism was bad enough, with its notion of God as an exalted monarch, made up of a lot of unintelligible or preposterous "attributes"; but, so long as it held strongly by the argument from design, it kept some touch with concrete realities. Since, however, Darwinism has once for all displaced design from the minds of the "scientific," theism has lost that foothold; and some kind of an immanent or pantheistic deity working *in* things rather than above them is, if any, the kind recommended to our contemporary imagination. Aspirants to a philosophic religion turn, as a rule, more hopefully nowadays towards idealistic pantheism than towards the older dualistic theism, in spite of the fact that the latter still counts able defenders.

But, as I said in my first lecture, the brand of pantheism offered is hard for them to assimilate if they are lovers of facts, or empirically minded. It is the absolutistic brand, spurning the dust and reared upon pure logic. It keeps no connexion whatever with concreteness. Affirming the Absolute Mind, which is its substitute for God, to be the rational presupposition of all particulars of fact, whatever they may be, it remains supremely indifferent to what the particular facts in our world actually are. Be they what they may, the

Absolute will father them. Like the sick lion in Esop's fable, all footprints lead into his den, but *nulla vestigia retrorsum*. You cannot redescend into the world of particulars by the Absolute's aid, or deduce any necessary consequences of detail important for your life from your idea of his nature. He gives you indeed the assurance that all is well with *Him*, and for his eternal way of thinking; but thereupon he leaves you to be finitely saved by your own temporal devices.

Far be it from me to deny the majesty of this conception, or its capacity to yield religious comfort to a most respectable class of minds. But from the human point of view, no one can pretend that it doesn't suffer from the faults of remoteness and abstractness. It is eminently a product of what I have ventured to call the rationalistic temper. It disdains empiricism's needs. It substitutes a pallid outline for the real world's richness. It is dapper, it is noble in the bad sense, in the sense in which to be noble is to be inapt for humble service. In this real world of sweat and dirt, it seems to me that when a view of things is "noble," that ought to count as a presumption against its truth, and as a philosophic disqualification. The prince of darkness may be a gentleman, as we are told he is, but whatever the God of earth and heaven is, he can surely be no gentleman. His menial services are needed in the dust of our human trials, even more than his dignity is needed in the empyrean.

Now pragmatism, devoted though she be to facts, has no such materialistic bias as ordinary empiricism labors under. Moreover, she has no objection whatever to the realizing of abstractions, so long as you get about among particulars with their aid and they actually carry you somewhere. Interested in no conclusions but those which our minds and our experiences work out together, she has no *a priori* prejudices against theology. *If theological ideas prove to have a value for concrete life, they will be true, for pragmatism, in the sense of being good for so much. For how much more they are true, will depend entirely on their relations to the other truths that also have to be acknowledged.*

What I said just now about the Absolute, of transcendental idealism, is a case in point. First, I called it majestic and said it yielded religious comfort to a class of minds, and then I accused it of remoteness and sterility. But so far as it affords such comfort, it surely is not sterile; it has that amount of value; it performs a concrete function. As a good pragmatist, I myself ought to call the Absolute true "in so far forth," then; and I unhesitatingly now do so.

But what does *true in so far forth* mean in this case? To answer, we need only apply the pragmatic method. What do believers in the Absolute mean by saying that their belief affords them comfort? They mean that since, in the Absolute finite evil is "overruled" already, we may, therefore, whenever we wish, treat the temporal as if it were potentially the eternal, be sure that we can trust its outcome, and, without sin, dismiss our fear and drop the worry of our finite responsibility. In short, they mean that we have a right ever and anon to take a moral holiday, to let the world wag in its own way, feeling that its issues are in better hands than ours and are none of our business.

The universe is a system of which the individual members may relax their anxieties occasionally, in which the don't-care mood is also right for men, and moral holidays in order—that, if I mistake not, is part, at least, of what the Absolute is "known-as," that is the great difference in our particular experiences which his being true makes, for us, that is his cash-value when he is pragmatically interpreted. Farther than that the ordinary lay-reader in philosophy who thinks favorably of absolute idealism does not venture to sharpen his conceptions. He can use the Absolute for so much, and so much is very precious. He is pained at hearing you speak incredulously of the Absolute, therefore, and disregards your criticisms because they deal with aspects of the conception that he fails to follow.

If the Absolute means this, and means no more than this, who can possibly deny the truth of it? To deny it would be to insist that men should never relax, and that holidays are never in order.

I am well aware how odd it must seem to some of you to hear me say that an idea is "true" so long as to believe it is profitable to our lives. That it is *good,* for as much as it profits, you will gladly admit. If what we do by its aid is good, you will allow the idea itself to be good in so far forth, for we are the better for possessing it. But is it not a strange misuse of the word "truth," you will say, to call ideas also "true" for this reason?

To answer this difficulty fully is impossible at this stage of my account. You touch here upon the very central point of Messrs. Schiller's, Dewey's, and my own doctrine of truth, which I cannot discuss with detail until my sixth lecture. Let me now say only this, that truth is *one species of good*, and not, as is usually supposed, a category distinct from good, and co-ordinate with it. *The true is the name of whatever proves itself to be good in the way of belief, and good, too, for definite, assignable reasons.* Surely you must admit this, that if there were *no* good for life in true ideas, or if the knowledge of them were positively disadvantageous and false ideas the only useful ones, then the current notion that truth is divine and precious, and its pursuit a duty, could never have grown up or become a dogma. In a world like that, our duty would be to *shun* truth, rather. But in this world, just as certain foods are not only agreeable to our taste, but good for our teeth, our stomach, and our tissues; so certain ideas are not only agreeable to think about, or agreeable as supporting other ideas that we are fond of, but they are also helpful in life's practical struggles. If there be any life that it is really better we should lead, and if there be any idea which, if believed in, would help us to lead that life, then it would be really *better for us* to believe in that idea, *unless, indeed, belief in it incidentally clashed with other greater vital benefits.*

"What would be better for us to believe!" This sounds very like a definition of truth. It comes very near to saying "what we *ought* to believe"; and in *that* definition none of you would find any oddity. Ought we ever not to believe what it is *better for us* to believe? And can we then keep the notion of what is better for us, and what is true for us, permanently apart?

Pragmatism says no, and I fully agree with her. Probably you also agree, so far as the abstract statement goes, but with a suspicion that if we practically did believe everything that made for good in our own personal lives, we should be found indulging all kinds of fancies about this world's affairs, and all kinds of sentimental superstitions about a world hereafter. Your suspicion here is undoubtedly well founded, and it is evident that something happens when you pass from the abstract to the concrete that complicates the situation.

I said just now that what is better for us to believe is true *unless the belief incidentally clashes with some other vital benefit.* Now in real life what vital benefits is any particular belief of ours most liable to clash with? What indeed except the vital benefits yielded by *other beliefs* when these prove incompatible with the first ones? In other words, the greatest enemy of any one of our truths may be the rest of our truths. Truths have once for all this desperate instinct of self-preservation and of desire to extinguish whatever contradicts them. My belief in the Absolute, based on the good it does me, must run the gauntlet of all my other beliefs. Grant that it may be true in giving me a moral holiday. Nevertheless, as I conceive it —and let me speak now confidentially, as it were, and merely in my own private person—it clashes with other truths of mine whose benefits I hate to give up on its account. It happens to be associated with a kind of logic of which I am the enemy, I find that it entangles me in metaphysical paradoxes that are inacceptable, etc., etc. But as I have enough trouble in life already without adding the trouble of carrying these intellectual inconsistencies, I personally just give up the Absolute. I just *take* my moral holidays; or else as a professional philosopher, I try to justify them by some other principle.

If I could restrict my notion of the Absolute to its bare holiday-giving value, it wouldn't clash with my other truths. But we cannot easily thus restrict our hypotheses. They carry supernumerary features, and these it is that clash so. My disbelief in the Absolute means then disbelief in those other supernumerary features, for I fully believe in the legitimacy of taking moral holidays.

You see by this what I meant when I called pragmatism a mediator and reconciler and said, borrowing the word from Papini, that she "unstiffens" our theories. She has in fact no prejudices whatever, no obstructive dogmas, no rigid canons of what shall count as proof. She is completely genial. She will entertain any hypothesis, she will consider any evidence. It follows that in the religious field she is at a great advantage both over positivistic empiricism, with its anti-theological bias, and over religious rationalism, with its exclusive interest in the remote, the noble, the simple, and the abstract in the way of conception.

In short, she widens the field of search for God. Rationalism sticks to logic and the empyrean. Empiricism sticks to the external senses. Pragmatism is willing to take anything, to follow either logic or the senses and to count the humblest and most personal experiences. She will count mystical experiences if they have practical consequences. She will take a God who lives in the very dirt of private fact—if that should seem a likely place to find him.

Her only test of probable truth is what works best in the way of leading us, what fits every part of life best and combines with the collectivity of experience's demands, nothing being omitted. If theological ideas should do this, if the notion of God, in particular, should prove to do it, how could pragmatism possibly deny God's existence? She could see no meaning in treating as "not true" a notion that was pragmatically so successful. What other kind of truth could there be, for her, than all this agreement with concrete reality?

·VIII·

OLIVER WENDELL HOLMES

[1 8 4 1 - 1 9 3 5]

THE PATH OF THE LAW

NATURAL LAW

THE PATH OF THE LAW

When we study law we are not studing a mystery but a well-known profession. We are studying what we shall want in order to appear before judges, or to advise people in such a way as to keep them out of court. The reason why it is a profession, why people will pay lawyers to argue for them or to advise them, is that in societies like ours the command of the public force is intrusted to the judges in certain cases, and the whole power of the state will be put forth, if necessary, to carry out their judgments and decrees. People want to know under what circumstances and how far they will run the risk of coming against what is so much stronger than themselves, and hence it becomes a business to find out when this danger is to be feared. The object of our study, then, is prediction, the prediction of the incidence of the public force through the instrumentality of the courts.

The means of the study are a body of reports, of treatises, and of statutes, in this country and in England, extending back for six hundred years, and now increasing annually by hundreds. In these sibylline leaves are gathered the scattered prophecies of the past upon the cases in which the axe will fall. These are what properly have been called the oracles of the law. Far the most important and pretty nearly the whole meaning of every new effort of legal thought is to make these prophecies more precise, and to generalize them into a thoroughly connected system. The process is one, from a lawyer's statement of a case, eliminating as it does all the dramatic elements with which his client's story has clothed it, and retaining only the facts of legal import, up to the final analyses and abstract universals of theoretic jurisprudence. The reason why a lawyer does not mention that his client wore a white hat when he made a contract, while

An address delivered at the Boston University School of Law, January 8, 1897; from *Collected Legal Papers*, pp. 167-202, by Oliver Wendell Holmes. Copyright, 1920, Harcourt, Brace and Company, Inc.; reprinted by permission.

Mrs. Quickly would be sure to dwell upon it along with the parcel gilt goblet and the sea-coal fire, is that he foresees that the public force will act in the same way whatever his client had upon his head. It is to make the prophecies easier to be remembered and to be understood that the teachings of the decisions of the past are put into general propositions and gathered into text-books, or that statutes are passed in a general form. The primary rights and duties with which jurisprudence busies itself again are nothing but prophecies. One of the many evil effects of the confusion between legal and moral ideas, about which I shall have something to say in a moment, is that theory is apt to get the cart before the horse, and to consider the right or the duty as something existing apart from and independent of the consequences of its breach, to which certain sanctions are added afterward. But, as I shall try to show, a legal duty so called is nothing but a prediction that if a man does or omits certain things he will be made to suffer in this or that way by judgment of the court; and so of a legal right.

The number of our predictions when generalized and reduced to a system is not unmanageably large. They present themselves as a finite body of dogma which may be mastered within a reasonable time. It is a great mistake to be frightened by the ever-increasing number of reports. The reports of a given jurisdiction in the course of a generation take up pretty much the whole body of the law, and restate it from the present point of view. We could reconstruct the corpus from them if all that went before were burned. The use of the earlier reports is mainly historical, a use about which I shall have something to say before I have finished.

I wish, if I can, to lay down some first principles for the study of this body of dogma or systematized prediction which we call the law, for men who want to use it as the instrument of their business to enable them to prophesy in their turn, and, as bearing upon the study, I wish to point out an ideal which as yet our law has not attained.

The first thing for a business-like understanding of the matter is to understand its limits, and therefore I think it desirable at once to point out and dispel a confusion between morality and law, which sometimes rises to the height of conscious theory, and more often and indeed constantly is making trouble in detail without reaching the point of consciousness. You can see very plainly that a bad man has as much reason as a good one for wishing to avoid an encounter with the public force, and therefore you can see the practical importance of the distinction between morality and law. A man who cares nothing for an ethical rule which is believed and practised by his neighbors is likely nevertheless to care a good deal to avoid being made to pay money, and will want to keep out of jail if he can.

I take it for granted that no hearer of mine will misinterpret what I have to say as the language of cynicism. The law is the witness and external deposit of our moral life. Its history is the history of the moral development of the race. The practice of it, in spite of popular jests, tends to make good citizens and good men. When I emphasize the difference between law and morals I do so with reference to a single end, that of learning and understanding the law. For that purpose you must definitely master its specific marks, and it is for that I ask you for the moment to imagine yourselves indifferent to other and greater things.

I do not say that there is not a wider point of view from which the distinction between law and morals becomes of secondary or no importance, as all mathematical distinctions vanish in presence of the infinite. But I do say that that distinction is of the first importance for the object which we are here to consider—a right study and mastery of the law as a business with well understood limits, a body of dogma enclosed within definite lines. I have just shown the practical reason for saying so. If you want to know the law and nothing else, you must look at it as a bad man, who cares only for the material consequences which such knowledge enables him to predict, not as a good one, who finds his reasons for conduct, whether inside the law or outside of it, in the vaguer sanctions of conscience. The theoretical importance of the distinction is no less, if you would reason on your subject aright. The law is full of phraseology drawn from morals, and by the mere force of language continually invites us to pass from one domain to the other without perceiving it, as we are sure to do unless we have the boundary constantly before our minds. The law talks about rights, and duties, and malice, and intent, and negligence, and so forth, and nothing is easier, or, I may say, more common in legal reasoning, than to take these words in their moral senses at some stage of the argument, and so drop into fallacy. For instance, when we speak of the rights of man in a moral sense, we mean to mark the limits of interference with individual freedom which we think are prescribed by conscience, or by our ideal, however reached. Yet it is certain that many laws have been enforced in the past, and it is likely that some are enforced now, which are condemned by the most enlightened opinion of the time, or which at all events pass the limit of interference as many consciences would draw it. Manifestly, therefore, nothing but confusion of thought can result from assuming that the rights of man in a moral sense are equally rights in the sense of the Constitution and the law. No doubt simple and extreme cases can be put of imaginable laws which the statute-making power would not dare to enact, even in the absence of written constitutional prohibitions, because the community would rise in rebellion and fight; and this gives some plausibility to the proposition that the law, if not a part of morality, is limited by it. But this limit of power is not coextensive with any system of morals. For the most part it falls far within the lines of any such system, and in some cases may extend beyond them, for reasons drawn from the habits of a particular people at a particular time. I once heard the late Professor Agassiz say that a German population would rise if you added two cents to the price of a glass of beer. A statute in such a case would be empty words, not because it was wrong, but because it could not be enforced. No one will deny that wrong statutes can be and are enforced, and we should not all agree as to which were the wrong ones.

The confusion with which I am dealing besets confessedly legal conceptions. Take the fundamental question, What constitutes the law? You will find some text writers telling you that it is something different from what is decided by the courts of Massachusetts or England, that it is a system of reason, that it is a deduction from principles of ethics or admitted axioms or what not, which may or may not coincide with the decisions. But if we take the view of our friend the bad man we shall find that he does not care two straws for the axioms or deductions, but that he does want to know what the Massachusetts or English courts are likely to do in fact. I am much of his mind. The prophecies of what the courts will do in fact, and nothing more pretentious, are what I mean by the law.

Take again a notion which as popularly understood is the widest conception which the law contains—the notion of legal duty, to which already I have referred. We fill the word with all the content which we draw from morals. But what does it mean to a bad man? Mainly, and in the first place, a prophecy that if he does certain things he will be subjected to disagreeable consequences by way of imprisonment or compulsory payment of money. But from his point of view, what is the difference between fined and being taxed a certain sum for doing a certain thing? That his point of view is the test of legal principles is shown by the many discussions which have arisen in the courts on the very question whether a given statutory liability is a penalty or a tax. On the answer to this question depends the decision whether conduct is legally wrong or right, and also whether a man is under compulsion or free. Leaving the criminal law on one side, what is the difference between the liability under the mill acts or statutes authorizing a taking by eminent domain and the liability for what we call a wrongful conversion of property where restoration is out of the question. In both cases the party taking another man's property has to pay its fair value as assessed by a jury, and no more. What significance is there is in calling one taking right and another wrong from the point of view of the law? It does not matter, so far as the given consequence, the compulsory payment, is concerned, whether the act to which it is attached is described in terms of praise or in terms of blame, or whether the law purports to prohibit it or to allow it. If it matters at all, still speaking from the bad man's point of view, it must be because in one case and not in the other some further disadvantages, or at least some further consequences, are attached to the act by the law. The only other disadvantages thus attached to it which I ever have been able to think of are to found in two somewhat insignificant legal doctrines, both of which might be abolished without disturbance. One is, that a contract to do a prohibited act is unlawful, and the other, that, if one of two or more joint wrongdoers has to pay all the damages, he cannot recover contribution from his fellows. And that I believe is all. You see how the vague circumference of the notion of duty shrinks and at the same time grows more precise when we wash it with cynical acid and expel everything except the object of our study, the operations of the law.

Nowhere is the confusion between legal and moral ideas more manifest than in the law of contract. Among other things, here again the so called primary rights and duties are invested with a mystic significance beyond what can be assigned and explained. The duty to keep a contract at common law means a prediction that you must pay damages if you do not keep it—and nothing else. If you commit a tort, you are liable to pay a compensatory sum. If you commit a contract, you are liable to pay a compensatory sum unless the promised event comes to pass, and that is all the difference. But such a mode of looking at the matter stinks in the nostrils of those who think it advantageous to get as much ethics into the law as they can. It was good enough for Lord Coke, however, and here, as in many other cases, I am content to abide with him. In *Bromage v. Genning*, a prohibition was sought in the King's Bench against a suit in the marches of Wales for the specific performance of a covenant to grant a lease, and Coke said that it would subvert the intention of the covenantor, since he intends it to be at his election either to lose the damages or to make the lease. Sergeant Harris for the plaintiff confessed that he moved the matter against his conscience, and a prohibition was granted. This goes further than we should go now, but it shows what I venture to say has been the common law point of view from the beginning, although Mr. Harriman, in his very able little book upon Contracts has been misled, as I humbly think, to a different conclusion.

I have spoken only of the common law, because there are some cases in which a logical justification can be found for speaking of civil liabilities as imposing duties in an intelligible sense. These are the relatively few in which equity will grant an injunction, and will enforce it by putting the defendant in prison or otherwise punishing him unless he complies with the order of the court. But I hardly think it advisable to shape general theory from the exception, and I think it would be better to cease troubling ourselves about primary rights and sanctions altogether, than to describe our prophecies concerning the liabilities commonly imposed by the law in those inappropriate terms.

I mentioned, as other examples of the use by the law of words drawn from morals, malice, intent, and negligence. It is enough to take malice as it is used in the law of civil liability for wrongs—what we lawyers call the law of torts—to show that it means something different in law from what it means in morals, and also to show how the difference has been obscured by giving to principles which have little or nothing to do with each other the same name. Three hundred years ago a parson preached a sermon and told a story out of Fox's *Book of Martyrs* of a man who had assisted at the torture of one of the saints, and afterward died, suffering compensatory inward torment. It happened that Fox was wrong. The man was alive and chanced to hear the sermon, and thereupon sued the parson. Chief Justice Wray instructed the jury that the defendant was not liable, because the story was told innocently, without malice. He took malice in the moral sense, as importing a malevolent motive. But nowadays no one doubts that a man may be liable, without any malevolent motive at all, for false statements manifestly calculated to inflict temporal damage. In stating the case in pleading, we still should call the defendant's conduct malicious; but, in my opinion at least, the word means nothing about motives, or even about the defendant's attitude toward the future, but only signifies that the tendency of his conduct under the known circumstances was very plainly to cause the plaintiff temporal harm.

In the law of contract the use of moral phraseology has led to equal confusion, as I have shown in part already, but only in part. Morals deal with the actual internal state of the individual's mind, what he actually intends. From the time of the Romans down to now, this mode of dealing has affected the language of the law as to contract, and the language used has reacted upon the thought. We talk about a contract as a meeting of the minds of the parties, and thence it is inferred in various cases that there is no contract because their minds have not met; that is, because they have intended different things or because one party has not known of the assent of the other. Yet nothing is more certain than that parties may be bound by a contract to things which neither of them intended, and when one does not know of the other's assent. Suppose a contract is executed in due form and in writing to deliver a lecture, mentioning no time. One of the parties thinks that the promise will be construed to mean at once, within a week. The other thinks that it means when he is ready. The court says that it means within a reasonable time. The parties are bound by the contract as it is interpreted by the court, yet neither of them meant what the court declares that they have said. In my opinion no one will understand the true theory of contract or be able even to discuss some fundamental questions intelligently until he has understood that all contracts are formal, that the making of a contract depends not on the agreement of two minds in one intention, but on the agreement of two sets of external signs—not on the parties' having *meant* the same thing but on their having *said* the same thing. Furthermore, as the signs may be addressed to one sense or another—to sight or to hearing—on the nature of the sign will depend the moment when the contract is made. If the sign is tangible, for instance, a letter, the contract is made when the letter of acceptance is delivered. If it is necessary that the minds of the parties meet, there will be no contract until the acceptance can be read—none, for example, if the acceptance be snatched from the hand of the offerer by a third person.

This is not the time to work out a theory in detail, or to answer many obvious doubts and questions which are suggested by these general views. I know of none which are not easy to answer, but what I am trying to do now is only by a series of hints to throw some light on the narrow path of legal doctrine, and upon two pitfalls which, as it seems to me, lie perilously near to it. Of the first of these I have said enough. I hope that my illustrations have shown the danger, both to speculation and to practice, of confounding morality with law, and the trap which legal language lays for us on that side of our way. For my own part, I often doubt whether it would not be a gain if every word of moral significance could be banished from the law altogether, and other words adopted which should convey legal ideas uncolored by anything outside the law. We should lose the fossil records of a good deal of history and the majesty got from ethical associations, but by ridding ourselves of an unnecessary confusion we should gain very much in the clearness of our thought.

So much for the limits of the law. The next thing which I wish to consider is what are the forces which determine its content and its growth. You may assume, with Hobbes and Bentham and Austin, that all law emanates from the sovereign, even when the first human beings to enunciate it are the judges, or you may think that law is the voice of the Zeitgeist, or what you like. It is all one to my present purpose. Even if every decision required the sanction of an emperor with despotic power and a whimsical turn of mind, we should be interested none the less, still with a view to prediction, in discovering some order, some rational explanation, and some principle of growth for the rules which he laid down. In every system there are such explanations and principles to be found. It is with regard to them that a second fallacy comes in, which I think it important to expose.

The fallacy to which I refer is the notion that the only force at work in the development of the law is logic. In the broadest sense, indeed, that notion would be true. The postulate on which we think about the universe is that there is a fixed quantitative relation between every phenomenon and its antecedents and consequents. If there is such a thing as a phenomenon without these fixed quantitative relations, it is a miracle. It is outside the law of cause and effect, and as such transcends our power of thought, or at least is something to or from which we cannot reason. The condition of our thinking about the universe is that it is capable of being thought about rationally, or, in other words, that every part of it is effect and cause in the same sense in which those parts are with which we are most familiar. So in the broadest sense it is true that the law is a logical development, like everything else. The danger of which I speak is not the admission that the principles governing other phenomena also govern the law, but the notion that a given system, ours, for instance, can be worked out like mathematics from some general axioms of conduct. This is the natural error of the schools, but it is not confined to them. I once heard a very eminent judge say that he never let a decision go until he was absolutely sure that it was right. So judicial dissent often is blamed, as if it meant simply that one side or the other were not doing their sums right, and, if they would take more trouble, agreement inevitably would come.

This mode of thinking is entirely natural. The training of lawyers is a training in logic. The processes of analogy, discrimination, and deduction are those in which they are most at home. The language of judicial decision is mainly the language of logic. And the logical method and form flatter that longing for certainty and for repose which is in every human mind. But certainty generally is illusion, and repose is not the destiny of man. Behind the logical form lies a judgment as to the relative worth and importance of competing legislative grounds, often and inarticulate and unconscious judgment, it is true, and yet the very root and nerve of the whole proceeding. You can give any conclusion a logical form. You always can imply a condition in a contract. But why do you imply it? It is because of some belief as to the practice of the community or of a class, or because of some opinion as to policy, or, in short, because of some attitude of yours upon a matter not capable of exact quantitative measurement, and therefore not capable of founding exact logical conclusions. Such matters really are battle grounds where the means do not exist for determinations that shall be good for all time, and where the decision can do no more than embody the preference of a given body in a given time and place. We do not realize how large a part of our law is open to reconsideration upon a slight change in the habit of the public mind. No concrete proposition is self evident, no matter how ready we may be to accept it, not even Mr. Herbert Spencer's "Every man has a right to do what he wills, provided he interferes not with a like right on the part of his neighbors."

Why is a false and injurious statement privileged, if it is made honestly in giving information about a servant? It is because it has been thought more important that information should be given freely, than that a man should be protected from what under other circumstances would be an actionable wrong. Why is a man at liberty to set up a business which he knows will ruin his neighbor? It is because the public good is supposed to be best subserved by free competition. Obviously such judgments of relative importance may vary in different times and places. Why does a judge instruct a jury that an employer is not liable to an employee for an injury received in the course of his employment unless he is negligent, and why do the jury generally find for the plaintiff if the case is allowed to go to them? It is because the traditional policy of our law is to confine liability to cases where a prudent man might have foreseen the injury, or at least the danger, while the inclination of a very large part of the community is to make certain classes of persons insure the safety of those with whom they deal. Since the last words were written, I have seen the requirement of such insurance put forth as part of the programme of one of the best known labor organizations. There is a concealed, half conscious battle on the question of legislative policy, and if any one thinks that it can be settled deductively, or once for all, I only can say that I think he is theoretically wrong, and that I am certain that his conclusion will not be accepted in practice *semper ubique et ab omnibus*.

Indeed, I think that even now our theory upon this matter is open to reconsideration, although I am not prepared to say how I should decide if a reconsideration were proposed. Our law of torts comes from the old days of isolated, ungeneralized wrongs, assaults, slanders, and the like, where the damages might be taken to lie where they fell by legal judgment. But the torts with which our courts are kept busy to-day are mainly the incidents of certain well known businesses. They are injuries to person or property by railroads, factories, and the like. The liability for them is estimated, and sooner or later goes into the price paid by the public. The public really pays the damages, and the question of liability, if pressed far enough, is really the question how far it is desirable that the public should insure the safety of those whose work it uses. It might be said that in such cases the chance of a jury finding for the defendant is merely a chance, once in a while rather arbitrarily interrupting the regular course of recovery, most likely in the case of an unusually conscientious plaintiff, and therefore better done away with. On the other hand, the economic value even of a life to the community can be estimated, and no recovery, it may be said, ought to go beyond that amount. It is conceivable that some day in certain cases we may find ourselves imitating, on a higher plane, the tariff for life and limb which we see in the *Leges Barbarorum.*

I think that the judges themselves have failed adequately to recognize their duty of weighing considerations of social advantage. The duty is inevitable, and the result of the often proclaimed judicial aversion to deal with such considerations is simply to leave the very ground and foundation of judgments inarticulate, and often unconscious, as I have said. When socialism first began to be talked about, the comfortable classes of the community were a good deal frightened. I suspect that this fear has influenced judicial action both here and in England, yet it is certain that it is not a conscious factor in the decisions to which I refer. I think that something similar has led people who no longer hope to control the legislatures to look to the courts as expounders of the Constitutions, and that in some courts new principles have been discovered outside the bodies of those instruments, which may be generalized into acceptance of the economic doctrines which prevailed about fifty years ago, and a wholesale prohibition of what a tribunal of lawyers does not think about right. I cannot but believe that if the training of lawyers led them habitually to consider more definitely and explicitly the social advantage on which the rule they lay down must be justified, they sometimes would hesitate where now they are confident, and see that really they were taking sides upon debatable and often burning questions.

So much for the fallacy of logical form. Now let us consider the present condition of the law as a subject for study, and the ideal toward which it tends. We still are far from the point of view which I desire to see reached. No one has reached it or can reach it as yet. We are only at the beginning of a philosophical reaction, and of a reconsideration of the worth of doctrines which for the most part still are taken for granted without any deliberate, conscious, and systematic questioning of their grounds. The development of our law has gone on for nearly a thousand years, like the development of a plant, each generation taking the inevitable next step, mind, like matter, simply obeying a law of spontaneous growth. It is perfectly natural and right that it should have been so. Imitation is a necessity of human nature, as has been illustrated by a remarkable French writer, M. Tarde, in an admirable book, *Les Lois de l'Imitation*. Most of the things we do, we do for no better reason than that our fathers have done them or that our neighbors do them, and the same is true of a larger part than we suspect of what we think. The reason is a good one, because our short life gives us no time for a better, but it is not the best. It does not follow, because we all are compelled to take on faith at second hand most of the rules on which we base our action and our thought, that each of us may not try to set some corner of his world in the order of reason, or that all of us collectively should not aspire to carry reason as far as it will go throughout the whole domain. In regard to the law, it is true, no doubt, that an evolutionist will hesitate to affirm universal validity for his social ideals, or for the principles which he thinks should be embodied in legislation. He is content if he can prove them best for here and now. He may be ready to admit that he knows nothing about an absolute best in the cosmos, and even that he knows next to nothing about a permanent best for men. Still it is true that a body of law is more rational and more civilized when every rule it contains is referred articulately and definitely to an end which it subserves, and when the grounds for desiring that end are stated or are ready to be stated in words.

At present, in very many cases, if we want to know why a rule of law has taken its particular shape, and more or less if we want to know why it exists at all, we go to tradition. We follow it into the Year Books, and perhaps beyond them to the customs of the Salian Franks, and somewhere in the past, in the German forests, in the needs of Norman kings, in the assumptions of a dominant class, in the absence of generalized ideas, we find out the practical motive for what now best is justified by the mere fact of its acceptance and that men are accustomed to it. The rational study of law is still to a large extent the study of history. History must be a part of the study, because without it we cannot know the precise scope of rules which it is our business to know. It is a part of the rational study, because it is the first step toward an enlightened scepticism, that is, toward a deliberate reconsideration of the worth of those rules.

When you get the dragon out of his cave on to the plain and in the daylight, you can count his teeth and claws, and see just what is his strength. But to get him out is only the first step. The next is either to kill him, or to tame him and make him a useful animal. For the rational study of the law the black-letter man may be the man of the present, but the man of the future is the man of statistics and the master of economics. It is revolting to have no better reason for a rule of law than that so it was laid down in the time of Henry IV. It is still more revolting if the grounds upon which it was laid down have vanished long since, and the rule simply persists from blind imitation of the past. I am thinking of the technical rule as to trespass *ab initio,* as it is called, which I attempted to explain in a recent Massachusetts case.

Let me take an illustration, which can be stated in a few words, to show how the social end which is aimed at by a rule of law is obscured and only partially attained in consequence of the fact that the rule owes its form to a gradual historical development, instead of being reshaped as a whole, with conscious articulate reference to the end in view. We think it desirable to prevent one man's property being misappropriated by another, and so we make larceny a crime. The evil is the same whether the misappropriation is made by a man into whose hands the owner has put the property, or by one who wrongfully takes it away. But primitive law in its weakness did not get much beyond an effort to prevent violence, and very naturally made a wrongful taking, a trespass, part of its definition of the crime. In modern times the judges enlarged the definition a little by holding that, if the wrong-doer gets possession by a trick or device, the crime is committed. This really was giving up the requirement of a trespass, and it would have been more logical, as well as truer to the present object of the law, to abandon the requirement altogether. That, however, would have seemed too bold, and was left to statute. Statutes were passed making embezzlement a crime. But the force of tradition caused the crime of embezzlement to be regarded as so far distinct from larceny that to this day, in some jurisdictions at least, a slip corner is kept open for thieves to contend, if indicted for larceny, that they should have been indicted for embezzlement, and if indicted for embezzlement, that they should have been indicted for larceny, and to escape on that ground.

Far more fundamental questions still await a better answer than that we do as our fathers have done. What have we better than a blind guess to show that the criminal law in its present form does more good than harm? I do not stop to refer to the effect which it has had in degrading prisoners and in plunging them further into crime, or to the question whether fine and imprisonment do not fall more heavily on a criminal's wife and children than on himself. I have in mind more far-reaching questions. Does punishment deter? Do we deal with criminals on proper principles? A modern school of Continental criminalists plumes itself on the formula, first suggested, it is said, by Gall, that we must consider the criminal rather than the crime. The formula does not carry us very far, but the inquiries which have been started look toward an answer of my questions based on science for the first time. If the typical criminal is a degenerate, bound to swindle or to murder by as deep seated an organic necessity as that which makes the rattlesnake bite, it is idle to talk of deterring him by the classical method of imprisonment. He must be got rid of; he cannot be improved, or frightened out of his structural reaction. If, on the other hand, crime, like normal human conduct, is mainly a matter of imitation, punishment fairly may be expected to help to keep it out of fashion. The study of criminals has been thought by some well known men of science to sustain the former hypothesis. The statistics of the relative increase of crime in crowded places like large cities, where example has the greatest chance to work, and in less populated parts, where the contagion spreads more slowly, have been used with great force in favor of the latter view. But there is weighty authority for the belief that, however this may be, "not the nature of the crime, but the dangerousness of the criminal, constitutes the only reasonable legal criterion to guide the inevitable social reaction against the criminal." [1]

The impediments to rational generalization, which I illustrated

---

[1] Havelock Ellis, *The Criminal*, 41, citing Garofalo. See also Ferri, *Sociologie Criminelle, passim.* Compare Tarde, *La Philosophie Penale.* [Holmes' note.]

from the law of larceny, are shown in the other branches of the law, as well as in that of crime. Take the law of tort or civil liability for damages apart from contract and the like. Is there any general theory of such liability, or are the cases in which it exists simply to be enumerated, and to be explained each on its special ground, as is easy to believe from the fact that the right of action for certain well known classes of wrongs like trespass or slander has its special history for each class? I think that there is a general theory to be discovered, although resting in tendency rather than established and accepted. I think that the law regards the infliction of temporal damage by a responsible person as actionable, if under the circumstances known to him the danger of his act is manifest according to common experience, or according to his own experience if it is more than common, except in cases where upon special grounds of policy the law refuses to protect the plaintiff or grants a privilege to the defendant.[2] I think that commonly malice, intent, and negligence mean only that the danger was manifest to a greater or less degree, under the circumstances known to the actor, although in some cases of privilege malice may mean an actual malevolent motive, and such a motive may take away a permission knowingly to inflict harm, which otherwise would be granted on this or that ground of dominant public good. But when I stated my view to a very eminent English judge the other day, he said: "You are discussing what the law ought to be; as the law is, you must show a right. A man is not liable for negligence unless he is subject to a duty." If our difference was more than a difference in words, or with regard to the proportion between the exceptions and the rule, then, in his opinion, liability for an act cannot be referred to the manifest tendency of the act to cause temporal damage in general as a sufficient explanation, but must be referred to the special nature of the damage, or must be derived from some special circumstances outside of the tendency of the act, for which no generalized explanation exists. I

[2] An example of the law's refusing to protect the plaintiff is when he is interrupted by a stranger in the use of a valuable way, which he has travelled adversely for a week less than the period of prescription. A week later he will have gained a right, but now he is only a trespasser. Example of privilege I have given already. One of the best is competition in business. [Holmes' note.]

think that such a view is wrong, but it is familiar, and I dare say generally is accepted in England.

Everywhere the basis of principle is tradition, to such an extent that we even are in danger of making the rôle of history more important than it is. The other day Professor Ames wrote a learned article to show, among other things, that the common law did not recognize the defence of fraud in actions upon specialties, and the moral might seem to be that the personal character of that defence is due to its equitable origin. But if, as I have said, all contracts are formal, the difference is not merely historical, but theoretic, between defects of form which prevent a contract from being made, and mistaken motives which manifestly could not be considered in any system that we should call rational except against one who was privy to those motives. It is not confined to specialties, but is of universal application. I ought to add that I do not suppose that Mr. Ames would disagree with what I suggest.

However, if we consider the law of contract, we find it full of history. The distinctions between debt, covenant, and assumpsit are merely historical. The classification of certain obligations to pay money, imposed by the law irrespective of any bargain as quasi contracts, is merely historical. The doctrine of consideration is merely historical. The effect given to a seal is to be explained by history alone. Consideration is a mere form. Is it a useful form? If so, why should it not be required in all contracts? A seal is a mere form, and is vanishing in the scroll and in enactments that a consideration must be given, seal or no seal. Why should any merely historical distinction be allowed to affect the rights and obligations of business men?

Since I wrote this discourse I have come on a very good example of the way in which tradition not only overrides rational policy, but overrides it after first having been misunderstood and having been given a new and broader scope than it had when it had a meaning. It is the settled law of England that a material alteration of a written contract by a party avoids it as against him. The doctrine is contrary to the general tendency of the law. We do not tell a jury that if a man ever has lied in one particular he is to be presumed to lie in all. Even if a man has tried to defraud, it seems no sufficient reason for preventing him from proving the truth. Objections of like nature in general go to the weight, not to the admissibility, of evidence. Moreover, this rule is irrespective of fraud, and is not confined to evidence. It is not merely that you cannot use the writing, but that the contract is at an end. What does this mean? The existence of a written contract depends on the fact that the offerer and offeree have interchanged their written expressions. But in the case of a bond, the primitive notion was different. The contract was inseparable from the parchment. If a stranger destroyed it, or tore off the seal, or altered it, the obligee could not recover, however free from fault, because the defendant's contract, that is, the actual tangible bond which he had sealed, could not be produced in the form in which it bound him. About a hundred years ago Lord Kenyon undertook to use his reason on this tradition, as he sometimes did to the detriment of the law, and, not understanding it, said he could see no reason why what was true of a bond should not be true of other contracts. His decision happened to be right, as it concerned a promissory note, where again the common law regarded the contract as inseparable from the paper on which it was written, but the reasoning was general, and soon was extended to other written contracts, and various absurd and unreal grounds of policy were invented to account for the enlarged rule.

I trust that no one will understand me to be speaking with disrespect of the law, because I criticise it so freely. I venerate the law, and especially our system of law, as one of the vastest products of the human mind. No one knows better than I do the countless number of great intellects that have spent themselves in making some addition or improvement, the greatest of which is trifling when compared with the mighty whole. It has the final title to respect that it exists, that it is not a Hegelian dream, but a part of the lives of men. But one may criticise even what one reveres. Law is the business to which my life is devoted, and I should show less than devotion if I did not do what in me lies to improve it, and, when I perceive what seems to me the ideal of its future, if I hesitated to point it out and to press toward it with all my heart.

Perhaps I have said enough to show the part which the study of history necessarily plays in the intelligent study of the law as it is to-day. In the teaching of this school and at Cambridge it is in no danger of being undervalued. Mr. Bigelow here and Mr. Ames and Mr. Thayer there have made important contributions which will not be forgotten, and in England the recent history of early English law by Sir Frederick Pollock and Mr. Maitland has lent the subject an almost deceptive charm. We must beware of the pitfall of antiquarianism, and must remember that for our purposes our only interest in the past is for the light it throws upon the present. I look forward to a time when the part played by history in the explanation of dogma shall be very small, and instead of ingenious research we shall spend our energy on a study of the ends sought to be attained and the reasons for desiring them. As a step toward that ideal it seems to me that every lawyer ought to seek an understanding of economics. The present divorce between the schools of political economy and law seems to me an evidence of how much progress in philosophical study still remains to be made. In the present state of political economy, indeed, we come again upon history on a larger scale, but there we are called on to consider and weigh the ends of legislation, the means of attaining them, and the cost. We learn that for everything we have we give up something else, and we are taught to set the advantage we gain against the other advantage we lose, and to know what we are doing when we elect.

There is another study which sometimes is undervalued by the practical minded, for which I wish to say a good word, although I think a good deal of pretty poor stuff goes under that name. I mean the study of what is called jurisprudence. Jurisprudence, as I look at it, is simply law in its most generalized part. Every effort to reduce a case to a rule is an effort of jurisprudence, although the name as used in English is confined to the broadest rules and most fundamental conceptions. One mark of a great lawyer is that he sees the application of the broadest rules. There is a story of a Vermont justice of the peace before whom a suit was brought by one farmer against another for breaking a churn. The justice took time to consider, and then said that he had looked through the statutes and could find nothing about churns, and gave judgment for the defendant. The same state of mind is shown in all our common digests and text-books. Applications of rudimentary rules of contract or tort are tucked away under the head of Railroads or Telegraphs or go to swell treatises on historical subdivisions, such as Shipping or Equity, or are gathered under an arbitrary title which is thought likely to appeal to the practical mind, such as Mercantile Law. If a man goes into law it pays to be a master of it, and to be a master of it means to look straight through all the dramatic incidents and to discern the true basis for prophecy. Therefore, it is well to have an accurate notion of what you mean by law, by a right, by a duty, by malice, intent, and negligence, by ownership, by possession, and so forth. I have in mind cases in which the highest courts seem to me to have floundered because they had no clear ideas on some of these themes. I have illustrated their importance already. If a further illustration is wished, it may be found by reading the Appendix to Sir James Stephen's *Criminal Law* on the subject of possession, and then turning to Pollock and Wright's enlightened book. Sir James Stephen is not the only writer whose attempts to analyze legal ideas have been confused by striving for a useless quintessence of all systems, instead of an accurate anatomy of one. The trouble with Austin was that he did not know enough English law. But still it is a practical advantage to master Austin, and his predecessors, Hobbes and Bentham, and his worthy successors, Holland and Pollock. Sir Frederick Pollock's recent little book is touched with the felicity which marks all his works, and is wholly free from the perverting influence of Roman models.

The advice of the elders to young men is very apt to be as unreal as a list of the hundred best books. At least in my day I had my share of such counsels, and high among the unrealities I place the recommendation to study the Roman law. I assume that such advice means more than collecting a few Latin maxims with which to ornament the discourse—the purpose for which Lord Coke recommended Bracton. If that is all that is wanted, the title *De Regulis Juris Antiqui* can be read in an hour. I assume that, if it is well to study the Roman law, it is well to study it as a working system. That means mastering a set of technicalities more difficult and less understood than our own, and studying another course of history by which even more than our own the Roman law must be explained. If any one doubts me, let him read Keller's *Der Römische Civil*

203

Process und die Actionen, a treatise on the praetor's edict, Muirhead's most interesting *Historical Introduction to the Private Law of Rome,* and, to give him the best chance, Sohm's admirable *Institutes.* No. The way to gain a liberal view of your subject is not to read something else, but to get to the bottom of the subject itself. The means of doing that are, in the first place, to follow the existing body of dogma into its highest generalizations by the help of jurisprudence; next, to discover from history how it has come to be what it is; and, finally, so far as you can, to consider the ends which the several rules seek to accomplish, the reasons why those ends are desired, what is given up to gain them, and whether they are worth the price.

We have too little theory in the law rather than too much, especially on this final branch of study. When I was speaking of history, I mentioned larceny as an example to show how the law suffered from not having embodied in a clear form a rule which will accomplish its manifest purpose. In that case the trouble was due to the survival of forms coming from a time when a more limited purpose was entertained. Let me now give an example to show the practical importance, for the decision of actual cases, of understanding the reasons of the law, by taking an example from rules which, so far as I know, never have been explained or theorized about in any adequate way. I refer to statutes of limitation and the law of prescription. The end of such rules is obvious, but what is the justification for depriving a man of his rights, a pure evil as far as it goes, in consequence of the lapse of time? Sometimes the loss of evidence is referred to, but that is a secondary matter. Sometimes the desirability of peace, but why is peace more desirable after twenty years than before? It is increasingly likely to come without the aid of legislation. Sometimes it is said that, if a man neglects to enforce his rights, he cannot complain if, after a while, the law follows his example. Now if this is all that can be said about it, you probably will decide a case I am going to put, for the plaintiff; if you take the view which I shall suggest, you possibly will decide it for the defendant. A man is sued for trespass upon land, and justifies under a right of way. He proves that he has used the way openly and adversely for twenty years, but it turns out that the plaintiff had granted a license to a person whom he reasonably supposed to be the defendant's agent, although not so in fact, and therefore had assumed that the use of the way was permissive, in which case no right would be gained. Has the defendant gained a right or not? If his gaining it stands on the fault and neglect of the landowner in the ordinary sense, as seems commonly to be supposed, there has been no such neglect, and the right of way has not been acquired. But if I were the defendant's counsel, I should suggest that the foundation of the acquisition of rights by lapse of time is to be looked for in the position of the person who gains them, not in that of the loser. Sir Henry Maine has made it fashionable to connect the archaic notion of property with prescription. But the connection is further back than the first recorded history. It is in the nature of man's mind. A thing which you have enjoyed and used as your own for a long time, whether property or an opinion, takes root in your being and cannot be torn away without your resenting the act and trying to defend yourself, however you came by it. The law can ask no better justification than the deepest instincts of man. It is only by way of reply to the suggestion that you are disappointing the former owner, that you refer to his neglect having allowed the gradual dissociation between himself and what he claims, and the gradual association of it with another. If he knows that another is doing acts which on their face show that he is on the way toward establishing such an association, I should argue that in justice to that other he was bound at his peril to find out whether the other was acting under his permission, to see that he was warned, and if necessary, stopped.

I have been speaking about the study of the law, and I have said next to nothing of what commonly is talked about in that connection—text-books and the case system, and all the machinery with which a student comes most immediately in contact. Nor shall I say anything about them. Theory is my subject, not practical details. The modes of teaching have been improved since my time, no doubt, but ability and industry will master the raw material with any mode. Theory is the most important part of the dogma of the law, as the architect is the most important man who takes part in the building of a house. The most important improvements of the last twenty-five years are improvements in theory. It is not to be feared as unpractical, for, to the competent, it simply means going to the bottom of the subject. For the incompetent, it sometimes is true, as has been said, that an interest in general ideas means an absence of particular knowledge. I remember in army days reading of a youth who, being examined for the lowest grade and being asked a question about squadron drill, answered that he never had considered the evolutions of less than ten thousand men. But the weak and foolish must be left to their folly. The danger is that the able and practical minded should look with indifference or distrust upon ideas the connection of which with their business is remote. I heard a story, the other day, of a man who had a valet to whom he paid high wages, subject to deductions for faults. One of his deductions was, "For lack of imagination, five dollars." The lack is not confined to valets. The object of ambition, power, generally presents itself nowadays in the form of money alone. Money is the most immediate form, and is a proper object of desire. "The fortune," said Rachel, "is the measure of the intelligence." That is a good text to waken people out of a fool's paradise. But, as Hegel says, "It is in the end not the appetite, but the opinion, which has to be satisfied." To an imagination of any scope the most far-reaching form of power is not money, it is the command of ideas. If you want great examples, read Mr. Leslie Stephen's *History of English Thought in the Eighteenth Century,* and see how a hundred years after his death the abstract speculations of Descartes had become a practical force controlling the conduct of men. Read the works of the great German jurists, and see how much more the world is governed to-day by Kant than by Bonaparte. We cannot all be Descartes or Kant, but we all want happiness. And happiness, I am sure from having known many successful men, cannot be won simply by being counsel for great corporations and having an income of fifty thousand dollars. An intellect great enough to win the prize needs other food besides success. The remoter and more general aspects of the law are those which give it universal interest. It is through them that you not only become a great master in your calling, but connect your subject with the universe and catch an echo of the infinite, a glimpse of its unfathomable process, a hint of the universal law.

NATURAL LAW

It is not enough for the knight of romance that you agree that his lady is a very nice girl—if you do not admit that she is the best that God ever made or will make, you must fight. There is in all men a demand for the superlative, so much so that the poor devil who has no other way of reaching it attains it by getting drunk. It seems to me that this demand is at the bottom of the philosopher's effort to prove that truth is absolute and of the jurist's search for criteria of universal validity which he collects under the head of natural law.

I used to say, when I was young, that truth was the majority vote of that nation that could lick all others. Certainly we may expect that the received opinion about the present war will depend a good deal upon which side wins (I hope with all my soul it will be mine), and I think that the statement was correct in so far as it implied that our test of truth is a reference to either a present or an imagined future majority in favor of our view. If, as I have suggested elsewhere, the truth may be defined as the system of my (intellectual) limitations, what gives it objectivity is the fact that I find my fellow man to a greater or less extent (never wholly) subject to the same *Can't Helps*. If I think that I am sitting at a table I find that the other persons present agree with me; so if I say that the sum of the angles of a triangle is equal to two right angles. If I am in a minority of one they send for a doctor or lock me up; and I am so far able to transcend the to me convincing testimony of my senses or my reason as to recognize that if I am alone probably something is wrong with my works.

Certitude is not the test of certainty. We have been cock-sure of many things that were not so. If I may quote myself again, property, friendship, and truth have a common root in time. One

From *The Harvard Law Review*, Vol. XXXII, 1918; reprinted in *Collected Legal Papers*, pp. 310-316, by Oliver Wendell Holmes. Copyright, 1920, Harcourt, Brace and Company, Inc.; reprinted by permission.

can not be wrenched from the rocky crevices into which one has grown for many years without feeling that one is attacked in one's life. What we most love and revere generally is determined by early associations. I love granite rocks and barberry bushes, no doubt because with them were my earliest joys that reach back through the past eternity of my life. But while one's experience thus makes certain preferences dogmatic for oneself, recognition of how they came to be so leaves one able to see that others, poor souls, may be equally dogmatic about something else. And this again means scepticism. Not that one's belief or love does not remain. Not that we would not fight and die for it if important—we all, whether we know it or not—are fighting to make the kind of a world that we should like—but that we have learned to recognize that others will fight and die to make a different world, with equal sincerity or belief. Deep-seated preferences can not be argued about—you can not argue a man into liking a glass of beer—and therefore, when differences are sufficiently far reaching we try to kill the other man rather than let him have his way. But that is perfectly consistent with admitting that, so far as appears, his grounds are just as good as ours.

The jurists who believe in natural law seem to me to be in that naïve state of mind that accepts what has been familiar and accepted by them and their neighbors as something that must be accepted by all men everywhere. No doubt it is true that, so far as we can see ahead, some arrangements and the rudiments of familiar institutions seem to be necessary elements in any society that may spring from our own and that would seem to us to be civilized—some form of permanent association between the sexes—some residue of property individually owned—some mode of binding oneself to specified future conduct—at the bottom of all, some protection for the person. But without speculating whether a group is imaginable in which all but the last of these might disappear and the last be subject to qualifications that most of us would abhor, the question remains as to the *Ought* of natural law.

It is true that beliefs and wishes have a transcendental basis in the sense that their foundation is arbitrary. You can not help entertaining and feeling them, and there is an end of it. As an arbitrary fact people wish to live, and we say with various degrees of certainty that they can do so only on certain conditions. To do it they must eat and drink. That necessity is absolute. It is a necessity of less degree but practically general that they should live in society. If they live in society, so far as we can see, there are further conditions. Reason working on experience does tell us, no doubt, that if our wish to live continues, we can do it only on those terms. But that seems to me the whole of the matter. I see no *a priori* duty to live with others and in that way, but simply a statement of what I must do if I wish to remain alive. If I do live with others they tell me that I must do and abstain from doing various things or they will put the screws on to me. I believe that they will, and being of the same mind as to their conduct I not only accept the rules but come in time to accept them with sympathy and emotional affirmation and begin to talk about duties and rights. But for legal purposes a right is only the hypostasis of a prophecy—the imagination of a substance supporting the fact that the public force will be brought to bear upon those who do things said to contravene it—just as we talk of the force of gravitation accounting for the conduct of bodies in space. One phrase adds no more than the other to what we know without it. No doubt behind these legal rights is the fighting will of the subject to maintain them, and the spread of his emotions to the general rules by which they are maintained; but that does not seem to me the same thing as the supposed *a priori* discernment of a duty or the assertion of a preëxisting right. A dog will fight for his bone.

The most fundamental of the supposed preëxisting rights—the right to life—is sacrificed without a scruple not only in war, but whenever the interest of society, that is, of the predominant power in the community, is thought to demand it. Whether that interest is the interest of mankind in the long run no one can tell, and as, in any event, to those who do not think with Kant and Hegel it is only an interest, the sanctity disappears. I remember a very tender-hearted judge being of opinion that closing a hatch to stop a fire and the destruction of a cargo was justified even if it was known that doing so would stifle a man below. It is idle to illustrate further, because to those who agree with me I am uttering commonplaces and to those who disagree I am ignoring the necessary foundations of thought. The *a priori* men generally call the dissentients superficial. But I do agree with them in believing that one's attitude on these matters is closely connected with one's general attitude toward the universe. Proximately, as has been suggested, it is determined largely by early associations and temperament, coupled with the desire to have an absolute guide. Men to a great extent believe what they want to—although I see in that no basis for a philosophy that tells us what we should want to want.

Now when we come to our attitude toward the universe I do not see any rational ground for demanding the superlative—for being dissatisfied unless we are assured that our truth is cosmic truth, if there is such a thing—that the ultimates of a little creature on this earth are the last word of the unimaginable whole. If a man sees no reason for believing that significance, consciousness and ideals are more than marks of the finite, that does not justify what has been familiar in French sceptics: getting upon a pedestal and professing to look with haughty scorn upon a world in ruins. The real conclusion is that the part can not swallow the whole—that our categories are not, or may not be, adequate to formulate what we cannot know. If we believe that we come out of the universe, not it out of us, we must admit that we do not know what we are talking about when we speak of brute matter. We do know that a certain complex of energies can wag its tail and another can make syllogisms. These are among the powers of the unknown, and if, as may be, it has still greater powers that we can not understand, as Fabre in his studies of instinct would have us believe, studies that gave Bergson one of the strongest strands for his philosophy and enabled Maeterlinck to make us fancy for a moment that we heard a clang from behind phenomena—if this be true, why should we not be content? Why should we employ the energy that is furnished to us by the cosmos to defy it and shake our fist at the sky? It seems to me silly.

That the universe has in it more than we understand, that the private soldiers have not been told the plan of the campaign, or even that there is one, rather than some vaster unthinkable to which every predicate is an impertinence, has no bearing upon our conduct. We still shall fight—all of us because we want to live, some, at least, because we want to realize our spontaneity and prove our powers, for the joy of it, and we may leave to the unknown the supposed final valuation of that which in any event has value to us. It is enough for us that the universe has produced us and has within it, as less than it, all that we believe and love. If we think of our existence not as that of a little god outside, but as that of a ganglion within, we have the infinite behind us. It gives us our only but our adequate significance. A grain of sand has the same, but what competent person supposes that he understands a grain of sand? That is as much beyond our grasp as man. If our imagination is strong enough to accept the vision of ourselves as parts inseverable from the rest, and to extend our final interest beyond the boundary of our skins, it justifies the sacrifice even of our lives for ends outside of ourselves. The motive, to be sure, is the common wants and ideals that we find in man. Philosophy does not furnish motives, but it shows men that they are not fools for doing what they already want to do. It opens to the forlorn hopes on which we throw ourselves away, the vista of the farthest stretch of human thought, the chords of a harmony that breathes from the unknown.

·IX·

JOHN DEWEY

[1 8 5 9 · 1 9 5 2]

THE INFLUENCE OF DARWINISM ON PHILOSOPHY

INTELLIGENCE AND MORALS

THE INFLUENCE OF DARWINISM ON PHILOSOPHY

I

That the publication of the *Origin of Species* marked an epoch in the development of the natural sciences is well known to the layman. That the combination of the very words origin and species embodied an intellectual revolt and introduced a new intellectual temper is easily overlooked by the expert. The conceptions that had reigned in the philosophy of nature and knowledge for two thousand years, the conceptions that had become the familiar furniture of the mind, rested on the assumption of the superiority of the fixed and final; they rested upon treating change and origin as signs of defect and unreality. In laying hands upon the sacred ark of absolute permanency, in treating the forms that had been regarded as types of fixity and perfection as originating and passing away, the *Origin of Species* introduced a mode of thinking that in the end was bound to transform the logic of knowledge, and hence the treatment of morals, politics, and religion.

No wonder, then, that the publication of Darwin's book, a half century ago, precipitated a crisis. The true nature of the controversy is easily concealed from us, however, by the theological clamor that attended it. The vivid and popular features of the anti-Darwinian row tended to leave the impression that the issue was between science on the one side and theology on the other. Such was not the case—the issue lay primarily within science itself, as Darwin himself early recognized. The theological outcry he discounted from the start, hardly noticing it save as it bore upon the "feelings of his female relatives." But for two decades before final publication he con-

---

A lecture delivered at Columbia University in a series observing the fiftieth anniversary of *The Origin of the Species,* 1909; reprinted from *The Influence of Darwin on Philosophy,* pp. 1-19, by John Dewey. Copyright, 1910, Henry Holt and Company, Inc.; reprinted by permission.

templated the possibility of being put down by his scientific peers as a fool or as crazy; and he set, as the measure of his success, the degree in which he should affect three men of science: Lyell in geology, Hooker in botany, and Huxley in zoology.

Religious considerations lent fervor to the controversy, but they did not provoke it. Intellectually, religious emotions are not creative but conservative. They attach themselves readily to the current view of the world and consecrate it. They steep and dye intellectual fabrics in the seething vat of emotions; they do not form their warp and woof. There is not, I think, an instance of any large idea about the world being independently generated by religion. Although the ideas that rose up like armed men against Darwinism owed their intensity to religious associations, their origin and meaning are to be sought in science and philosophy, not in religion.

II

Few words in our language foreshorten intellectual history as much as does the word species. The Greeks, in initiating the intellectual life of Europe, were impressed by characteristic traits of the life of plants and animals; so impressed indeed that they made these traits the key to defining nature and to explaining mind and society. And truly, life is so wonderful that a seemingly successful reading of its mystery might well lead men to believe that the key to the secrets of heaven and earth was in their hands. The Greek rendering of this mystery, the Greek formulation of the aim and standard of knowledge, was in the course of time embodied in the word species, and it controlled philosophy for two thousand years. To understand the intellectual face-about expressed in the phrase *Origin of Species,* we must, then, understand the long dominant idea against which it is a protest.

Consider how men were impressed by the facts of life. Their eyes fell upon certain things slight in bulk, and frail in structure. To every appearance, these perceived things were inert and passive. Suddenly, under certain circumstances, these things—henceforth known as seeds or eggs or germs—begin to change, to change rapidly in size, form, and qualities. Rapid and extensive changes occur, however, in many things—as when wood is touched by fire. But the changes in the living thing are orderly; they are cumulative; they tend constantly in one direction; they do not, like other changes, destroy or consume, or pass fruitless into wandering flux; they realize and fulfill. Each successive stage, no matter how unlike its predecessor, preserves its net effect and also prepares the way for a fuller activity on the part of its successor. In living beings, changes do not happen as they seem to happen elsewhere, any which way; the earlier changes are regulated in view of later results. This progressive organization does not cease till there is achieved a true final term, a τελὸς, a completed, perfected end. This final form exercises in turn a plenitude of functions, not the least noteworthy of which is production of germs like those from which it took its own origin, germs capable of the same cycle of self-fulfilling activity.

But the whole miraculous tale is not yet told. The same drama is enacted to the same destiny in countless myriads of individuals so sundered in time, so severed in space, that they have no opportunity for mutual consultation and no means of interaction. As an old writer quaintly said, "things of the same kind go through the same formalities"—celebrate, as it were, the same ceremonial rites.

This formal activity which operates throughout a series of changes and holds them to a single course; which subordinates their aimless flux to its own perfect manifestation; which, leaping the boundaries of space and time, keeps individuals distant in space and remote in time to a uniform type of structure and function: this principle seemed to give insight into the very nature of reality itself. To it Aristotle gave the name, εἶδος. This term the scholastics translated as *species*.

The force of this term was deepened by its application to everything in the universe that observes order in flux and manifests constancy through change. From the casual drift of daily weather, through the uneven recurrence of seasons and unequal return of seed time and harvest, up to the majestic sweep of the heavens—the image of eternity in time—and from this to the unchanging pure and contemplative intelligence beyond nature lies one unbroken fulfillment of ends. Nature as a whole is a progressive realization of purpose strictly comparable to the realization of purpose in any single plant or animal.

The conception of εἶδος, species, a fixed form and final cause, was the central principle of knowledge as well as of nature. Upon it rested the logic of science. Change as change is mere flux and lapse; it insults intelligence. Genuinely to know is to grasp a permanent end that realizes itself through changes, holding them thereby within the metes and bounds of fixed truth. Completely to know is to relate all special forms to their one single end and good: pure contemplative intelligence. Since, however, the scene of nature which directly confronts us is in change, nature as directly and practically experienced does not satisfy the conditions of knowledge. Human experience is in flux, and hence the instrumentalities of sense-perception and of inference based upon observation are condemned in advance. Science is compelled to aim at realities lying behind and beyond the processes of nature, and to carry on its search for these realities by means of rational forms transcending ordinary modes of perception and inference.

There are, indeed, but two alternative courses. We must either find the appropriate objects and organs of knowledge in the mutual interactions of changing things; or else, to escape the infection of change, we *must* seek them in some transcendent and supernal region. The human mind, deliberately as it were, exhausted the logic of the changeless, the final, and the transcendent, before it essayed adventure on the pathless wastes of generation and transformation. We dispose all too easily of the efforts of the schoolmen to interpret nature and mind in terms of real essences, hidden forms, and occult faculties, forgetful of the seriousness and dignity of ideas that lay behind. We dispose of them by laughing at the famous gentleman who accounted for the fact that opium put people to sleep on the ground it had a dormitive faculty. But the doctrine, held in our day, that knowledge of the plant that yields the poppy consists in referring the peculiarities of an individual to a type, to a universal form, a doctrine so firmly established that any other method of knowing was conceived to be unphilosophical and unscientific, is a survival of precisely the same logic. This identity of conception in the scholastic and anti-Darwinian theory may well suggest greater sympathy for what has become unfamiliar as well as greater humility regarding the further unfamiliarities that history has in store.

Darwin was not, of course, the first to question the classic philosophy of nature and of knowledge. The beginnings of the revolution are in the physical science of the sixteenth and seventeenth centuries. When Galileo said: "It is my opinion that the earth is very noble and admirable by reason of so many and so different alterations and generations which are incessantly made therein," he expressed the changed temper that was coming over the world; the transfer of interest from the permanent to the changing. When Descartes said: "The nature of physical things is much more easily conceived when they are beheld coming gradually into existence, than when they are only considered as produced at once in a finished and perfect state," the modern world became self-conscious of the logic that was henceforth to control it, the logic of which Darwin's *Origin of Species* is the latest scientific achievement. Without the methods of Copernicus, Kepler, Galileo, and their successors in astronomy, physics, and chemistry, Darwin would have been helpless in the organic sciences. But prior to Darwin the impact of the new scientific method upon life, mind, and politics, had been arrested, because between these ideal or moral interests and the inorganic world intervened the kingdom of plants and animals. The gates of the garden of life were barred to the new ideas; and only through this garden was there access to mind and politics. The influence of Darwin upon philosophy resides in his having conquered the phenomena of life for the principle of transition, and thereby freed the new logic for application to mind and morals and life. When he said of species what Galileo had said of the earth, *e pur se muove,* he emancipated, once for all, genetic and experimental ideas as an organon of asking questions and looking for explanations.

III

The exact bearings upon philosophy of the new logical outlook are, of course, as yet, uncertain and inchoate. We live in the twilight of intellectual transition. One must add the rashness of the prophet to the stubbornness of the partizan to venture a systematic exposition of the influence upon philosophy of the Darwinian method. At best, we can but inquire as to its general bearing—the effect upon mental temper and complexion, upon that body of half-conscious, half-instinctive intellectual aversions and preferences which determine, after all, our more deliberate intellectual enterprises. In this vague inquiry there happens to exist as a kind of touchstone a problem of long historic currency that has also been much discussed in Darwinian literature. I refer to the old problem of design *versus* chance, mind *versus* matter, as the causal explanation, first or final, of things.

As we have already seen, the classic notion of species carried with it the idea of purpose. In all living forms, a specific type is present directing the earlier stages of growth to the realization of its own perfection. Since this purposive regulative principle is not visible to the senses, it follows that it must be an ideal or rational force. Since, however, the perfect form is gradually approximated through the sensible changes, it also follows that in and through a sensible realm a rational ideal force is working out its own ultimate manifestation. These inferences were extended to nature: (*a*) She does nothing in vain; but all for an ulterior purpose. (*b*) Within natural sensible events there is therefore contained a spiritual causal force, which as spiritual escapes perception, but is apprehended by an enlightened reason. (*c*) The manifestation of this principle brings about a subordination of matter and sense to its own realization, and this ultimate fulfillment is the goal of nature and of man. The design argument thus operated in two directions. Purposefulness accounted for the intelligibility of nature and the possibility of science, while the absolute or cosmic character of this purposefulness gave sanction and worth to the moral and religious endeavors of man. Science was underpinned and morals authorized by one and the same principle, and their mutual agreement was eternally guaranteed.

This philosophy remained, in spite of sceptical and polemic outbursts, the official and regnant philosophy of Europe for over two thousand years. The expulsion of fixed first and final causes from astronomy, physics, and chemistry had indeed given the doctrine something of a shock. But, on the other hand, increased acquaintance with the details of plant and animal life operated as a counterbalance and perhaps even strengthened the argument from design. The marvelous adaptations of organisms to their environment, of organs to the organism, of unlike parts of a complex organ—like the eye—to the organ itself; the foreshadowing by lower forms of the higher; the preparation in earlier stages of growth for organs that only later had their functioning—these things were increasingly recognized with the progress of botany, zoology, paleontology, and embryology. Together, they added such prestige to the design argument that by the late eighteenth century it was, as approved by the sciences of organic life, the central point of theistic and idealistic philosophy.

The Darwinian principle of natural selection cut straight under this philosophy. If all organic adaptations are due simply to constant variation and the elimination of those variations which are harmful in the struggle for existence that is brought about by excessive reproduction, there is no call for a prior intelligent causal force to plan and preordain them. Hostile critics charged Darwin with materialism and with making chance the cause of the universe.

Some naturalists, like Asa Gray, favored the Darwinian principle and attempted to reconcile it with design. Gray held to what may be called design on the installment plan. If we conceive the "stream of variations" to be itself intended, we may suppose that each successive variation was designed from the first to be selected. In that case, variation, struggle, and selection simply define the mechanism of "secondary causes" through which the "first cause" acts; and the doctrine of design is none the worse off because we know more of its *modus operandi*.

Darwin could not accept this mediating proposal. He admits or rather he asserts that it is "impossible to conceive this immense and wonderful universe including man with his capacity of looking far backwards and far into futurity as the result of blind chance or necessity." But nevertheless he holds that since variations are in useless as well as useful directions, and since the latter are sifted out simply by the stress of the conditions of struggle for existence, the design argument as applied to living beings is unjustifiable;

and its lack of support there deprives it of scientific value as applied to nature in general. If the variations of the pigeon, which under artificial selection give the pouter pigeon, are not preordained for the sake of the breeder, by what logic do we argue that variations resulting in natural species are pre-designed?

IV

So much for some of the more obvious facts of the discussion of design *versus* chance, as causal principles of nature and of life as a whole. We brought up this discussion, you recall, as a crucial instance. What does our touchstone indicate as to the bearing of Darwinian ideas upon philosophy? In the first place, the new logic outlaws, flanks, dismisses—what you will—one type of problems and substitutes for it another type. Philosophy forswears inquiry after absolute origins and absolute finalities in order to explore specific values and the specific conditions that generate them.

Darwin concluded that the impossibility of assigning the world to chance as a whole and to design in its parts indicated the insolubility of the question. Two radically different reasons, however, may be given as to why a problem is insoluble. One reason is that the problem is too high for intelligence; the other is that the question in its very asking makes assumptions that render the question meaningless. The latter alternative is unerringly pointed to in the celebrated case of design *versus* chance. Once admit that the sole verifiable or fruitful object of knowledge is the particular set of changes that generate the object of study together with the consequences that then flow from it, and no intelligible question can be asked about what, by assumption, lies outside. To assert—as is often asserted—that specific values of particular truths, social bonds and forms of beauty, if they can be shown to be generated by concretely knowable conditions, are meaningless and in vain; to assert that they are justified only when they and their particular causes and effects have all at once been gathered up into some inclusive first cause and some exhaustive final goal, is intellectual atavism. Such argumentation is reversion to the logic that explained the extinction of fire by water through the formal essence of aqueousness and the quenching of thirst by water through the final cause of aqueousness. Whether used in the case of the special event or that of life as a whole, such logic only abstracts some aspect of the existing course of events in order to reduplicate it as a petrified eternal principle by which to explain the very changes of which it is the formalization.

When Henry Sidgwick casually remarked in a letter that as he grew older his interest in what or who made the world was altered into interest in what kind of a world it is anyway, his voicing of a common experience of our own day illustrates also the nature of that intellectual transformation effected by the Darwinian logic. Interest shifts from the wholesale essence back of special changes to the question of how special changes serve and defeat concrete purposes; shifts from an intelligence that shaped things once for all to the particular intelligences which things are even now shaping; shifts from an ultimate goal of good to the direct increments of justice and happiness that intelligent administration of existent conditions may beget and that present carelessness or stupidity will destroy or forego.

In the second place, the classic type of logic inevitably set philosophy upon proving that life *must* have certain qualities and values—no matter how experience presents the matter—because of some remote cause and eventual goal. The duty of wholesale justification inevitably accompanies all thinking that makes the meaning of special occurrences depend upon something that once and for all lies behind them. The habit of derogating from present meanings and uses prevents our looking the facts of experience in the face; it prevents serious acknowledgment of the evils they present and serious concern with the goods they promise but do not as yet fulfill. It turns thought to the business of finding a wholesale transcendent remedy for the one and guarantee for the other. One is reminded of the way many moralists and theologians greeted Herbert Spencer's recognition of an unknowable energy from which welled up the phenomenal physical processes without and the conscious operations within. Merely because Spencer labeled his unknowable energy "God," this faded piece of metaphysical goods was greeted as an important and grateful concession to the reality of the spiritual realm. Were it not for the deep hold of the habit of seeking justification for ideal values in the remote and transcendent, surely this reference of them to an unknowab.. absolute would be despised in comparison with the demonstrations of experience that knowable energies are daily generating about us precious values.

The displacing of this wholesale type of philosophy will doubtless not arrive by sheer logical disproof, but rather by growing recognition of its futility. Were it a thousand times true that opium produces sleep because of its dormitive energy, yet the inducing of sleep in the tired, and the recovery to waking life of the poisoned, would not be thereby one least step forwarded. And were it a thousand times dialectically demonstrated that life as a whole is regulated by a transcendent principle to a final inclusive goal, none the less truth and error, health and disease, good and evil, hope and fear in the concrete, would remain just what and where they now are. To improve our education, to ameliorate our manners, to advance our politics, we must have recourse to specific conditions of generation.

Finally, the new logic introduces responsibility into the intellectual life. To idealize and rationalize the universe at large is after all a confession of inability to master the courses of things that specifically concern us. As long as mankind suffered from this impotency, it naturally shifted a burden of responsibility that it could not carry over to the more competent shoulders of the transcendent cause. But if insight into specific conditions of value and into specific consequences of ideas is possible, philosophy must in time become a method of locating and interpreting the more serious of the conflicts that occur in life, and a method of projecting ways for dealing with them: a method of moral and political diagnosis and prognosis.

The claim to formulate *a priori* the legislative constitution of the universe is by its nature a claim that may lead to elaborate dialectic developments. But it is also one that removes these very conclusions from subjection to experimental test, for, by definition, these results make no differences in the detailed course of events. But a philosophy that humbles its pretensions to the work of projecting hypotheses for the education and conduct of mind, individual and social, is thereby subjected to test by the way in which the ideas it propounds work out in practice. In having modesty forced upon it, philosophy also acquires responsibility.

Doubtless I seem to have violated the implied promise of my earlier remarks and to have turned both prophet and partizan. But in anticipating the direction of the transformations in philosophy to be wrought by the Darwinian genetic and experimental logic, I do not profess to speak for any save those who yield themselves consciously or unconsciously to this logic. No one can fairly deny that at present there are two effects of the Darwinian mode of thinking. On the one hand, there are making many sincere and vital efforts to revise our traditional philosophic conceptions in accordance with its demands. On the other hand, there is as definitely a recrudescence of absolutistic philosophies; an assertion of a type of philosophic knowing distinct from that of the sciences, one which opens to us another kind of reality from that to which the sciences give access; an appeal through experience to something that essentially goes beyond experience. This reaction affects popular creeds and religious movements as well as technical philosophies. The very conquest of the biological sciences by the new ideas has led many to proclaim an explicit and rigid separation of philosophy from science.

Old ideas give way slowly; for they are more than abstract logical forms and categories. They are habits, predispositions, deeply engrained attitudes of aversion and preference. Moreover, the conviction persists—though history shows it to be a hallucination—that all the questions that the human mind has asked are questions that can be answered in terms of the alternatives that the questions themselves present. But in fact intellectual progress usually occurs through sheer abandonment of questions together with both of the alternatives they assume—an abandonment that results from their decreasing vitality and a change of urgent interest. We do not solve them: we get over them. Old questions are solved by disappearing, evaporating, while new questions corresponding to the changed attitude of endeavor and preference take their place. Doubtless the greatest dissolvent in contemporary thought of old questions, the greatest precipitant of new methods, new intentions, new problems,

is the one effected by the scientific revolution that found its climax
in the *Origin of Species*.

INTELLIGENCE AND MORALS

"Except the blind forces of nature," said Sir Henry Maine, "nothing moves in this world which is not Greek in its origin." And if
we ask why this is so, the response comes that the Greek discovered
the business of man to be pursuit of good, and intelligence to be
central in this quest. The utmost to be said in praise of Plato and
Aristotle is not that they invented excellent moral theories, but that
they rose to the opportunity which the spectacle of Greek life afforded. For Athens presented an all but complete microcosm for the
study of the interaction of social organization and individual character. A public life of rich diversity in concentrated and intense
splendor trained the civic sense. Strife of faction and the rapid
oscillations of types of polity provided the occasion for intellectual
inquiry and analysis. The careers of dramatic personalities, habits
of discussion, ease of legislative change, facilities for personal ambitions, distraction by personal rivalries, fixed attention upon the elements of character, and upon consideration of the effect of individual character on social vitality and stability. Happy exemption from
ecclesiastical preoccupations, susceptibility to natural harmony, and
natural piety conspired with frank and open observation to acknowledgment of the rôle played by natural conditions. Social
instability and shock made equally pertinent and obvious the re-
mark that only intelligence can confirm the values that natural
conditions generate, and that intelligence is itself nurtured and
matured only in a free and stable society.

In Plato the resultant analysis of the mutual implications of the
individual, the social and the natural, converged in the ideas that

From a lecture delivered at Columbia University, March, 1908; reprinted
from *The Influence of Darwin on Philosophy*, pp. 46-76, by John Dewey.
Copyright, 1910, Henry Holt and Company, Inc.; reprinted by permission.

morals and philosophy are one: namely, a love of that wisdom which is the source of secure and social good; that mathematics and the natural sciences focused upon the problem of the perception of the good furnish the materials of moral science; that logic is the method of the pregnant organization of social conditions with respect to good; that politics and psychology are sciences of one and the same human nature, taken first in the large and then in the little. So far that large and expansive vision of Plato.

But projection of a better life must be based upon reflection of the life already lived. The inevitable limitations of the Greek city-state were inevitably wrought into the texture of moral theory.

The business of thought was to furnish a substitute for customs which were then relaxing from the pressure of contact and inter-course without and the friction of strife within. Reason was to take the place of custom as a guide of life; but it was to furnish rules as final, as unalterable as those of custom. In short, the thinkers were fascinated by the afterglow of custom. They took for their own ideal the distillation from custom of its essence—ends and laws which should be rigid and invariable. Thus Morals was set upon the track which it dared not leave for nigh twenty-five hundred years: search for *the* final good, and for *the* single moral force.

Aristotle's assertions that the state exists by nature, and that in the state alone does the individual achieve independence and com-pleteness of life, are indeed pregnant sayings. But as uttered by Aristotle they meant that, in an isolated state, the Greek city-state, set a garlanded island in the waste sea of *barbaroi,* a community indifferent when not hostile to all other social groupings, individuals attain their full end. In a social unity which signified social con-traction, contempt, and antagonism, in a social order which despised intercourse and glorified war, is realized the life of excellence!

There is likewise a profound saying of Aristotle's that the indi-vidual who otherwise than by accident is not a member of a state is either a brute or a god. But it is generally forgotten that else-where Aristotle identified the highest excellence, the chief virtue, with pure thought, and identifying this with the divine, isolated it in lonely grandeur from the life of society. That man, so far as in him lay, should be godlike, meant that he should be non-social,

...cause supra-civic. Plato the idealist had shared the belief that reason is the divine; but he was also a reformer and a radical and he would have those who attained rational insight descend again into the civic cave, and in its obscurity labor patiently for the enlightenment of its blear-eyed inhabitants. Aristotle, the conservative and the definer of what is, gloried in the exaltation of intelligence in man above civic excellence and social need; and thereby isolated the life of truest knowledge from contact with social experience and from responsibility for discrimination of values in the course of life.

Moral theory, however, accepted from social custom more than its cataleptic rigidity, its exclusive area of common good, and its unfructified and irresponsible reason. The city-state was a superficial layer of cultured citizens, cultured through a participation in affairs made possible by relief from economic pursuits, superimposed upon the dense mass of serfs, artizans, and laborers. For this division, moral philosophy made itself spiritual sponsor, and thus took it up into its own being. Plato wrestled valiantly with the class problem; but his outcome was the necessity of decisive demarcation, after education of the masses in whom reason was asleep and appetite much awake, from the few who were fit to rule because alertly wise. The most generously imaginative soul of all philosophy could not far outrun the institutional practices of his people and his times. This might have warned his successors of the danger of deserting the sober path of a critical discernment of the better and the worse within contemporary life for the more exciting adventure of a final determination of absolute good and evil. It might have taught the probability that some brute residuum or unrationalized social habit would be erected into an apotheosis of pure reason. But the lesson was not learned. Aristotle promptly yielded to the besetting sin of all philosophers, the idealization of the existent: he declared that the class distinctions of superiority and inferiority as between man and woman, master and slave, liberal-minded and base mechanic, exist and are justified by nature—a nature which aims at embodied reason.

What, finally, is this Nature to which the philosophy of society and the individual so bound itself? It is the nature which figures in Greek customs and myth; the nature resplendent and adorned which confronts us in Greek poetry and art: the animism of savage man purged of grossness and generalized by unerring esthetic taste into beauty and system. The myths had told of the loves and hates, the caprices and desertions of the gods, and behind them all, inevitable Fate. Philosophy translated these tales into formulae of the brute fluctuation of rapacious change held in bounds by the final and supreme end: the rational good. The animism of the popular mind died to reappear as cosmology.

Repeatedly in this course we have heard of sciences which began as parts of philosophy and which gradually won their independence. Another statement of the same history is that both science and philosophy began in subjection to mythological animism. Both began with acceptance of a nature whose irregularities displayed the meaningless variability of foolish wants held within the limits of order and uniformity by an underlying movement toward a final and stable purpose. And when the sciences gradually assumed the task of reducing irregular caprice to regular conjunction, philosophy bravely took upon itself the task of substantiating, under the caption of a spiritual view of the universe, the animistic survival. Doubtless Socrates brought philosophy to earth; but his injunction to man to know himself was incredibly compromised in its execution by the fact that later philosophers submerged man in the world to which philosophy was brought: a world which was the heavy and sunken center of hierarchic heavens located in their purity and refinement as remotely as possible from the gross and muddy vesture of earth.

The various limitations of Greek custom, its hostile indifference to all outside the narrow city-state, its assumption of fixed divisions of wise and blind among men, its inability socially to utilize science, its subordination of human intention to cosmic aim—all of these things were worked into moral theory. Philosophy had no active hand in producing the condition of barbarism in Europe from the fifth to the fifteenth centuries. By an unwitting irony which would have shocked none so much as the lucid moralists of Athens, their philosophic idealization, under the captions of Nature and Reason, of the inherent limitations of Athenian society and Greek science, furnished the intellectual tools for defining, standardizing, and justifying all the fundamental clefts and antagonisms of feudalism. When practical conditions are not frozen in men's imagination into crystalline truths, they are naturally fluid. They come and go. But when intelligence fixes fluctuating circumstances into final ideals, petrifaction is likely to occur; and philosophy gratuitously took upon itself the responsibility for justifying the worst defects of barbarian Europe by showing their necessary connection with divine reason.

The division of mankind into the two camps of the redeemed and the condemned had not needed philosophy to produce it. But the Greek cleavage of men into separate kinds on the basis of their position within or without the city-state was used to rationalize this harsh intolerance. The hierarchic organization of feudalism, within church and state, of those possessed of sacred rule and those whose sole excellence was obedience, did not require moral theory to generate or explain it. But it took philosophy to furnish the intellectual tools by which such chance episodes were emblazoned upon the cosmic heavens as a grandiose spiritual achievement. No; it is all too easy to explain bitter intolerance and desire for domination. Stubborn as they are, it was only when Greek moral theory had put underneath them the distinction between the irrational and the rational, between divine truth and good and corrupt and weak human appetite, that intolerance on system and earthly domination for the sake of eternal excellence were philosophically sanctioned. The health and welfare of the body and the securing for all of a sure and a prosperous livelihood were not matters for which medieval conditions fostered care in any case. But moral philosophy was prevailed upon to damn the body on principle, and to relegate to insignificance as merely mundane and temporal the problem of a just industrial order. Circumstances of the times bore with sufficient hardness upon successful scientific investigation; but philosophy added the conviction that in any case truth is so supernal that it must be supernaturally revealed, and so important that it must be authoritatively imparted and enforced. Intelligence was diverted from the critical consideration of the natural sources and social consequences of better and worse into the channel of metaphysical subtleties and systems, acceptance of which was made essential to participation in the social order and in rational excellence. Philosophy bound the once erect form of human endeavor and progress to the chariot wheels of cosmology and theology.

Since the Renaissance, moral philosophy has repeatedly reverted to the Greek ideal of natural excellence realized in social life, under the fostering care of intelligence in action. The return, however, has taken place under the influence of democratic polity, commercial expansion, and scientific reorganization. It has been a liberation more than a reversion. This combined return and emancipation, having transformed our practice of life in the last four centuries, will not be content till it has written itself clear in our theory of that practice. Whether the consequent revolution in moral philosophy be termed pragmatism or be given the happier title of the applied and experimental habit of mind is of little account. What is of moment is that intelligence has descended from its lonely isolation at the remote edge of things, whence it operated as unmoved mover and ultimate good, to take its seat in the moving affairs of men. Theory may therefore become responsible to the practices that have generated it; the good be connected with nature, but with nature naturally, not metaphysically, conceived, and social life be cherished in behalf of its own immediate possibilities, not on the ground of its remote connections with a cosmic reason and an absolute end.

There is a notion, more familiar than correct, that Greek thought sacrificed the individual to the state. None has ever known better than the Greek that the individual comes to himself and to his own only in association with others. But Greek thought subjected, as we have seen, both state and individual to an external cosmic order; and thereby it inevitably restricted the free use in doubt, inquiry, and experimentation, of the human intelligence. The *anima libera*, the free mind of the sixteenth century, of Galileo and his successors, was the counterpart of the disintegration of cosmology and its animistic teleology. The lecturer on political economy reminded us that his subject began, in the Middle Ages, as a branch of ethics, though, as he hastened to show, it soon got into better association. Well, the same company was once kept by all the sciences, mathematical and physical as well as social. According to all accounts it was the integrity of the number one and the rectitude of the square that attracted the attention of Pythagoras to arithmetic and geometry as promising fields of study. Astronomy was the projected picture book of a cosmic object lesson in morals, Dante's transcript of which is none the less literal because poetic. If physics alone remained outside the moral fold, while noble essences redeemed chemistry, occult forces blessed physiology, and the immaterial soul exalted psychology, physics is the exception that proves the rule: matter was so inherently immoral that no high-minded science would demean itself by contact with it.

If we do not join with many in lamenting the stripping from nature of those idealistic properties in which animism survived, if we do not mourn the secession of the sciences from ethics, it is because the abandonment by intelligence of a fixed and static moral end was the necessary precondition of a free and progressive science of both things and morals; because the emancipation of the sciences from ready made, remote, and abstract values was necessary to make the sciences available for creating and maintaining more and specific values here and now. The divine comedy of modern medicine and hygiene is one of the human epics yet to be written; but when composed it may prove no unworthy companion of the medieval epic of other worldly beatific visions. The great ideas of the eighteenth century, that expansive epoch of moral perception which ranks in illumination and fervor along with classic Greek thought, the great ideas of the indefinitely continuous progress of humanity and of the power and significance of freed intelligence, were borne by a single mother—experimental inquiry.

The growth of industry and commerce is at once cause and effect of the growth in science. Democritus and other ancients conceived the mechanical theory of the universe. The notion was not only bland and repellent, because it ignored the rich social material which Plato and Aristotle had organized into their rival idealistic views; but it was scientifically sterile, a piece of dialectics. Contempt for machines as the accouterments of despised mechanics kept the mechanical conception aloof from these specific and controllable experiences which alone could fructify it. This conception, then, like the idealistic, was translated into a speculative cosmology and thrown like a vast net around the universe at large, as if to keep it from coming to pieces. It is from respect for the lever, the pulley, and the screw that modern experimental and mathematical mechanics derives itself. Motion, traced through the workings of a machine, was followed out into natural events and studied just as motion, not as a poor yet necessary device for realizing final causes. So studied, it was found to be available for new machines and new applications, which in creating new ends also promoted new wants, and thereby stimulated new activities, new discoveries, and new inventions. The recognition that natural energy can be systematically applied, through experimental observation, to the satisfaction and multiplication of concrete wants is doubtless the greatest single discovery ever imported into the life of man—save perhaps the discovery of language. Science, borrowing from industry, repaid the debt with interest, and has made the control of natural forces for the aims of life so inevitable that for the first time man is relieved from overhanging fear, with its wolflike scramble to possess and accumulate, and is freed to consider the more gracious question of securing to all an ample and liberal life. The industrial life had been condemned by Greek exaltation of abstract thought and by Greek contempt for labor, as representing the brute struggle of carnal appetite for its own satiety. The industrial movement, offspring of science, restored it to its central position in morals. When Adam Smith made economic activity the moving spring of man's unremitting effort, from the cradle to the grave, to better his own lot, he recorded this change. And when he made sympathy the central spring in man's conscious moral endeavor, he reported the effect which the increasing intercourse of men, due primarily to commerce, had in breaking down suspicion and jealousy and in liberating man's kindlier impulses.

Democracy, the crucial expression of modern life, is not so much an addition to the scientific and industrial tendencies as it is the perception of their social or spiritual meaning. Democracy is an absurdity where faith in the individual as individual is impossible; and this faith is impossible when intelligence is regarded as a cosmic power, not an adjustment and application of individual tendencies. It is also impossible when appetites and desires are conceived to be the dominant factor in the constitution of most men's characters, and when appetite and desire are conceived to be manifestations of the disorderly and unruly principle of nature. To put the intellectual center of gravity in the objective cosmos, outside of men's own experiments and tests, and then to invite the application of individual intelligence to the determination of society, is to invite chaos. To hold that want is mere negative flux and hence requires external fixation by reason, and then to invite the wants to give free play to themselves in social construction and intercourse, is to call down anarchy. Democracy is estimable only through the changed conception of intelligence, that forms modern science, and of want, that forms modern industry. It is essentially a changed psychology. The substitution, for *a priori* truth and deduction, of fluent doubt and inquiry meant trust in human nature in the concrete; in individual honesty, curiosity, and sympathy. The substitution of moving commerce for fixed custom meant a view of wants as the dynamics of social progress, not as the pathology of private greed. The nineteenth century indeed turned sour on that somewhat complacent optimism in which the eighteenth century rested: the ideas that the intelligent self-love of individuals would conduce to social cohesion, and competition among individuals usher in the kingdom of social welfare. But the conception of a social harmony of interests in the achievement by each individual of his own freedom should contribute to a like perfecting of the powers of all, through a fraternally organized society, is the permanent contribution of the industrial movement to morals—even though so far it be but the contribution of a problem.

Intellectually speaking, the centuries since the fourteenth are the true middle ages. They mark the transitional period of mental habit, as the so-called medieval period represents the petrifaction, under changed outward conditions, of Greek ideas. The conscious articulation of genuinely modern tendencies has yet to come, and till it comes the ethic of our own life must remain undescribed. But the system of morals which has come nearest to the reflection of the movements of science, democracy, and commerce is doubtless the utilitarian. Scientific, after the modern mode, it certainly would be. Newton's influence dyes deep the moral thought of the eighteenth century. The arrangements of the solar system had been described in terms of a homogeneous matter and motion, worked by two opposed and compensating forces: all because a method of analysis, of generalization by analogy, and of mathematical deduction back to new empirical details had been followed. The imagination of the eighteenth century was a Newtonian imagination; and this no less in social than in physical matters. Hume proclaims that morals is about to become an experimental science. Just as, almost in our own day, Mill's interest in a method for social science led him to reformulate the logic of experimental inquiry, so all the great men of the Enlightenment were in search for the organon of morals which should repeat the physical triumphs of Newton. Bentham notes that physics has had its Bacon and Newton; that morals has had its Bacon in Helvétius, but still awaits its Newton; and he leaves us in no doubt that at the moment of writing he was ready, modestly but firmly, to fill the waiting niche with its missing figure.

The industrial movement furnished the concrete imagery for this ethical renovation. The utilitarians borrowed from Adam Smith the notion that through industrial exchange in a free society the individual pursuing his own good is led, under the guidance of the "invisible hand," to promote the general good more effectually than if he had set out to do it. This idea was dressed out in the atomistic psychology which Hartley built out from Locke—and was returned at usurious rates to later economists.

From the great French writers who had sought to justify and promote democratic individualism, came the conception that, since it is perverted political institutions which deprave individuals and bring them into hostility, nation against nation, class against class, individual against individual, the great political problem is such a reform of law and legislation, civil and criminal, of administration, and of education as will force the individual to find his own interests in pursuits conducing to the welfare of others.

Tremendously effective as a tool of criticism, operative in abolition and elimination, utilitarianism failed to measure up to the constructive needs of the time. Its theoretical equalization of the good of each with that of every other was practically perverted by its excessive interest in the middle and manufacturing classes. Its specu-lative defect of an atomistic psychology combined with this narrow-ness of vision to make light of the constructive work that needs to be done by the state, before all can have, otherwise than in name, an equal chance to count in the common good. Thus the age-long subordination of economics to politics was revenged in the sub-merging of both politics and ethics in a narrow theory of economic profit; and utilitarianism, in its orthodox descendants, proffered the disjointed pieces of a mechanism, with a monotonous reiteration that looked at aright they form a beautifully harmonious organism.

Prevision, and to some extent experience, of this failure, conjoined with differing social traditions and ambitions, evoked German idealism, the transcendental morals of Kant and his successors. German thought strove to preserve the traditions which bound the culture to the past, while revising these traditions to render them capable of meeting novel conditions. It found weapons at hand in the conceptions borrowed by Roman law from Stoic philosophy, and in the conceptions by which Protestant humanism had re-edited scholastic Catholicism. Grotius had made the idea of natural law, natural right and obligation, the central idea of German morals, as thoroughly as Locke had made the individual desire for liberty and happiness the focus of English and then of French speculation. Materialized idealism is the happy monstrosity in which the popular demand for vivid imagery is most easily reconciled with the equally strong demand for supremacy of moral values; and the complete idealistic materialism of Stoicism has always given its ideas a practi-cal influence out of all proportion to their theoretical vogue as a system. To the Protestant, that is the German, humanist, Natural Law, the bond of harmonious reason in nature, the spring of social intercourse among men, the inward light of individual conscience, united Cicero, St. Paul, and Luther in blessed union; gave a rational, not superrational basis for morals, and provided room for social legislation which at the same time could easily be held back from too ruthless application to dominant class interests.

Kant saw the mass of empirical and hence irrelevant detail that had found refuge within this liberal and diffusive reason. He saw that the idea of reason could be made self-consistent only by stripping it naked of these empirical accretions. He then provided, in his critiques, a somewhat cumbrous moving van for transferring the resultant pure or naked reason out of nature and the objective world, and for locating it in new quarters, with a new stock of goods and new customers. The new quarters were particular subjects, individuals; the stock of goods were the forms of perception and the functions of thought by which empirical flux is woven into durable fabrics; the new customers were a society of individuals in which all are ends in themselves. There ought to be an injunction issued that Kant's saying about Hume's awakening of him should not be quoted save in connection with his other saying that Rousseau brought him to himself, in teaching him that the philosopher is of less account than the laborer in the fields unless he contributes to human freedom. But none the less, the new tenant, the universal reason, and the old homestead, the empirical tumultuous individual, could not get on together. Reason became a mere voice which, having nothing in particular to say, said Law, Duty, in general, leaving to the existing social order of the Prussia of Frederick the Great the congenial task of declaring just what was obligatory in the concrete. The marriage of freedom and authority was thus celebrated with the understanding that sentimental primacy went to the former and practical control to the latter.

The effort to force a universal reason that had been used to the broad domains of the cosmos into the cramped confines of individuality conceived as merely "empirical," a highly particularized creation of sense, could have but one result: an explosion. The products of that explosion constitute the Post-Kantian philosophies. It was the work of Hegel to attempt to fill in the empty reason of Kant with the concrete contents of history. The voice sounded like the voice of Aristotle, Thomas of Aquino, and Spinoza translated into Swabian German; but the hands were as the hands of Montesquieu, Herder, Condorcet, and the rising historical school. The outcome was the assertion that history is reason, and reason is history: the actual is rational, the rational is the actual. It gave the pleasant appearance (which Hegel did not strenuously discourage) of being specifically an idealization of the Prussian nation, and incidentally a systematized apologetic for the universe at large. But in intellectual and practical effect, it lifted the idea of process above that of fixed origins and fixed ends, and presented the social and moral order, as well as the intellectual, as a scene of becoming, and it located reason somewhere within the struggles of life.

Unstable equilibrium, rapid fermentation, and a succession of explosive reports are thus the chief notes of modern ethics. Scepticism and traditionalism, empiricism and rationalism, crude naturalism and all-embracing idealisms, flourish side by side—all the more flourish, one suspects, because side by side. Spencer exults because natural science reveals that a rapid transit of evolution is carrying us automatically to the goal of perfect man in perfect society; and his English idealistic contemporary, Green, is so disturbed by the removal from nature of its moral qualities, that he tries to show that this makes no difference, since nature in any case is constituted and known through a spiritual principle which is as permanent as nature is changing. An Amiel genteelly laments the decadence of the inner life, while his neighbor Nietzsche brandishes in rude ecstasy the banner of brute survival as a happy omen of the final victory of nobility of mind. The reasonable conclusion from such a scene is that there is taking place a transformation of attitude towards moral theory rather than mere propagation of varieties among theories. The classic theories all agreed in one regard. They all alike assumed the existence of *the* end, the *summum bonum*, the final goal; and of *the* separate moral force that moves to that goal. Moralists have disputed as to whether the end is an aggregate of pleasurable states of consciousness, enjoyment of the divine essence, acknowledgment of the law of duty, or conformity to environment. So they have disputed as to the path by which the final goal is to be reached: fear or benevolence? reverence for pure law or pity for others? self-love or altruism? But these very controversies implied that there was but the one end and the one means.

The transformation in attitude, to which I referred, is the growing belief that the proper business of intelligence is discrimination of multiple and present goods and of the varied immediate means of their realization; not search for the one remote aim. The progress of biology has accustomed our minds to the notion that intelligence is not an outside power presiding supremely but statically over the desires and efforts of man, but is a method of adjustment of capacities and conditions within specific situations. History . . . has discovered itself in the idea of process. The genetic standpoint makes us aware that the systems of the past are neither fraudulent impostures nor absolute revelations; but are the products of political, economic, and scientific conditions whose change carries with it change of theoretical formulations. The recognition that intelligence is properly an organ of adjustment in difficult situations makes us aware that past theories were of value so far as they helped to carry to an issue the social perplexities from which they emerged. But the chief impact of the evolutionary method is upon the present. Theory having learned what it cannot do, is made responsible for the better performance of what needs to be done, and what only a broadly equipped intelligence can undertake: study of the conditions out of which come the obstacles and the resources of adequate life, and developing and testing the ideas that, as working hypotheses, may be used to diminish the causes of evil and to buttress and expand the sources of good. This program is indeed vague, but only unfamiliarity with it could lead one to the conclusion that it is less vague than the idea that there is a single moral ideal and a single moral motive force.

From this point of view there is no separate body of moral rules; no separate system of motive powers; no separate subject-matter of moral knowledge, and hence no such thing as an isolated ethical science. If the business of morals is not to speculate upon man's final end and upon an ultimate standard of right, it is to utilize physiology, anthropology, and psychology to discover all that can be discovered of man, his organic powers and propensities. If its business is not to search for the one separate moral motive, it is to converge all the instrumentalities of the social arts, of law, education, economics, and political science upon the construction of intelligent methods of improving the common lot.

If we still wish to make our peace with the past, and to sum up the plural and changing goods of life in a single word, doubtless the term happiness is the one most apt. But we should again exchange free morals for sterile metaphysics, if we imagine that "happiness" is any less unique than the individuals who experience it; any less complex than the constitution of their capacities, or any less variable than the objects upon which their capacities are directed.

To many timid, albeit sincere, souls of an earlier century, the decay of the doctrine that all true and worthful science is knowledge of final causes seemed fraught with danger to science and to morals. The rival conception of wide open universe, a universe without bounds in time or space, without final limits of origin or destiny, a universe with the lid off, was a menace. We now face in moral science a similar crisis and like opportunity, as well as share in a like dreadful suspense. The abolition of a fixed and final goal and causal force in nature did not, as a matter of fact, render rational conviction less important or less attainable. It was accompanied by the provision of a technique of persistent and detailed inquiry in all special fields of fact, a technique which led to the detection of unsuspected forces and the revelation of undreamed of uses. In like fashion we may anticipate that the abolition of *the* final goal and *the* single motive power and *the* separate and infallible faculty in morals, will quicken inquiry into the diversity of specific goods of experience, fix attention upon their conditions, and bring to light values now dim and obscure. The change may relieve men from responsibility for what they cannot do, but it will promote thoughtful consideration of what they may do and the definition of responsibility for what they do amiss because of failure to think straight and carefully. Absolute goods will fall into the background, but the question of making more sure and extensive the share of all men in natural and social goods will be urgent, a problem not to be escaped nor evaded.

Morals, philosophy, returns to its first love; love of the wisdom that is nurse, as nature is mother, of good. But it returns to the Socratic principle equipped with a multitude of special methods of inquiry and testing; with an organized mass of knowledge, and with control of the arrangements by which industry, law, and education may concentrate upon the problem of the participation by all men and women, up to their capacity of absorption, in all attained values. Morals may then well leave to poetry and to art, the task (so unartistically performed by philosophy since Plato) of gathering together and rounding out, into one abiding picture, the separate and special goods of life. It may leave this task with the assurance that the resultant synthesis will not depict any final and all-inclusive good, but will add just one more specific good to the enjoyable excellencies of life.

Humorous irony shines through most of the harsh glances turned towards the idea of an experimental basis and career for morals. Some shiver in the fear that morals will be plunged into anarchic confusion—a view well expressed by a recent writer in saying that if the *a priori* and transcendental basis of morals be abandoned "we shall have merely the same certainty that now exists in physics and chemistry"! Elsewhere lurks the apprehension that the progress of scientific method will deliver the purposive freedom of man bound hand and foot to the fatal decrees of iron necessity, called natural law. The notion that laws govern and forces rule is an animistic survival. It is a product of reading nature in terms of politics in order to turn around and then read politics in the light of supposed sanctions of nature. This idea passed from medieval theology into the science of Newton, to whom the universe was the dominion of a sovereign whose laws were the laws of nature. From Newton it passed into the deism of the eighteenth century, whence it migrated into the philosophy of the Enlightenment, to make its last stand in Spencer's philosophy of the fixed environment and the static goal.

No, nature is not an unchangeable order, unwinding itself majestically from the reel of law under the control of deified forces. It is an indefinite congeries of changes. Laws are not governmental regulations which limit change, but are convenient formulations of selected portions of change followed through a longer or shorter period of time, and then registered in statistical forms that are amenable to mathematical manipulation. That this device of shorthand symbolization presages the subjection of man's intelligent effort to fixity of law and environment is interesting as a culture survival, but is not important for moral theory. Savage and child delight in creating bogeys from which, their origin and structure being conveniently concealed, interesting thrills and shudders may be had. Civilized man in the nineteenth century outdid these bugaboos in his image of a fixed universe hung on a cast-iron framework of fixed, necessary, and universal laws. Knowledge of nature does not mean subjection to predestination, but insight into courses of change; an insight which is formulated in "laws," that is, methods of subsequent procedure.

Knowledge of the process and conditions of physical and social change through experimental science and genetic history has one result with a double name: increase of control, and increase of responsibility; increase of power to direct natural change, and increase of responsibility for its equitable direction toward fuller good. Theory located within progressive practice instead of reigning statically supreme over it, means practice itself made responsible to intelligence; to intelligence which relentlessly scrutinizes the consequences of every practice, and which exacts liability by an equally relentless publicity. As long as morals occupies itself with mere ideals, forces and conditions as they are will be good enough for "practical" men, since they are then left to their own devices in turning these to their own account. As long as moralists plume themselves upon possession of the domain of the categorical imperative with its bare precepts, men of executive habits will always be at their elbows to regulate the concrete social conditions through which the form of law gets its actual filling of specific injunctions. When freedom is conceived to be transcendental, the coercive restraint of immediate necessity will lay its harsh hand upon the mass of men.

In the end, men do what they can do. They refrain from doing what they cannot do. They do what their own specific powers in conjunction with the limitations and resources of the environment permit. The effective control of their powers is not through precepts, but through the regulation of their conditions. If this regulation is to be not merely physical or coercive, but moral, it must consist of the intelligent selection and determination of the environments in which we act; and in an intelligent exaction of responsibility for the use of men's powers. Theorists inquire after the "motive" to morality, to virtue and the good, under such circumstances. What then, one wonders, is their conception of the make-up of human nature and of its relation to virtue and to goodness? The pessimism that dictates such a question, if it be justified, precludes any consideration of morals.

The diversion of intelligence from discrimination of plural and concrete goods, from noting their conditions and obstacles, and from devising methods for holding men responsible for their concrete use of powers and conditions, has done more than brute love of power to establish inequality and injustice among men. It has done more, because it has confirmed with social sanctions the principle of feudal domination. All men require moral sanctions in their conduct: the consent of their kind. Not getting it otherwise, they go insane to feign it. No man ever lived with the exclusive approval of his own conscience. Hence the vacuum left in practical matters by the remote irrelevancy of transcendental morals has to be filled in somehow. It is filled in. It is filled in with class-codes, class-standards, class-approvals—with codes which recommend the practices and habits already current in a given circle, set, calling, profession, trade, industry, club, or gang. These class-codes always lean back upon and support themselves by the professed ideal code. This latter meets them more than half-way. Being in its pretense a theory for regulating practice, it must demonstrate its practicability. It is uneasy in isolation, and travels hastily to meet with compromise and accommodation the actual situation in all its brute unrationality. Where the pressure is greatest—in the habitual practice of the political and economic chieftains—there it accommodates the most.

Class-codes of morals are sanctions, under the caption of ideals, of uncriticised customs; they are recommendations, under the head of duties, of what the members of the class are already most given to doing. If there are to obtain more equable and comprehensive principles of action, exacting a more impartial exercise of natural power and resource in the interests of a common good, members of a class must no longer rest content in responsibility to a class whose traditions constitute its conscience, but be made responsible to a society whose conscience is its free and effectively organized intelligence.

In such a conscience alone will the Socratic injunction to man to know himself be fulfilled.

·X·

BROOKS ADAMS

[1 8 4 8 - 1 9 2 7]

INTRODUCTION TO
"THE NEW EMPIRE"

INFERENCES

INTRODUCTION TO
"THE NEW EMPIRE"

During the last decade the world has traversed one of those periodic crises which attend an alteration in the social equilibrium. The seat of energy has migrated from Europe to America. The phenomenon is not new, as similar perturbations have occurred from the earliest times; its peculiarity lies in its velocity and its proportions. A change of equilibrium has heretofore occupied at least the span of a human lifetime, so that a new generation has gradually become habituated to the novel environment. In this instance the revolution came so suddenly that few realized its presence before it ended. Nevertheless, it has long been in preparation, and it appears to be fundamental, for it is the effect of that alteration in mental processes which we call the advance of science.

American supremacy has been made possible only through applied science. The labors of successive generations of scientific men have established a control over nature which has enabled the United States to construct a new industrial mechanism, with processes surpassingly perfect. Nothing has ever equalled in economy and energy the administration of the great American corporations. These are the offspring of scientific thought. On the other hand, wherever scientific criticism and scientific methods have not penetrated, the old processes prevail, and these show signs of decrepitude. The national government may be taken as an illustration.

When Englishmen first settled upon this continent they came as pioneers, and they developed an extreme individuality. Thinly scattered in widely separated colonies along the coast, little independent communities came into being which had few interests in common. Consolidation began late and took an imperfect form, the conditions then existing generating a peculiar administrative mechanism. The organization reached after the Revolution was rather negative than

From *The New Empire*, pp. 1-43, by Brooks Adams (New York: The Macmillan Company, 1902). Reprinted by permission of the Massachusetts Historical Society.

positive. The people suffered from certain effects of decentralization which interfered with commercial exchanges. These they tried to remedy, but they deprecated corporate energy. They provided against discriminations in trade, violations of contract, bad money, and the like, and they made provision for the common defence, but they manifested jealousy of consolidated power.

Each state feared interference in local concerns more than it craved aid in schemes which transcended its borders, and accordingly the framers of the Constitution intentionally made combined action slow and difficult. They devised three coördinate departments, each of which could stop the other two, and none of which could operate alone. And they did this under the conviction that they had reached certain final truths in government, and in the face of the law that friction bears a ratio to the weight moved.

Even with such concessions to tradition, no little energy was required to overcome the inertia of that primitive society, for on such societies tradition has preponderating influence. Patrick Henry well represented conservative Virginia, and Henry denounced the Constitution day by day "as the most fatal plan which could possibly be conceived for enslaving a free people." Henry could not comprehend the change in the conditions of life about him, because he had been bred to believe that the institutions he knew were intrinsically good. He revered them much as he revered revealed religion; as an end in themselves, and not as means to an end. Every considerable political innovation must thus affect a portion of the population, for men always live to whom a change in what they have been trained to respect is tantamount to sacrilege. This temper of the mind is conservatism. It resists change instinctively and not intelligently, and it is this conservatism which largely causes those violent explosions of pent-up energy which we term revolutions. Still, changes, peaceful or bloody, must come, and it behooves each generation to take care that such as it shall have to deal with shall be accepted without shock. Intellectual rigidity is the chief danger, for resistance to the inevitable is proportionate to intellectual rigidity.

The Romans were rigid, and the massacres which attended their readjustments are memorable. The slaughter of the Gracchi, the

245

proscriptions of Marius and Sulla, and the lists of the Triumvirs are examples. On the other hand, Caesar miscarried because of too high intelligence. He measured circumstances accurately, and because he did so, he misjudged others. Had he comprehended the stupidity of Brutus, he would have killed him. With conservative populations slaughter is nature's remedy. Augustus applied it. He substantially exterminated the opposition; then the new organization operated.

Similarly the French, in emergency, have always resorted to massacre to overcome obstruction, from the crusades against the Albigenses in the thirteenth century to the Commune of Paris in the nineteenth. It was not only Saint Bartholomew, and the persecutions which followed the revocation of the Edict of Nantes, which brought about the Terror of 1793; it was rather a thousand nameless butcheries like those which occurred during the reign of Louis XIV. The incapacity of the French to ameliorate their fiscal system generated an unequal taxation which provoked revolt, and revolt caused repression frightful in ferocity. At Rennes in 1675, as a punishment for insubordination, the town was given up to pillage, and la Rue Haute, the main street, was destroyed. The inhabitants, old men, women, and children, were driven forth into the fields "without a refuge, without food, and without a place to sleep." They perished from exposure and want.

Rome and France are extreme examples of conservation, but they illustrate the better the working of a law. All administrative systems tend toward induration; more especially political systems, because they are most cumbersome. Conversely, nature is in eternal movement. Therefore, the disparity between any given government and its environment is apt to be proportionate to the time which has elapsed since the last period of active change. When a population is flexible, adjustment is peaceful, as in the case of the adoption of our Constitution, or the passage of the first English Reform Bill; when a population is rigid, a catastrophe occurs, like the civil wars in Rome, or the Terror of 1793 in France.

Measure the United States by this standard. Since the Constitution went into operation in 1789 every civilized nation has undergone reorganization, some, like France and Germany, more than once. And yet nowhere have all the conditions of life altered so fundamentally as in North America.

In 1789 the United States was a wilderness lying upon the outskirts of Christendom; she is now the heart of civilization and focus of energy. The Union forms a gigantic and growing empire which stretches half round the globe, an empire possessing the greatest mass of accumulated wealth, the most perfect means of transportation, and the most delicate yet powerful industrial system which has ever been developed. By the products of that system she must be brought into competition with rivals at the ends of the earth. The nation, in its corporate capacity, has to deal with problems domestic and foreign, more vast and complicated than were ever before presented for solution. In a word, the conditions of the twentieth century are almost precisely the reverse of those of the eighteenth, and yet the national organization not only remains unaltered, but is prevented from automatic adjustment by the provisions of a written document, which, in practice, cannot be amended.

For the present generation the manner in which change shall come is a matter only of speculative interest, since before the existing structure can crumble, those now in middle life will have passed away. To the rising generation it is of supreme moment, for the forces at work are gigantic, and the velocity extreme.

Man cannot shape his own environment, but he alone of all animals can consciously adapt himself to the demands of nature. He does so by education. This faculty is an incalculable advantage in the struggle for existence, for by education the young can be trained to dexterity in almost any manual or mental process. Intellectual flexibility may be developed as readily as intellectual rigidity. Science has won her triumphs through such training. The scientific schools perform their functions well. Their discipline creates an open mind; scientific methods of thought are now paramount in our industries, and it is to this faculty that America, in a very large measure, owes her industrial success.

It is an axiom that the manufacturer who is least bound by tradition is the man who, other things being equal, will succeed. He who can cast aside the prepossessions of a lifetime, abandon his old equipment, and adopt what is newest, is held to be enlightened. The doctrine is reduced to a rule of conduct. The railway manager reckons that his locomotives are capable of a given amount of work. He extracts that work as fast as possible, because he can replace an old machine by a better. The British manager acts on the opposite principle. He rests his engines, repairs them, cares for them, and boasts that he can exhibit some relic of the time of Stephenson.

Penetrate the recesses of British society, and one chief cause of this conservatism is disclosed. The nation is intellectually inelastic, and it cultivates rigidity by confiding its education to the clergy, who are preëminently a rigid class. The result is that Englishmen fall behind. They own, for example, the South African gold mines, but they do not work them.

In England the old processes of so-called liberal thought still prevail. In America these have been superseded in science, and in those walks of life which are regulated by scientific methods. They still survive in colleges, as distinguished from technical schools, and colleges very largely shape opinion in the United States, not only on political, but on a great variety of other subjects. No better illustration of this tendency can be chosen than the attitude maintained toward history.

History presents a double aspect: First, the commercial and literary; second, the educational and scientific. The man who writes a history either as a social or political speculation, or else for sale, differs from no other adventurer. He writes for a market, as another man manufactures for a market, and most of the best historical work has been done under these conditions. Thucydides, Tacitus, Caesar, Gibbon, and Macaulay produced their books for private ends or else for sale, and in either case the result was the same. No one bought who did not care to read, and no one read without the inclination. It was a trade in luxuries like the trade in spices.

Modern educational and scientific history stands on a different basis. It is assumed that there are facts in the past which it imports all the world to know, and much money and time are spent in unearthing them. For many years governments, corporations, and individuals have vied with each other in publishing archives and editing documents, while monographs on all sorts of special subjects abound; but no attempt has been made to digest what has been gathered. Meanwhile the mass of material is accumulating rapidly. Libraries are no longer able to buy and catalogue the volumes which appear, and he who would read intelligently must first learn to eliminate. Apparently it is assumed that the accumulation of facts for the facts' sake is an adequate end, and yet nothing serves so little purpose as undigested facts. A fact in itself has no significance; neither have a thousand facts. What gives facts their value is their relation to each other; for when enough have been collected to suggest a sequence of cause and effect, a generalization can be made which scientific men call a "law." The law amounts only to this, that certain phenomena have been found to succeed each other with sufficient regularity to enable us to count with reasonable certainty on their recurrence in a determined order.

Science is constructed from such approximations. History as taught in our colleges ignores the advantage of generalization, and discourages all attempts to generalize. Yet it may be doubted whether advantage accrues to any one from the mere accumulation of historical details. Unless reduced to order, so as to offer a basis of comparison, past facts bear little upon present events. The change of conditions impairs their relevancy. Certainly it is fatuous to burden the memory with them, for a gazetteer is fuller and more accurate than any human memory, and is always at hand.

To such reasoning the teaching profession objects that their speciality differs from all others in that it deals with human actions. These actions either are not regulated by the same laws which pervade the rest of nature, or, if they are, the causes of which they are effects are so complicated as to elude us, unless we gather a very much larger number of observations from which to generalize than we now possess, or are likely to possess in the immediate future. A dilemma is thus presented. Either human experience cannot be formulated; or, at best, it can be only by amassing more facts than the mind can grasp. In either case the same conclusion is reached. Generalization must be abandoned, and the collection of "historical material" must be accepted as the end for which so much money and time are spent. If this be true, it is doubtful whether the sums expended on historical research and on professional salaries might not be made to yield a better return.

Possibly, however, professional historians are mistaken in their estimate of the difficulty of historical generalization; possibly, also, the reasons they allege against making the attempt are not those which influence them most. Still, as these reasons are seriously advanced, they must be seriously examined.

On their face the objections proposed seem inconclusive, for they rest on fallacious premises. They assume, in the first place, that human actions are the effects of peculiarly complicated causes; and in the second, that an imperfect generalization is valueless. Both assumptions are incorrect. The causes which have combined to cast a single grain of sand upon the shore are infinite, and the infinite can neither be surpassed nor understood. We cannot understand what the sand is or how it comes to be where it lies, and yet we can make geology useful. Also it is a maxim of science that results are obtained by approximation through error, and that the truths of one generation are the errors of the next.

The scientific man accepts his limitations and does not expect to arrive at absolute verity. He observes, and when he has advanced far enough to begin to generalize, he formulates his ideas as an hypothesis to serve as a basis on which to work until some one has suggested something better. There is hardly a general scientific proposition which is not called in question, and it is precisely by such questioning that knowledge is reduced to a serviceable shape.

For example, one of the most cherished postulates of science has been that "a thing cannot act where it is not," a postulate which Newton himself agreed to; and yet that postulate is directly contradicted by gravity. Nobody can guess what gravity is, or how it operates, and yet laws can be formulated which enable us to use it for multifarious purposes.

The atomic theory was at one time generally adopted, and now chemists are discussing whether it is not more of a hindrance than a help. The famous nebular hypothesis of Kant and La Place played a great part in astronomy, but it is conceded that there are fatal objections to receiving it as a solution of the secret of the formation of stars. The work of the astronomer is based on fictions. "In calculating the attraction of a homogeneous sphere upon a material point . . . the astronomer begins with two fictions—the fiction of a 'material point' (which is, in truth, a contradiction in terms), . . . and the fiction of the finite differences representing the molecular constitution of the sphere." The theory of the conservation of energy is expected to "prove the great theoretical solvent of chemical as well as physical phenomena," and yet in regard to the planetary system Lord Kelvin has formulated his conclusions thus:—

"1. There is at present in the material world a universal tendency to the dissipation of mechanical energy.

"2. Any restoration of mechanical energy, without more than an equivalent of dissipation, is impossible in inanimate material processes, and is probably never effected by material masses either endowed with vegetable life, or subjected to the will of an animated creature.

"3. Within a finite time past the earth must have been, and within a finite period of time to come the earth must again be, unfit for the habitation of man as at present constituted, unless operations have been, or are to be, performed which are impossible under the laws to which the known operations going on at present in the material world are subject."

The axioms of mathematics are disputed. A school of geometers now conceive of space as curved, so that lines which we have regarded as straight may prove to be a closed curve, and parallel lines meet. "A whole pencil of shortest lines may [thus] be drawn through the same point." Moreover, mathematicians regard space as having various dimensions, so that the solar system in its march through the universe may be approaching regions where there will be four dimensions.

The list might be prolonged, but to little purpose, as the principle is undisputed. All scientific men agree to the tentative condition of generalizations, and yet science advances, the proof being the control obtained over natural forces. If satisfactory results can be reached elsewhere by using well-established methods of observation and generalization, there seems no reason, at first sight, why the same methods should not be applied to humanity, especially as

Darwin drew his inferences regarding evolution by these processes. On considering more attentively, however, the possibilities which are disclosed by such investigations, the hesitation of the universities appears less inexplicable. Certainly no fundamental religious dogmas are threatened, since neither the attributes of the soul nor of the mind are in question; but if communities of men are to be studied as though they were communities of ants, learned bodies might be forced into positions which would make untenable their present tacitly accepted platform of principles.

Submission to tradition is one of the strong instincts. In primitive ages it is absolute; life is regulated by ritual. The code of Leviticus instructs men how to eat, and wash, and shave, and reap, and the law was changeless, to be kept by "thy son and thy son's son all the days of thy life."

A religious truth, of course, cannot vary, for truth is immutable and eternal, and no believer in an inspired church could tolerate having her canons examined as we should examine human laws. But it is not only in religion that tradition wields power. It is often preponderant in politics, and a political principle is not seldom preached as a tenet of faith. Not so very long ago the Anglican clergy maintained as orthodox doctrine the divine right of kings, and, to come nearer home, the language of the Declaration of Independence varies little from that of a Catholic council. The Declaration lays down an immutable law, "We hold these truths to be self-evident." The Church enunciates a verity in slightly different terms, but no more dogmatically, "This holy Synod doth now declare." Even in science tradition has not been altogether eradicated. Some years ago, on retiring from the presidency of the American Association for the Advancement of Science, Professor Langley took the occasion to remonstrate against this tendency.

"The final conclusion was irresistible, that the universal statement of this alleged well-known fact, inexplicable as this might seem, in so simple a matter, was directly contradicted by experiment. I had some natural curiosity to find how every one knew this to be a fact; but search only showed the same statement (that the earth's atmosphere absorbed dark heat like glass) repeated everywhere, with absolutely nowhere any observation or evidence whatever to prove it, but each writer quoting from an earlier one, till I was almost ready to believe it a dogma superior to reason, and resting on the well-known '*Quod semper, quod ubique, quod ab omnibus, creditum est.*'"

Professor Langley went on to say: "The question of fact here, though important, is, I think, quite secondary to the query it raises as to the possible unsuspected influence of mere tradition in science, when we do not recognize it as such. Now, members of any church are doubtless consistent in believing in traditions, if they believe that these are presented to them by an infallible guide; but are we, who have no infallible guide, quite safe in believing all we do, from our fond persuasion that in the scientific body mere tradition has no weight?"

Here lies the divergence between the scientific and the liberal training. Professor Langley insists that nothing must be taken as fixed, and that the mind should be held open to proceed to successive generalizations as the range of observation expands. The College proceeds on nearly an opposite principle.

The College assumes certain ethical premises, and the conclusions of a study must be made to square with these. This is as it should be from the inductive standpoint, for the College is the offspring of the Church and the daughter of the medieval convent. Nevertheless such an assumption places liberal in antagonism to scientific methods, and especially between inductive and ethical history the gulf cannot be bridged.

If men are to be observed scientifically, the standard by which customs and institutions must be gauged cannot be abstract moral principles, but success. Those instincts are judged advantageous to animals which help them in their struggle for life, and those prejudicial which hamper them. They are means to an end. So with physical peculiarities. A beast's color is good if it serves to protect; and bad if it make him conspicuous to his enemy. Similarly with men. Institutions are good which lead to success in competition, and are bad when they hinder. No series of institutions are *a priori* to be preferred to others; the criterion is the practical one of success.

The same rule applies to men themselves. They are the best who conform most perfectly to the demands of nature, or who, in other words, succeed best. Nature eliminates those who do not satisfy her requirements, and from Nature's decree there is no appeal.

These generalizations can with difficulty be reconciled with any body of fixed ethical principles. Evidently they form a doctrine of expediency founded on necessity. The theory is that men will arrive at precisely the same end, in either case; only by flexibility will they avoid suffering. In fact, nothing is more sensitive to the exigencies of an environment than a moral law. According to conditions of time and place murder, cruelty, piracy, slaving, polygamy, celibacy, deceit, and their like, have been exalted into virtues; while it is not so very long since the Church declared the healing of the sick by scientific means and the taking of interest for money to be crimes before God. As the environment changes, those men are gradually selected who conform thereto; the rest perish more or less miserably. The scientific education would tend to diminish the agony of adaptation.

Followed to their root, also, the two systems of thought will be found to be as opposed in their practical methods as they are in regard to the temper of mind which they propagate. The one is analytical and administrative, the other idealistic and slack. A few examples will explain the differences between them.

Large public libraries are now admittedly in an unsatisfactory condition. Libraries may indeed speculate in curiosities, or be used for amusement, but here they are considered only as educational institutions or workshops. Viewed thus, none are complete, for the books printed outrun the means of buying, cataloguing, and housing. Administration has broken down; and administration has broken down because it is unscientific. Men of liberal education have collected libraries who have never been taught to generalize. These men look on a book as a unit, precisely as in history they look on a fact as a unit. When a book is supposed to have a certain degree of merit, it is deemed worthy of purchase, almost regardless of its subject. Thus the whole range of knowledge is thrown open, and the result is bewilderment.

On no principle of generalization can the book, apart from ordinary books of reference, be considered as the unit. The subject is the unit, and the book has a value only in relation to its subject. A single book, like a single chapter, word, or fact, needs a context to explain it; therefore a library collected on the basis of individual books must be incomplete, and an indifferent workshop, because no man can thoroughly finish any task therein. To find all his tools he must travel elsewhere, and everywhere he is met with the same difficulty, because all general libraries are collected on much the same system, and all duplicate each other.

Supposing, however, that liberal education like science were based on a series of generalizations, a different result would be attained. The book would not then be regarded as the unit, nor of value, as a thing in itself, but only of value in so far as it related to the contents of the collection to which it might be added. The department of knowledge would thus become the unit; and in growing the library would grow not by volumes but by departments. The next generalization would be uniting several libraries, covering many departments, under one management, so that their books might be mutually accessible and few duplicated. This generalization might be broadened indefinitely so as, at last, by an exchange of books of many libraries, to make an almost perfect collection in all important departments, and that at the lowest cost.

Precisely the same phenomena are disclosed in museums devoted to the fine arts. Like libraries, museums devoted may speculate in bric-a-brac, but the true function of an art museum is conceded to be education. The theory on which they have been formed has been a liberal *a priori* theory. It has been taught that certain objects are in themselves beautiful, because they conform to a conventional aesthetic standard, and that such objects should be purchased for their own intrinsic merit, apart from the contents of the museum. Such a theory conflicts with the inductive method.

If art be viewed as a product of an environment, art is, like language, a form of expression; therefore a heterogeneous mass of pictures, laces, statues, porcelain, and coins has no more significance than would have stray lines taken at random from the poets of a thousand languages and printed side by side. The carvings and glass of the cathedral of Chartres spoke as clearly and more emphatically to the mediaeval peasant than any book can speak to us, and we cannot appreciate that masterpiece unless we comprehend the language in which the Church of the twelfth century addressed the people. To the Greek likewise the coin had a meaning. We cannot exhibit a few Greek coins as a model of what coinage should be, for those coins would be unserviceable now. They convey no lesson unless they be read in the light of Greek economic civilization.

Our architecture, when dealing with iron and steel, with matter of fact factories, railway stations, and warehouses, is admirable. When it strives after an aesthetic ideal, it is a failure; and, logically, it could be nothing but a failure, because it is unintelligent.

A body of material produced during certain epochs is arbitrarily selected as worthy, and from this material architects are thought to be justified in borrowing whatever may suit their purpose, or strike their fancy, irrespective of the language which their predecessors spoke, or the ideas which they conveyed. The arms of a pope may be used to adorn the front of a New England library, or the tomb of the Virgin for a booth at an international commercial exhibition.

If men would translate or adapt a poem, they must first soak themselves in the language and the temper of the poet, and artists who would borrow with effect must first be archaeologists and students of history. Approached thus, the heterogeneous collection of aesthetic objects can only be a stumbling-block. The value of the museum must be proportionate to the perfection with which it displays the development of the artistic side of any civilization, and the intelligence with which it offers the key to the form of expression which it undertakes to explain. This is generalization.

The same defective administration arising from imperfect generalization appears in the University. Until within about a generation the American College retained substantially the methods and the curriculum which had been in use when it served as a divinity school. About 1870 an expansion took place, based on the theory of the intrinsic value of the fact, precisely as the expansion of the library has been based on the theory of the intrinsic value of the book. The aim of the new University came to be to teach everything, little attention being given to the coördination of the parts. The result could not be other than wasteful and disjointed. Suppose two foundations each teach one hundred subjects, those subjects being substantially identical; they obviously duplicate each other, while they divide their resources by one hundred. Suppose each, on the contrary, to teach but fifty subjects, the original hundred being distributed between them, they double their teaching power, and still offer to the public precisely the same field as before. They suppress waste and increase efficiency.

The theory on which the modern University system rests is fallacious. The worth of the University lies not in the multitude of units taught, but in the coördination of parts and the intensity of effort. What our civilization demands is the maximum of energy, and that maximum cannot be attained when the money which would bring one department to the standard is divided between two. American universities would have now abundant funds for all necessary work of the highest grade were there no waste. They are poor because of bad administration.

It is true that the worst examples of duplicate foundations are effects of the clerical *a priori* reasoning, yet, when all allowances have been made for sectarian narrowness, the fact remains that colleges do not attempt to add to their efficiency and stop their waste by intelligent coöperation among themselves, as manufacturers would coöperate who did not mean to be ruined. They do not even go so far as to coördinate their instruction by departments and by sub-departments, so that every student who receives tuition shall receive it with that degree of intelligence which comes from knowing where he stands in regard to the sum of human knowledge. And yet such a generalization, at least in regard to departments, would be easy. Every science is so generalized that each specialist can know at any moment how his part stands to the whole. If he need to broaden his sphere of knowledge by examining other branches, he can choose those most advantageous with celerity and certainty. The student at college is launched upon an unknown sea, like a mariner without chart or compass. He has little to guide him in ascertaining what departments are really kindred. Even the courses of history are often arranged according to the taste of professors, and with no relation to historical sequence.

Take economics as an example. During the eighteenth century Adam Smith, having carefully observed the conditions which prevailed in Europe and especially in Great Britain, wrote a book admirably suited to his environment, and the book met with success.

Then men undertook to erect the principles of that book into an universal law, irrespective of environment. Then others theorized on these commentators, and their successors upon them, until the most practical of business problems has been lost in a metaphysical fog.

Now men are apt to lecture on political economy as if it were a dogma, much as the nominalists and realists lectured in mediaeval schools. But *a priori* theories can avail little in matters which are determined by experiment.

Political economy as a dogma is as absurd as would be a dogma which taught an infallible way to manipulate the stock market. Success in competition comes solely through a comprehension of existing conditions and the capacity to take advantage of opportunities. One community, such as Rome, may do well by robbery; another, like Great Britain, when she enjoyed a monopoly of minerals and of manufactures, may flourish upon free trade; a third, like Germany with her sugar policy, may find her advantage in attacking a rival by export bounties; while a fourth may thrive by seclusion, as did Japan, as long as circumstances favored. No one can say *a priori* what will succeed; the criterion is success.

The inference is that if a man would study economics to some purpose, he must study them practically, as he would any other business. He must begin by learning the principles of trade and finance as they are presented by actual daily experience, just as the soldier, the sailor, the lawyer, and the doctor learn their professions. Then if he wish to generalize, he can examine into the experience of other countries, past and present, and observe how they won or lost. In other words, he can read geography, history, archaeology, numismatics, and kindred branches, and extend his horizon at his pleasure. Thus men work who expect to earn their bread in the walks of active life, but colleges do not classify.

History, geography, and economics are related branches which mutually explain each other, and none of which can be well understood alone. They also aid each other, for the sequence of cause and effect sustains the memory; and yet they are never taught together, although to learn the three combined would take little longer, and demand less effort, than to learn any one singly. It is a curious commentary on liberal methods, that geography, which is eminently practical, is only applied in military or possibly technical schools. There is, perhaps, no thorough collection of maps made on scientific principles in any public library in the United States.

Lastly, it remains to consider how the introduction of inductive methods in social matters would affect the community at large by the destruction of its ideals; for ideals would probably suffer.

He who is dominated by tradition exalts the past. In the concrete case of an American he believes more or less implicitly that the contemporaries of Washington and Jefferson arrived at political truths which, at least so far as he is concerned, may be received as final. The man who reasons by induction views the work of Washington and Jefferson otherwise. He views it as the product of the conditions of the eighteenth century, and as having no more necessary relation to the conduct of affairs in the twentieth, than Franklin's methods in electricity would have to the manipulation of a modern dynamo. The United States now occupies a position of extraordinary strength. Favored alike by geographical position, by deposits of minerals, by climate, and by the character of her population, she has little to fear, either in peace or war, from rivals, provided the friction created by the movement of the masses with which she has to deal does not neutralize her energy.

Masses accumulate in the United States because administration by masses is cheaper than administration by detail. Masses take the form of corporations, and the men who rise to the control of these corporations rise because they are fittest. The process is natural selection. The life of the community lies in these masses. Derange them, and there would immediately follow an equivalent loss of energy. They are there because the conditions of our civilization are such as to make it cheaper that they should be there, and if our political institutions are ill-adapted to their propagation and development, then political institutions must be readjusted, or the probability is that the whole fabric of society will be shattered by the dislocation of the economic system. America holds its tenure of prosperity only on condition that she can undersell her rivals, and she cannot do so if her administrative machinery generates friction unduly.

Political institutions and political principles are but a conventional dial on whose face the hands revolve which mark the movement of the mechanism within. Most governments and many codes have been adored as emanating from the deity. All were ephemeral, and all which survived their purpose became a jest or a curse to the children of the worshippers; things to be cast aside like worn-out garments.

Under any circumstances an organism so gigantic as the American Union must generate friction. In American industry friction will infallibly exist between capital and labor; but that necessary friction may be indefinitely increased by conservatism. History teems with examples of civilizations which have been destroyed through an unreasoning inertia like that of Brutus, or the French privileged classes, or Patrick Henry. A slight increase in the relative cost of production caused by an imperfect mechanical adjustment is usually sufficient to give some rival an advantage, and when a country is undersold, misery sets in. People who cannot earn their daily bread are revolutionary, and disorders bred by violence achieve the series of disasters which began with the diversion of trade. Such was the fate of the great cities of Flanders, of Bruges, of Ghent, and of Ypres.

The alternative presented is plain. Men may cherish ideals and risk substantial benefits to realize them. Such is the emotional instinct. Or they may regard their government dispassionately, as they would any other matter of business.

Americans in former generations led a simple agricultural life. Possibly such a life was happier than ours. Very probably keen competition is not a blessing. We cannot alter our environment. Nature has cast the United States into the vortex of the fiercest struggle which the world has ever known. She has become the heart of the economic system of the age, and she must maintain her supremacy by wit and by force, or share the fate of the discarded. . . .

The liberal education tends to instil a reverence for fixed standards; therefore an adherence to these methods must encourage rigidity and make innovations proportionately difficult, and this in the face of a huge, complex society, moving with unexampled velocity. An extension of scientific training to branches hitherto controlled by conservatism would doubtless alter moral standards, but probably only by anticipating by a few years an inevitable intellectual transformation. The advantage would be that we should facilitate adjustment and distance our rivals by reaching first a predestined goal.

The following essay is an attempt to deal, by inductive methods, with the consolidation and dissolution of those administrative masses which we call empires. The same method might be applied to any phase of civilization, artistic, literary, or military. My observation leads me to surmise that the intellectual stimulus of an environment acts very uniformly, and that where a community is roused to activity in one direction, it will be active in all directions in which it has capacity to succeed, or in which opportunity for success is afforded. . . .

From the days of Roger Bacon to those of Darwin scientific methods and scientific theories have not commended themselves to the conservative. They could hardly do so, since they undermine tradition. Among many examples which might be cited of resistance to innovation one might suffice. It is, perhaps, the most memorable. On June 22, 1633, the Holy Office enunciated the following decree in the trial of Galileo for heresy:—

1. That the sun is the centre of the world and immovable is a proposition absurd and false in philosophy, and formally heretical, as being expressly contrary to Holy Scripture.

2. That the earth is not the centre of the world, nor immovable, but that it moves even with a diurnal motion, is in like manner a proposition absurd and false in philosophy, and, considered in theology, at least erroneous in faith.

To escape torture Galileo recanted, but still he murmured, "e pur si muove."

Brooks Adams

INFERENCES

As the universe, which at once creates and destroys life, is a complex of infinitely varying forces, history can never repeat itself. It is vain, therefore, to look in the future for some paraphrase of the past. Yet if society be, as I assume it to be, an organism operating on mechanical principles, we may perhaps, by pondering upon history, learn enough of those principles to enable us to view, more intelligently than we otherwise should, the social phenomena about us. What we call civilization is, I suspect, only, in proportion to its perfection, a more or less thorough social centralization, while centralization, very clearly, is an effect of applied science. Civilization is accordingly nearly synonymous with centralization, and is caused by mechanical discoveries, which are applications of scientific knowledge, like the discovery of how to kindle fire, how to build and sail ships, how to smelt metals, how to prepare explosives, how to make paper and print books and the like. And we perceive on a little consideration that from the first great and fundamental discovery of how to kindle fire, every advance in applied science has accelerated social movement, until the discovery of steam and electricity in the eighteenth and nineteenth centuries quickened movement as movement had never been quickened before. And this quickening has caused the rise of those vast cities, which are at once our pride and our terror.

Social consolidation is, however, not a simple problem, for social consolidation implies an equivalent capacity for administration. I take it to be an axiom, that perfection in administration must be commensurate to the bulk and momentum of the mass to be administered, otherwise the centrifugal will overcome the centripetal force and the mass will disintegrate. In other words, civilization would

Concluding chapter of *The Theory of Social Revolutions*, pp. 203-230, by Brooks Adams (New York: The Macmillan Company, 1913). Reprinted by permission of the Massachusetts Historical Society.

dissolve. It is in dealing with administration, as I apprehend, that civilizations have usually, though not always, broken down, for it has been on administrative difficulties that revolutions have for the most part supervened. Advances in administration seem to presuppose the evolution of new governing classes, since, apparently, no established type of mind can adapt itself to changes in environment, even in slow-moving civilizations, as fast as environments change. Thus a moment arrives when the minds of any given dominant type fail to meet the demands made upon them, and are superseded by a younger type, which in turn is set aside by another still younger, until the limit of the administrative genius of that particular race has been reached. Then disintegration sets in, the social momentum is gradually relaxed and society sinks back to a level at which it can cohere. To us, however, the most distressing aspect of the situation is, that the social acceleration is progressive in proportion to the activity of the scientific mind which makes mechanical discoveries, and it is, therefore, a triumphant science which produces those ever more rapidly recurring changes in environment to which men must adapt themselves at their peril. As, under the stimulant of modern science, the old types fail to sustain themselves, new types have to be equally rapidly evolved, and the rise of a new governing class is always synonymous with a social revolution and a redistribution of property. The Industrial Revolution began almost precisely a century and a half ago, since when the scientific mind has continually gained in power, and, during that period, on an average of once in two generations, the environment has so far shifted that a social revolution has occurred, accompanied by the advent of a new favored class, and a readjustment of wealth. I think that a glance at American history will show this estimate to be within the truth. At the same time such rapidity of intellectual mutation is without precedent, and I should suppose that the mental exhaustion incident thereto must be very considerable.

In America, in 1770, a well-defined aristocracy held control. As an effect of the Industrial Revolution upon industry and commerce, the Revolutionary War occurred, the colonial aristocracy misjudged the environment, adhered to Great Britain, were exiled, lost their property, and perished. Immediately after the American Revolution and also as a part of the Industrial Revolution, the cotton gin was invented, and the cotton gin created in the South another aristocracy, the cotton planters, who flourished until 1860. At this point the changing of the environment, caused largely by the railway, brought a pressure upon the slave-owners against which they, also failing to comprehend their situation, rebelled. They were conquered, suffered confiscation of their property, and perished. Furthermore, the rebellion of the aristocracy at the South was caused, or at all events was accompanied by, the rise of a new dominant class at the North, whose power rested upon the development of steam in transportation and industry. This is the class which has won high fortune by the acceleration of the social movement, and the consequent urban growth of the nineteenth century, and which has now for about two generations dominated in the land. If this class, like its predecessors, has in its turn mistaken its environment, a redistribution of property must occur, distressing, as previous redistributions have been, in proportion to the inflexibility of the sufferers. The last two redistributions have been painful, and, if we examine passing phenomena from this standpoint, they hardly appear to promise much that is reassuring for the future.

Administration is the capacity of coördinating many, and often conflicting, social energies in a single organism, so adroitly that they shall operate as a unity. This presupposes the power of recognizing a series of relations between numerous special social interests, with all of which no single man can be intimately acquainted. Probably no very highly specialized class can be strong in this intellectual quality because of the intellectual isolation incident to specialization; and yet administration or generalization is not only the faculty upon which social stability rests, but is, possibly, the highest faculty of the human mind. It is precisely in this preëminent requisite for success in government that I suspect the modern capitalistic class to be weak. The scope of the human intellect is necessarily limited, and modern capitalists appear to have been evolved under the stress of an environment which demanded excessive specialization in the direction of a genius adapted to money-making under highly complex industrial conditions. To this money-making attribute all else has been sacrificed, and the modern capitalist not only thinks in terms of money, but he thinks in terms of money more exclusively than the French aristocrat or lawyer ever thought in terms of caste. The modern capitalist looks upon life as a financial combat of a very specialized kind, regulated by a code which he understands and has indeed himself concocted, but which is recognized by no one else in the world. He conceives sovereign powers to be for sale. He may, he thinks, buy them; and if he buys them, he may use them as he pleases. He believes, for instance, that it is the lawful, nay more! in America, that it is the constitutional right of the citizen to buy the national highways, and, having bought them, to use them as a common carrier might use a horse and cart upon a public road. He may sell his service to whom he pleases at what price may suit him, and if by doing so he ruins men and cities, it is nothing to him. He is not responsible, for he is not a trustee for the public. If he be restrained by legislation, that legislation is in his eye an oppression and an outrage, to be annulled or eluded by any means which will not lead to the penitentiary. He knows nothing and cares less, for the relation which highways always have held, and always must hold, to every civilized population, and if he be asked to inform himself on such subjects he resents the suggestion as an insult. He is too specialized to comprehend a social relation, even a fundamental one like this, beyond the narrow circle of his private interests. He might, had he so chosen, have evolved a system of governmental railway regulation, and have administered the system personally, or by his own agents, but he could never be brought to see the advantage to himself of rational concession to obtain a resultant of forces. He resisted all restraint, especially national restraint, believing that his one weapon—money—would be more effective in obtaining what he wanted in state legislatures than in Congress. Thus, of necessity, he precipitates a conflict, instead of establishing an adjustment. He is, therefore, in essence, a revolutionist without being aware of it. The same specialized thinking appears in his reasoning touching actual government. New York City will serve as an illustration.

New York has for two generations been noted for a civic corruption which has been, theoretically, abominable to all good citizens, and which the capitalistic class has denounced as abominable to itself. I suspect this to be an imaginative conception of the situation. Tammany Hall is, I take it, the administrative bureau through which capital purchases its privileges. An incorruptible government would offend capital, because, under such a government, capital would have to obey the law, and privilege would cease. Occasionally, Tammany grows rapacious and exacts too much for its services. Then a reform movement is undertaken, and finally a new management is imposed on Tammany; but when Tammany has consented to a satisfactory scale of prices, the reform ends. To change the system would imply a shift in the seat of power. In fine, money is the weapon of the capitalist as the sword was the weapon of the mediaeval soldier; only, as the capitalist is more highly specialized than the soldier ever was, he is more helpless when his single weapon fails him. From the days of William the Conqueror to our own, the great soldier has been, very commonly, a famous statesman also, but I do not now remember, in English or American history, a single capitalist who has earned eminence for comprehensive statesmanship. On the contrary, although many have participated in public affairs, have held high office, and have shown ability therein, capitalists have not unusually, however unjustly, been suspected of having ulterior objects in view, unconnected with the public welfare, such as tariffs or land grants. Certainly, so far as I am aware, no capitalist has ever acquired such influence over his contemporaries as has been attained with apparent ease by men like Cromwell, Washington, or even Jackson.

And this leads, advancing in an orderly manner step by step, to what is, perhaps, to me, the most curious and interesting of all modern intellectual phenomena connected with the specialized mind,—the attitude of the capitalist toward the law. Naturally the capitalist, of all men, might be supposed to be he who would respect and uphold the law most, considering that he is at once the wealthiest and most vulnerable of human beings, when called upon to defend himself by physical force. How defenceless and how incompetent he is in such exigencies, he proved to the world some years ago when he plunged himself and the country into the great Pennsylvania coal strike, with absolutely no preparation. Nevertheless, in spite of his vulnerability, he is of all citizens the most lawless.[1] He appears to assume that the law will always be enforced when he has need of it, by some special personnel whose duty lies that way, while he may evade the law, when convenient, or bring it into contempt, with impunity. The capitalist seems incapable of feeling his responsibility, as a member of the governing class, in this respect, and that he is bound to uphold the law, no matter what the law may be, in order that others may do the like. If the capitalist has bought some sovereign function, and wishes to abuse it for his own behoof, he regards the law which restrains him as a despotic invasion of his constitutional rights, because, with his specialized mind, he cannot grasp the relation of a sovereign function to the nation as a whole. He, therefore, looks upon the evasion of a law devised for public protection, but inimical to him, as innocent or even meritorious.

If an election be lost, and the legislature, which has been chosen by the majority, cannot be pacified by money, but passes some act which promises to be annoying, the first instinct of the capitalist is to retain counsel, not to advise him touching his duty under the law, but to devise a method by which he may elude it, or, if he cannot elude it, by which he may have it annulled as unconstitutional by the courts. The lawyer who succeeds in this branch of practice is certain to win the highest prizes at the bar. And as capital has had now, for more than one or even two generations, all the prizes of the law within its gift, this attitude of capital has had a profound effect upon shaping the American legal mind. The capitalist, as I infer, regards the constitutional form of government which exists in the United States, as a convenient method of obtaining his own way against a majority, but the lawyer has learned to worship it as a fetich. Nor is this astonishing, for, were written constitutions suppressed, he would lose most of his importance and much of his income. Quite honestly, therefore, the American lawyer has come to believe that a sheet of paper soiled with printer's ink and interpreted by half-a-dozen elderly gentlemen snugly dozing in armchairs, has

---

[1] In these observations on the intellectual tendencies of capital I speak generally. Not only individual capitalists, but great corporations, exist, who are noble examples of law-abiding and intelligent citizenship. Their rarity, however, and their conspicuousness, seem to prove the general rule.

some inherent and marvellous virtue by which it can arrest the march of omnipotent Nature. And capital gladly accepts this view of American civilization, since hitherto capitalists have usually been able to select the magistrates who decide their causes, perhaps directly through the intervention of some president or governor whom they have had nominated by a convention controlled by their money, or else, if the judiciary has been elective, they have caused sympathetic judges to be chosen by means of a mechanism like Tammany, which they have frankly bought.

I wish to make myself clearly understood. Neither capitalists nor lawyers are necessarily, or even probably, other than conscientious men. What they do is to think with specialized minds. All dominant types have been more or less specialized, if none so much as this, and this specialization has caused, as I understand it, that obtuseness of perception which has been their ruin when the environment which favored them has changed. All that is remarkable about the modern capitalist is the excess of his eccentricity or his deviation from that resultant of forces to which he must conform. To us, however, at present, neither the morality nor the present mental eccentricity of the capitalist is so material as the possibility of his acquiring flexibility under pressure, for it would seem to be almost mathematically demonstrable that he will, in the near future, be subjected to a pressure under which he must develop flexibility or be eliminated.

There can be no doubt that the modern environment is changing faster than any environment ever previously changed; therefore, the social centre of gravity constantly tends to shift more rapidly; and therefore, modern civilization has unprecedented need of the administrative or generalizing mind. But, as the mass and momentum of modern society is prodigious, it will require a correspondingly prodigious energy to carry it safely from an unstable to a stable equilibrium. The essential is to generate the energy which brings success; and the more the mind dwells upon the peculiarities of the modern capitalistic class, the more doubts obtrude themselves touching their ability to make the effort, even at present, and still more so to make it in the future as the magnitude of the social organism grows.

One source of capitalistic weakness comes from a lack of proper instruments wherewith to work, even supposing the will of capital to be good; and this lack of administrative ability is somewhat due to the capitalistic attitude toward education. In the United States capital has long owned the leading universities by right of purchase, as it has owned the highways, the currency, and the press, and capital has used the universities, in a general way, to develop capitalistic ideas. This, however, is of no great moment. What is of moment is that capital has commercialized education. Apparently modern society, if it is to cohere, must have a high order of generalizing mind,—a mind which can grasp a multitude of complex relations,—but this is a mind which can, at best, only be produced in small quantity and at high cost. Capital has preferred the specialized mind, and that not of the highest quality, since it has found it profitable to set quantity before quality to the limit which the market will endure. Capitalists have never insisted upon raising an educational standard save in science and mechanics, and the relative overstimulation of the scientific mind has now become an actual menace to order because of the inferiority of the administrative intelligence.

Yet, even supposing the synthetic mind of the highest power to be increasing in proportion to the population, instead of, as I suspect, pretty rapidly decreasing, and supposing the capitalist to be fully alive to the need of administrative improvements, a phalanx of Washingtons would be impotent to raise the administrative level of the United States materially, as long as the courts remain censors of legislation; because the province of the censorial court is to dislocate any comprehensive body of legislation, whose effect would be to change the social status. That was the fundamental purpose which underlay the adoption of a written constitution whose object was to keep local sovereignties intact, especially at the South. Jefferson insisted that each sovereignty should by means of nullification protect itself. It was a long step in advance when the nation conquered the prerogative of asserting its own sovereign power through the Supreme Court. Now the intervention of the courts in legislation has become, by the change in environment, as fatal to administration as would have been, in 1800, the success of nullification. I find it difficult to believe that capital, with its specialized view of what constitutes its advantages, its duties and its responsibilities, and stimulated by a bar moulded to meet its prejudices and requirements, will ever voluntarily assent to the consolidation of the United States to the point at which the interference of the courts with legislation might be eliminated; because, as I have pointed out, capital finds the judicial veto useful as a means of at least temporarily evading the law, while the bar, taken as a whole, quite honestly believes that the universe will obey the judicial decree. No delusion could be profounder and none, perhaps, more dangerous. Courts, I need hardly say, cannot control nature, though by trying to do so they may, like the Parliament of Paris, create a friction which shall induce an appalling catastrophe.

True judicial courts, whether in times of peace or of revolution, seldom fail to be substantial protection to the weak, because they enforce an established *corpus juris* and conduct trials by recognized forms. It is startling to compare the percentage of convictions to prosecutions, for the same class of offences, in the regular criminal courts during the French Revolution, with the percentage in the Revolutionary Tribunal. And once a stable social equilibrium is reached, all men tend to support judicial courts, if judicial courts exist, from an instinct of self-preservation. This has been amply shown by French experience, and it is here that French history is so illuminating to the American mind. Before the Revolution France had semi-political courts which conduced to the overthrow of Turgot, and, therefore, wrought for violence; but more than this, France, under the old régime, had evolved a legal profession of a cast of mind incompatible with an equal administration of the law. The French courts were, therefore, when trouble came, supported only by a faction, and were cast aside. With that the old régime fell.

The young Duke of Chartres, the son of Égalité Orleans, and the future Louis Philippe, has related in his journal an anecdote which illustrates that subtle poison of distrust which undermines all legal authority, the moment that suspicion of political partiality in the judiciary enters the popular mind. In June, 1791, the Duke went down from Paris to Vendôme to join the regiment of dragoons of which he had been commissioned colonel. One day, soon after he joined, a messenger came to him in haste to tell him that a mob had gathered near by who were about to hang two priests. "I ran thither at once," wrote the Duke; "I spoke to those who seemed most excited and impressed upon them how horrible it was to hang men without trial; besides, to act as hangmen was to enter a trade which they all thought infamous; that they had judges, and that this was their affair. They answered that their judges were aristocrats, and that they did not punish the guilty." That is to say, although the priests were non-jurors, and, therefore, criminals in the eye of the law, the courts would not enforce the law because of political bias.[1] "It is your fault," I said to them, "since you elected them (the judges), but that is no reason why you should do justice yourselves."

Danton explained in the Convention that it was because of the deep distrust of the judiciary in the public mind, which this anecdote shows, that the September massacres occurred, and it was because all republicans knew that the state and the army were full of traitors like Dumouriez, whom the ordinary courts would not punish, that Danton brought forward his bill to organize a true political tribunal to deal with them summarily. When Danton carried through this statute he supposed himself to be at the apex of power and popularity, and to be safe, if any man in France were safe. Very shortly he learned the error in his calculation. Billaud was a member of the Committee of Public Safety, while Danton had allowed himself to be dropped from membership. Danton had just been married, and to an aristocratic wife, and the turmoil of office had grown to be distasteful to him. On March 30, 1794, Billaud somewhat casually remarked, "We must kill Danton;" for in truth Danton, with conservative leanings, was becoming a grave danger to the extreme Jacobins. Had he lived a few months longer he would have been a Thermidorist. Billaud, therefore, only expressed the prevailing Jacobin opinion; so the Jacobins arrested Danton, Camille Desmoulins, and his other friends, and Danton at

---

[1] By the Law of November 27, 1790, priests refusing to swear allegiance to the "civil constitution" of the clergy were punished by loss of pay and of rights of citizenship if they continued their functions. By Law of August 26, 1792, by transportation to Cayenne.

once anticipated what would be his doom. As he entered his cell he said to his jailer: "I erected the Tribunal. I ask pardon of God and men." But even yet he did not grasp the full meaning of what he had done. At his trial he wished to introduce his evidence fully, protesting "that he should understand the Tribunal since he created it;" nevertheless, he did not understand the Tribunal, he still regarded it as more or less a court. Topino-Lebrun, the artist, did understand it. Topino sat on the jury which tried Danton, and observed that the heart of one of his colleagues seemed failing him. Topino took the waverer aside and said: "This is not a *trial*, it is a *measure*. Two men are impossible; one must perish. Will you kill Robespierre?—No.—Then by that admission you condemn Danton." Lebrun in these few words went to the root of the matter, and stated the identical principle which underlies our whole doctrine of the Police Power. A political court is not properly a court at all, but an administrative board whose function is to work the will of the dominant faction for the time being. Thus a political court becomes the most formidable of all engines for the destruction of its creators the instant the social equilibrium shifts. So Danton found, in the spring of 1794, when the equilibrium shifted; and so Robespierre, who slew Danton, found the next July, when the equilibrium shifted again.

Danton died on the 5th April, 1794; about three months later Jourdan won the Fleurus campaign. Straightway Thermidor followed, and the Tribunal worked as well for the party of Thermidor as it had for the Jacobins. Carrier, who had wallowed in blood at Nantes, as the ideal Jacobin, walked behind the cart which carried Robespierre to the scaffold, shouting, "Down with the tyrant;" but that did not save him. In vain he protested to the Convention that, were he guilty, the whole Convention was guilty, "down to the President's bell." By a vote of 498 out of 500, Carrier was sent before the Tribunal which, even though reorganized, condemned him. Thérézia Cabarrus gaily presided at the closing of the Jacobin Club, Tallien moved over to the benches on the right, and therefore the court was ruthless to Fouquier. On the 11 Thermidor, seventy members, officers, or partisans of the Commune of Paris, were sent to the guillotine in only two batches. On the next day twelve more followed, four of whom were jurymen. Fouquier's turn came later. It may also be worth while for Americans to observe that a political court is quite as effective against property as against life. The Duke of Orleans is only the most celebrated example of a host of Frenchmen who perished, not because of revenge, fear, or jealousy, but because the party in power wanted their property. The famous Law touching Suspected Persons (loi des suspects) was passed on September 17, 1793. On October 10, 1793, that is three weeks afterward, Saint-Just moved that additional powers should be granted, by the Convention, to the Committee of Public Safety, defining, by way of justification for his motion, those who fell within the purview of this law. Among these, first of all, came "the rich," who by that fact alone were to be considered, *prima facie,* enemies to their country.

As I stated at the beginning of this chapter, history never can repeat itself; therefore, whatever else may happen in the United States, we certainly shall have no Revolutionary Tribunal like the French Tribunal of 1793, but the mechanical principle of the political court always remains the same; it is an administrative board, the control of which is useful, or may be even essential, to the success of a dominant faction, and the instinctive comprehension which the American people have of this truth is demonstrated by the determination with which they have, for many years, sought to impose the will of the majority upon the judiciary. Other means failing to meet their expectations, they have now hit on the recall, which is as revolutionary in essence as were the methods used during the Terror. Courts, from the Supreme Court downward, if purged by recall, or a process tantamount to recall, would, under proper stress, work as surely for a required purpose as did the tribunal supervised by Fouquier-Tinville.

These considerations rather lead me to infer that the extreme complexity of the administrative problems presented by modern industrial civilization is beyond the compass of the capitalistic mind. If this be so, American society, as at present organized, with capitalists for the dominant class, can concentrate no further, and, as nothing in the universe is at rest, if it does not concentrate, it must, probably, begin to disintegrate. Indeed we may perceive incipient signs of disintegration all about us. We see, for example, an universal contempt for law, incarnated in the capitalistic class itself, which is responsible for order, and in spite of the awful danger which impends over every rich and physically helpless type should the coercive power collapse. We see it even more distinctly in the chronic war between capital and labor, which government is admittedly unable to control; we see it in the slough of urban politics, inseparable from capitalistic methods of maintaining its ascendancy; and, perhaps, most disquieting of all, we see it in the dissolution of the family which has, for untold ages, been the seat of discipline and the foundation of authority. For the dissolution of the family is peculiarly a phenomenon of our industrial age, and it is caused by the demand of industry for the cheap labor of women and children. Napoleon told the lawyers who drafted the Code that he insisted on one thing alone. They must fortify the family, for, said he, if the family is responsible to the father and the father to me, I can keep order in France. One of the difficulties, therefore, which capital has to meet, by the aid of such administrative ability as it can command, is how to keep order when society no longer rests on the cohesive family, but on highly volatilized individuals as incohesive as grains of sand.

Meditating upon these matters, it is hard to resist the persuasion that unless capital can, in the immediate future, generate an intellectual energy, beyond the sphere of its specialized calling, very much in excess of any intellectual energy of which it has hitherto given promise, and unless it can besides rise to an appreciation of diverse social conditions, as well as to a level of political sagacity, far higher than it has attained within recent years, its relative power in the community must decline. If this be so the symptoms which indicate social disintegration will intensify. As they intensify, the ability of industrial capital to withstand the attacks made upon it will lessen, and this process must go on until capital abandons the contest to defend itself as too costly. Then nothing remains but flight. Under what conditions industrial capital would find migration from America possible, must remain for us beyond the bounds even of speculation. It might escape with little or no loss. On the other hand, it might fare as hardly as did the southern slaveholders. No man can foresee his fate. In the event of adverse fortune, however, the position of capitalists would hardly be improved by the existence of political courts serving a malevolent majority. Whatever may be in store for us, here at least we reach an intelligible conclusion. Should Nature follow such a course as I have suggested, she will settle all our present perplexities as simply and as drastically as she is apt to settle human perturbations, and she will follow logically in the infinitely extended line of her own most impressive precedents.

·XI·

HENRY ADAMS

[1 8 3 8 - 1 9 1 8]

THE RULE OF PHASE
APPLIED TO HISTORY

THE RULE OF PHASE
APPLIED TO HISTORY

In 1876–1878 Willard Gibbs, Professor of Mathematical Physics at Yale, published in the Transactions of the Connecticut Academy his famous memoir on the "Equilibrium of Heterogeneous Substances," containing the short chapter "On Existent Phases of Matter," which, in the hands of the Dutch chemists, became, some ten years afterwards, a means of greatly extending the science of Static Chemistry. Although the name of Willard Gibbs is probably to-day the highest in scientific fame of all Americans since Benjamin Franklin, his Rule of Phases defies translation into literary language. The mathematical formulas in which he hid it were with difficulty intelligible to the chemists themselves, and are quite unintelligible to an unmathematical public, while the sense in which the word Phase was used, confused its meaning to a degree that alters its values, and reduces it to a chemical relation. Willard Gibbs helped to change the face of science, but his Phase was not the Phase of History.

As he used it, the word meant Equilibrium, which is in fact the ordinary sense attached to it, but his equilibrium was limited to a few component parts. Ice, water, and water-vapor were three phases of a single substance, under different conditions of temperature and pressure; but if another element were added,—if one took sea-water, for instance,—the number of phases was increased according to the nature of the components. The chemical phase thus became a distinct physical section of a solution, and as many sections existed as there were independent components.

The common idea of phase is that of the solution itself, as when salt is dissolved in water. It is the whole equilibrium or state of apparent rest. It means, perhaps, when used of movement, a vari-

From *The Degradation of the Democratic Dogma*, pp. 267-311, by Henry Adams (New York: The Macmillan Company, 1920). Reprinted by permission of the Massachusetts Historical Society.

ance of direction, but it seems not to have been so much employed to indicate a mere change in speed. Yet the word would apply in literature as well as it does in physical chemistry to the three stages of equilibrium: ice, water, and steam. Where only one component is concerned, the Rule of Phase is the same for chemistry as for general usage. A change of phase, in all cases, means a change of equilibrium.

Whether the equilibrium or phase is temporary or permanent,—whether the change is rapid or slow,—whether the force at work for the purpose is a liquid solvent, or heat, or a physical attraction or repulsion,—the interest of the equilibrium lies in its relations, and the object of study is the behavior of each group under new relations. Chemists and physicists have turned their studies, for twenty or thirty years past, to these relations, and the various conditions of temperature, pressure, and volume have become more important than the atoms and molecules themselves, while new processes,—osmosis, electrolysis, magnetic action,—have made a new world that is slowly taking the place of the world as it existed fifty years ago; though as yet the old curriculum of thought has been hardly touched by the change.

The new field can be entered only by timid groping for its limits, and with certainty of constant error; but in order to enter it at all, one must begin by following the lines given by physical science. If the Rule of Phase is to serve for clue, the first analogy which imposes itself as the starting-point for experiment is the law of solutions, which seems to lie on the horizon of science as the latest and largest of possible generalizations. As science touches every material or immaterial substance, each in its turn dissolves, until the ether itself becomes an ocean of discontinuous particles.

A solution is defined as a homogeneous mixture, which can pass through continuous variations of composition within the limits that define its existence. Solids, as we all know, may be dissolved, but we do not all realize that liquids and gases may also be dissolved, or that a change in composition must accompany a change of phase. As early as 1662, Isaac Voss, in his work, "De Lucis Natura," on the Nature of Light, defined Heat as "actus dissolvens corpora," the solvent of material bodies; and in 1870, the French chemist Rosentiehl published a paper in the Comptes Rendues of the French Academy (vol. LXX) suggesting that any gas might be likened to a body dissolved in the medium of the universal solvent, the ether. Reversing the theory, the English and Dutch physicists have solidified every gas, including even helium. The solvent has been suggested or found for every form of matter, even the most subtle, until it trembles on the verge of the ether itself; and a by-stander, who is interested in watching the extension of this new synthesis, cannot help asking himself where it can find a limit. If every solid is soluble into a liquid, and every liquid into a gas, and every gas into corpuscles which vanish in an ocean of ether,—if nothing remains of energy itself except potential motion in absolute space,—where can science stop in the application of this fecund idea?

Where it can stop is its own affair, dependent on its own will or convenience; but where it must stop is a larger question that interests philosophy. There seems to be no reason for insisting that it must necessarily stop anywhere within the region of experience. Certainly it cannot stop with static electricity, which is itself more obviously a mere phase than water-vapor. The physicists cannot conceive it without conceiving something more universal behind or above it. The logic of former thought, in its classic simplicity, would have taken for granted that electricity must be capable of reduction to a solid,—that it can be frozen,—and that it must also be soluble in ether. One has learned to distrust logic, and to expect contradiction from nature, but we cannot easily prevent thought from behaving as though sequence were probable until the contrary becomes still more probable; and the mind insists on asking what would happen if, in the absence of known limit, every substance that falls within human experience should be soluble successively in a more volatile substance, or under more volatile conditions. Supposing the mechanical theories of matter to be carried out as far as experience warrants,—supposing each centre of motion capable of solution in a less condensed motion,—supposing every vortex-centre treated as a phase or stage of equilibrium which passes, more or less abruptly, into another phase, under changed conditions; must all motion merge at least into ultimate static energy existing only as potential force in absolute space?

The reply of the physicist is very simple as a formula of experiment; he can carry his theory no further than he can carry his experience; but how far does he, as a matter of fact, carry his habitual, ordinary experience? Time was when experiment stopped with matter perceptible to the senses; but the chemist long ago lost sight of matter so limited. Vehemently resisting, he had been dragged into regions where supersensual forces alone had play. Very unwillingly, after fifty years of struggle, chemists had been forced to admit the existence of inconceivable and incredible substances, and their convulsive efforts to make these substances appear comprehensible had measured the strain on their thought. Static electricity already lay beyond the legitimate domain of sensual science, while beyond static electricity lay a vast supersensual ocean roughly called the ether which the physicists and chemists, on their old principles, were debarred from entering at all, and had to be dragged into, by Faraday and his school. Beyond the ether, again, lay a vast region, known to them as the only substance which they knew or could know—their own thought,—which they positively refused to touch.

Yet the physicists here, too, were helpless to escape the step, for where they refused to go as experimenters, they had to go as mathematicians. Without the higher mathematics they could no longer move, but with the higher mathematics, metaphysics began. There the restraints of physics did not exist. In the mathematical order, infinity became the invariable field of action, and not only did the mathematician deal habitually and directly with all sorts of infinities, but he also built up hyper-infinities, if he liked, or hyperspaces, or infinite hierarchies of hyper-space. The true mathematician drew breath only in the hyper-space of Thought; he could exist only by assuming that all phases of material motion merged in the last conceivable phase of immaterial motion—pure mathematical thought.

The physicist, in self-defence, though he may not deny, prefers to ignore this rigorous consequence of his own principles, as he refused for many years to admit the consequences of Faraday's experiments; but at least he can surely rely upon this admission being the last he will ever be called upon to make. No phase of hyper-substance more subtle than thought can ever be conceived, since it could exist only as his own thought returning into itself. Possibly, in the inconceivable domains of abstraction, the ultimate substance may show other sides or extensions, but to man it can be known only as hyperthought,—the region of pure mathematics and metaphysics,—the last and universal solvent.

There even mathematics must stop. Motion itself ended; even thought became merely potential in this final solution. The hierarchy of phases was complete. Each phase, measured by its rapidity of vibration, arranged itself in the physical sequence familiar to physicists, such as that sketched by Stoney in his well-known memoirs of 1885, 1890, and 1899, and as reasonable as the solar spectrum. The hierarchy rose in an order more or less demonstrable, from:—

1. The *Solids,* among which the Rule of Phases offers ice as a convenient example of its first phase, because under a familiar change of temperature it passes instantly into its next phase:—

2. The *Fluid,* or water, which by a further change of temperature transforms itself suddenly into the third phase:—

3. *Vapor,* or gas, which has laws and habits of its own forming the chief subject of chemical study upon the molecule and atom. Thus far, each phase falls within the range of human sense, but the gases, under new conditions, seem to resolve themselves into a fourth phase:—

4. The Electron or *Electricity,* which is not within the range of any sense except when set in motion. Another form of the same phase is Magnetism; and some psychologists have tried to bring animal consciousness or thought into relation with electro-magnetism, which would be very convenient for scientific purposes. The most prolonged and painful effort of the greatest geniuses has not yet succeeded in uniting Electricity with Magnetism, much less with Mind, but all show the strongest signs of a common origin in the next phase of undifferentiated energy or energies called:—

5. The *Ether,* endowed with qualities which are not so much substantial or material as they are concepts of thought,—self-contradictions in experience. Very slowly and unwillingly have the scientists yielded to the necessity of admitting that this form of

potential energy—this undifferentiated substance supporting matter and mind alike—exists, but it now forms the foundation of physics, and in it both mind and matter merge. Yet even this semi-sensual, semi-concrete, inconceivable complex of possibilities, the agent or home of infinite and instantaneous motion like gravitation,—infinitely rigid and infinitely elastic at once,—is solid and concrete compared with its following phase:—

6. *Space,* knowable only as a concept of extension, a thought, a mathematical field of speculation, and yet almost the only concrete certainty of man's consciousness. Space can be conceived as a phase of potential strains of disturbances of equilibrium, but whether studied as static substance or substance in motion, it must be endowed with an infinite possibility of strain. That which is infinitely formless must produce form. That which is only intelligible as thought, must have a power of self-induction or disturbance that can generate motion.

7. Finally, the last phase conceivable is that which lies beyond motion altogether as Hyper-space, knowable only as Hyper-thought, or pure mathematics, which, whether a subjective idea or an objective theme, is the only phase that man can certainly know and about which he can be sure. Whether he can know it from more than one side, or otherwise than as his own self-consciousness, or whether he can ever reach higher phases by developing higher powers, is a matter for mathematicians to decide; but, even after reducing it to pure negation, it must still possess, in the abstractions of ultimate and infinite equilibrium, the capacity for self-disturbance; it cannot be absolutely dead.

The Rule of Phases lends itself to mathematical treatment, and the rule of science which is best suited to mathematical treatment will always be favored by physicists, or merits being equal. Though the terms be as general as those of Willard Gibbs' formulas, if they hold good for every canonical system they will be adopted. The Rule itself assumes the general fact, ascertained by experiment or arbitrarily taken as starting point, that every equilibrium, or phase, begins and ends with what is called a critical point, at which, under a given change of temperature or pressure, a mutation occurs into another phase; and that this passage from one to the other can always be expressed mathematically. The time required for establishing a new equilibrium varies with the nature or conditions of the substance, and is sometimes very long in the case of solids, but the formula does not vary.

In chemistry the Rule of Phase applied only to material substances, but in physics no such restriction exists. Down to the moment of Hertz's experiments in 1887 and 1888, common-sense vigorously rejected the idea that material substance could be reduced to immaterial energy, but this resistance had to be abandoned with the acceptance of magneto-electricity and ether, both of which were as immaterial as thought itself; and the surrender became final with the discovery of radium, which brought the mutation of matter under the closest direct observation. Thenceforward nothing prevented the mathematical physicist from assuming the existence of as many phases, and calculating the values of as many mutations, as he liked, up to the last thinkable stage of hyper-thought and hyper-space which he knew as pure mathematics, and in which all motion, all relation, and all form, were merged.

The laws governing potential strains and stresses in an ideal equilibrium infinitely near perfection, or the volatility of an ideal substance infinitely near a perfect rest, or the possibilities of self-induction in an infinitely attenuated substance, may be left to mathematitcs for solution; but the ether, with its equally contradictory qualities, is admitted to exist; it is a real substance—or series of substances,—objective and undeniable as a granite rock. It is an equilibrium, a phase with laws of its own which are not the laws of Newtonian mechanics; it requires new methods, perhaps new mind; but, as yet, the physicist has found no reason to exclude it from the sequence of substances. The dividing line between static electricity and ether is hardly so sharp as that between any of the earlier phases,—solid, fluid, gaseous, or electric.

The physicist has been reluctantly coerced into this concession, and if he had been also a psychologist he would have been equally driven, under the old laws of association formerly known as logic, to admit that what he conceded to motion in its phase as matter, he must concede to motion in its form as mind. Without this extension, any new theory of the universe based on mechanics must be as ill-balanced as the old. Whatever dogmatic confidence the mechanist had professed in his mechanical theory of the universe, his own mind had always betrayed an uneasy protest against being omitted from its own mechanical creation. This neglect involved not only a total indifference to its claim to exist as a material—or immaterial—vibration, although such mere kinetic movement was granted in theory to every other substance it knew; but it ignored also the higher claim, which was implied in its own definition, that it existed as the sole source of Direction, or Form, without which all mechanical systems must remain forever as chaotic as they show themselves in a thousand nebulae. The matter of Direction was more vital to science than all kinematics together. The question how order could have got into the universe at all was the chief object of human thought since thought existed; and order,—to use the expressive figure of Rudolph Goldscheid,—was but Direction regarded as stationary, like a frozen waterfall. The sum of motion without direction is zero, as in the motion of a kinetic gas where only Clerk Maxwell's demon of Thought could create a value. Possibly, in the chances of infinite time and space, the law of probabilities might assert that, sooner or later, some volume of kinetic motion must end in the accident of Direction, but no such accident has yet affected the gases, or imposed a general law on the visible universe. Down to our day Vibration and Direction remain as different as Matter and Mind. Lines of force go on vibrating, rotating, moving in waves, up and down, forward and back, indifferent to control and pure waste of energy,—forms of repulsion,—until their motion becomes guided by motive, as an electric current is induced by a dynamo.

History, so far as it recounts progress, deals only with such induction or direction, and therefore in history only the attractive or inductive mass, as Thought, helps to construct. Only attractive forces have a positive, permanent value for the advance of society on the path it has actually pursued. The processes of History being irreversible, the action of Pressure can be exerted only in one direction, and therefore the variable called Pressure in physics has its equivalent in the Attraction, which, in the historical rule of phase, gives to human society its forward movement. Thus in the historical formula, Attraction is equivalent to Pressure, and takes its place.

In physics, the second important variable is Temperature. Always a certain temperature must coincide with a certain pressure before the critical point of change in phase can be reached. In history, and possibly wherever the movement is one of translation in a medium, the Temperature is a result of acceleration, or its equivalent, and in the Rule of historical phase Acceleration takes its place.

The third important variable in the physico-chemical phase is Volume, and it reappears in the historical phase unchanged. Under the Rule of Phase, therefore, man's Thought, considered as a single substance passing through a series of historical phases, is assumed to follow the analogy of water, and to pass from one phase to another through a series of critical points which are determined by the three factors Attraction, Acceleration, and Volume, for each change of equilibrium. Among the score of figures that might be used to illustrate the idea, that of a current is perhaps the nearest; but whether the current be conceived as a fluid, a gas, or as electricity,—whether it is drawn on by gravitation or induction,—whether it be governed by the law of astronomical or electric mass,—it must always be conceived as a solvent, acting like heat or electricity, and increasing in volume by the law of squares.

This solvent, then,—this ultimate motion which absorbs all other forms of motion is an ultimate equilibrium,—this ethereal current of Thought,—is conceived as existing, like ice on a mountain range, and trickling from every pore of rock, in innumerable rills, uniting always into larger channels and always dissolving whatever it meets, until at last it reaches equilibrium in the ocean of ultimate solution. Historically the current can be watched for only a brief time, at most ten thousand years. Inferentially it can be divined for perhaps a hundred thousand. Geologically, it can be followed back perhaps a hundred million years, but however long the time, the origin of consciousness is lost in the rocks before we can reach more than a fraction of its career.

In this long and—for our purposes—infinite stretch of time, the substance called Thought has,—like the substance called water or gas,—passed through a variety of phases, or changes, or states of equilibrium, with which we are all, more or less, familiar. We live in a world of phases, so much more astonishing than the explosion of rockets, that we cannot, unless we are Gibbs or Watts, stop every moment to ask what becomes of the salt we put in our soup, or the water we boil in our teapot, and we are apt to remain stupidly stolid when a bulb bursts into a tulip, or a worm turns into a butterfly. No phase compares in wonder with the mere fact of our own existence, and this wonder has so completely exhausted the powers of Thought that mankind, except in a few laboratories, has ceased to wonder, or even to think. The Egyptians had infinite reason to bow down before a beetle; we have as much reason as they, for we know no more about it; but we have learned to accept our beetle Phase, and to recognize that everything, animate or inanimate, spiritual or material, exists in Phase; that all is equilibrium more or less unstable, and that our whole vision is limited to the bare possibility of calculating in mathematical form the degree of a given instability.

Thus results the plain assurance that the future of Thought, and therefore of History, lies in the hands of the physicists, and that the future historian must seek his education in the world of mathematical physics. Nothing can be expected from further study on the old lines. A new generation must be brought up to think by new methods, and if our historical department in the Universities cannot enter this next Phase, the physical department will have to assume the task alone.

Meanwhile, though quite without the necessary education, the historical inquirer or experimenter may be permitted to guess for a moment,—merely for the amusement of guessing,—what may perhaps turn out to be a possible term of the problem as the physicist will take it up. He may assume, as his starting-point, that Thought is a historical substance, analogous to an electric current, which has obeyed the laws,—whatever they are,—of Phase. The hypothesis is not extravagant. As a fact, we know only too well that our historical Thought has obeyed, and still obeys, some law of Inertia, since it has habitually and obstinately resisted deflection by new forces or motives; we know even that it acts as though it felt friction from resistance, since it is constantly stopped by all sorts of obstacles; we can apply to it, letter for letter, one of the capital laws of physical chemistry, that, where an equilibrium is subjected to conditions which tend to change, it reacts internally in ways that tend to resist the external constraint, and to preserve its established balance; often it is visibly set in motion by sympathetic forces which act upon it as a magnet acts on soft iron, by induction; the commonest school-history takes for granted that it has shown periods of unquestioned acceleration. If, then, society has in so many ways obeyed the ordinary laws of attraction and inertia, nothing can be more natural than to inquire whether it obeys them in all respects, and whether the rules that have been applied to fluids and gases in general, apply also to society as a current of Thought. Such a speculative inquiry is the source of almost all that is known of magnetism, electricity and ether, and all other possible immaterial substances, but in history the inquiry has the vast advantage that a Law of Phase has been long established for the stages of human thought.

No student of history is so ignorant as not to know that fully fifty years before the chemists took up the study of Phases, Auguste Comte laid down in sufficiently precise terms a law of phase for history which received the warm adhesion of two authorities,—the most eminent of that day,—Émile Littré and John Stuart Mill. Nearly a hundred and fifty years before Willard Gibbs announced his mathematical formulas of phase to the physicists and chemists, Turgot stated the Rule of historical Phase as clearly as Franklin stated the law of electricity. As far as concerns theory, we are not much further advanced now than in 1750, and know little better what electricity or thought is, as substance, than Franklin and Turgot knew it; but this failure to penetrate the ultimate synthesis of nature is no excuse for professors of history to abandon the field which is theirs by prior right, and still less can they plead their ignorance of the training in mathematics and physics which it was their duty to seek. The theory of history is a much easier study than the theory of light.

It was about 1830 that Comte began to teach the law that the human mind, as studied in the current of human thought, had passed through three stages or phases:—theological, metaphysical, and what he called positive as developed in his own teaching; and that this was the first principle of social dynamics. His critics tacitly accepted in principle the possibility of some such division, but they fell to disputing Comte's succession of phases as though this were essential to the law. Comte's idea of applying the rule had nothing to do with the validity of the rule itself. Once it was admitted that human thought had passed through three known phases,—analogous to the chemical phases of solid, liquid, and gaseous,—the standard of measurement which was to be applied might vary with every experimenter until the most convenient should be agreed upon. The commonest objection to Comte's rule,—the objection that the three phases had always existed and still exist, together,—had still less to do with the validity of the law. The residuum of every distillate contains all the original elements in equilibrium with the whole series, if the process is not carried too far. The three phases always exist together in equilibrium; but their limits on either side are fixed by changes of temperature and pressure, manifesting themselves in changes of Direction or Form.

Discarding, then, as unessential, the divisions of history suggested by Comte, the physicist-historian would assume that a change of phase was to be recognized by a change of Form; that is, by a change of Direction; and that it was caused by Acceleration, and increase of Volume or Concentration. In this sense the experimenter is restricted rigidly to the search for changes of Direction or Form of thought, but has no concern in its acceleration except as one of the three variables to which he has to assign mathematical values in order to fix the critical point of change. The first step in experiment is to decide upon some particular and unquestioned change of Direction or Form in human thought.

By common consent, one period of history has always been regarded, even by itself, as a Renaissance, and has boasted of its singular triumph in breaking the continuity of Thought. The exact date of this revolution varies within a margin of two hundred years or more, according as the student fancies the chief factor to have been the introduction of printing, the discovery of America, the invention of the telescope, the writings of Galileo, Descartes, and Bacon, or the mechanical laws perfected by Newton, Huyghens, and the mathematicians as late as 1700; but no one has ever doubted the fact of a distinct change in direction and form of thought during that period; which furnishes the necessary starting-point for any experimental study of historical Phase.

Any one who reads half a dozen pages of Descartes or Bacon sees that these great reformers expressly aimed at changing the Form of thought; that they had no idea but to give it new direction, as Columbus and Galileo had expressly intended to affect direction in space; and even had they all been unconscious of intent, the Church would have pointed it out to them, as it did with so much emphasis to Galileo in 1633. On this point there was no difference of opinion; the change of direction in Thought was not a mere acceleration; it was an angle or tangent so considerable that the Church in vain tried to ignore it. Galileo proved it, and the Church agreed with him on that point if on no other. Nothing could be more unanimously admitted than the change of direction between the thought of St. Augustine and that of Lord Bacon.

Since the Rule of historical Phase has got to rest on this admission, theory cannot venture on the next step unless this one is abundantly proved; but, in fact, no one as yet has ever doubted it. The moment was altogether the most vital that history ever recorded, and left the deepest impression on men's memory, but this popular impression hardly expresses its scientific value. As a change of phase it offered singular interest, because, in this case alone, the process could be followed as though it were electrolytic, and the path of each separate molecule were visible under the microscope. Any school-boy could plot on a sheet of paper in abscissae and ordinates the points through which the curve of thought passed, as fixed by the values of the men and their inventions or discoveries. History offers no other demonstration to compare with it, and the more because the curve shows plainly that the new lines of Force or Thought were induced lines, obeying the laws of mass, and not those of self-induction. On this obedience Lord Bacon dwelt with tireless persistence; "the true and legitimate object of science is only to endow human life with new inventions and forces"; but he defined the attractive power of this magnet as equal to the sum of nature's forces, so far as they could serve man's needs or wishes; and he followed that attraction precisely as Columbus followed the attraction of a new world, or as Newton suffered the law of gravitation on his mind as he did on his body. As each newly appropriated force increased the attraction between the sum of nature's forces and the volume of human mind, by the usual law of squares, the acceleration hurried society towards the critical point that marked the passage into a new phase as though it were heat impelling water to explode as steam.

Only the electrolytic process permits us to watch such movements in physics and chemistry, and the change of phase in 1500-1700 is marvellously electrolytic, but the more curious because we can even give names to the atoms or molecules that passed over to the positive or negative electrode, and can watch the accumulation of force which ended at last by deflecting the whole current of Thought. The maximum movement possible in the old channel was exceeded; the acceleration and concentration, or volume, reached the point of sudden expansion, and the new phase began.

The history of the new phase has no direct relation with that which preceded it. The gap between theology and mathematics was so sharp in its rapid separation that history is much perplexed to maintain the connection. The earlier signs of the coming change, —before 1500—were mostly small additions to the commoner mechanical resources of society; but when, after 1500, these additions assumed larger scope and higher aim, they still retained mechanical figure and form even in expanding the law of gravitation into astronomical space. If a direct connection between the two phases is more evident on one line than on another, it is in the curious point of view that society seemed to take of Newton's extension of the law of gravitation to include astronomical mass, which, for two hundred years, resembled an attribute of divinity, and grew into a mechanical theory of the universe amounting to a religion. The connection of thought lay in the human reflection of itself in the universe; yet the acceleration of the seventeenth century, as compared with that of any previous age, was rapid, and that of the eighteenth was startling. The acceleration became even measurable, for it took the form of utilizing heat as force, through the steam-engine, and this addition of power was measurable in the coal output. Society followed the same lines of attraction with little change, down to 1840, when the new chemical energy of electricity began to deflect the thought of society again, and Faraday rivalled Newton in the vigor with which he marked out the path of changed attractions, but the purely mechanical theory of the universe typified by Newton and Dalton held its own, and reached its highest authority towards 1870, or about the time when the dynamo came into use.

Throughout these three hundred years, and especially in the nine-

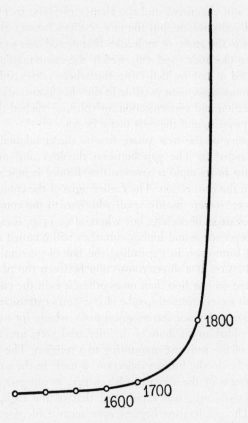

1800

1700

1600

teenth century, the acceleration suggests at once the old, familiar law of squares. The curve resembles that of the vaporization of water. The resemblance is too close to be disregarded, for nature loves the logarithm, and perpetually recurs to her inverse square. For convenience, if only as a momentary refuge, the physicist-historian will probably have to try the experiment of taking the law of inverse squares as his standard of social acceleration for the nineteenth century, and consequently for the whole phase, which obliges him to accept it experimentally as a general law of history. Nature is rarely so simple as to act rigorously on the square, but History, like Mathematics, is obliged to assume that eccentricities more or less balance each other, so that something remains constant at last, and it is compelled to approach its problems by means of some fiction,—some infinitesimal calculus,—which may be left as general and undetermined as the formulas of our greatest master, Willard Gibbs, but which gives a hypothetical movement for an ideal substance that can be used for relation. Some experimental starting-point must always be assumed, and the mathematical historian will be at liberty to assume the most convenient, which is likely to be the rule of geometrical progression.

Thus the first step towards a Rule of Phase for history may be conceived as possible. In fact the Phase may be taken as admitted by all society and every authority since the condemnation of Galileo in 1633; it is only the law, or rule, that the mathematician and physicist would aim at establishing. Supposing, then, that he were to begin by the Phase of 1600-1900, which he might call the Mechanical Phase, and supposing that he assumes for the whole of it the observed acceleration of the nineteenth century, the law of squares, his next step would lead him backward to the far more difficult problem of fixing the limits of the Phase that preceded 1600.

Here was the point which Auguste Comte and all other authorities have failed to agree upon. Although no one denies that at some moment between 1500 and 1700 society passed from one form of thought to another, every one may reasonably hesitate to fix upon the upper limit to be put on the earlier. Comte felt the difficulty so strongly that he subdivided his scale into a fetish, polytheistic, monotheistic, and metaphysical series, before arriving at himself, or Positivism. Most historians would admit the change from polytheism to monotheism, about the year 500, between the establishment of Christianity and that of Mohammedanism as a distinct change in the form or direction of thought, and perhaps in truth society never performed a more remarkable feat than when it consciously unified its religious machinery as it had already concentrated its political and social organism. The concentration certainly marked an era; whether it marked a change of Direction may be disputed. The physicist may prefer to regard it as a refusal to change direction; an obedience to the physico-chemical law that when an equilibrium is subjected to conditions which tend towards change, it reacts internally in ways that tend to resist the external constraint; and, in fact, the establishment of monotheism was regarded by the philosophers even in its own day rather as a reaction than an advance. No doubt the Mohammedan or the Christian felt the change of deity as the essence of religion; but the mathematician might well think that the scope and nature of religion had little to do with the number of Gods. Religion is the recognition of unseen power which has control of man's destiny, and the power which man may, at different times or in different regions, recognize as controlling his destiny, in no way alters his attitude or the form of the thought. The physicist, who affects psychology, will regard religion as the self-projection of mind into nature in one direction, as science is the projection of mind into nature in another. Both are illusions, as the metaphysician conceives, and in neither case does—or can—the mind reach anything but a different reflection of its own features; but in changing from polytheism to monotheism the mind merely concentrated the image; it was an acceleration, not a direction that was changed. From first to last the fetish idea inhered in the thought; the idea of an occult power to which obedience was due,—a reflection of the human self from the unknown depths of nature—was as innate in the Allah of Mohammed as in the fetish serpent which Moses made of brass.

The reflection or projection of the mind in nature was the earliest and will no doubt be the last motive of man's mind, whether as religion or as science, and only the attraction will vary according to the value which the mind assigns to the image of the thing that moves it; but the mere concentration of the image need not change the direction of movement, any more than the concentration of converging paths into one single road need change the direction of travel or traffic. The direction of the social movement may be taken, for scientific purposes, as unchanged from the beginning of history to the condemnation of Galileo which marked the conscious recognition of break in continuity; but in that case the physicist-historian will probably find nowhere the means of drawing any clean line of division across the current of thought, even if he follows it back to the lowest known archaic race. Notoriously, during this enormously long Religious Phase, the critical point seemed to be touched again and again,—by Greeks and Romans, in Athens, Alexandria, and Constantinople, long before it was finally passed in 1600; but also, in following the stream backwards to its source, the historian will probably find suggestions of a critical point in ethnology long before such a critical point can be fixed. So far as he will see, man's thought began by projecting its own image, in this form, into the unknown of nature. Yet nothing in science is quite so firmly accepted as the fact that such a change of phase took place. Whether evolution was natural or supernatural, the leap of nature from the phase of instinct to the phase of thought was so immense as to impress itself on every imagination. No one denies that it must have been relatively ancient;—few anthropologists would be content with less than a hundred thousand years;—and no one need be troubled by admitting that it may have been relatively sudden, like many other mutations, since all the intermediate steps have vanished and the line of connection is obliterated. Yet the anthropoid ape remains to guide the physical historian, and, what is more convincing than the ape, the whole phase of instinct survives, not merely as a force in actual evidence, but as the foundation of the whole geological record. As an immaterial force, Instinct was so strong as to overcome obstacles that Intellect has been helpless to affect. The bird, the beetle, the butterfly accomplished feats that still defy all the resources of human reason. The attractions that led instinct to pursue so many and such varied lines to such great distances, must have been intensely strong and indefinitely lasting. The quality that developed the eye and the wing of the bee and the condor has no known equivalent in man. The vast perspective of time opened by the most superficial study of this phase has always staggered belief; but geology itself breaks off abruptly in the middle of the story, when already the fishes and crustaceans astonish by their modern airs.

Yet the anthropoid ape is assumed to have potentially contained the future, as he actually epitomized the past; and to him, as to us, the phase to which he belonged was the last and briefest. Behind him and his so-called instinct oi consciousness, stretched other phases of vegetable and mechanical motion,—more or less organic,—phases of semi-physical, semi-material, attractions and repulsions,—that could have, in the concept, no possible limitation of time. Neither bee, nor monkey, nor man, could conceive a time when stones could not fall. The anthropoid ape could look back, as certainly as the most scientific modern historian, to a critical point at which his own phase must have begun, when the rudimentary forces that had developed in the vegetables had acquired a volume and complexity which could no longer be enclosed in rigid forms, and had expanded into freer movement. The ape might have predicted his own expansion into new force, for, long before the first man was sketched, the monkeys and their companions in instinct had peopled every continent, and civilized—according to their standards—the whole world.

The problem to the anthropoid ape a hundred thousand years ago was the same as that addressed to the physicist-historian of 1900:—How long could he go on developing indefinite new phases in response to the occult attractions of an infinitely extended universe? What new direction could his genius take? To him, the past was a miraculous development, and, to perfect himself, he needed only to swim like a fish and soar like a bird; but probably he felt no conscious need of mind. His phase had lasted unbroken for millions of years, and had produced an absolutely miraculous triumph of instinct. Had he been so far gifted as to foresee his next mutation, he would have possibly found in it only a few meagre pages, telling of impoverished life, at the end of his own enormous library of records, the bulk of which had been lost. Had he studied these past records, he would probably have admitted that thus far, by some mechanism totally incomprehensible, the series of animated beings had in some directions responded to nature's call, and had thrown out tentacles on many sides; but he, as a creature of instinct, would have instinctively wished to develop in the old directions,—he could have felt no conscious wish to become a mathematician.

Thus the physicist-historian seems likely to be forced into admitting that an attractive force, like gravitation, drew these trickling rivulets of energy into new phases by an external influence which tended to concentrate and accelerate their motion by a law with which their supposed wishes or appetites had no conscious relation. At a certain point the electric corpuscle was obliged to become a gas, the gas a liquid, the liquid a solid. For material mass, only one law was known to hold good. Ice, water, and gas, all have weight; they obey the law of astronomical mass; they are guided by the attraction of matter. If the current of Thought has shown obedience to the law of gravitation it is material, and its phases should be easily calculated.

The physicist will, therefore, have to begin by trying the figure of the old Newtonian or Cartesian vortices, or gravitating group of heterogeneous substances moving in space as though in a closed receptacle. Any nebula or vortex-group would answer his purpose,— say the great nebula of Orion, which he would conceive as containing potentially every possible phase of substance. Here the various local centres of attraction would tend to arrange the diffused elements like iron-filings round a magnet in a phase of motion which, if the entire equilibrium were perfect, would last forever; but if, at any point, the equilibrium were disturbed, the whole volume would be set in new motion, until, under the rise in pressure and temperature, one phase after another must mechanically,—and more and more suddenly,—occur with the increasing velocity of movement.

That such sudden changes of phase do in fact occur is one of the articles of astronomical faith, but the reality of the fact has little to do with the convenience of the figure. The nebula is beyond human measurements. A simple figure is needed, and our solar system offers none. The nearest analogy would be that of a comet, not so much because it betrays marked phases, as because it resembles Thought in certain respects since, in the first place, no one knows what it is, which is also true of Thought, and it seems in some cases to be immaterial, passing in a few hours from the cold of space to actual contact with the sun at a temperature some two thousand times that of incandescent iron, and so back to the cold of space, without apparent harm, while its tail sweeps round an inconceivable circle with almost the speed of thought,—certainly the speed of light,—and its body may show no nucleus at all. If not a Thought, the comet is a sort of brother of Thought, an early condensation of the ether itself, as the human mind may be another, traversing the infinite without origin or end, and attracted by a sudden object of curiosity that lies by chance near its path. If such elements are subject to the so-called law of gravitation, no good reason can exist for denying gravitation to the mind.

Such a typical comet is that of 1668, or 1843, or Newton's comet of 1680; bodies which fall in a direct line,—itself a miracle,—from space, for some hundreds of years, with an acceleration given by the simple formula $k\,\dfrac{M}{r^2}$ where k is the constant of gravitation, M the mass of the sun and r the distance between the comet and the centre of the sun. If not deflected from its straight course by any of the planets, it penetrates at last within the orbit of Venus and approaches the sun.

At five o'clock one winter morning in 1843, the comet began to show deflection at about two-and-a-half diameters distance from the sun; at ten o'clock it was abreast of the sun, and swung about at a right angle; at half past ten it passed perihelion at a speed of about 350 miles a second; and at noon, after having passed three hours in a temperature exceeding 5000° Centrigrade, it appeared unharmed on its return course, until at five o'clock in the afternoon it was flying back to the space it came from, on the same straight line, parallel to that by which it came.

Nothing in the behavior of Thought is more paradoxical than that of these planets, or shows direction or purpose more flagrantly, and it happens that they furnish the only astronomical parallel for the calculated acceleration of the last Phase of Thought. No other heavenly body shows the same sharp curve or excessive speed. Yet, if the calculated curve of deflection of Thought in 1600-1900 were put on that of the planet, it would show that man's evolution had passed perihelion, and that his movement was already retrograde. To some minds, this objection might not seem fatal, and in fact another fifty years must elapse before the rate of human movement would sensibly relax; but another objection would be serious, if not for the theory, at least for the figure. The acceleration of the comet is much slower than that of society. The world did not double or treble its movement between 1800 and 1900, but, measured by any standard known to science—by horse-power, calories, volts, mass in any shape,—the tension and vibration and volume and so-called

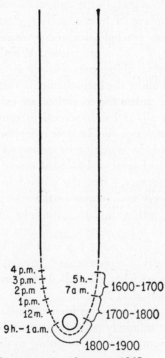

PASSAGE OF THE COMET OF 1843
February 27, twelve hours

progression of society were fully a thousand times greater in 1900 than in 1800;—the force had doubled ten times over, and the speed, when measured by electrical standards as in telegraphy, approached infinity, and had annihilated both space and time. No law of material movement applied to it.

Some such result was to be expected. Nature is not so simple as to obey only one law, or to apply necessarily a law of material mass to immaterial substance. The result proves only that the comet is material, and that thought is less material than the comet. The figure serves the physicist only to introduce the problem. If the laws of material mass do not help him, he will seek for a law of immaterial mass, and here he has, as yet, but one analogy to follow,—that of electricity. If the comet, or the current of water, offers some suggestion for the current of human society, electricity offers one so much stronger that psychologists are apt instinctively to study the mind as a phase of electro-magnetism. Whether such a view is sound or not matters nothing to its convenience as a figure. Thought has always moved under the incumbrance of matter, like an electron in a solution, and, unless the conditions are extremely favorable, it does not move at all, as has happened in many solutions,—as in China,—or in some cases may become enfeebled and die out, without succession. Only by watching its motion on the enormous scale of historical and geological or biological time can one see,—across great gulfs of ignorance,—that the current has been constant as measured by its force and volume in the absorption of nature's resources, and that, within the last century, its acceleration has been far more rapid than before,—more rapid than can be accounted for by the laws of material mass; but only highly trained physicists could invent a model to represent such motion. The ignorant student can merely guess what the skilled experimenter would do; he can only imagine an ideal case.

This ideal case would offer to his imagination the figure of nature's power as an infinitely powerful dynamo, attracting or inducing a current of human thought according to the usual electric law of squares,—that is to say, that the average motion of one phase is the square of that which precedes it. The curve is thus:—

Assuming that the change of phase began in 1500, and that the new Mechanical Phase dates in its finished form from Galileo, Bacon, and Descartes, with a certain lag in its announcement by them,—say from 1600,—the law of squares gives a curve like that of ice, water, and steam, running off to the infinite in almost straight lines at either end, like the comet but at right angles. Supposing a value in numbers of any sort,—say 6, 36, 1296,—and assigning 1296 to the period 1600-1900, the preceding religious phase would have a value of only 36 as the average of many thousand years, representing therefore nearly a straight line, while the twentieth century would be represented by the square of 1296, or what is equivalent to a straight line to infinity.

Reversing the curve to try the time-sequence by the same rule, the Mechanical Phase being represented by 300 years, the Religious Phase would require not less than 90,000. Perhaps this result might not exactly suit a physicist's views, but if he accepts the sequence 90,000 and 300 for these two phases in time, he arrives at some curious results for the future, and in calculating the period of the fourth, or electric phase, he must be prepared for extreme figures.

No question in the series is so vital as that of fixing the limits of the Mechanical Phase. Assuming, as has been done, the year 1600 for its beginning, the question remains to decide the probable date of its close. Perhaps the physicist might regard it as already closed. He might say that the highest authority of the mechanical universe was reached about 1870, and that, just then, the invention of the dynamo turned society sharply into a new channel of electric thought as different from the mechanical as electric mass is different from astronomical mass. He might assert that Faraday, Clerk Maxwell, Hertz, Helmholz, and the whole electro-magnetic school, thought in terms quite unintelligible to the old chemists, and mechanists. The average man, in 1850, could understand what Davy or Carwin had to say; he could not understand what Clerk Maxwell meant. The later terms were not translatable into the earlier; even the mathematics became hyper-mathematical. Possibly a physicist might go so far as to hold that the most arduous intellectual effort ever made by man with a distinct consciousness of needing new mental powers, was made after 1870 in the general effort to acquire habits of electro-magnetic thought,—the familiar use of formulas carrying indefinite self-contradiction into the conception of force. The physicist knows best his own difficulties, and perhaps to him the process of evolution may seem easy, but to the mere by-stander the gap between electric and astronomic mass seems greater than that between Descartes and St. Augustine, or Lord Bacon and Thomas Aquinas. The older ideas, though hostile, were intelligible; the idea of electro-magnetic-ether is not.

Thus it seems possible that another generation, trained after 1900 in the ideas and terms of electro-magnetism and radiant matter, may regard that date as marking the sharpest change of direction, taken at the highest rate of speed, ever effected by the human mind; a change from the material to the immaterial,—from the law of gravitation to the law of squares. The Phases were real: the change of direction was measured by the consternation of physicists and chemists at the discovery of radium which was quite as notorious as the consternation of the Church at the discovery of Galileo; but it is the affair of science, not of historians, to give it a mathematical value.

Should the physicist reject the division, and insist on the experience of another fifty or a hundred years, the consequence would still be trifling for the fourth term of the series. Supposing the Mechanical Phase to have lasted 300 years, from 1600 to 1900, the next or Electric Phase would have a life equal to $\sqrt{300}$, or about seventeen years, and a half, when—that is, in 1917—it would pass into another or Ethereal Phase, which, for half a century, science has been promising, and which would last only $\sqrt{17.5}$, or about four years and bring Thought to the limit of its possibilities in the year 1921. It may well be! Nothing whatever is beyond the range of possibility; but even if the life of the previous phase, 1600-1900, were extended another hundred years, the difference to the last term of the series would be negligible. In that case, the Ethereal Phase would last till about 2025.

The mere fact that society should think in terms of Ether or the higher mathematics might mean little or much. According to the Phase Rule, it lived from remote ages in terms of fetish force, and passed from that into terms of mechanical force, which again led to terms of electric force, without fairly realizing what had happened except in slow social and political revolutions. Thought in terms of Ether means only Thought in terms of itself, or, in other words, pure Mathematics and Metaphysics, a stage often reached by individuals. At the utmost it could mean only the subsidence of the current into an ocean of potential thought, or mere consciousness, which is also possible, like static electricity. The only consequence might be an indefinitely long stationary period, such as John Stuart Mill foresaw. In that case, the current would merely cease to flow.

But if, in the prodigiously rapid vibration of its last phases, Thought should continue to act as the universal solvent which it is, and should reduce the forces of the molecule, the atom, and the electron to that costless servitude to which it has reduced the old elements of earth and air, fire and water; if man should continue to set free the infinite forces of nature, and attain the control of cosmic forces on a cosmic scale, the consequences may be as surprising as the change of water to vapor, of the worm to the butterfly, of radium to electrons. At a given volume and velocity, the forces that are concentrated on his head must act.

Such seem to be, more or less probably, the lines on which any physical theory of the universe would affect the study of history, according to the latest direction of physics. Comte's Phases adapt themselves easily to some such treatment, and nothing in philosophy or metaphysics forbids it. The figure used for illustration is immaterial except so far as it limits the nature of the attractive force. In any case the theory will have to assume that the mind has always figured its motives as reflections of itself, and that this is as true in its conception of electricity, as in its instinctive imitation of a God. Always and everywhere the mind creates its own universe, and pursues its own phantoms; but the force behind the image is always a reality, —the attractions of occult power. If values can be given to these attractions, a physical theory of history is a mere matter of physical formula, no more complicated than the formulas of Willard Gibbs or Clerk Maxwell; but the task of framing the formula and assigning the values belongs to the physicist, not to the historian; and if one such arrangement fails to accord with the facts, it is for him to try another, to assign new values to his variables, and to verify the results. The variables themselves can hardly suffer much change.

If the physicist-historian is satisfied with neither of the known laws of mass,—astronomical or electric,—and cannot arrange his variables in any combination that will conform with a phase-sequence, no resource seems to remain but that of waiting until his physical problems shall be solved, and he shall be able to explain what Force is. As yet he knows almost as little of material as of immaterial substance. He is as perplexed before the phenomena of Heat, Light, Magnetism, Electricity, Gravitation, Attraction, Repulsion, Pressure, and the whole schedule of names used to indicate unknown elements, as before the common, infinitely familiar fluctuations of his own Thought whose action is so astounding on the directions of his energies. Probably the solution of any one of the problems will give the solution for them all.

·XII·

THORSTEIN VEBLEN

[1 8 5 7 - 1 9 2 9]

THE PLACE OF SCIENCE IN
MODERN CIVILIZATION

THE PLACE OF SCIENCE IN
MODERN CIVILIZATION

It is commonly held that modern Christendom is superior to any and all other systems of civilized life. Other ages and other cultural regions are by contrast spoken of as lower, or more archaic, or less mature. The claim is that the modern culture is superior on the whole, not that it is the best or highest in all respects and at every point. It has, in fact, not an all-around superiority, but a superiority within a closely limited range of intellectual activities, while outside this range many other civilizations surpass that of the modern occidental peoples. But the peculiar excellence of the modern culture is of such a nature as to give it a decisive practical advantage over all other cultural schemes that have gone before or that have come into competition with it. It has proved itself fit to survive in a struggle for existence as against those civilizations which differ from it in respect of its distinctive traits.

Modern civilization is peculiarly matter-of-fact. It contains many elements that are not of this character, but these other elements do not belong exclusively or characteristically to it. The modern civilized peoples are in a peculiar degree capable of an impersonal, dispassionate insight into the material facts with which mankind has to deal. The apex of cultural growth is at this point. Compared with this trait the rest of what is comprised in the cultural scheme is adventitious, or at the best it is a by-product of this hard-headed apprehension of facts. This quality may be a matter of habit or of racial endowment, or it may be an outcome of both; but whatever be the explanation of its prevalence, the immediate consequence is much the same for the growth of civilization. A civilization which is

From *The Place of Science in Modern Civilization, and other Essays,* by Thorstein Veblen, pp. 3-36; as included in *What Veblen Taught,* by Wesley C. Mitchell. Copyright, 1919, by B. W. Huebsch; 1947, by Becky Meyers and Ann B. Sims. Reprinted by permission of The Viking Press, Inc., New York. Originally printed in *American Journal of Sociology,* March, 1906.

dominated by this matter-of-fact insight must prevail against any cultural scheme that lacks this element. This characteristic of western civilization comes to a head in modern science, and it finds its highest material expression in the technology of the machine industry. In these things modern culture is creative and self-sufficient; and these being given, the rest of what may seem characteristic in western civilization follows by easy consequence. The cultural structure clusters about this body of matter-of-fact knowledge as its substantial core. Whatever is not consonant with these opaque creations of science is an intrusive feature in the modern scheme, borrowed or standing over from the barbarian past.

Other ages and other peoples excel in other things and are known by other virtues. In creative art, as well as in critical taste, the faltering talent of Christendom can at the best follow the lead of the ancient Greeks and the Chinese. In deft workmanship the handicraftsmen of the middle Orient, as well as of the Far East, stand on a level securely above the highest European achievement, old or new. In myth-making, folklore, and occult symbolism many of the lower barbarians have achieved things beyond what the latter-day priests and poets know how to propose. In metaphysical insight and dialectical versatility many orientals, as well as the Schoolmen of the Middle Ages, easily surpass the highest reaches of the New Thought and the Higher Criticism. In a shrewd sense of the religious verities, as well as in an unsparing faith in devout observances, the people of India or Tibet, or even the medieval Christians, are past-masters in comparison even with the select of the faith of modern times. In political finesse, as well as in unreasoning, brute loyalty, more than one of the ancient peoples give evidence of a capacity to which no modern civilized nation may aspire. In warlike malevolence and abandon the hosts of Islam, the Sioux Indian, and the "heathen of the northern sea" have set the mark above the reach of the most strenuous civilized warlord.

To modern civilized men, especially in their intervals of sober reflection, all these things that distinguish the barbarian civilizations seem of dubious value and are required to show cause why they should not be slighted. It is not so with the knowledge of facts. The making of states and dynasties, the founding of families, the prosecution of feuds, the propagation of creeds and the creation of sects, the accumulation of fortunes, the consumption of superfluities— these have all in their time been felt to justify themselves as an end of endeavour; but in the eyes of modern civilized men all these things seem futile in comparison with the achievements of science. They dwindle in men's esteem as time passes, while the achievements of science are held higher as time passes. This is the one secure holding-ground of latter-day conviction, that "the increase and diffusion of knowledge among men" is indefeasibly right and good. When seen in such perspective as will clear it of the trivial perplexities of workday life, this proposition is not questioned within the horizon of the western culture, and no other cultural idea holds a similar unquestioned place in the convictions of civilized mankind.

On any large question which is to be disposed of for good and all the final appeal is by common consent taken to the scientist. The solution offered in the name of science is decisive so long as it is not set aside by a still more searching scientific inquiry. This state of things may not be altogether fortunate, but such is the fact. There are other, older grounds of finality that may conceivably be better, nobler, worthier, more profound, more beautiful. It might conceivably be preferable, as a matter of cultural ideals, to leave the last word with the lawyer, the duelist, the priest, the moralist, or the college of heraldry. In past times people have been content to leave their weightiest questions to the decision of some one or other of these tribunals, and, it cannot be denied, with very happy results in those respects that were then looked to with the greatest solicitude. But whatever the common-sense of earlier generations may have held in this respect, modern common-sense holds that the scientist's answer is the only ultimately true one. In the last resort enlightened common-sense sticks by the opaque truth and refuses to go behind the returns given by the tangible facts.

Quasi lignum vitae in paradiso Dei, et quasi lucerna fulgoris in domo Domini, such is the place of science in modern civilization. This latter-day faith in matter-of-fact knowledge may be well grounded or it may not. It has come about that men assign it this high place, perhaps idolatrously, perhaps to the detriment of the best and most intimate interests of the race. There is room for much more than a vague doubt that this cult of science is not altogether a wholesome growth—that the unmitigated quest of knowledge, of this matter-of-fact kind, makes for race-deterioration and discomfort on the whole, both in its immediate effects upon the spiritual life of mankind, and in the material consequences that follow from a great advance in matter-of-fact knowledge.

But we are not here concerned with the merits of the case. The question here is: How has this cult of science arisen? What are its cultural antecedents? How far is it in consonance with hereditary human nature? and, What is the nature of its hold on the convictions of civilized men?

In dealing with pedagogical problems and the theory of education, current psychology is nearly at one in saying that all learning is of a "pragmatic" character; that knowledge is inchoate action inchoately directed to an end; that all knowledge is "functional"; that it is of the nature of use. This, of course, is only a corollary under the main postulate of the latter-day psychologists, whose catchword is that the Idea is essentially active. There is no need of quarrelling with this "pragmatic" school of psychologists. Their aphorism may not contain the whole truth, perhaps, but at least it goes nearer to the heart of the epistemological problem than any earlier formulation. It may confidently be said to do so because, for one thing, its argument meets the requirements of modern science. It is such a concept as matter-of-fact science can make effective use of; it is drawn in terms which are, in the last analysis, of an impersonal, not to say tropismatic, character; such as is demanded by science, with its insistence on opaque cause and effect. While knowledge is construed in teleological terms, in terms of personal interest and attention, this teleological aptitude is itself reducible to a product of unteleological natural selection. The teleological bent of intelligence is an hereditary trait settled upon the race by the selective action of forces that look to no end. The foundations of pragmatic intelligence are not pragmatic, nor even personal or sensible.

This impersonal character of intelligence is, of course, most evident on the lower levels of life. If we follow Mr. Loeb, e.g., in his inquiries into the psychology of that life that lies below the threshold of intelligence, what we meet with is an aimless but unwavering motor response to stimulus. The response is of the nature of motor impulse, and in so far it is "pragmatic," if that term may fairly be applied to so rudimentary a phase of sensibility. The responding organism may be called an "agent" in so far. It is only by a figure of speech that these terms are made to apply to tropismatic reactions. Higher in the scale of sensibility and nervous complication instincts work to a somewhat similar outcome. On the human plane, intelligence (the selective effect of inhibitive complication) may throw the response into the form of a reasoned line of conduct looking to an outcome that shall be expedient for the agent. This is naïve pragmatism of the developed kind. There is no longer a question but that the responding organism is an "agent" and that his intelligent response to stimulus is of a teleological character. But that is not all. The inhibitive nervous complication may also detach another chain of response to the given stimulus, which does not spend itself in a line of motor conduct and does not fall into a system of uses. Pragmatically speaking, this outlying chain of response is unintended and irrelevant. Except in urgent cases, such an idle response seems commonly to be present as a subsidiary phenomenon. If credence is given to the view that intelligence is, in its elements, of the nature of an inhibitive selection, it seems necessary to assume some such chain of idle and irrelevant response to account for the further course of the elements eliminated in giving the motor response the character of a reasoned line of conduct. So that associated with the pragmatic attention there is found more or less of an irrelevant attention, or idle curiosity. This is more particularly the case where a higher range of intelligence is present. This idle curiosity is, perhaps, closely related to the aptitude for play observed both in man and in the lower animals. The aptitude for play, as well as the functioning of idle curiosity, seems peculiarly lively in the young, whose aptitude for sustained pragmatism is at the same time relatively vague and unreliable.

This idle curiosity formulates its response to stimulus, not in terms of an expedient line of conduct, nor even necessarily in a chain of motor activity, but in terms of the sequence of activities going on in the observed phenomena. The "interpretation" of the facts under the guidance of this idle curiosity may take the form of anthropomorphic or animistic explanations of the "conduct" of the objects observed. The interpretation of the facts takes a dramatic form. The facts are conceived in an animistic way, and a pragmatic animus is imputed to them. Their behaviour is construed as a reasoned procedure on their part looking to the advantage of these animistically conceived objects, or looking to the achievement of some end which these objects are conceived to have at heart for reasons of their own.

Among the savage and lower barbarian peoples there is commonly current a large body of knowledge organized in this way into myths and legends, which need have no pragmatic value for the learner of them and no intended bearing on his conduct of practical affairs. They may come to have a practical value imputed to them as a ground of superstitious observances, but they may also not. All students of the lower cultures are aware of the dramatic character of the myths current among these peoples, and they are also aware that, particularly among the peaceable communities, the great body of mythical lore is of an idle kind, as having very little intended bearing on the practical conduct of those who believe in these myth-dramas. The myths on the one hand, and the workday knowledge of uses, materials, appliances, and expedients on the other hand, may be nearly independent of one another. Such is the case in a special degree among those peoples who are prevailingly of a peaceable habit of life, among whom the myths have not in any great measure been canonized into precedents of divine malevolence.

The lower barbarian's knowledge of the phenomena of nature, in so far as they are made the subject of deliberate speculation and are organized into a consistent body, is of the nature of life-histories. This body of knowledge is in the main organized under the guidance of an idle curiosity. In so far as it is systematized under the canons of curiosity rather than of expediency, the test of truth applied throughout this body of barbarian knowledge is the test of dramatic consistency. In addition to their dramatic cosmology and folk legends, it is needless to say, these peoples have also a considerable body of worldly wisdom in a more or less systematic form. In this the test of validity is usefulness.[1]

The pragmatic knowledge of the early days differs scarcely at all in character from that of the maturest phases of culture. Its highest achievements in the direction of systematic formulation consist of didactic exhortations to thrift, prudence, equanimity, and shrewd management—a body of maxims of expedient conduct. In this field there is scarcely a degree of advance from Confucius to Samuel Smiles. Under the guidance of the idle curiosity, on the other hand, there has been a continued advance toward a more and more comprehensive system of knowledge. With the advance in intelligence and experience there come closer observation and more detailed analysis of facts. The dramatization of the sequence of phenomena may then fall into somewhat less personal, less anthropomorphic formulations of the processes observed; but at no stage of its growth —at least at no stage hitherto reached—does the output of this work of the idle curiosity lose its dramatic character. Comprehensive generalizations are made and cosmologies are built up, but always in dramatic form. General principles of explanation are settled on, which in the earlier days of theoretical speculation seem invariably to run back to the broad vital principle of generation. Procreation, birth, growth, and decay constitute the cycle of postulates within which the dramatized processes of natural phenomena run their course. Creation is procreation in these archaic theoretical systems, and causation is gestation and birth. The archaic cosmological schemes of Greece, India, Japan, China, Polynesia, and America all

---

[1] "Pragmatic" is here used in a more restricted sense than the distinctively pragmatic school of modern psychologists would commonly assign the term. "Pragmatic," "teleological," and the like terms have been extended to cover imputation of purpose as well as conversion to use. It is not intended to criticize this ambiguous use of terms, nor to correct it; but the terms are here used only in the latter sense, which alone belongs to them by force of early usage and etymology. "Pragmatic" knowledge, therefore, is such as is designed to serve an expedient end for the knower, and is here contrasted with the imputation of expedient conduct to the facts observed. The reason for preserving this distinction is simply the present need of a simple term by which to mark the distinction between worldly wisdom and idle learning.

run to the same general effect on this head. The like seems true for the Elohistic elements in the Hebrew scriptures.

Throughout this biological speculation there is present, obscurely in the background, the tacit recognition of a material causation, such as conditions the vulgar operations of workday life from hour to hour. But this causal relation between vulgar work and product is vaguely taken for granted and not made a principle for comprehensive generalizations. It is overlooked as a trivial matter of course. The higher generalizations take their colour from the broader features of the current scheme of life. The habits of thought that rule in the working-out of a system of knowledge are such as are fostered by the more impressive affairs of life, by the institutional structure under which the community lives. So long as the ruling institutions are those of blood-relationship, descent, and clannish discrimination, so long the canons of knowledge are of the same complexion.

When presently a transformation is made in the scheme of culture from peaceable life which sporadic predation to a settled scheme of predaceous life, involving mastery and servitude, gradations of privilege and honour, coercion and personal dependence, then the scheme of knowledge undergoes an analogous change. The predaceous, or higher barbarian, culture is, for the present purpose, peculiar in that it is ruled by an accentuated pragmatism. The institutions of this cultural phase are conventionalized relations of force and fraud. The questions of life are questions of expedient conduct as carried on under the current relations of mastery and subservience. The habitual distinctions are distinctions of personal force, advantage, precedence, and authority. A shrewd adaptation to this system of graded dignity and servitude becomes a matter of life and death, and men learn to think in these terms as ultimate and definitive. The system of knowledge, even in so far as its motives are of a dispassionate or idle kind, falls into the like terms, because such are the habits of thought and the standards of discrimination enforced by daily life.[2]

The theoretical work of such a cultural era as, for instance, the Middle Ages still takes the general shape of dramatization, but the

---

[2] Cf. James, *Psychology,* chap. 9, esp. sec. 5.

postulates of the dramaturgic theories and the tests of theoretic validity are no longer the same as before the scheme of graded servitude came to occupy the field. The canons which guide the work of the idle curiosity are no longer those of generation, blood-relationship, and homely life, but rather those of graded dignity, authenticity, and dependence. The higher generalizations take on a new complexion, it may be without formally discarding the older articles of belief. The cosmologies of these higher barbarians are cast in terms of a feudalistic hierarchy of agents and elements, and the causal nexus between phenomena is conceived animistically after the manner of sympathetic magic. The laws that are sought to be discovered in the natural universe are sought in terms of authoritative enactment. The relation in which the deity, or deities, are conceived to stand to facts is no longer the relation of progenitor, so much as that of suzerainty. Natural laws are corollaries under the arbitrary rules of status imposed on the natural universe by an all-powerful Providence with a view to the maintenance of his own prestige. The science that grows in such a spiritual environment is of the class represented by alchemy and astrology, in which the imputed degree of nobility and prepotency of the objects and the symbolic force of their names are looked to for an explanation of what takes place.

The theoretical output of the Schoolmen has necessarily an accentuated pragmatic complexion, since the whole cultural scheme under which they lived and worked was of a strenuously pragmatic character. The current concepts of things were then drawn in terms of expediency, personal force, exploit, prescriptive authority, and the like, and this range of concepts was by force of habit employed in the correlation of facts for purposes of knowledge even where no immediate practical use of the knowledge so gained was had in view. At the same time a very large proportion of the scholastic researches and speculations aimed directly at rules of expedient conduct, whether it took the form of a philosophy of life under temporal law and custom, or of a scheme of salvation under the decrees of an autocratic Providence. A naïve apprehension of the dictum that all knowledge is pragmatic would find more satisfactory corroboration in the intellectual output of scholasticism than in any system of knowledge of an older or a later date.

With the advent of modern times a change comes over the nature of the inquiries and formulations worked out under the guidance of the idle curiosity—which from this epoch is often spoken of as the scientific spirit. The change in question is closely correlated with an analogous change in institutions and habits of life, particularly with the changes which the modern era brings in industry and in the economic organization of society. It is doubtful whether the characteristic intellectual interests and teachings of the new era can properly be spoken of as less "pragmatic," as that term is sometimes understood, than those of the scholastic times; but they are of another kind, being conditioned by a different cultural and industrial situation.[3] In the life of the new era conceptions of authentic rank and differential dignity have grown weaker in practical affairs, and notions of preferential reality and authentic tradition similarly count for less in the new science. The forces at work in the external world are conceived in a less animistic manner, although anthropomorphism still prevails, at least to the degree required in order to give a dramatic interpretation of the sequence of phenomena.

The changes in the cultural situation which seem to have had the most serious consequences for the methods and animus of scientific inquiry are those changes that took place in the field of industry. Industry in early modern times is a fact of relatively greater preponderance, more of a tone-giving factor, than it was under the regime of feudal status. It is the characteristic trait of the modern culture, very much as exploit and fealty were the characteristic cultural traits of the earlier time. This early-modern industry is, in an obvious and convincing degree, a matter of workmanship. The same has not been true in the same degree either before or since.

---

[3] As currently employed, the term "pragmatic" is made to cover both conduct looking to the agent's preferential advantage, expedient conduct, and workmanship directed to the production of things that may or may not be of advantage to the agent. If the term be taken in the latter meaning, the culture of modern times is no less "pragmatic" than that of the Middle Ages. It is here intended to be used in the former sense.

The workman, more or less skilled and with more or less specialized efficiency, was the central figure in the cultural situation of the time; and so the concepts of the scientists came to be drawn in the image of the workman. The dramatizations of the sequence of external phenomena worked out under the impulse of the idle curiosity were then conceived in terms of workmanship. Workmanship gradually supplanted differential dignity as the authoritative canon of scientific truth, even on the higher levels of speculation and research. This, of course, amounts to saying in other words that the law of cause and effect was given the first place, as contrasted with dialectical consistency and authentic tradition. But this early-modern law of cause and effect—the law of efficient causes—is of an anthropomorphic kind. "Like causes produce like effects," in much the same sense as the skilled workman's product is like the workman; "nothing is found in the effect that was not contained in the cause," in much the same manner.

These dicta are, of course, older than modern science, but it is only in the early days of modern science that they come to rule the field with an unquestioned sway and to push the higher grounds of dialectical validity to one side. They invade even the highest and most recondite fields of speculation, so that at the approach to the transition from the early-modern to the late-modern period, in the eighteenth century, they determine the outcome even in the counsels of the theologians. The deity, from having been in medieval times primarily a suzerain concerned with the maintenance of his own prestige, becomes primarily a creator engaged in the workmanlike occupation of making things useful for man. His relation to man and the natural universe is no longer primarily that of a progenitor, as it is in the lower barbarian culture, but rather that of a talented mechanic. The "natural laws" which the scientists of that era make so much of are no longer decrees of a preternatural legislative authority, but rather details of the workshop specifications handed down by the master-craftsman for the guidance of handicraftsmen working out his designs. In the eighteenth-century science these natural laws are laws specifying the sequence of cause and effect, and will bear characterization as a dramatic interpretation of the activity of the causes at work, and these causes are conceived in a quasi-personal manner. In later modern times the formulations of causal sequence grow more impersonal and more objective, more matter-of-fact; but the imputation of activity to the observed objects never ceases, and even in the latest and maturest formulations of scientific research the dramatic tone is not wholly lost. The causes at work are conceived in a highly impersonal way, but hitherto no science (except ostensibly mathematics) has been content to do its theoretical work in terms of inert magnitude alone. Activity continues to be imputed to the phenomena with which science deals; and activity is, of course, not a fact of observation, but is imputed to the phenomena by the observer.[4] This is, also of course, denied by those who insist on a purely mathematical formulation of scientific theories, but the denial is maintained only at the cost of consistency. Those eminent authorities who speak for a colourless mathematical formulation invariably and necessarily fall back on the (essentially metaphysical) preconception of causation as soon as they go into the actual work of scientific inquiry.[5]

Since the machine technology has made great advances, during the nineteenth century, and has become a cultural force of wide-reaching consequence, the formulations of science have made another move in the direction of impersonal matter-of-fact. The machine process has displaced the workman as the archetype in whose image causation is conceived by the scientific investigators. The dramatic interpretation of natural phenomena has thereby become less anthropomorphic; it no longer constructs the life-history of a cause working to produce a given effect—after the manner of a skilled workman producing a piece of wrought goods—but it constructs the life-history of a process in which the distinction between cause and effect need scarcely be observed in an itemized and specific way, but in which the run of causation unfolds itself in an unbroken sequence of cumulative change. By contrast with the

---

[4] Epistemologically speaking, activity is imputed to phenomena for the purpose of organizing them into a dramatically consistent system.

[5] Cf., e.g., Karl Pearson, *Grammar of Science,* and compare his ideal of inert magnitudes as set forth in his exposition with his actual work as shown in chaps. 9, 10, and 12, and more particularly in his discussions of "Mother Right" and related topics in *The Chances of Death.*

pragmatic formulations of worldly wisdom these latter-day theories of the scientists appear highly opaque, impersonal, and matter-of-fact; but taken by themselves they must be admitted still to show the constraint of the dramatic prepossessions that once guided the savage myth-makers.

In so far as touches the aims and the animus of scientific inquiry, as seen from the point of view of the scientist, it is a wholly fortuitous and insubstantial coincidence that much of the knowledge gained under machine-made canons of research can be turned to practical account. Much of this knowledge is useful, or may be made so, by applying it to the control of the processes in which natural forces are engaged. This employment of scientific knowledge for useful ends is technology, in the broad sense in which the term includes, besides the machine industry proper, such branches of practice as engineering, agriculture, medicine, sanitation, and economic reforms. The reason why scientific theories can be turned to account for these practical ends is not that these ends are included in the scope of scientific inquiry. These useful purposes lie outside the scientist's interest. It is not that he aims, or can aim, at technological improvements. His inquiry is as "idle" as that of the Pueblo myth-maker. But the canons of validity under whose guidance he works are those imposed by the modern technology, through habituation to its requirements; and therefore his results are available for the technological purpose. His canons of validity are made for him by the cultural situation; they are habits of thought imposed on him by the scheme of life current in the community in which he lives; and under modern conditions this scheme of life is largely machine-made. In the modern culture, industry, industrial processes, and industrial products have progressively gained upon humanity, until these creations of man's ingenuity have latterly come to take the dominant place in the cultural scheme; and it is not too much to say that they have become the chief force in shaping men's daily life, and therefore the chief factor in shaping men's habits of thought. Hence men have learned to think in the terms in which the technological processes act. This is particularly true of those men who by virtue of a peculiarly strong susceptibility in this direction become addicted to that habit of matter-of-fact inquiry that constitutes scientific research.

Modern technology makes use of the same range of concepts, thinks in the same terms, and applies the same tests of validity as modern science. In both, the terms of standardization, validity, and finality are always terms of impersonal sequence, not terms of human nature or of preternatural agencies. Hence the easy copartnership between the two. Science and technology play into one another's hands. The processes of nature with which science deals and which technology turns to account, the sequence of changes in the external world, animate and inanimate, run in terms of brute causation, as do the theories of science. These processes take no thought of human expediency or inexpediency. To make use of them they must be taken as they are, opaque and unsympathetic. Technology, therefore, has come to proceed on an interpretation of these phenomena in mechanical terms, not in terms of imputed personality nor even of workmanship. Modern science, deriving its concepts from the same source, carries on its inquiries and states its conclusions in terms of the same objective character as those employed by the mechanical engineer.

So it has come about, through the progressive change of the ruling habits of thought in the community, that the theories of science have progressively diverged from the formulations of pragmatism, ever since the modern era set in. From an organization of knowledge on the basis of imputed personal or animistic propensity the theory has changed its base to an imputation of brute activity only, and this latter is conceived in an increasingly matter-of-fact manner; until, latterly, the pragmatic range of knowledge and the scientific are more widely out of touch than ever, differing not only in aim, but in matter as well. In both domains knowledge runs in terms of activity, but it is on the one hand knowledge of what had best be done, and on the other hand knowledge of what takes place; on the one hand knowledge of ways and means, on the other hand knowledge without any ulterior purpose. The latter range of knowledge may serve the ends of the former, but the converse does not hold true.

These two divergent ranges of inquiry are to be found together in all phases of human culture. What distinguishes the present phase is that the discrepancy between the two is now wider than ever before. The present is nowise distinguished above other cultural eras by any exceptional urgency or acumen in the search for pragmatic expedients. Neither is it safe to assert that the present excels all other civilizations in the volume or the workmanship of that body of knowledge that is to be credited to the idle curiosity. What distinguishes the present in these premises is (1) that the primacy in the cultural scheme has passed from pragmatism to a disinterested inquiry whose motive is idle curiosity, and (2) that in the domain of the latter the making of myths and legends in terms of imputed personality, as well as the construction of dialectical systems in terms of differential reality, has yielded the first place to the making of theories in terms of matter-of-fact sequence.[6]

Pragmatism creates nothing but maxims of expedient conduct. Science creates nothing but theories. It knows nothing of policy or utility, of better or worse. None of all that is comprised in what is today accounted scientific knowledge. Wisdom and proficiency of the pragmatic sort does not contribute to the advance of a knowledge of fact. It has only an incidental bearing on scientific research, and its bearing is chiefly that of inhibition and misdirection. Wherever canons of expediency are intruded into or are attempted to be incorporated in the inquiry, the consequence is an unhappy one for science, however happy it may be for some other purpose extraneous to science. The mental attitude of worldly wisdom is at cross-purposes with the disinterested scientific spirit, and the pursuit of it induces an intellectual bias that is incompatible with scientific insight. Its intellectual output is a body of shrewd rules of conduct, in great part designed to take advantage of human infirmity. Its habitual terms of standardization and validity are terms of human nature, of human preference, prejudice, aspiration, endeavour, and disability, and the habit of mind that goes with it is such as is consonant with these terms. No doubt, the all-pervading pragmatic animus of the older and non-European civilizations has had more

---

[6] Cf. James, *Psychology,* vol. II, chap. 28, pp. 633-71, esp. p. 640 note.

than anything else to do with their relatively slight and slow advance in scientific knowledge. In the modern scheme of knowledge it holds true, in a similar manner and with analogous effect, that training in divinity, in law, and in the related branches of diplomacy, business tactics, military affairs, and political theory is alien to the sceptical scientific spirit and subversive of it.

The modern scheme of culture comprises a large body of worldly wisdom, as well as of science. This pragmatic lore stands over against science with something of a jealous reserve. The pragmatists value themselves somewhat on being useful as well as being efficient for good and evil. They feel the inherent antagonism between themselves and the scientists, and look with some doubt on the latter as being merely decorative triflers, although they sometimes borrow the prestige of the name of science—as is only good and well, since it is of the essence of worldly wisdom to borrow anything that can be turned to account. The reasoning in these fields turns about questions of personal advantage of one kind or another, and the merits of the claims canvassed in these discussions are decided on grounds of authenticity. Personal claims make up the subject of the inquiry, and these claims are construed and decided in terms of precedent and choice, use and wont, prescriptive authority, and the like. The higher reaches of generalization in these pragmatic inquiries are of the nature of deductions from authentic tradition, and the training in this class of reasoning gives discrimination in respect of authenticity and expediency. The resulting habit of mind is a bias for substituting dialectical distinctions and decisions *de jure* in the place of explanations *de facto*. The so-called "sciences" associated with these pragmatic disciplines, such as jurisprudence, political science, and the like, are a taxonomy of credenda. Of this character was the greater part of the "science" cultivated by the Schoolmen, and large remnants of the same kind of authentic convictions are, of course, still found among the tenets of the scientists, particularly in the social sciences, and no small solicitude is still given to their cultivation. Substantially the same value as that of the temporal pragmatic inquiries belongs also, of course, to the "science" of divinity. Here the questions to which an answer is sought, as well as the aim and method of inquiry, are of the same pragmatic character, although the argument runs on a higher plane of personality, and seeks a solution in terms of a remoter and more metaphysical expediency.

In the light of what has been said above, the questions recur: How far is the scientific quest of matter-of-fact knowledge consonant with the inherited intellectual aptitudes and propensities of the normal man? and, What foothold has science in the modern culture? The former is a question of the temperamental heritage of civilized mankind, and therefore it is in large part a question of the circumstances which have in the past selectively shaped the human nature of civilized mankind. Under the barbarian culture, as well as on the lower levels of what is currently called civilized life, the dominant note has been that of competitive expediency for the individual or the group, great or small, in an avowed struggle for the means of life. Such is still the ideal of the politician and business man, as well as of other classes whose habits of life lead them to cling to the inherited barbarian traditions. The upper-barbarian and lower-civilized culture, as has already been indicated, is pragmatic, with a thoroughness that nearly bars out any non-pragmatic ideal of life or of knowledge. Where this tradition is strong, there is but a precarious chance for any consistent effort to formulate knowledge in other terms than those drawn from the prevalent relations of personal mastery and subservience and the ideals of personal gain.

During the Dark and Middle Ages, for instance, it is true in the main that any movement of thought not controlled by considerations of expediency and conventions of status is to be found only in the obscure depths of vulgar life, among those neglected elements of the population that lived below the reach of the active class struggle. What there is surviving of this vulgar, non-pragmatic intellectual output takes the form of legends and folk-tales, often embroidered on the authentic documents of the Faith. These are less alien to the latest and highest culture of Christendom than are the dogmatic, dilectical, and chivalric productions that occupied the attention of the upper classes in medieval times. It may seem a curious paradox that the latest and most perfect flower of the western civilization is more nearly akin to the spiritual life of the serfs and villeins than it is to that of the grange or the abbey. The courtly life and the chivalric habits of thought of that past phase of culture have left as nearly no trace in the cultural scheme of later modern times as could well be. Even the romancers who ostensibly rehearse the phenomena of chivalry unavoidably make their knights and ladies speak the language and the sentiments of the slums of that time, tempered with certain schematized modern reflections and speculations. The gallantries, the genteel inanities and devout imbecilities, of medieval high-life would be insufferable even to the meanest and most romantic modern intelligence. So that in a later, less barbarian age the precarious remnants of folklore that have come down through that vulgar channel—half savage and more than half pagan—are treasured as containing the largest spiritual gains which the barbarian ages of Europe have to offer.

The sway of barbarian pragmatism has, everywhere in the western world, been relatively brief and relatively light; the only exceptions would be found in certain parts of the Mediterranean seaboard. But wherever the barbarian culture has been sufficiently long-lived and unmitigated to work out a thoroughly selective effect in the human material subjected to it, there the pragmatic animus may be expected to have become supreme and to inhibit all movement in the direction of scientific inquiry and eliminate all effective aptitude for other than worldly wisdom. What the selective consequences of such a protracted regime of pragmatism would be for the temper of the race may be seen in the human flotsam left by the great civilizations of antiquity, such as Egypt, India, and Persia. Science is not at home among these leavings of barbarism. In these instances of its long and unmitigated dominion the barbarian culture has selectively worked out a temperamental bias and a scheme of life from which objective, matter-of-fact knowledge is virtually excluded in favour of pragmatism, secular and religious. But for the greater part of the race, at least for the greater part of civilized mankind, the regime of the mature barbarian culture has been of relatively short duration, and has had a correspondingly superficial and transient selective effect. It has not had force and time to eliminate certain elements of human nature handed down from an earlier phase of life, which are not in full consonance with the barbarian animus or with the demands of the pragmatic scheme of thought. The barbarian-pragmatic habit of mind, therefore, is not properly speaking a temperamental trait of the civilized peoples, except possibly within certain class limits (as, e.g., the German nobility). It is rather a tradition, and it does not constitute so tenacious a bias as to make head against the strongly materialistic drift of modern conditions and set aside that increasingly urgent resort to matter-of-fact conceptions that makes for the primacy of science. Civilized mankind does not in any great measure take back atavistically to the upper-barbarian habit of mind. Barbarism covers too small a segment of the life-history of the race to have given an enduring temperamental result. The unmitigated discipline of the higher barbarism in Europe fell on a relatively small proportion of the population, and in the course of time this select element of the population was crossed and blended with the blood of the lower elements whose life always continued to run in the ruts of savagery rather than in those of the high-strung, finished barbarian culture that gave rise to the chivalric scheme of life.

Of the several phases of human culture the most protracted, and the one which has counted for most in shaping the abiding traits of the race, is unquestionably that of savagery. With savagery, for the purpose in hand, is to be classed that lower, relatively peaceable barbarism that is not characterized by wide and sharp class discrepancies or by an unremitting endeavour of one individual or group to get the better of another. Even under the full-grown barbarian culture—as, for instance, during the Middle Ages—the habits of life and the spiritual interests of the great body of the population continue in large measure to bear the character of savagery. The savage phase of culture accounts for by far the greater portion of the life-history of mankind, particularly if the lower barbarism and the vulgar life of later barbarism be counted in with savagery, as in a measure they properly should. This is particularly true of those racial elements that have entered into the composition of the leading peoples of Christendom.

The savage culture is characterized by the relative absence of pragmatism from the higher generalizations of its knowledge and beliefs. As has been noted above, its theoretical creations are chiefly of the nature of mythology shading off into folklore. This genial spinning of apocryphal yarns is, at its best, an amiably inefficient formulation of experiences and observations in terms of something like a life-history of the phenomena observed. It has, on the one hand, little value, and little purpose, in the way of pragmatic expediency, and so it is not closely akin to the pragmatic-barbarian scheme of life; while, on the other hand, it is also ineffectual as a systematic knowledge of matter-of-fact. It is a quest of knowledge, perhaps of systematic knowledge, and it is carried on under the incentive of the idle curiosity. In this respect it falls in the same class with the civilized man's science; but it seeks knowledge not in terms of opaque matter-of-fact, but in terms of some sort of spiritual life imputed to the facts. It is romantic and Hegelian rather than realistic and Darwinian. The logical necessities of its scheme of thought are necessities of spiritual consistency rather than of quantitative equivalence. It is like science in that it has no ulterior motive beyond the idle craving for a systematic correlation of data; but it is unlike science in that its standardization and correlation of data run in terms of the free play of imputed personal initiative rather than in terms of the constraint of objective cause and effect.

By force of the protracted selective discipline of this past phase of culture, the human nature of civilized mankind is still substantially the human nature of savage man. The ancient equipment of congenital aptitudes and propensities stands over substantially unchanged, though overlaid with barbarian traditions and conventionalities and readjusted by habituation to the exigencies of civilized life. In a measure, therefore, but by no means altogether, scientific inquiry is native to civilized man with his savage heritage, since scientific inquiry proceeds on the same general motive of idle curiosity as guided the savage myth-makers, though it makes use of concepts and standards in great measure alien to the myth-makers' habit of mind. The ancient human predilection for discovering a dramatic play of passion and intrigue in the phenomena of nature still asserts itself. In the most advanced communities, and even among the adepts of modern science, there comes up persistently the revulsion of the native savage against the inhumanly dispassionate sweep of the scientific quest, as well as against the inhumanly ruthless fabric of technological processes that have come out of this search for matter-of-fact knowledge. Very often the savage need of a spiritual interpretation (dramatization) of phenomena breaks through the crust of acquired materialistic habits of thought, to find such refuge as may be had in articles of faith seized on and held by sheer force of instinctive conviction. Science and its creations are more or less uncanny, more or less alien, to that fashion of craving for knowledge that by ancient inheritance animates mankind. Furtively or by an overt breach of consistency, men still seek comfort in marvellous articles of savage-born lore, which contradict the truths of that modern science whose dominion they dare not question, but whose findings at the same time go beyond the breaking-point of their jungle-fed spiritual sensibilities.

The ancient ruts of savage thought and conviction are smooth and easy; but however sweet and indispensable the archaic ways of thinking may be to the civilized man's peace of mind, yet such is the binding force of matter-of-fact analysis and inference under modern conditions that the findings of science are not questioned on the whole. The name of science is after all a word to conjure with. So much so that the name and the mannerisms, at least, if nothing more of science, have invaded all fields of learning and have even overrun territory that belongs to the enemy. So there are "sciences" of theology, law, and medicine, as has already been noted above. And there are such things as Christian Science, and "scientific" astrology, palmistry, and the like. But within the field of learning proper there is a similar predilection for an air of scientific acumen and precision where science does not belong. So that even that large range of knowledge that has to do with general information rather than with theory—what is loosely termed scholarship—tends strongly to take on the name and forms of theoretical statement. However decided the contrast between these branches of knowledge on the one hand, and science properly so called on the other hand, yet even the classical learning, and the humanities generally, fall in with this predilection more and more with each succeeding generation of students. The students of literature, for instance, are more and more prone to substitute critical analysis and linguistic speculation, as the end of their endeavours, in the place of that discipline of taste and that cultivated sense of literary form and literary feeling that must always remain the chief end of literary training, as distinct from philology and the social sciences. There is, of course, no intention to question the legitimacy of a science of philology or of the analytical study of literature as a fact in cultural history, but these things do not constitute training in literary taste, nor can they take the place of it. The effect of this straining after scientific formulations in a field alien to the scientific spirit is as curious as it is wasteful. Scientifically speaking, these quasi-scientific inquiries necessarily begin nowhere and end in the same place; while in point of cultural gain they commonly come to nothing better than spiritual abnegation. But these blindfold endeavours to conform to the canons of science serve to show how wide and unmitigated the sway of science is in the modern community.

Scholarship—that is to say, an intimate and systematic familiarity with past cultural achievements—still holds its place in the scheme of learning, in spite of the unadvised efforts of the short-sighted to blend it with the work of science, for it affords play for the ancient genial propensities that ruled men's quest of knowledge before the coming of science or of the outspoken pragmatic barbarism. Its place may not be so large in proportion to the entire field of learning as it was before the scientific era got fully under way. But there is no intrinsic antagonism between science and scholarship, as there is between pragmatic training and scientific inquiry. Modern scholarship shares with modern science the quality of not being pragmatic in its aim. Like science it has no ulterior end. It may be difficult here and there to draw the line between science and scholarship, and it may even more be unnecessary to draw such a line; yet while the two ranges of discipline belong together in many ways, and while there are many points of contact and sympathy between the two; while the two together make up the modern scheme of learning; yet there is no need of confounding the one with the other, nor can the one do the work of the other. The scheme of learning has changed in such manner as to give science the more commanding place, but the scholar's domain has not thereby been invaded, nor has it suffered contraction at the hands of science, whatever may be said of the weak-kneed abnegation of some whose place, if they have one, is in the field of scholarship rather than of science.

All that has been said above has of course nothing to say as to the intrinsic merits of this quest of matter-of-fact knowledge. In point of fact, science gives its tone to modern culture. One may approve or one may deprecate the fact that this opaque, materialistic interpretation of things pervades modern thinking. That is a question of taste, about which there is no disputing. The prevalence of this matter-of-fact inquiry is a feature of modern culture, and the attitude which critics take toward this phenomenon is chiefly significant as indicating how far their own habit of mind coincides with the enlightened common-sense of civilized mankind. It shows in what degree they are abreast of the advance of culture. Those in whom the savage predilection of the barbarian tradition is stronger than their habituation to civilized life will find that this dominant factor of modern life is perverse, if not calamitous; those whose habits of thought have been fully shaped by the machine process and scientific inquiry are likely to find it good. The modern western culture, with its core of matter-of-fact knowledge, may be better or worse than some other cultural scheme, such as the classic Greek, the medieval Christian, the Hindu, or the Pueblo Indian. Seen in certain lights, tested by certain standards, it is doubtless better; by other standards, worse. But the fact remains that the current cultural scheme, in its maturest growth, is of that complexion; its characteristic force lies in this matter-of-fact insight; its highest discipline and its maturest aspirations are these.

In point of fact, the sober common-sense of civilized mankind accepts no other end of endeavour as self-sufficient and ultimate. That such is the case seems to be due chiefly to the ubiquitous presence of the machine technology and its creations in the life of modern communities. And so long as the machine process continues to hold its domiant place as a disciplinary factor in modern culture, so long must the spiritual and intellectual life of this cultural era maintain the character which the machine process gives it.

But while the scientist's spirit and his achievements stir an unqualified admiration in modern men, and while his discoveries carry conviction as nothing else does, it does not follow that the manner of man which this quest of knowledge produces or requires comes near answering to the current ideal of manhood, or that his conclusions are felt to be as good and beautiful as they are true. The ideal man, and the ideal of human life, even in the apprehension of those who most rejoice in the advances of science, is neither the finikin sceptic in the laboratory nor the animated slide-rule. The quest of science is relatively new. It is a cultural factor not comprised, in anything like its modern force, among those circumstances whose selective action in the far past has given to the race the human nature which it now has. The race reached the human plane with little of this searching knowledge of facts; and throughout the greater part of its life-history on the human plane it has been accustomed to make its higher generalizations and to formulate its larger principles of life in other terms than those of passionless matter-of-fact. This manner of knowledge has occupied an increasing share of men's attention in the past, since it bears in a decisive way upon the minor affairs of workday life; but it has never until now been put in the first place, as the dominant note of human culture. The normal man, such as his inheritance has made him, has therefore good cause to be restive under its dominion.

·XIII·

LOUIS DEMBITZ BRANDEIS

[1 8 5 6 - 1 9 4 1]

THE OPPORTUNITY IN THE LAW

TRUE AMERICANISM

THE OPPORTUNITY IN THE LAW

I assume that in asking me to talk to you on the Ethics of the Legal Profession, you do not wish me to enter upon a discussion of the relation of law to morals, or to attempt to acquaint you with those detailed rules of ethics which lawyers have occasion to apply from day to day in their practice. What you want is this: Standing not far from the threshold of active life, feeling the generous impulse for service which the University fosters, you wish to know whether the legal profession would afford you special opportunities for usefulness to your fellow-men, and, if so, what the obligations and limitations are which it imposes. I say special opportunities, because every legitimate occupation, be it profession or business or trade, furnishes abundant opportunities for usefulness, if pursued in what Matthew Arnold called "the grand manner." It is, as a rule, far more important *how* men pursue their occupation than *what* the occupation is which they select.

But the legal profession does afford in America unusual opportunities for usefulness. That this has been so in the past, no one acquainted with the history of our institutions can for a moment doubt. The great achievement of the English-speaking people is the attainment of liberty through law. It is natural, therefore, that those who have been trained in the law should have borne an important part in that struggle for liberty and in the government which resulted. Accordingly, we find that in America the lawyer was in the earlier period almost omnipresent in the State. Nearly every great lawyer was then a statesman; and nearly every statesman, great or small, was a lawyer. DeTocqueville, the first important foreign observer of American political institutions, said of the United States seventy-five years ago:

An address delivered at Phillips Brooks House, Harvard University, May 4, 1905; printed in *Business—A Profession,* by Louis D. Brandeis (Boston: Charles T. Branford Co., 1925). Reprinted by permission of the publishers.

In America there are no nobles or literary men, and the people are apt to mistrust the wealthy; lawyers, consequently, form the highest political class. . . . As the lawyers form the only enlightened class whom the people do not mistrust, they are naturally called upon to occupy most of the public stations. They fill the legislative assemblies and are at the head of the administration; they consequently exercise a powerful influence upon the formation of the law and upon its execution.

For centuries before the American Revolution the lawyer had played an important part in England. His importance in the State became much greater in America. One reason for this, as DeTocqueville indicated, was the fact that we possessed no class like the nobles, which took part in government through privilege. A more potent reason was that with the introduction of a written constitution the law became with us a far more important factor in the ordinary conduct of political life than it did in England. Legal questions were constantly arising and the lawyer was necessary to settle them. But I take it the paramount reason why the lawyer has played so large a part in our political life is that his training fits him especially to grapple with the questions which are presented in a democracy.

The whole training of the lawyer leads to the development of judgment. His early training—his work with books in the study of legal rules—teaches him patient research and develops both the memory and the reasoning faculties. He becomes practised in logic; and yet the use of the reasoning faculties in the study of law is very different from their use, say, in metaphysics. The lawyer's processes of reasoning, his logical conclusions, are being constantly tested by experience. He is running up against facts at every point. Indeed it is a maxim of the law: Out of the facts grows the law; that is, propositions are not considered abstractly, but always with reference to facts.

Furthermore, in the investigation of the facts the lawyer differs very materially from the scientist or the scholar. The lawyer's investigations into the facts are limited by time and space. His investigations have reference always to some practical end. Unlike the scientist, he ordinarily cannot refuse to reach a conclusion on the ground that he lacks the facts sufficient to enable one to form an opinion. He must form an opinion from those facts which he has gathered; he must reason from the facts within his grasp.

If the lawyer's practice is a general one, his field of observation extends, in course of time, into almost every sphere of business and of life. The facts so gathered ripen his judgment. His memory is trained to retentiveness. His mind becomes practised in discrimination as well as in generalization. He is an observer of men even more than of things. He not only sees men of all kinds, but knows their deepest secrets; sees them in situations which "try men's souls." He is apt to become a good judge of men.

Then, contrary to what might seem to be the habit of the lawyer's mind, the practice of law tends to make the lawyer judicial in attitude and extremely tolerant. His profession rests upon the postulate that no contested question can be properly decided until both sides are heard. His experience teaches him that nearly every question has two sides; and very often he finds—after decision of judge or jury—that both he and his opponent were in the wrong. The practice of law creates thus a habit of mind, and leads to attainments which are distinctly different from those developed in most professions or outside of the profession. These are the reasons why the lawyer has acquired a position materially different from that of other men. It is the position of the adviser of men.

Your chairman said: "People have the impression to-day that the lawyer has become mercenary." It is true that the lawyer has become largely a part of the business world. Mr. Bryce said twenty years ago when he compared the America of 1885 with the America of DeTocqueville:

Taking a general survey of the facts of to-day, as compared with the facts of sixty years ago, it is clear that the Bar counts for less as a guiding and restraining power, tempering the crudity or haste of democracy by its attachment to rule and precedent, than it did.

And in reviewing American conditions after his recent visit Mr. Bryce said:

Lawyers are now to a greater extent than formerly business men, a part of the great organized system of industrial and financial enterprise. They are less than formerly the students of a particular kind of learning, the practitioners of a particular art. And they do not seem to be so much of a distinct professional class.

That statement was made by a very sympathetic observer of American institutions; but it is clear that Mr. Bryce coincides in the view commonly expressed, that the Bar had become commercialized through its connection with business. I am inclined to think that this view is not altogether correct. Probably business has become professionalized as much as the Bar has become commercialized. Is it not this which has made the lawyer so important a part of the business world?

The ordinary man thinks of the Bar as a body of men who are trying cases, perhaps even trying criminal cases. Of course there is an immense amount of litigation going on; and a great deal of the time of many lawyers is devoted to litigation. But by far the greater part of the work done by lawyers is done not in court, but advising men on important matters, and mainly in business affairs. In guiding these affairs industrial and financial, lawyers are needed, not only because of the legal questions involved, but because the particular mental attributes and attainments which the legal profession develops are demanded in the proper handling of these large financial or industrial affairs. The magnitude and scope of these operations remove them almost wholly from the real of "petty trafficking" which people formerly used to associate with trade. The questions which arise are more nearly questions of statesmanship. The relations created call in many instances for the exercise of the highest diplomacy. The magnitude, difficulty and importance of the problems involved are often as great as in the matters of state with which lawyers were formerly frequently associated. The questions appear in different guise; but they are similar. The relations between rival railroad systems are like the relations between neighboring kingdoms. The relations of the great trusts to the consumers or to their employees is like that of feudal lords to commoners or dependents. The relations of public-service corporations to the people raise questions not unlike those presented by the monopolies of old.

So some of the ablest American lawyers of this generation, after acting as professional advisers of great corporations, have become finally their managers. . . . Their legal training was called for in the business world, because business has tended to become professionalized. And thus, although the lawyer is not playing in affairs of state the part he once did, his influence is, or at all events may be, quite as important as it ever was in the United States; and it is simply a question how that influence is to be exerted.

It is true that at the present time the lawyer does not hold as high a position with the people as he held seventy-five or indeed fifty years ago; but the reason is not lack of opportunity. It is this: Instead of holding a position of independence, between the wealthy and the people, prepared to curb the excesses of either, able lawyers have, to a large extent, allowed themselves to become adjuncts of great corporations and have neglected the obligation to use their powers for the protection of the people. We hear much of the "corporation lawyer," and far too little of the "people's lawyer." The great opportunity of the American Bar is and will be to stand again as it did in the past, ready to protect also the interests of the people.

Mr. Bryce, in discussing our Bar, said, in his *American Commonwealth:*

But I am bound to add that some judicious American observers hold that the last thirty years have witnessed a certain decadence in the Bar of the great cities. They say that the growth of the enormously rich and powerful corporations willing to pay vast sums for questionable services has seduced the virtue of some counsel whose eminence makes their example important.

The leading lawyers of the United States have been engaged mainly in supporting the claims of the corporations; often in endeavoring to evade or nullify the extremely crude laws by which legislators sought to regulate the power or curb the excesses of corporations.

Such questions as the regulation of trusts, the fixing of railway rates, the municipalization of public utilities, the relation between capital and labor, call for the exercise of legal ability of the highest order. Up to the present time the legal ability of a high order which has been expended on those questions has been almost wholly in opposition to the contentions of the people. The leaders of the Bar, without any preconceived intent on their part, and rather as an incident to their professional standing, have, with rare exceptions, been ranged on the side of the corporations, and the people have been represented, in the main, by men of very meagre legal ability.

If these problems are to be settled right, this condition cannot continue. Our country is, after all, not a country of dollars, but of ballots. The immense corporate wealth will necessarily develop a hostility from which much trouble will come to us unless the excesses of capital are curbed, through the respect for law, as the excesses of democracy were curbed seventy-five years ago. There will come a revolt of the people against the capitalists, unless the aspirations of the people are given some adequate legal expression; and to this end coöperation of abler lawyers is essential.

For nearly a generation the leaders of the Bar have, with few exceptions, not only failed to take part in constructive legislation designed to solve in the public interest our great social, economic and industrial problems; but they have failed likewise to oppose legislation prompted by selfish interests. They have often gone further in disregard of common weal. They have often advocated, as lawyers, legislative measures which as citizens they could not approve, and have endeavored to justify themselves by a false analogy. They have erroneously assumed that the rule of ethics to be applied to a lawyer's advocacy is the same where he acts for private interests against the public, as it is in litigation between private individuals.

The ethical question which laymen most frequently ask about the legal profession is this: How can a lawyer take a case which he does not believe in? The profession is regarded as necessarily somewhat immoral, because its members are supposed to be habitually taking cases of that character. As a practical matter, the lawyer is not often harassed by this problem; partly because he is apt to believe, at the time, in most of the cases that he actually tries; and partly because he either abandons or settles a large number of those he does not believe in. But the lawyer recognizes that in trying a case his prime duty is to present his side to the tribunal fairly and as well as he can, relying upon his adversary to present the other side fairly and as well as he can. Since the lawyers on the two sides are usually reasonably well matched the judge or jury may ordinarily be trusted to make such a decision as justice demands.

But when lawyers act upon the same principle in supporting the attempts of their private clients to secure or to oppose legislation, a very different condition is presented. In the first place, the counsel selected to represent important private interests possesses usually ability of a high order, while the public is often inadequately represented or wholly unrepresented. Great unfairness to the public is apt to result from this fact. Many bills pass in our legislatures which would not have become law, if the public interest had been fairly represented; and many good bills are defeated which if supported by able lawyers would have been enacted. Lawyers have, as a rule, failed to consider this distinction between practice in courts involving only private interests, and practice before the legislature or city council involving public interests. Some men of high professional standing have even endeavored to justify their course in advocating professionally legislation which in their character as citizens they would have voted against.

Furthermore, lawyers of high standing have often failed to apply in connection with professionl work before the legislature or city council a rule of ethics which they would deem imperative in practice before the court. Lawyers who would indignantly retire from a court case in the justice of which they believed, if they had reason to think that a juror had been bribed or a witness had been suborned by their client, are content to serve their client by honest arguments before a legislative committee, although they have as great reason to believe that their client has bribed members of the legislature or corrupted public opinion. This confusion of ethical ideas is an important reason why the Bar does not now hold the position which it formerly did as a brake upon democracy, and which I believe it must take again if the serious questions now before us are to be properly solved.

Here, consequently, is the great opportunity in the law. The next generation must witness a continuing and ever-increasing contest between those who have and those who have not. The industrial world is in a state of ferment. The ferment is in the main peaceful, and, to a considerable extent, silent; but there is felt to-day very widely the inconsistency in this condition of political democracy and industrial absolutism. The people are beginning to doubt whether in the long run democracy and absolutism can co-exist in the same community; beginning to doubt whether there is a justification for the wealth, for the rapid creation of fortunes, more mysterious than the deeds of Aladdin's lamp. The people have begun to think; and they show evidences on all sides of a tendency to act. Those of you who have not had an opportunity of talking much with laboring men can hardly form a conception of the amount of thinking that they are doing. With many these problems are all-absorbing. Many workingmen, otherwise uneducated, talk about the relation of employer and employee far more intelligently than most of the best educated men in the community. The labor question involves for them the whole of life, and they must in the course of a comparatively short time realize the power which lies in them. Often their leaders are men of signal ability, men who can hold their own in discussion or in action with the ablest and best-educated men in the community. The labor movement must necessarily progress. The people's thought will take shape in action; and it lies with us, with you to whom in part the future belongs, to say on what lines the action is to be expressed; whether it is to be expressed wisely and temperately, or wildly and intemperately; whether it is to be expressed on lines of evolution or on lines of revolution. Nothing can better fit you for taking part in the solution of these problems, than the study and preëminently the practice of law. Those of you who feel drawn to that profession may rest assured that you will find in it an opportunity for usefulness which is probably unequalled. There is a call upon the legal profession to do a great work for this country.

Louis Dembitz Brandeis

TRUE AMERICANISM

E pluribus unum—Out of many one—was the motto adopted by
the founders of the Republic when they formed a union of the
thirteen states. To these we have added, from time to time, thirty-
five more. The founders were convinced, as we are, that a strong
nation could be built through federation. They were also convinced,
as we are, that in America, under a free government, many peoples
would make one nation. Throughout all these years we have admitted to our country and to citizenship immigrants from the diverse
lands of Europe. We have had faith that thereby we would best
serve ourselves and mankind. This faith has been justified. The
United States has grown great. The immigrants and their immediate descendants have proved themselves as loyal as any citizens of
the country. Liberty has knit us closely together as Amercans.
Note the common devotion to our country's emblem expressed at the
recent Flag Day celebration in New York by boys and girls representing more than twenty different nationalities warring abroad.

On the nation's birthday it is customary for us to gather together
for the purpose of considering how we may better serve our country.
This year we are asked to address ourselves to the newcomers and
to make this Fourth of July what has been termed Americanization
Day.

What is Americanization? It manifests itself, in a superficial way,
when the immigrant adopts the clothes, the manners, and the customs generally prevailing here. Far more important is the manifestation presented when he substitutes for his mother tongue the
English language as the common medium of speech. But the adoption of our language, manners and customs is only a small part of
the process. To become Americanized the change wrought must be

An address delivered at Faneuil Hall, Boston, July 4, 1915; printed in
Business—A Profession, by Louis D. Brandeis (Boston: Charles T. Branford Co., 1925). Reprinted by permission of the publishers.

fundamental. However great his outward conformity, the immigrant is not Americanized unless his interests and affections have become deeply rooted here. And we properly demand of the immigrant even more than this,—he must be brought into complete harmony with our ideals and aspirations and coöperate with us for their attainment. Only when this has been done will he possess the national consciousness of an American.

I say "he must be brought into complete harmony." But let us not forget that many a poor immigrant comes to us from distant lands, ignorant of our language, strange in tattered clothes and with jarring manners, who is already truly American in this most important sense; who has long shared our ideals and who, oppressed and persecuted abroad, has yearned for our land of liberty and for the opportunity of aiding in the realization of its aims.

What are the American ideals? They are the development of the individual for his own and the common good; the development of the individual through liberty, and the attainment of the common good through democracy and social justice.

Our form of government, as well as humanity, compels us to strive for the development of the individual man. Under universal suffrage (soon to be extended to women) every voter is a part ruler of the state. Unless the rulers have, in the main, education and character, and are free men, our great experiment in democracy must fail. It devolves upon the state, therefore, to fit its rulers for their task. It must provide not only facilities for development but the opportunity of using them. It must not only provide opportunity, it must stimulate the desire to avail of it. Thus we are compelled to insist upon the observance of what we somewhat vaguely term the American standard of living; we become necessarily our brothers' keepers.

What does this standard imply? In substance, the exercise of those rights which our Constitution guarantees—the right to life, liberty and the pursuit of happiness. Life, in this connection, means living, not existing; liberty, freedom in things industrial as well as political; happiness includes, among other things, that satisfaction which can come only through the full development and utilization of one's faculties. In order that men may live and not merely exist, in order that men may develop their faculties, they must have a reasonable income; they must have health and leisure. High wages will not meet the worker's need unless employment be regular. The best of wages will not compensate for excessively long working hours which undermine health. And working conditions may be so bad as to nullify the good effects of high wages and short hours. The essentials of American citizenship are not satisfied by supplying merely the material needs or even the wants of the worker.

Every citizen must have education—broad and continuous. This essential of citizenship is not met by an education which ends at the age of fourteen, or even at eighteen or twenty-two. Education must continue throughout life. A country cannot be governed well by rulers whose education and mental development are gained only from their attendance at the common school. Whether the education of the citizen in later years is to be given in classes or from the public platform, or is to be supplied through discussion in the lodges and the trade unions, or is to be gained from the reading of papers, periodicals and books, in any case, freshness of mind is indispensable to its attainment. And to the preservation of freshness of mind a short workday is as essential as adequate food and proper conditions of working and of living. The worker must, in other words, have leisure. But leisure does not imply idleness. It means ability to work not less but more, ability to work harder while working at breadwinning, and ability to work more years at breadwinning. Leisure, so defined, is an essential of successful democracy.

Furthermore, the citizen in a successful democracy must not only have education, he must be free. Men are not free if dependent industrially upon the arbitrary will of another. Industrial liberty on the part of the worker cannot, therefore, exist if there be overweening industrial power. Some curb must be placed upon capitalistic combination. Nor will even this curb be effective unless the workers coöperate, as in trade unions. Control and coöperation are both essential to industrial liberty.

And if the American is to be fitted for his task as ruler, he must have besides education and industrial liberty also some degree of financial independence. Our existing industrial system is converting an ever increasing percentage of the population into wage-earners;

and experience teaches us that a large part of these become at some time financial dependents, by reason of sickness, accident, invalidity, super-annuation, unemployment or premature death of the bread-winner of the family. Contingencies like these, which are generally referred to in the individual case as misfortunes, are now recognized as ordinary incidents in the life of the wage-earner. The need of providing indemnity against financial losses from such ordinary contingencies in the workingman's life has become apparent and is already being supplied in other countries. The standard worthy to be called American implies some system of social insurance.

And since the child is father of the man, we may bear constantly in mind that the American standard of living cannot be attained or preserved unless the child is not only well fed but well born; unless he lives under conditions wholesome morally as well as physically; unless he is given education adequate both in quantity and in character to fit him for life's work.

Such are our ideals and the standard of living we have erected for ourselves. But what is there in these ideals which is peculiarly American? Many nations seek to develop the individual man for himself and the common good. Some are as liberty-loving as we. Some pride themselves upon institutions more democratic than our own. Still others, less conspicuous for liberty or democracy, claim to be more successful in attaining social justice. And we are not the only nation which combines love of liberty with the practice of democracy and a longing for social justice. But there is one feature in our ideals and practices which is peculiarly American,—it is inclusive brotherhood.

Other countries, while developing the individual man, have assumed that their common good would be attained only if the privileges of their citizenship should be limited practically to natives or to persons of a particular nationality. America, on the other hand, has always declared herself for equality of nationalities as well as for equality of individuals. It recognizes racial equality as an essential of full human liberty and true brotherhood, and that racial equality is the complement of democracy. America has, therefore, given like welcome to all the peoples of Europe.

Democracy rests upon two pillars: one, the principle that all men are equally entitled to life, liberty and the pursuit of happiness; and the other, the conviction that such equal opportunity will most advance civilization. Aristocracy, on the other hand, denies both these postulates. It rests upon the principle of the superman. It willingly subordinates the many to the few, and seeks to justify sacrificing the individual by insisting that civilization will be advanced by such sacrifices.

The struggles of the eighteenth and nineteenth centuries both in peace and war were devoted largely to overcoming the aristocratic position as applied to individuals. In establishing the equal right of every person to development it became clear that equal opportunity for all involves this necessary limitation: each man may develop himself so far, but only so far, as his doing so will not interfere with the exercise of a like right by all others. Thus liberty came to mean the right to enjoy life, to acquire property, to pursue happiness in such manner and to such extent only as the exercise of the right in each is consistent with the exercise of a like right by every other of our fellow citizens. Liberty thus defined underlies twentieth-century democracy. Liberty thus defined exists in a large part of the western world. And even where this equal right of each individual has not yet been accepted as a political right, its ethical claim is gaining recognition.

America, dedicated to liberty and the brotherhood of man, rejected the aristocratic principle of the superman as applied to peoples as it rejected the principle when applied to individuals. America has believed that each race had something of peculiar value which it can contribute to the attainment of those high ideals for which it is striving. America has believed that we must not only give to the immigrant the best that we have, but must preserve for America the good that is in the immigrant and develop in him the best of which he is capable. America has believed that in differentiation, not in uniformity, lies the path of progress. It acted on this belief; it has advanced human happiness, and it has prospered.

On the other hand, the aristocratic theory as applied to peoples survived generally throughout Europe. It was there assumed by the stronger countries that the full development of one people necessarily involved its domination over another, and that only by such domination would civilization advance. Strong nationalities, assuming their own superiority, came to believe that they possessed the divine right to subject other peoples to their sway; and the belief in the existence of such a right ripened into a conviction that there was also a duty to exercise it. The Russianizing of Finland, the Prussianizing of Poland and Alsace, and the Magyarizing of Croatia, the persecution of the Jews in Russia and Rumania, are the fruits of this arrogant claim of superiority; and that claim is also the underlying cause of the present war.

The movements of the last century have proved that whole peoples have individuality no less marked than that of the single person; that the individuality of a people is irrepressible, and that the misnamed internationalism which seeks the obliteration of nationalities or peoples is unattainable. The new nationalism adopted by America proclaims that each race or people, like each individual, has the right and duty to develop, and that only through such differentiated development will high civilization be attained. Not until these principles of nationalism, like those of democracy, are generally accepted will liberty be fully attained and minorities be secure in their rights. Not until then can the foundation be laid for a lasting peace among the nations.

The world longs for an end of this war, and even more for a peace that will endure. It turns anxiously to the United States, the one great neutral country and bids us point the way. And may we not answer: Go the way of liberty and justice—led by democracy and the new nationalism. Without these, international congresses and supreme courts will prove vain and disarmament "The Great Illusion."

And let us remember the poor parson of whom Chaucer says:

> But Christe's loore, and his Apostles twelve,
> He taughte, but first he followed it hymselve.

Rinehart Editions